ACCA

Paper
P1

Professional Accountant

Welcome to IFP's study text for Paper P1 *Professional Accountant* which is:

- Written by tutors
- Comprehensive but concise
- In simple English
- Used around the world by Emile Woolf Colleges including China, Russia and the UK

D1425856

International Financial Publishing

in association with

EW **Emile Woolf** International
Training Professionals

First edition published by
International Financial Publishing Limited
Hitherbury House, 97 Portsmouth Road, Guildford, Surrey GU2 5DL
Email: info@ifpbooks.com
www.ifpbooks.com

© International Financial Publishing Limited, May 2007

All rights reserved. No part of this publication may be reproduced, stored in a retrieval system, or transmitted, in any form or by any means, electronic, mechanical, photocopying, recording, scanning or otherwise, without the prior permission in writing of International Financial Publishing Limited, or as expressly permitted by law, or under the terms agreed with the appropriate reprographics rights organisation.

You must not circulate this book in any other binding or cover and you must impose the same condition on any acquirer.

Notice
International Financial Publishing Limited has made every effort to ensure that at the time of writing the contents of this study text are accurate, but neither International Financial Publishing Limited nor its directors or employees shall be under any liability whatsoever for any inaccurate or misleading information this work could contain.

British Library Cataloguing in Publications Data
A catalogue record for this book is available from the British Library

ISBN: 978-1-905623-40-2

Printed and bound in Great Britain

Acknowledgements
The syllabus and study guide are reproduced by kind permission of the Association of Chartered Certified Accountants.

The UK Combined Code on Corporate Governance is © Financial Reporting Council (FRC). Adapted and reproduced with the kind permission of the Financial Reporting Council. All rights reserved.

The Singapore Code of Corporate Governance is © the Accounting and Corporate Regulatory Authority, Singapore. Extracts are reproduced with their kind permission.

C

Contents

International Financial Publishing Limited

S

Syllabus and study guide

The syllabus for Professional Accountant (P1) has been called the 'gateway syllabus' for the professional level of the ACCA examinations.

It is concerned with the cultural environment within which the professional accountant works. Without getting into the detail of financial methods and techniques, or strategic decision-making, it looks at the 'proper way' to run a business entity or not-for-profit entity. There are several aspects to this.

- **Corporate governance**. This is the way that companies are governed, mainly by their directors. Similar concepts apply to non-corporate entities. There is 'good' and 'bad' corporate governance, and the professional accountant needs to understand the issues involved.

- **Internal control and risk management**. Well-managed entities should have a culture of risk awareness. Business is not just about making profits: it is also concerned with risk management and control. The general concepts of risk management apply to much of the work of the professional accountant – in financial reporting, auditing, financial management and performance management.

- **Professional ethics**. Accountancy is a profession, and accountants are required to apply professional values and ethical standards to the work that they do.

- **Business ethics**. Accountants should also understand the nature of ethics in business. There are differing views about how business entities should 'behave'. For example, to what extent should companies be responsible for the general well-being of society and for the protection of the environment?

Aim

To apply relevant knowledge, skills and exercise professional judgement in carrying out the role of the accountant relating to governance, internal control, compliance and the management of risk within an organisation, in the context of an overall ethical framework.

Main capabilities

On successful completion of this paper, candidates should be able to:

A Define governance and explain its function in the effective management and control of organisations and of the resources for which they are accountable

B Evaluate the professional accountant's role in internal control, review and compliance

C Explain the role of the accountant in identifying and assessing risk

D Explain and evaluate the role of the accountant in controlling and mitigating risk

E Demonstrate the application of professional values and judgement through an ethical framework that is in the best interests of society and the profession, in compliance with relevant professional codes, laws and regulations.

Rationale

The syllabus for Paper P1, *Professional Accountant*, acts as the gateway syllabus into the professional level. It sets the other Essentials and Options papers into a wider professional, organisational, and societal context.

The syllabus assumes essential technical skills and knowledge acquired at the Fundamentals level where the core technical capabilities will have been acquired, and where ethics, corporate governance, internal audit, control, and risk will have been introduced in a subject-specific context.

The PA syllabus begins by examining the whole area of governance within organisations in the broad context of the agency relationship. This aspect of the syllabus focuses on the respective roles and responsibilities of directors and officers to organisational stakeholders and of accounting and auditing as support and control functions.

The syllabus then explores internal review, control, and feedback to implement and support effective governance, including compliance issues related to decision-making and decision-support functions. The syllabus also examines the whole area of identifying, assessing, and controlling risk as a key aspect of responsible management.

Finally, the syllabus covers personal and professional ethics, ethical frameworks – and professional values – as applied in the context of the accountant's duties and as a guide to appropriate professional behaviour and conduct in a variety of situations.

© International Financial Publishing Limited

Syllabus

A Governance and responsibility

1 The scope of governance

2 Agency relationships and theories

3 The board of directors

4 Board committees

5 Directors' remuneration

6 Different approaches to corporate governance

7 Corporate governance and corporate social responsibility

8 Governance: reporting and disclosure

B Internal control and review

1 Management control systems in corporate governance

2 Internal control, audit and compliance in corporate governance

3 Internal control and reporting

4 Management information in audit and internal control

C Identifying and assessing risk

1 Risk and the risk management process

2 Categories of risk

3 Identification, assessment and measurement of risk

D Controlling risk

1 Targeting and monitoring risk

2 Methods of controlling and reducing risk

3 Risk avoidance, retention and modelling

E Professional values and ethics

1 Ethical theories

2 Different approaches to ethics and social responsibility

3 Professions and the public interest

4 Professional practice and codes of ethics

5 Conflicts of interest and the consequences of unethical behaviour

6   Ethical characteristics of professionalism

7   Social and environmental issues in the conduct of business and of ethical behaviour

Approach to examining the syllabus

The syllabus will be assessed by a three-hour paper-based examination. The examination paper will be structured in two sections. Section A will be based on a case study style question comprising a compulsory 50 mark question, with requirements based on several parts with all parts relating to the same case information. The case study will usually assess a range of subject areas across the syllabus and will require the candidate to demonstrate high level capabilities to evaluate, relate and apply the information in the case study to several of the requirements.

Section B comprises three questions of 25 marks each, of which candidates must answer two. These questions will be more likely to assess a range of discrete subject areas from the main syllabus section headings, but may require application, evaluation and the synthesis of information contained within short scenarios in which some requirements may need to be contextualised.

		Number of marks
Section A	Compulsory case study	50
Section B	Choice of 2 from 3 questions, 25 marks each	50
		100

© International Financial Publishing Limited

Study guide

This study guide provides more detailed guidance on the syllabus. You should use this as the basis of your studies.

A   GOVERNANCE AND RESPONSIBILITY
1   The scope of governance

(a)   Define and explain the meaning of corporate governance.

(b)   Explain, and analyse the issues raised by the development of the joint stock company as the dominant form of business organisation and the separation of ownership and control over business activity.

(c)   Analyse the purposes and objectives of corporate governance.

(d)   Explain, and apply in context of corporate governance, the key underpinning concepts of:

   i)   fairness

   ii)   openness/transparency

   iii)   independence

   iv)   probity/honesty

   v)   responsibility

   vi)   accountability

   vii)   reputation

   viii)   judgment

   ix)   integrity

(e)   Explain and assess the major areas of organisational life affected by issues in corporate governance.

   (i)   duties of directors and functions of the board (including performance measurement)

   (ii)   the composition and balance of the board (and board committees)

   (iii)   reliability of financial reporting and external auditing

   (iv)   directors' remuneration and rewards

   (v)   responsibility of the board for risk management systems and internal control

   (vi)   the rights and responsibilities of shareholders, including institutional investors

   (vii)   corporate social responsibility and business ethics.

(f) Compare, and distinguish between public, private and non-governmental organisations (NGO) sectors with regard to the issues raised by, and scope of, governance.

(g) Explain and evaluate the roles, interests and claims of, the internal parties involved in corporate governance.

    (i) Directors

    (ii) Company secretaries

    (iii) Sub-board management

    (iv) Employee representatives (e.g. trade unions)

(h) Explain and evaluate the roles, interests and claims of, the external parties involved in corporate governance.

    (i) Shareholders (including shareholders' rights and responsibilities)

    (ii) Auditors

    (iii) Regulators

    (iv) Government

    (v) Stock exchanges

    (vi) Small investors (and minority rights)

    (vii) Institutional investors (see also next point)

(i) Analyse and discuss the role and influence of institutional investors in corporate governance systems and structures, for example the roles and influences of pension funds, insurance companies and mutual funds.

2 Agency relationships and theories

(a) Define agency theory.

(b) Define and explain the key concepts in agency theory.

    (i) Agents

    (ii) Principals

    (iii) Agency

    (iv) Agency costs

    (v) Accountability

    (vi) Fiduciary responsibilities

    (vii) Stakeholders

(c) Explain and explore the nature of the principal- agent relationship in the context of corporate governance.

 © International Financial Publishing Limited

(d) Analyse and critically evaluate the nature of agency accountability in agency relationships.

(e) Explain and analyse the following other theories used to explain aspects of the agency relationship.

(i) Transaction costs theory

(ii) Stakeholder theory

3 The board of directors

(a) Explain and evaluate the roles and responsibilities of boards of directors.

(b) Describe, distinguish between and evaluate the cases for and against, unitary and two-tier board structures.

(c) Describe the characteristics, board composition and types of, directors (including defining executive and non-executive directors (NED).

(d) Describe and assess the purposes, roles and responsibilities of NEDs.

(e) Describe and analyse the general principles of legal and regulatory frameworks within which directors operate on corporate boards:

(i) legal rights and responsibilities

(ii) time-limited appointments

(iii) retirement by rotation

(iv) service contract

(v) removal

(vi) disqualification

(vii) conflict and disclosure of interests

(viii) insider dealing/trading

(f) Define, explore and compare the roles of the chief executive officer and company chairman.

(g) Describe and assess the importance and execution of, induction and continuing professional development of directors on boards of directors.

(h) Explain and analyse the frameworks for assessing the performance of boards and individual directors (including NEDs) on boards.

4 Board committees

(a) Explain and assess the importance, roles and accountabilities of, board committees in corporate governance.

(b) Explain and evaluate the role and purpose of the following committees in effective corporate governance:

    (i) Remuneration committees

    (ii) Nominations committees

    (iii) Risk committees.

5 Directors' remuneration

(a) Describe and assess the general principles of remuneration.

    (i) purposes

    (ii) components

    (iii) links to strategy

    (iv) links to labour market conditions.

(b) Explain and assess the effect of various components of remuneration packages on directors' behaviour.

    (i) basic salary

    (ii) performance related

    (iii) shares and share options

    (iv) loyalty bonuses

    (v) benefits in kind

(c) Explain and analyse the legal, ethical, competitive and regulatory issues associated with directors' remuneration.

6 Different approaches to corporate governance

(a) Describe and compare the essentials of 'rules' and 'principles' based approaches to corporate governance. Includes discussion of 'comply or explain'.

(b) Describe and analyse the different models of business ownership that influence different governance regimes (e.g. family firms versus joint stock company-based models).

(c) Describe and critically evaluate the reasons behind the development and use of codes of practice in corporate governance (acknowledging national differences and convergence).

(d) Explain and briefly explore the development of corporate governance codes in principles-based jurisdictions.

    (i) impetus and background

    (ii) major corporate governance codes

    (iii) effects of

© International Financial Publishing Limited

(e)   Explain and explore the Sarbanes-Oxley Act (2002) as an example of a rules-based approach to corporate governance.

     (i)   impetus and background

     (ii)   main provisions/contents

     (iii)   effects of

(f)   Describe and explore the objectives, content and limitations of, corporate governance codes intended to apply to multiple national jurisdictions.

     (i)   Organisation for economic cooperation and development (OECD) Report (2004)

     (ii)   International corporate governance network (ICGN) Report (2005)

7   Corporate governance and corporate social responsibility

(a)   Explain and explore social responsibility in the context of corporate governance.

(b)   Discuss and critically assess the concept of stakeholders and stakeholding in organisations and how this can affect strategy and corporate governance.

(c)   Analyse and evaluate issues of 'ownership,' 'property' and the responsibilities of ownership in the context of shareholding.

(d)   Explain the concept of the organisation as a corporate citizen of society with rights and responsibilities.

8   Governance: reporting and disclosure

(a)   Explain and assess the general principles of disclosure and communication with shareholders.

(b)   Explain and analyse 'best practice' corporate governance disclosure requirements (for example under the UK Combined Code 2003 Schedule C).

(c)   Define and distinguish between mandatory and voluntary disclosure of corporate information in the normal reporting cycle.

(d)   Explain and explore the nature of, and reasons and motivations for, voluntary disclosure in a principles-based reporting environment (compared to, for example, the reporting regime in the USA).

(e)   Explain and analyse the purposes of the annual general meeting and extraordinary general meetings for information exchange between board and shareholders.

(f)   Describe and assess the role of proxy voting in corporate governance.

B   INTERNAL CONTROL AND REVIEW

1   Management control systems in corporate governance

(a)   Define and explain internal management control.

(b)   Explain and explore the importance of internal control and risk management in corporate governance.

(c)   Describe the objectives of internal control systems.

(d)   Identify, explain and evaluate the corporate governance and executive management roles in risk management (in particular the separation between responsibility for ensuring that adequate risk management systems are in place and the application of risk management systems and practices in the organisation).

(e)   Identify and assess the importance of the elements or components of internal control systems.

2   Internal control, audit and compliance in corporate governance

(a)   Describe the function and importance of internal audit.

(b)   Explain, and discuss the importance of, auditor independence in all client-auditor situations (including internal audit).

(c)   Explain, and assess the nature and sources of risks to, auditor independence. Assess the hazard of auditor capture.

(d)   Explain and evaluate the importance of compliance and the role of the internal audit committee in internal control.

(e)   Explore and evaluate the effectiveness of internal control systems.

(f)   Describe and analyse the work of the internal audit committee in overseeing the internal audit function.

(g)   Explain and explore the importance and characteristics of, the audit committee's relationship with external auditors.

3   Internal control and reporting

(a)   Describe and assess the need to report on internal controls to shareholders.

(b)   Describe the content of a report on internal control and audit.

     © International Financial Publishing Limited

4   Management information in audit and internal control

(a)   Explain and assess the need for adequate information flows to management for the purposes of the management of internal control and risk.

(b)   Evaluate the qualities and characteristics of information required in internal control and risk management and monitoring.

C   IDENTIFYING AND ASSESSING RISK

1   Risk and the risk management process

(a)   Define and explain risk in the context of corporate governance.

(b)   Define and describe management responsibilities in risk management.

2   Categories of risk

(a)   Define and compare (distinguish between) strategic and operational risks.

(b)   Define and explain the sources and impacts of common business risks.

    (i)   market

    (ii)   credit

    (iii)   liquidity

    (iv)   technological

    (v)   legal

    (vi)   health, safety and environmental

    (vii)   reputation

    (viii) business probity

    (ix)   derivatives

(c)   Recognise and analyse the sector or industry specific nature of many business risks

3   Identification, assessment and measurement of risk

(a)   Identify, and assess the impact upon, the stakeholders involved in business risk.

(b)   Explain and analyse the concepts of assessing the severity and probability of risk events.

(c) Describe and evaluate a framework for board level consideration of risk.

(d) Describe the process of (externally) reporting internal control and risk.

D CONTROLLING RISK

1 Targeting and monitoring of risk

(a) Explain and assess the role of a risk manager in identifying and monitoring risk.

(b) Explain and evaluate the role of the risk committee in identifying and monitoring risk.

(c) Describe and assess the role of internal or external risk auditing in monitoring risk.

2 Methods of controlling and reducing risk

(a) Explain the importance of risk awareness at all levels in an organisation.

(b) Describe and analyse the concept of embedding risk in an organisation's systems and procedures

(c) Describe and evaluate the concept of embedding risk in an organisation's culture and values.

(d) Explain and analyse the concepts of spreading and diversifying risk and when this would be appropriate.

3 Risk avoidance, retention and modelling

(a) Define the terms 'risk avoidance' and 'risk retention'.

(b) Explain and evaluate the different attitudes to risk and how these can affect strategy.

(c) Explain and assess the necessity of incurring risk as part of competitively managing a business organisation.

(d) Explain and assess attitudes towards risk and the ways in which risk varies in relation to the size, structure and development of an organisation

© International Financial Publishing Limited

E   PROFESSIONAL VALUES AND ETHICS

1   Ethical theories

(a)   Explain and distinguish between the ethical theories of relativism and absolutism.

(b)   Explain, in an accounting and governance context, Kohlberg's stages of human moral development.

(c)   Describe and distinguish between deontological and teleological/consequentialist approaches to ethics.

2   Different approaches to ethics and social responsibility.

(a)   Describe and evaluate Gray, Owen & Adams (1996) seven positions on social responsibility.

(b)   Describe and evaluate other constructions of corporate and personal ethical stance:

     (i)   short-term shareholder interests

     (ii)   long-term shareholder interests

     (iii)   multiple stakeholder obligations

     (iv)   shaper of society

(c)   Describe and analyse the variables determining the cultural context of ethics and corporate social responsibility (CSR).

3   Professions and the public interest

(a)   Explain and explore the nature of a 'profession' and 'professionalism'.

(b)   Describe and assess what is meant by 'the public interest'.

(c)   Describe the role of, and assess the widespread influence of, accounting as a profession in the organisational context.

(d)   Analyse the role of accounting as a profession in society.

(e)   Recognise accounting's role as a value-laden profession capable of influencing the distribution of power and wealth in society.

(f)   Describe and critically evaluate issues surrounding accounting and acting against the public interest.

4   Professional practice and codes of ethics

(a)   Describe and explore the areas of behaviour covered by corporate codes of ethics.

(b)   Describe and assess the content of, and principles behind, professional codes of ethics.

(c)   Describe and assess the codes of ethics relevant to accounting professionals such as the IFAC or professional body codes eg ACCA.

5   Conflicts of interest and the consequences of unethical behaviour

(a)   Describe and evaluate issues associated with conflicts of interest and ethical conflict resolution.

(b)   Explain and evaluate the nature and impacts of ethical threats and safeguards.

(c)   Explain and explore how threats to independence can affect ethical behaviour.

6   Ethical characteristics of professionalism

(a)   Explain and analyse the content and nature of ethical decision-making using content from Kohlberg's framework as appropriate.

(b)   Explain and analyse issues related to the application of ethical behaviour in a professional context.

(c)   Describe and discuss 'rules based' and 'principles based' approaches to resolving ethical dilemmas encountered in professional accounting.

7   Social and environmental issues in the conduct of business and ethical behaviour

(a)   Describe and assess the social and environmental effects that economic activity can have (in terms of social and environmental 'footprints').

(b)   Explain and assess the concept of sustainability and evaluate the issues concerning accounting for sustainability (including the contribution of 'full cost' accounting).

(c)   Describe the main features of internal management systems for underpinning environmental accounting such as EMAS and ISO 14000.

(d)   Explain the nature of social and environmental audit and evaluate the contribution it can make to the development of environmental accounting.

     © International Financial Publishing Limited

CHAPTER

1

The scope of governance

Contents
1   The meaning of governance
2   Concepts of good governance
3   Stakeholders

> ## The meaning of governance
>
> - Corporate governance
> - The separation of ownership from control
> - Corporate governance: laws and guidelines
> - Corporate governance issues
> - Governance issues in public sector entities and in government

1 The meaning of governance

1.1 Corporate governance

Corporate governance has been defined (in the Cadbury Report, 1992) as follows: 'Corporate governance is the system by which companies are directed and controlled.'

Governance should not be confused with management.

- Management is concerned with running the business operations of a company.
- Governance is about giving a lead to the company and monitoring and controlling management decisions, so as to ensure that the company achieves its intended purpose and aims.

Management is about making business decisions: governance is about monitoring and controlling decisions, as well as giving leadership and direction. 'If management is about running business, governance is about seeing that it is run properly': (Professor Bob Tricker, 1984). In order to understand what corporate governance is, it might be helpful to think about what it is not.

- Corporate governance is not about management activities, and management skills and techniques. The powers of executive management to direct a business is an aspect of governance, but how they use those powers to direct business activities is not.
- Corporate governance is not about formulating business strategies for the company. However, the responsibility of the board of directors and other senior managers for deciding strategy is an aspect of governance.

Corporate governance is concerned with matters such as:

- In whose interests is a company governed?
- Who has the power to make decisions for a company?
- For what aims or purposes are those powers used?
- In what manner are those powers used?
- Who else might influence the governance of a company?
- Are the governors of a company held accountable for the way in which they use their powers?
- How are risks managed?

© International Financial Publishing Limited

The term 'corporate governance' means the governance of companies (corporate bodies). Similar issues arise for the governance of other entities, such as government bodies, state-owned entities and non-government organisations such as charities.

1.2   The separation of ownership from control

Problems arise with corporate governance because of the separation of ownership of a company from control of the company. This is a basic feature of company law.

- A company is a legal person. In law, a company exists independently of its shareholders, who own it.

- The constitution of a company usually delegates the powers to manage a company to its board of directors. The board of directors in turn delegates many of these management powers and responsibilities to executive managers.

- The directors act as agents for the company. Their responsibilities are to the company, not the company's shareholders.

- However, it is widely accepted that companies should be governed in the interests of their owners, the shareholders. However the interests of other groups, such as the company's employees, might also have a strong influence on the directors.

Problems arising from the separation of ownership and control

The separation of ownership and control creates problems for good corporate governance, because:

- the directors of a company might be able to run the company in a way that is not in the best interests of the shareholders

- but the shareholder might not be able to prevent the directors from doing this, because the directors have most of the powers to control what the company does.

When the shareholders of a company are also its directors, problems with corporate governance will not arise.

When a company is controlled by a majority shareholder, problems with governance are unlikely, because the majority shareholder has the power to remove any directors and so can control decisions by the board of directors.

Problems with corporate governance arise when a company has many different shareholders, and there is no majority shareholder. In these companies, the board of directors have extensive powers for controlling the company but the shareholders are relatively weak. The directors ought to be accountable to the shareholders for the way they are running the company. However in practice the shareholders might have little or no influence and do not have the ability to prevent the directors from running the company in the way that the directors themselves consider to be best.

Problems of corporate governance are therefore particularly severe in large companies where shareholders continually buy and sell their shares, so that many shareholders are not long-term investors in the company that, for a time at least, they partly own. This is why attempts to improve corporate governance have focused mainly on stock market companies (listed companies) and to a lesser extent on smaller public companies and large private companies.

Ownership and control in non-corporate entities

The separation of ownership from control can affect the quality of governance in non-corporate entities, as well as companies.

In any entity, it is should be possible to identify owners and controllers:

- The owners might be the government, or the 'public'. In the case of a charity organisation, the owners might be a section of the public.

- Those in control. The power to govern a non-corporate body might be given to a management committee (or in the UK, a board of trustees). Appointments to the management committee might be made by the owners, or by means of a procedure that is specified by the constitutional rules of the entity.

The relationship between owners and controllers is different in a non-corporate entity compared with a company. The aims of a non-corporate entity also differ from the profit-seeking aims of a company. Even so, the possibility of governance problems can arise. There is a risk that the controllers of an entity will not run its affairs in a way that meets the needs or expectations of its owners.

1.3 Corporate governance: laws and guidelines

It is well recognised that there is good governance and bad governance.

- Bad governance occurs when an entity is governed in a way that is inconsistent with certain concepts and practices. Often, bad governance means that a company is governed in the interests of its directors personally, rather than in the best interests of its owners (or other important interest groups).

- Good governance is based on certain key concepts and practices, which are described later.

To some extent, good governance is supported by **the law**. In the UK, for example, the directors of a company owe certain duties to their company. (These duties are now included in the Companies Act 2006.) UK law also requires the directors of a company to present an annual report and accounts to the shareholders; this helps to make the directors accountable to the shareholders of their company. The Sarbanes-Oxley Act 2002 in the USA introduced a range of legal measures designed to improve the quality of corporate governance in the US, following the spectacular collapse of several large corporations (such as Enron and WorldCom) where bad corporate governance was held largely to blame.

In some countries, such as the UK, where laws on corporate governance are not strong, **guidelines or codes of governance principles and practice** have been issued. The guidelines are voluntary, but are backed by major financial institutions, stock exchanges and investment organisations. For example:
- The UK has a Combined Code on corporate governance and listed companies are required to comply with its provisions or explain why they have failed to do so.

- Similarly, Singapore has a Code of Corporate Governance, issued by the Ministry of Finance.

© International Financial Publishing Limited

- A more general set of corporate governance guidelines has been issued by the Organisation for Economic Co-operation and Development (OECD), which all countries are encouraged to adopt as a minimum standard for good corporate governance.

These Codes will be described in more detail later.

Example

What makes a good company?

A good company is not necessarily a company that is well-governed. However, it is useful to think about what you would consider to be a good company. Which of the following characteristics would you consider to be a feature of a 'good' company?

1   A company that earns good profits.
2   A company that responds to the needs of its customers.
3   A company that is a good employer.
4   A company that is environmentally-friendly.

You might think that a good company is any or all of these. Or you might have a different opinion about what makes a good company. However, your views on what makes a good company will probably also affect your opinions about how companies ought to be governed.

1.4   Corporate governance issues

So what are the key issues in corporate governance, which establish how well or badly a company is governed? The main areas covered by codes of corporate governance are as follows:

- **The role and responsibilities of the board of directors**. The board of directors should have a clear understanding of its responsibilities and it should fulfil these responsibilities and provide suitable leadership to the company. Governance is therefore concerned with establishing what the responsibilities of the board should be, and making sure that these are carried out properly.

- **The composition and balance of the board of directors**. A board of directors collectively, and individual directors, should act with integrity, and bring independence of thought and judgment to their role. The board should not be dominated by a powerful chief executive and/or chairman. It is therefore important that the board should have a suitable balance, and consist of individuals with a range of backgrounds and experience.

- **Financial reporting, narrative reporting and auditing**. The board should be properly accountable to its shareholders, and should be open and transparent with investors generally. To make a board properly accountable, high standards of financial reporting (and narrative reporting) and external auditing must be upheld. The major 'scandals' of corporate governance in the past have been characterised by misleading financial information in the company's accounts – in the UK, for example, Maxwell Communications Corporation and Polly Peck

International, more recently in Enron and WorldCom in the US and Parmalat in Italy. Enron filed for bankruptcy in 2001 after 'adjusting' its accounts. WorldCom, which collapsed in 2002 admitted to fraud in its accounting and its chief executive officer was subsequently convicted and jailed.

- **Directors' remuneration**. Directors work for a reward. To encourage their commitment to achieving the objectives of their company, they should be given suitable incentives. Linking remuneration to performance is considered essential for successful corporate governance. However, linking directors' pay to performance is complex, and remuneration schemes for directors have not been particularly successful. Directors' pay is an aspect of corporate governance where companies are frequently criticised.

- **Risk management and internal control**. The directors should ensure that their company operates within acceptable levels of risk, and should ensure through a system of internal control that the resources of the company are properly used and its assets are protected.

- **Shareholders' rights**. Shareholders' rights vary between countries. These rights might be weak, or might not be exercised fully. Another aspect of corporate governance is encouraging the involvement of shareholders in the companies in which they invest, through more dialogue with the directors and through greater use of shareholder powers – such as voting powers at general meetings of the company.

Corporate social responsibility and ethical behaviour by companies (**business ethics**) are also issues related to corporate governance.

All these issues will be explained in more detail in the chapters that follow.

Example

In 2001, US corporation Enron collapsed unexpectedly. The collapse was blamed to a large extent on poor corporate governance. Failings that occurred in corporate governance included:

- False accounting. Executive managers encouraged or allowed incorrect and misleading treatments of transactions in the company's accounts.

- The audit committee of the board gave its approval to seriously misleading annual financial statements.

- Executives in the company, and professional advisers, profited personally (but secretly) from transactions involving the company.

- The board was ineffective in supervising the actions of the company's senior executives.

- The board ignored information from 'whistleblowers' about serious problems and dubious transactions.

© International Financial Publishing Limited

1.5   Governance issues in public sector entities and in government

Similar issues apply to governance in public sector entities and government. In the UK, a Good Governance Standard was published by the Independent Commission for Good Governance in Public Service. This sets out six core principles of good corporate governance for public service corporations.

1   'Good governance means focusing on the organisation's purpose and on outcomes for citizens and service users'. This means having a clear understanding of the purpose of the organisation, and making sure that users of the service receive a high-quality service and that taxpayers (who pay for the service) get value for money.

2   'Good governance means performing effectively in clearly defined functions and roles'. The governing body of the organisation is comparable to the board of directors in a company. It must be clear about what its responsibilities are, and it should carry these out. The responsibilities of executive management should also be clear, and the governing body is responsible for making sure that management fulfils its responsibilities properly.

3.   'Good governance means promoting values for the whole organisation and demonstrating the values of good governance through behaviour'. Integrity and ethical behaviour are therefore seen as core governance issues in public sector entities.

4   'Good governance means taking informed, transparent decisions and managing risk'. Risk management and the responsibility of the governing body for the internal control system is as much a core feature of governance in public sector entities as in companies.

5   'Good governance means developing the capacity and capability of the governing body to be effective'. This issue is concerned with the composition and balance of the governing body.

6   'Good governance means engaging stakeholders and making accountability real'. In companies, the relationship between shareholders and the board of directors is an important aspect of governance, and companies and shareholders are encouraged to engage in constructive dialogue with each other. In public sector organisations, the constructive dialogue should exist between the governing body and the general public and particular interest groups.

There are clear similarities between governance issues in companies and those in the public sector.

Concepts of good governance
■ Fairness
■ Openness/transparency
■ Independence
■ Honesty and integrity
■ Responsibility and accountability
■ Reputation
■ Judgment
■ Nolan's Seven Principles of Public Life

2 Concepts of good governance

There are several concepts of good governance. In companies, these concepts should be evident in the relationship between the shareholders and the board of directors. Some of these concepts should also apply to the company's dealings with its employees, customers, suppliers and the general public.

The concepts described briefly here might seem 'obvious'. However, it is useful to think about what might happen if these concepts are not applied. In particular, how the absence of these concepts might affect the relationship between the board of directors and the shareholders.

2.1 Fairness

In corporate governance, fairness refers to the principle that all shareholders should receive fair treatment from the directors. At a basic level, it means that all the equity shareholders in a company should be entitled to equal treatment, such as one vote per share at general meetings of the company and the right to the same dividend per share.

In the UK, the concept of fair treatment for shareholders is supported by the law (which provides some protection for minority shareholders against unjust treatment by the directors or the majority shareholders). However, in some countries, the law provides little or no protection for minority shareholders. For example, in a takeover bid for a company, the law might permit a higher price to be offered to large shareholders than the price offered to small shareholders.

2.2 Openness/transparency

Openness or transparency means 'not hiding anything'. Intentions should be clear, and information should not be withheld from individuals who ought to have a right to receive it.

Transparency means clarity. In corporate governance, it should refer not only to the ability of the shareholders to see what the directors are trying to achieve. It also refers to the ease with which an 'outsider', such as a potential investor or an

© International Financial Publishing Limited

employee, can make a meaningful analysis of the company and its intentions. Transparency therefore means providing information about what the company has done, what it intends to do in the future, and what risks it faces.

- In public sector organisations and government, openness means telling the public, and not making decisions 'behind closed doors'.

- In listed companies (stock market companies) openness includes matters such as:

  - requiring major shareholders to declare the size of their shareholding in the company, and

  - requiring the board of directors to announce to the stock market information about any major new developments in the company's affairs, so that all shareholders and other investors are kept informed.

2.3 Independence

Independence means freedom from the influence of someone else. A principle of good corporate governance is that a substantial number of the directors of a company should be independent, which means that they are able to make judgements and give opinions that are in the best interests of the company, without bias or pre-conceived ideas.

Similarly, professional advisers to a company such as external auditors and solicitors should be independent of the company, and should give honest and professional opinions and advice.

- The independence of a director is threatened by having a connection to a special interest group. Executive directors can never be independent, because their views will represent the opinions of the management team. Similarly, a retired former executive might still be influenced by the views of management, because he or she shares the 'management culture'. Directors who represent the interests of major shareholders are also incapable of being independent.

- The independence of external auditors can be threatened by over-reliance on fee income from a client company. When a firm of auditors, or a regional office of a national firm, earns most of its income from one corporate client there is a risk that the auditors might choose to accept what they are told by the company's management, rather than question them rigorously and risk an argument. It has been suggested that this occurred in the Houston office of Andersen's, the audit firm that collapsed in 2002 as a result of the Enron scandal.

- Familiarity can also remove an individual's independence, because when one person knows another well he is more likely to accept what that person tells him and support his point of view. Auditors are at risk of losing their independence if they work on the audit of the same corporate client for too many years.

2.4 Honesty and integrity

It might seem obvious that honesty should be an essential quality for directors and their advisers. An individual who is honest, and who is known to be honest, is believed by others and is therefore more likely to be trusted.

However, honesty is not as widespread as it might be. Business leaders, as well as political leaders, may prefer to 'put a spin' on the facts, and manipulate facts for the purpose of presenting a more favourable impression.

Integrity is similar to honesty, but it also means behaving in accordance with high standards of behaviour and a strict moral or ethical code of conduct. Professional accountants, for example, are expected to act with integrity, by being honest and acting in accordance with their professional code of ethics.

If shareholders in a company suspect that the directors are not acting honestly or with integrity, there can be no trust, and good corporate governance is impossible.

2.5 Responsibility and accountability

The directors of a company are given most of the powers for running the company. Many of these powers are delegated to executive managers, but the directors remain responsible for the way in which those powers are used.

- An important role of the board of directors is to monitor the decisions of executive management, and to satisfy themselves that the decisions taken by management are in the best interests of the company and its shareholders.

- The board of directors should also retain the responsibility for certain key decisions, such as setting strategic objectives for their company and approving major capital investments.

A board of directors should not ignore their responsibilities by delegating too many powers to executive management, and letting the management team 'get on with the job'. The board should accept its responsibilities.

With responsibility, there should also be accountability. In a company, the board of directors should be accountable to the shareholders. Shareholders should be able to consider reports from the directors about what they have done, and how the company has performed under their stewardship, and give their approval or show their disapproval. Some of the ways in which the board are accountable are as follows:

- Presenting the annual report and accounts to the shareholders, for the shareholders to consider and discuss with the board. In the UK, this happens at the annual general meeting of the company.

- If shareholders do not approve of a director, they are able to remove him from office. Individual directors may be required to submit themselves for re-election by the shareholders at regular intervals. In the UK for example, it is common practice for directors to be required to retire every three years and stand for re-election at the company's annual general meeting.

In the UK, it is recognised that individual directors should be made accountable for the way in which they have acted as a director. The Combined Code on corporate governance includes a provision that all directors should be subject to an annual performance review, and should be accountable to the chairman of the company for they way in which they have carried out their duties in the previous year.

© International Financial Publishing Limited

It might be argued that a board of directors is not sufficiently accountable to the shareholders, and that there should be much more accountability.

2.6 Reputation

A large company is known widely by its reputation or character. A reputation may be good or bad. The reputation of a company is based on a combination of several qualities, including commercial success and management competence. However, a company might earn a good reputation with investors, employees, customers and suppliers in other ways. As concerns for the environment have grown, companies have recognised the importance of being 'environment-friendly' or 'eco-friendly'. Reputation is also based on honesty and fair dealing, and on being a good employer.

- Investors might be more inclined to buy shares and bonds in a company they respect and trust. Some investment institutions are 'ethical funds' that are required to invest only in 'ethical' companies.

- Employees are more likely to want to work for an employer that treats its employees well and fairly. As a result, companies with a high reputation can often choose better-quality employees, because they have more applicants to choose from.

- Consumers are more likely to buy goods or services from a company they respect, and that has a reputation for good quality and fair prices, and for being customer-friendly or environment-friendly.

Companies that are badly governed can be at risk of losing goodwill – from investors, employees and customers.

2.7 Judgment

Directors make judgments in reaching their opinions. All directors are expected to have sound judgment and to be objective in making their judgements (avoiding bias and conflicts of interest). In its principles of corporate governance, for example, the OECD states that: 'the board should be able to exercise objective judgment on corporate affairs independent, in particular, from management.'

Independent non-executive directors are expected to show judgment that is both sound and independent. Rolls Royce, for example, in an annual report on its corporate governance, stated that: 'The Board applies a rigorous process in order to satisfy itself that its non-executive directors remain independent. Having undertaken this review in [Year], the Board confirms that all the non-executive directors are considered to be independent in character and judgment.'

2.8 Nolan's Seven Principles of Public Life

The concepts described above apply to public sector entities and not-for-profit entities, as well as to companies. This is evident in Nolan's Seven Principles of Public Life. These were issued in the UK by the Nolan Committee on Standards in Public Life, which was set up in 1995 to report on standards of behaviour amongst politicians and in the civil service and other public sector bodies.

The seven principles are as follows:

1 **Selflessness**. Holders of public office should not make decisions that are in their personal self-interest. Their decisions should be based entirely on concern for the public interest.

2 **Integrity**. Holders of public office should not put themselves under any financial obligation or other obligation to another individual or organisation, that might influence how they act in the course of carrying out their duties.

3 **Objectivity**. Holders of public office, in awarding contracts or making recommendations, should base their decisions on merit.

4 **Accountability**. Holders of public office are accountable to the public and should submit themselves to public scrutiny.

5 **Openness**. Holders of public office should be as open as possible about the decisions they take and the reasons for those decisions. They should only withhold information when this is in the public interest.

6 **Honesty**. Holders of public office have a duty to declare any conflicts of interest they might have, and should take steps to resolve them whenever they arise.

7 **Leadership**. Holders of public office should promote and support these principles by setting an example with their own behaviour and giving a lead to others.

© International Financial Publishing Limited

Stakeholders

- Stakeholders and their influence on corporate governance
- Shareholders and directors
- Other internal stakeholders
- External stakeholders
- Institutional investors

---

3 Stakeholders

3.1 Stakeholders and their influence on corporate governance

A stakeholder in a company is someone who has a 'stake' in the company and an interest in what the company does.

- A company must offer something to all its stakeholders. If a company does not give its stakeholders something of what they want, the stakeholders might cease to have an interest in it.
- All stakeholders in a company have some expectations from the company.
- If a company wishes to remain associated with its stakeholders, it must do something to satisfy these expectations.

The expectations of different groups of stakeholders are not the same, and they are often inconsistent with each other. One of the objectives of corporate governance should be to provide enough satisfaction for each stakeholder group.

For example, two stakeholder groups in a company are the shareholders and the employees of the company. Employees expect a fair wage or salary, and often expect job security or career prospects. Shareholders expect a reasonable return on their investment in the company. The directors and management of a company need to satisfy the expectations of both shareholders (for high profits and dividends) and employees (for high salaries).

Each stakeholder or stakeholder group might expect to have some influence over the company and the actions that it takes. A feature of corporate governance in any company is the balance of power between the stakeholder groups and the relative power and influence of each group.

3.2 Shareholders and directors

The main stakeholder groups in a company are usually the shareholders and the directors of the company. The shareholders own the company and the directors are its leaders.

The shareholders

The influence of shareholders over their company varies with circumstances.

- In a small company the shareholders and directors might be the same individuals.

- In some companies, there may be a majority shareholder (controlling shareholder). A majority shareholder should be able to influence the decisions of the board of directors, because he has the power to remove directors who disagree with them.

- In quoted companies (stock market companies) the interests of shareholders are likely to be focused on the value of their shares and the size of dividends. However, the shareholders might have little influence over the decisions of the board of directors.

The directors

The board of directors is a significant stakeholder group in a company because they have the power to direct the company. Directors act as agents for the company and represent the interests of the company.

- A board of directors consists of both **executive and non-executive directors**. Executive directors have executive responsibilities as managers in the company, in addition to their role as director. They are usually full-time employees of the company. Non-executives are not involved in executive management and are very much 'part time' and in many countries (for example the UK and US) they are not company employees. Since executive directors combine their role as director with their full-time job as company employee, their interests are likely to differ from those of the non-executive directors.

- On the board of directors, some individuals might have considerably more influence than others. Typically, the most influential members of the board are the **company chairman** (board chairman) and the managing director (often called the **chief executive officer** or CEO).

The board of directors take many decisions as a group, but they also have individual interests in the company. Directors are therefore stakeholders in their company both as a unit and as separate individuals.

3.3 Other internal stakeholders

Internal stakeholders are stakeholders who work within the entity. Employees can be an important stakeholder group. It might be possible to divide employees into sub-groups, each with a different set of interests and expectations, and each with a different amount of influence over the actions of the company.

- It might be appropriate to separate **senior management** and **other employees** into two separate stakeholder groups. Senior management might have a bigger interest in the profits and share price of the company because they belong to a share incentive scheme or share option scheme, or because they receive annual bonus payments based on the company's profitability. Other employees who do not have such incentives will have much less interest in the financial performance of the company or its share price.

© International Financial Publishing Limited

■ Some employees might be able to demand large rewards from the company or might exercise strong influence because of their value to the company. For example, in the UK some individual investment bankers have a strong influence within their bank because of the specialist skills they possess and the income they are able to earn or the bank.

In some companies, there might be a strong **trade union influence**. The ability of a company to alter its working practices, for example, may depend on obtaining the co-operation and support of the trade unions.

3.4 External stakeholders

A company has external stakeholders as well as internal stakeholders. External stakeholders are individuals or groups who do not work for the company but who nevertheless have an interest in what the company does and who might be able to influence the way in which the company is governed.

■ **Lenders** have an interest in a company to which they lend money. They expect to be paid what they are owed. Usually a lender will not be closely involved in the governance or management of a company, but they will monitor its financial performance and financial position. Lenders will also become significant stakeholders if the company gets into financial difficulties and is faced with the risk of insolvency.

■ **Suppliers** have an interest in companies who are their major customers, although their influence over its governance might be small.

■ **Regulators** have an interest in companies whose activities they are required to regulate. Some aspects of regulation have a major impact on the way in which a company is governed. For example, quoted companies must comply with the rules set by the securities regulator (such as the Securities Exchange Commission in the US and the Financial Services Authority in the UK).

■ **Government** has a stake in companies. Companies are a source of tax revenue and also collect tax (income taxes and sales taxes) for the government from employees and customers. For some companies, such as companies that manufacture defence equipment, the government might have an influence as a major customer for the goods that the company produces.

■ **Customers, the general public or special interest groups** might have a significant influence over a company, especially a company that relies for success on the high reputation of its products or services.

■ **Stock exchanges** have an influence over the governance of quoted companies, because companies must comply with the rules of the stock exchange on which their shares are traded.

■ A company's **auditors** should also have some influence over the governance of a company, by making sure that the board of directors presents financial statements to the shareholders that present a true and fair view of the company's financial position and performance.

■ **Investors** are a major influence over companies whose shares are traded on a stock exchange. Investors decide what the market price of a company's shares should be. A company needs to satisfy the expectations not only of its shareholders, but of the investing community in general, if it wishes to sustain or increase the share price (and so the total value of the company).

3.5 Institutional investors

Institutional investors are entities that specialise in investing, mainly in shares and bonds. There are several types of institutional investor.

- **Pension funds**. These institutions hold funds that will be used to provide pensions to individuals after their retirement. Pension funds may be sponsored by an employer, or may be private pension schemes of individuals. Until the money is needed to pay a pension, it is invested to earn a return.

- **Insurance companies**. The funds of insurance companies come from insurance policy premiums and life assurance premiums. Until the money is needed for payment to the insurance policy holders, it is invested.

- **Mutual funds**. Mutual funds are funds of many individual investors, who invest relatively small amounts of money in the fund. The investments of the many different individuals are combined and invested collectively. In the UK, the main types of mutual funds are unit trusts and Open-Ended Investment Companies or OEICs.

Institutional investors are significant stakeholders on companies, in any country where they invest large funds. They are particularly influential in the US and UK.

- Individually, an institutional investor might hold only a small proportion of the shares in a large public company. However, by joining together and speaking collectively, a group of institutional investors might be able to have some influence over the decisions of a company's board of directors.

- Most institutional investors belong to a 'trade association'. In the UK, for example, most pension funds are members of the National Association of Pension Funds (NAPF) and most insurance companies are members of the Association of British Insurers (ABI). Each of these trade associations give information and advice to their members about corporate governance matters, and might recommend how they should vote on certain issues at the general meetings of companies. Collectively, bodies such as the NAPF and ABI (and their members) can have a major influence on companies because of the significance of their members as investors and shareholders.

In the UK for example, the influence of the institutional investors has been significance in persuading listed companies to adopt (most of) the provisions of the Combined Code on corporate governance. Their role in promoting good corporate governance has therefore been critically important.

- In the UK, a section of the Combined Code on corporate governance contains principles about the role of institutional investors in contributing to good corporate governance.

- The institutional shareholder bodies have issued guidelines on corporate governance to their members, which they encourage their members to apply.

- The institutional shareholder bodies issue regular advice to members on how they should consider voting on certain issues at general meetings of particular

© International Financial Publishing Limited

companies. For example, the NAPF or ABI might recommend to their members that they should vote against the re-election of a particular director, or should vote against the directors' remuneration report, or against a proposed takeover bid.

Corporate governance and investor confidence

Institutional investors are also important because their views are a good reflection of investor confidence in the stock market. Bad corporate governance could eventually damage the confidence of investors and make them much less willing to invest in shares. This in turn will keep share prices – and company values – down, and will make it difficult for companies to raise fresh capital in the financial markets when they need it.

Arthur Levitt, a former chairman of the US Securities and Exchange Commission, made the following comments at the time of the Enron collapse (and a heavy fall in stock market prices generally in the US): 'If a country does not have a reputation for strong corporate governance practice, capital will flow elsewhere. If investors are not confident with the level of disclosure, capital will flow elsewhere. If a country opts for lax accounting and reporting standards, capital will flow elsewhere. All enterprises in that country, regardless of how steadfast a particular company's practices, may suffer the consequences.... Markets exist by the grace of investors and it is today's more empowered investors who will determine which companies and which markets will stand the test of time and endure the weight of greater competition. It serves us well to remember that no market has a divine right to investors' capital.'

© International Financial Publishing Limited

CHAPTER

2

Agency relationships and theories

Contents
1   Agency theory
2   Transaction cost economics theory
3   Stakeholder theory

> ### Agency theory
>
> - The law of agency
> - Concepts in agency theory: the agency relationship
> - Agency conflicts
> - Agency costs
> - Reducing the agency problem
> - Accountability of agents
> - Ethics and agency theory

1 Agency theory

1.1 The law of agency

An agent is a person who acts on behalf of another person, the principal, in dealing with other people. For example, a selling agent acts on behalf of a principal, a manufacturer of goods, to sell goods on the manufacturer's behalf. Similarly, a stock broker is an agent who acts on behalf of a client (the principal) to buy or sell shares on the client's behalf. The agent acts on the name of the principal, and commits the principal to agreements and transactions.

In company law, the directors act as agents of the company. The board of directors as a whole, and individual directors, have the authority to bind the company to contractual agreements with other parties.

Since most of the powers to act on behalf of the company are given to the board of directors, the directors (and the management of a company) have extensive powers in deciding what the company should do, what its objectives should be, what its business strategies should be, how it should invest and what its targets for performance should be.

The powerful position of the directors raises questions about the use of this power, especially where the owners of the company (its shareholders) and the directors are different individuals.

- How can the owners of the company make sure that the directors are acting in the best interests of the shareholders?
- If the directors act in ways that the shareholders do not agree with, what can the shareholders do to make the directors act differently?

Fiduciary duty of directors

As agents of the company, directors have a fiduciary duty to the company. A fiduciary duty is a duty of trust. A director must act on behalf of the company in total good faith, and must not put his personal interests before the interests of the company.

© International Financial Publishing Limited

If a director is in breach of this fiduciary duty he could be held liable in law, if the company were to take legal action against him. Legal action by a company against a director for breach of fiduciary duty would normally be taken by the rest of the board of directors or, possibly, a majority of the shareholders acting in the name of the company.

Agency law and challenging the actions of directors

In practice, it is very difficult for shareholders to use the law to challenge the decisions and actions of the company's directors. If shareholders believe that the directors are not acting in the best interests of the company, their ability to do something about the problem is restricted.

- The shareholders can vote to remove any director from office, but this requires a majority vote by the shareholders, which might be difficult to obtain.

- In a court of law, shareholders would have to demonstrate that the directors were actually acting against the interests of the company, or against the clear interests of particular shareholders, in order to persuade the court to take legal measures against the directors.

In summary, although there is a legal relationship between the board of directors and their company, the shareholders cannot easily use the law to control the decisions or actions that the directors take on behalf of the company.

1.2 Concepts in agency theory: the agency relationship

Whereas agency law deals with the legal relationship between a company and its directors, the theory of agency deals with the relationship between:

- a company's owners and
- its managers (directors).

Agency theory is based on the idea that when a company is first established, its owners are usually also its managers. As a company grows, the owners appoint managers to run the company. The owners expect the managers to run the company in the best interests of the owners; therefore a form of agency relationship exists between the owners and the managers.

Many companies borrow, and a significant proportion of the long-term capital of a company might come from various sources of debt capital, such as bank loans, lease finance and bond issues (debentures, loan stock and so on). Major lenders also have an interest in how the company is managed, because they want to be sure that the company will be able to repay the debt with interest.

The agency relationship

Agency theory was developed by **Jensen and Meckling** (1976). They suggested a theory of how the governance of a company is based on the conflicts of interest between the company's owners (shareholders), its managers and major providers of debt finance.

Each of these groups has different interests and objectives.

- The **shareholders** want to increase their income and wealth. Their interest is with the returns that the company will provide in the form of dividends, and also in the value of their shares. The value of their shares depends on the long-term financial prospects for the company. Shareholders are therefore concerned about dividends, but they are even more concerned about long-term profitability and financial prospects, because these affect the value of their shares.

- The **managers** are employed to run the company on behalf of the shareholders. However, if the managers do not own shares in the company, they have no direct interest in future returns for shareholders, or in the value of the shares. Managers have an employment contract and earn a salary. Unless they own shares, or unless their remuneration is linked to profits or share values, their main interests are likely to be the size of their remuneration package and their status as company managers.

- The **major** providers of debt have an interest in sound financial management by the company's managers, so that the company will be able to pay its debts in full and on time.

Jensen and Meckling defined the agency relationship as a form of contract between a company's owners and its managers, where the owners (as principal) appoint an agent (the managers) to manage the company on their behalf. As a part of this arrangement, the owners must delegate decision-making authority to the management.

The owners expect the agents to act in the best interests of the owners. Ideally, the 'contract' between the owners and the managers should ensure that the managers always act in the best interests of the owners. However, it is impossible to arrange the 'perfect contract', because decisions by the managers (agents) affect their own personal welfare as well as the interests of the owners.

This raises a fundamental question. How can managers, as agents of their company, be induced or persuaded to act in the best interests of the shareholders?

1.3 Agency conflicts

Agency conflicts are differences in the interests of a company's owners and managers. They arise in several ways.

- **Moral hazard**. A manager has an interest in receiving benefits from his or her position as a manager. These include all the benefits that come from status, such as a company car, a private chauffeur, use of a company airplane, lunches, attendance at sponsored sporting events, and so on. Jensen and Meckling suggested that a manger's incentive to obtain these benefits is higher when he has no shares, or only a few shares, in the company. The biggest problem is in large companies.

- **Effort level**. Managers may work less hard than they would if they were the owners of the company. The effect of this 'lack of effort' could be lower profits and a lower share price. The problem will exist in a large company at middle levels of management as well as at senior management level. The interests of middle managers and the interests of senior managers might well be different,

© International Financial Publishing Limited

especially if senior management are given pay incentives to achieve higher profits, but the middle managers are not.

- **Earnings retention**. The remuneration of directors and senior managers is often related to the size of the company, rather than its profits. This gives managers an incentive to grow the company, and increase its sales turnover and assets, rather than to increase the returns to the company's shareholders. Management are more likely to want to re-invest profits in order to make the company bigger, rather than pay out the profits as dividends. When this happens, companies might invest in capital investment projects where the expected profitability is quite small, and the net present value might be negative.

- **Risk aversion**. Executive directors and senior managers usually earn most of their income from the company they work for. They are therefore interested in the stability of the company, because this will protect their job and their future income. This means that management might be risk-averse, and reluctant to invest in higher-risk projects. In contrast, shareholders might want a company to take bigger risks, if the expected returns are sufficiently high. Shareholders often invest in a portfolio of different companies; therefore it matters less to them if an individual company takes risks.

- **Time horizon**. Shareholders are concerned about the long-term financial prospects of their company, because the value of their shares depends on expectations for the long-term future. In contrast, managers might only be interested in the short-term. This is partly because they might receive annual bonuses based on short-term performance, and partly because they might not expect to be with the company for more than a few years. Managers might therefore have an incentive to increase accounting return on capital employed (or return on investment), whereas shareholders have a greater interest in long-term value as measured by net present value.

1.4 Agency costs

Agency costs are the costs of having an agent to make decisions on behalf of a principal. Applying this to corporate governance, agency costs are the costs that the shareholders incur by having managers to run the company instead of running the company themselves.

- Agency costs do not exist when the owners and the managers are exactly the same individuals.

- Agency costs start to arise as soon as some of the shareholders are not also directors of the company.

- Agency costs are potentially very high in large companies, where there are many different shareholders and a large professional management.

Agency costs can therefore be defined as the 'value loss' to shareholders that arises from the divergence of interests between the shareholders and the company's management.

There are three aspects to agency costs:

■ They include the **costs of monitoring**. The owners of a company can establish systems for monitoring the actions and performance of management, to try to ensure that management are acting in their best interests. An example of monitoring is the requirement for the directors to present an annual report and accounts to the shareholders, setting out the financial performance and financial position of the company. These accounts are audited, and the auditors present a report to the shareholders. Preparing accounts and having them audited has a cost.

■ Agency costs also include the costs to the shareholder that arise when the managers take decisions that are not in the best interests of the shareholders (but are in the interests of the managers themselves). For example, agency costs arise when a company's directors decide to acquire a new subsidiary, and pay more for the acquisition than it is worth. The managers would gain personally from the enhanced status of managing a larger group of companies. The cost to the shareholders comes from the fall in share price that would result from paying too much for the acquisition.

■ The third aspect of agency costs is costs that might be incurred to provide incentives to managers to act in the best interests of the shareholders. These are sometimes called **bonding costs**. These costs are intended to reduce the size of the agency problem. Directors and other senior managers might be given incentives in the form of free shares in the company, or share options. In addition, directors and senior managers might be paid cash bonuses if the company achieves certain specified financial targets. The remuneration packages for directors and senior managers are therefore an important element of agency costs.

Agency costs: summary

Agency costs can be summarised as follows

Monitoring costs	Costs of measuring, observing and controlling the behaviour of management. Some costs are imposed by law (annual accounts, annual audit) and some arise from compliance with codes of corporate governance.
+ Bonding costs	Costs of arrangements that help to align the interests of the shareholders and managers.
+ Residual loss	Losses occur for the owners, such as the losses arising from a lower share price, because the managers take decisions and actions that are not in the best interests of the shareholders. Monitoring costs and bonding costs will not prevent some residual loss from occurring.

1.5 Reducing the agency problem

Jensen and Meckling argued that when they act in the interest of the shareholders, managers bear the entire cost of failing to pursue goals that are in their own best interests, but gain only a few of the benefits. Incentives should therefore be provided to management to increase their willingness to take 'value-maximising decisions' – in other words, to take decisions that benefit the shareholders by maximising the value of their shares.

© International Financial Publishing Limited

Several methods of reducing the agency problem have been suggested. These include:

■ Devising a remuneration package for executive directors and senior managers that gives them an incentive to act in the best interests of the shareholders. Remuneration packages may therefore provide rewards for achieving a mixture of both long-term and short-term financial targets and non-financial targets.

■ Having a large proportion of debt on the long-term capital structure of the company.

■ Having a board of directors that will monitor the decisions taken for the company by its executive management.

In addition, agents (management) should be held **accountable** to the principal (shareholders).

Providers of debt

Jensen and Meckling argued that the problems of the agency relationship are bigger in companies that are profitable but have low growth in profits. These companies generate a large amount of free cash flow.

Free cash flow is cash that can be spent at the discretion of management, and does not have to be spent on essential items such a payment of debt interest, taxation and the replacement of ageing non-current assets.

It is in the interest of shareholders that free cash flow should be either:

■ invested in projects that will earn a high return (a positive net present value), or

■ paid to the shareholders as dividends.

The directors and other senior managers of a company might want to invest free cash flow in projects that will increase the size of the company. These could be projects that will earn a high return. In a low-growth company, however, it is likely that managers will want to invest in projects that increase the size of the company but are only marginally profitable and would have a negative net present value.

One way of reducing this problem would be to have a high proportion of debt capital in the capital structure of the company. Interest must be paid on debt, and this reduces the free cash flow. Management must also ensure that new investments are sufficiently profitable so that the company can continue to pay the interest costs on its debt capital.

The board of directors

A different method of reducing the agency problem is to make the board of directors more effective at monitoring the decisions of the executive management.

■ A board will be ineffective at monitoring the decisions of management if it is dominated by the chief executive officer (CEO). This is because the CEO is the head of the executive management team. The board would be especially ineffective in a monitoring role if the CEO is also the chairman of the board.

- Fama and Jensen (1983) argued that an effective board must consist largely of **independent non-executive directors**. Independent non-executive directors have no executive role in the company and are not full-time employees. They are able to act in the best interests of the shareholders.

- Independent non-executive directors should also take the decisions where there is (or could be) a conflict of interest between executive directors and the best interests of the company. For example, non-executive directors should be responsible for the remuneration packages for executive directors and other senior managers.

Jensen also argued (1993) that the board of directors becomes less effective as it grows in size. This is because a large board is often slow to react to events and will often be incapable of taking action quickly when it is needed. The directors on a large board are also less likely to be critical of each other than directors on small boards.

These ideas for reducing the agency problem are contained in codes of corporate governance, and will be considered in more detail in later chapters.

1.6 Accountability of agents

Agents should be accountable to their principal for their decisions and actions. Accountability means:

- Having to report back to the principal and give an account of what has been achieved.

- Having to answer questions from the principal about performance and achievements.

- The principal having power to reward or punish an agent for good or bad performance.

Greater accountability should reduce the agency problem, because it provides management with a greater incentive (obtaining rewards or avoiding punishments) to achieve performance levels that are in the best interests of the shareholders.

However, the costs of accountability (which are monitoring costs) should not be excessive and should not exceed the value of the benefits that the monitoring provides.

Accountability and the source of authority in an entity

Accountability also determines where the centre of authority lies within an entity. Day and Klein (1987) made the following comment about accountability in public services, but the same principle applies to companies: 'The ability to call people to account defines the [centre] of authority in any given society…. But the notion of the **right** to call people to account needs to be complemented by the notion of power in the **ability** to call people to account.'

The accountability of management depends on both the right of the shareholders to call the directors to account, but also on their ability to do so.

　　　　　　　　　　　　　　　　　　© International Financial Publishing Limited

1.7   Ethics and agency theory

Agency theory may be summarised as follows.

- In many companies there is a separation of ownership from control. Professional managers are appointed to act as agents for the owners of the company.

- Individuals are driven by self-interest.

- Conflicts of self-interest arise between shareholders and managers.

- Managers, because they are driven by self-interest, cannot be relied on to act in the best interests of the shareholders. This creates problems in the agency relationship between shareholders and management.

- These agency problems create costs for the shareholders. The aim should be to minimise these costs, by improving the monitoring of management and/or providing management with incentives that bring their interests closer to those of the shareholders.

- Concepts of agency theory are now applied in various codes of corporate governance, in many different countries.

'In brief, agency theory suggests that the prime role of the board is to ensure that executive behaviour is aligned with the interests of the shareholder-owners. Otherwise, self-interested managers will use their superior information to line their own pockets. This is the justification for the separation of the chairman and CEO roles, huge senior executive salaries and the over-riding requirement for [independence of non-executive directors], and much more' (Simon Caulkin, The Observer, 27 November 2005).

There is an ethical aspect to agency theory. The theory is based on the view that individuals cannot be trusted to act in any way that is not in their own best interests.

Transaction cost economics theory
■ Costs of the firm: production costs and transaction costs
■ Assumptions in transaction cost economics
■ The variables in transaction cost economics
■ Comparison of transaction cost economics with agency theory

2   Transaction cost economics theory

Agency theory explains the relationship between the owners of a company and its management as the resolution of a conflict of interests. Shareholders delegate the task of running the company to their managers, but need to ensure that agency costs are minimised.

Transaction cost economics provides a different basis for explaining the relationship between the owners of a company and its management. Although it is an economic theory, it also attempts to explain companies not just as 'economic units', but as an organisation consisting of people with differing views and objectives. You need to know a little about transaction cost economics, in order to contrast it with agency theory.

The theory of transaction cost economics (TCE) is most closely associated with the work of **Oliver Williamson**, who based his ideas on the earlier work of Coase. Williamson began writing on TCE in the 1970s.

2.1   Costs of the firm: production costs and transaction costs

The operations of a business entity can be performed either through market transactions or by doing the work in-house. For example, a business entity could obtain its raw materials from an external supplier, or it could make the materials itself. Similarly, an entity could hire self-employed contractors to do work, or it could hire full-time employees. An entity might sell its finished goods to a retail organisation, or it might sell directly to the end-consumer.

Logically, a firm's decision about whether to arrange transactions in the open market or whether to do the work 'in-house' (itself) depends on which is cheaper.

When a firm does work 'in-house', it needs a management structure and a hierarchy of authority. Senior management are at the top of this hierarchy. According to the theory of transaction cost economics, the structure of a firm and the relationship between the owners of a firm and its management depends on the extent to which transactions are performed internally.

Total costs are defined as the sum of production costs and transaction costs.

■ Production costs are the costs that would be incurred in an ideal economic market, to make and sell goods of the firm. In an ideal economic market, production costs are minimised.

                                                 © International Financial Publishing Limited

- Transaction costs are additional costs incurred whenever the 'perfect' situation is not achieved. For example, if a company might buy goods from a supplier who is not the cheapest available, because it was not aware of the existence of the cheapest supplier. A company might sell goods on credit to a customer, not knowing that the trade receivable will become a bad debt.

Transaction costs are sometimes higher when a transaction is arranged in the market, and they are sometimes higher when the transaction is done 'in-house'. Carrying out activities in-house rather than arranging contracts externally is referred to as **vertical integration**.

Total costs are minimised when transaction costs are minimised. This should determine the optimal size of the firm and the size of the management hierarchy in the firm. The way in which a company is organised, and the extent to which it is vertically integrated, also affect the control the company has over its transactions.

The way in which transaction costs are minimised depends on a number of variables. These are described later.

As a general rule, it is in the interests of a company's management to carry out transactions internally, and not in the external market. Performing transactions internally:

- removes the risks and uncertainties about the future prices of products and about product quality
- removes all the risks and costs of dealing with external suppliers.

2.2 Assumptions in transaction cost economics (TCE)

Traditional economic theory is based on the assumptions that all behaviour is rational and that profit maximisation is the rational objective of all businesses. Transaction cost economics changes these assumptions, by trying to allow for human behaviour, and the fact that individuals do not always act rationally.

Williamson based his theory on two assumptions about behaviour:

- bounded rationality, and
- opportunism.

Bounded rationality

It is assumed in TCE that humans act rationally, but only within certain limits of understanding. This means for example that the managers of a company will in theory act rationally in seeking to maximise the value of the company for its shareholders, but their bounded rationality might make them act differently. Business is very complex and large businesses are much more complex than small businesses. However, in any business, there is a limit to the amount of information that individuals can remember, understand and deal with. No one is capable of assessing all the possible courses of action and no one can anticipate what will happen in the future. In a competitive market, no one can anticipate with certainty what competitors will do.

Playing the game of chess has been used as an example of bounded rationality. The game is very complex, and there are many different possible moves. The actions of the opponent in a game of chess cannot be predicted, so it is impossible to predict what the opponent will do in response to a particular move. The same problem applies to managing a company. It is impossible to predict with certainty what will happen, because there are too many factors and too many possibilities to consider.

Williamson was mainly concerned with what happens when individuals reach the boundaries of their understanding, because a situation is too complex or too uncertain. He wrote: 'Bounds on rationality are interesting ... only to the extent that the limits of rationality are reached – which is to say under conditions of uncertainty and/or complexity.'

When uncertainty is high, or when a situation is very complex, there is a greater tendency to carry out transactions 'in-house' and to have vertical integration.

Opportunism

Williamson also argued that individuals will act in a self-interested way, and 'with guile'. In other words, people will not always be honest and truthful about their intentions. Williamson defined opportunism as: 'an effort to realise individual gains through a lack of candour or honesty in transactions.' An individual might try to take advantage of an opportunity to gain a benefit at the expense of someone else.

Williamson also argued that it is not possible to predict in advance who might act with opportunism, or when. However, managers are opportunistic by nature. Given the opportunity, they will take advantage of available ways of improving their own benefits and privileges.

In terms of transaction cost economics, a problem with opportunism is that external parties – such as contractors and suppliers of goods – cannot always be trusted to act honestly. As a result, there may be a tendency for a firm to carry out transactions itself, rather than rely on external suppliers. However, there is also a risk that by taking control of transactions internally, managers will have opportunities to take decisions and actions that are in their own personal interests.

This self-interest needs to be controlled. When managers act in their own interests, investors will be discouraged from providing finance to the company. In this respect, transaction cost theory has similarities with agency theory.

2.3 The variables in transaction cost economics

Williamson argued that there are three factors or variables which determine the extent to which a firm is 'integrated vertically' and does the work itself. These factors are:

- frequency of transactions
- uncertainty
- asset specificity.

© International Financial Publishing Limited

Frequency of transactions

A firm will never wish to bring 'in house' a service or the production of an item that is very rarely used. Rare transactions will always be arranged in the market with another individual or entity.

For example, a company will rarely ever want to establish its own department for management consultancy. This is because the services of management consultants should be required only rarely, and they can be provided much better by external specialists. The transaction costs of a market transaction are therefore much lower.

However, when goods are purchased very frequently, or services are used frequently, there is a much stronger case for vertical integration and bringing the work 'in house' because the transaction costs should be lower.

Uncertainty

As indicated earlier, uncertainty creates problems partly because of bounded rationality. Uncertainty about transactions will affect a decision about whether the transactions should be done in house or arranged in the market. As a general rule, greater uncertainty makes it more likely that the transactions will be done in-house.

For example, suppose that a holiday tour operator wants to arrange a long-term contract for the supply of ski instructors for customers on its winter skiing holidays. The tour operator might consider negotiating a long-term contract with a company that employs and trains ski instructors. However, with such a long term contract there would inevitably be some uncertainties. How can the tour operator be sure that the other company will remain in business? What will guarantee that a sufficient number of ski instructors will always be available? Who will guarantee the quality of the ski instruction? Who will be responsible in the event of a skiing accident, caused by an instructor? Depending on circumstances – and the extent of the uncertainty – the tour operator might decide to hire and train its own ski instructors, to improve the probability that it can obtain a long-term supply of enough ski instructors of a suitable quality.

Asset specificity

Asset specificity refers to assets that are only valuable for a specific transaction. When an asset has only one specific use, transaction costs are likely to be reduced by vertical integration.

For example, a professional football club will use a football stadium for its football matches. The stadium has only one specific use – to host football matches for that particular football club. In such circumstances, transaction costs should be lower if the football club owns and operates the stadium itself, rather than hires the stadium from an independent stadium owner.

2.4   Comparison of transaction cost economics with agency theory

Transaction cost economics provides a theory to explain how a company develops into the size and structure that it has, and what might make the size and structure change. It assumes that management behaviour is determined by a combination of bounded rationality and opportunism, with the result that managers will act in their own self interests when the opportunities arise. This self-interested behaviour must be controlled.

Agency theory uses the conflict of interests between shareholders and managers to explain the nature of a company and its governance. Managers will often try to increase the size of their company, even though this is not in the best interests of the shareholders, because they benefit personally from growth in the size of the company.

Although they are based on different assumptions, both agency theory and transaction cost theory support the need for controls over corporate governance practices.

© International Financial Publishing Limited

> ## Stakeholder theory
>
> - Stakeholder approach to corporate governance
> - Definition of stakeholder theory
> - Rights for stakeholders
> - Stakeholder theory and agency theory

3 Stakeholder theory

3.1 Stakeholder approach to corporate governance

Agency theory is based on the assumption that the main objective of a company should be to maximise the wealth of shareholders. Management should therefore act and take decisions in the best interests of the shareholders. Corporate governance should therefore be concerned with minimising agency costs, by improving the monitoring of management and by bringing the self-interests of management more into line with the interests of the company's shareholders.

The stakeholder view is that the purpose of corporate governance should be to achieve, as far as possible, the aims of all key stakeholders – employees, investors, major creditors, customers, major suppliers, the government, local communities and the general public. A role of the company's directors is therefore to consider the interests of all the major stakeholders. However, some stakeholders (for example, employees) might be more important than others, so that management should give priority to their interests above the interests of other stakeholder groups.

In the introduction to its principles of corporate governance, the OECD commented that an aim of government policy ('public policy') should be 'to provide firms with the incentives and discipline to minimise divergence between private and social returns and to protect the interest of stakeholders.'

The OECD Principles themselves recognise the role of stakeholders in corporate governance and state that the corporate governance framework should:

- recognise the rights of stakeholders that are recognised in law or through mutual agreements, and also

- encourage active co-operation between corporations and stakeholders in creating wealth, jobs and the sustainability of financially sound enterprises.

3.2 Definition of stakeholder theory

Stakeholder theory can therefore be explained as follows.

The theory states that a company's managers should take decisions that take into consideration the interests of all the stakeholders. This means trying to achieve a range of different objectives, not just the aim of maximising the value of the company for its shareholders. This is because different stakeholders each have their own (different) expectations from the company, which the company's management should attempt to satisfy.

It has been suggested that in stakeholder theory, the company should have an individual set of values that provide an environment in which the interests of different stakeholders can co-exist, and stakeholders can co-operate to achieve their differing objectives.

Stakeholder theory can be seen as a mix of a variety of disciplines which produces a blend of sociological and organisational ideas. As companies are so large, they have an impact not just on their own shareholders, but on many more sectors of society.

3.3 Rights for stakeholders

Supporters of stakeholder approach to corporate governance recognise that only the senior managers and directors of a company, and the shareholders, have any significant power within the framework of corporate governance.

A stakeholder approach to corporate governance can therefore be implemented only by:

- negotiation and co-operation between management and employees, and
- legislation giving rights to stakeholders or protecting stakeholder rights.

3.4 Stakeholder theory and agency theory

Stakeholder theory, that a company has obligations to other stakeholders in addition to shareholders, is based on different assumptions from agency theory, which is based on the view that managers should act in the best interests of the shareholders. However, the two approaches to governance (and ethical theory) are not necessarily inconsistent.

Companies and their managers can act in the best interests of shareholders and at the same time attempt to satisfy interests of other stakeholders. For example, shareholders themselves might not have an objective of wealth maximisation. They might want to obtain satisfactory returns, but at the same time might want the companies they invest in to shown suitable concerns for society and the environment.

In other words, best practice in corporate governance and corporate social responsibility might be consistent with each other.

© International Financial Publishing Limited

CHAPTER

3

The board of directors

Contents

1	The role of the board
2	Composition of the board
3	The roles of chairman, chief executive officer and NEDs
4	Directors and the law
5	Induction, training and performance evaluation of directors

---

The role of the board

- Introductory note: codes of corporate governance
- Delegation of power within a company
- Corporate governance codes on the role of the board
- Decision-making and monitoring roles
- Unitary boards and two-tier board structures

---

1 The role of the board

1.1 Introductory note: codes of corporate governance

This chapter and the following chapters look at various aspects of corporate governance. These are relevant to all companies where there is a separation of the ownership from control, and the shareholders and directors are different individuals.

References will be made to codes of corporate governance, particularly the UK's Combined Code, which has provided a model for corporate governance codes in other countries.

When a country has a code of corporate governance, the code applies only to major stock market companies. In the UK, these are the 'listed' companies. A listed company is a company whose shares are on the Official List of the financial services regulator. A company's shares must be on the Official List before they can be traded on the main market of the London Stock Exchange. A listed company is therefore a major stock market company.

You should bear in mind that when references are made to corporate governance codes, these are likely to apply only to major companies. However, other companies (such as private companies or subsidiaries within a group) might choose voluntarily to comply with the principles or provisions of a corporate governance code, as a way of strengthening their corporate governance.

1.2 Delegation of power within a company

Within a company, all the powers are usually given to the board of directors. For example, this is an article in the standard articles of association (constitution) of UK companies. The board of directors then delegates some of its powers to executive management, and executive management are responsible for the day-to-day business operations.

There are no laws or standard rules, however, about what the role of the board of directors should be, or how much authority for decision-making should be retained by the board (and how much should be delegated to executive management).

                                                    © International Financial Publishing Limited

The delegation of power within a company may therefore vary between companies.

Students familiar with a unitary board (which is the form of board structure found in most countries) may have difficulty in identifying the difference between:

- the role of executive directors as managers of the company, and
- the role of the board of directors as a whole in the governance of the company.

The role of the board of directors is **not** to manage the company. This is the role of management.

Specifying the role of the board of directors, and making the board accountable for its performance in the role, is a key aspect of corporate governance.

1.3   Corporate governance codes on the role of the board

The role of the board of directors is specified in codes of corporate governance. There are many different codes or statements of corporate governance principles. This text will refer to some, but others are similar.

The Combined Code in the UK states that 'every company should be headed by an effective board, which is collectively responsible for the success of the company.' It then goes on to state that the role of the board is to:

- provide entrepreneurial leadership of the company; however this leadership should be provided within a framework of prudent and effective risk management
- set the strategic aims for the company
- ensure that the company has the necessary financial and human resources to meet its objectives
- review management performance
- set the company's values and standards and ensure that its 'obligations to its shareholders and others' are understood and met. (The Combined Code is therefore not specific about what the main objectives of the company should be.)

Singapore's Code of Corporate Governance specifies the role of the board in much the same way.

The OECD Principles of Corporate Governance state that the corporate governance framework should ensure:

- the strategic guidance of the company
- the effective monitoring of management by the board, and
- the board's accountability to the company and the shareholders.

1.4 Decision-making and monitoring roles

The role of a board of directors is a combination of decision-making and monitoring.

- A board should retain certain responsibilities, and should make decisions in these areas itself.

- Where the board delegates responsibilities to executive management, it should monitor the performance of management. For example, the board should expect senior management (usually the Chief Executive Officer) to account to the board for the performance of the company. In addition, the board should be responsible for monitoring the system of internal control that management has put in place.

In addition, the board should be accountable to the shareholders for its performance in carrying out these twin roles of decision-making and monitoring.

ICSA Guidance Note on matters reserved for the board

Corporate governance codes and principles are not specific about what exactly the decision-making responsibilities of the board should be. The Institute of Chartered Secretaries and Administrators (ICSA) has published a Guidance Note, suggesting that in each company there should be a formal, written list of matters for which the board will take the decisions, and will not delegate to management. These include monitoring responsibilities as well as decision-making responsibilities.

The Guidance Note ('Matters Reserved for the Board') provides a suggested schedule of board responsibilities, that it should not delegate. This is listed under 12 headings or categories.

Responsibility	Comment
Strategy and management	The board is responsible for the overall management of the company or group. This involves: ■ Approving the long-term objectives and commercial strategy ■ Approving the annual budget and capital expenditure budget ■ Oversight of operations ■ Review of the performance of the company or group ■ Decisions about expanding operations into new product areas or new markets, and decisions about closing down any significant part of operations.
Structure and capital	Changes relating to the capital structure of the group, or its management and control structure. Also decisions about any change in the company's status, such as going from private company to public company status.
Financial reporting and controls	Approval of financial statements and results. Approval of dividend policy. Approval of treasury policies, such as foreign currency exposures and the use of financial derivatives.
Internal controls	Ensuring that there is a sound system of internal control and risk management, by monitoring the systems that are in place.
Contracts	Approval of major capital projects and strategically-significant contracts. Approval of loans or foreign currency transactions above a stated amount. Approval of all major acquisitions and disposals.

© International Financial Publishing Limited

Communication	Approval of all communications to shareholders and the stock market, and all major press releases.
Board membership and other appointments	Decisions about appointments to the board, appointment of the company secretary and the appointment of the company's auditors.
Remuneration	Decisions about the remuneration of all directors and senior managers, including the approval of major share incentive schemes (which may also require approval by the shareholders).
Delegation of authority	The board is responsible for deciding what responsibilities should be delegated to board committees, and should decide on the division of responsibilities between the chief executive officer and the board chairman.
Corporate governance matters	The board is responsible for corporate governance matters such as communications with the company's shareholders, deciding the balance of interests between the shareholders and other stakeholders and ensuring that independent non-executive directors continue to be independent.
Policies	Approval of company policies, such as health and safety policy and environmental policy.
Other issues	There will probably be a number of other issues that the board should reserve for its own decision-making, such as decisions affecting the company's contributions to its employees' pension fund, the appointment of the company's main professional advisers, and decisions to prosecute, defend or settle major litigation disputes involving costs or payments above a specified amount.

This extract from the Institute of Chartered Secretaries and Administrators' guidance note on 'Matters Reserved for the Board' has been reproduced with the permission of ICSA and is available in full at www.icsa.org.uk.

1.5   Unitary boards and two-tier board structures

In most countries, companies have a unitary board. This means that there is a single board of directors, which is responsible for performing all the functions of the board.

Two-tier boards

In some countries (such as Germany and the Netherlands), all or most large companies have a two-tier board. A two-tier board structure consists of:

■   a management board, and

■   a supervisory board.

The **management board** is responsible for the oversight of management and business operations. It consists entirely of executive directors, and its chairman is the company's chief executive officer.

The **supervisory board** is responsible for the general oversight of the company and the management board. It consists entirely of non-executive directors, who have no executive management responsibilities in the company. Its chairman is the chairman of the company, who is the most significant figure in the corporate governance structure.

The responsibilities of the management board and supervisory board should be clearly defined. For example, it is a requirement of Germany's code of corporate governance (the Cromme Code) that the supervisory board should have a list of matters that require its attention.

A function of the chairman of the company (and supervisory board) is to work closely with the CEO. As chairman of the management board, the CEO reports to the chairman of the company. If there is a good relationship between the CEO and chairman, the chairman will speak for the company's management at meetings of the supervisory board.

Germany has been closely associated with a stakeholder approach to corporate governance, and the interests of stakeholder groups are recognised by representation on the supervisory board. Directors on the supervisory board normally include:

■ representatives of major shareholders of the company

■ representatives of the employees or a major trade union

■ former executive managers of the company, possibly former members of the management board who have now retired from the company.

In large companies, the supervisory board can be quite large, in order that it can represent a sufficient number of different stakeholder interests. Directors who represent an interest, such as the interests of a major shareholder or the company's employees, are not 'independent' – unlike most non-executive directors on the unitary boards of listed companies (stock market companies) in other countries.

Comparison of unitary boards and two-tier boards

An obvious question to ask is which type of board structure, a unitary board or a two-tier board structure, provides better corporate governance. Each type of board structure has its strengths and weaknesses. In the analysis below, the strengths of a two-tier board structure are, by implication, weaknesses of a unitary board, and vice versa.

The advantages of a two-tier board structure are as follows.

■ It separates two different roles for the board. The management board is responsible for operational issues, whereas the supervisory board is able to monitor the performance of management generally, including the executive directors on the management board.

■ It is an appropriate structure for a company that recognises the interests of different stakeholder groups. These stakeholder interests can be represented on the supervisory board, without having a direct impact on the management of the company.

■ The legal duties of non-executive directors on the supervisory board can be different from the legal duties of executive directors on the management board. This is sensible, because independent directors are part-time appointments and are not involved in the management of the company. In a unitary board, the legal duties of non-executive directors and executive directors are the same.

© International Financial Publishing Limited

The advantages of a unitary board are as follows.

- Unitary boards can be small in size, because there is no requirement to appoint directors who represent stakeholder interest groups. Small boards are more likely to act quickly in an emergency or when a fast decision is required.

- In a unitary board structure, it is easier for the non-executive directors and the executive directors to work co-operatively. With a two-tier structure, there is a risk that the two boards will not co-operate fully, especially when the chairman of the company and the CEO do not work well together.

- Unitary boards work towards a common purpose, which is what the board considers to be the best interests of the shareholders and others. With two-tier boards, there is more opportunity for disagreements on the supervisory board between directors who represent different stakeholder interests.

The remainder of this text on corporate governance will concentrate on companies with a unitary board. However, similar principles and issues arise in companies with a two-tier board structure.

Composition of the board
■ Composition and size of the board
■ Executive and non-executive directors
■ Independence
■ Independent directors
■ Board balance and independent directors

2 Composition of the board

2.1 Composition and size of the board

The composition of the (unitary) board of a major company in many countries consists of:

- A chairman, who may be an executive director but is more usually a non-executive director
- (Sometimes) a deputy chairman
- A chief executive officer, who is an executive director
- Other executive directors
- Other non-executive directors.

The board should include individuals who together provide a suitable balance of skills, experience and judgement.

However, a board of directors should not be too big. The UK Combined Code states that 'the board should not be so large as to be unwieldy.' The Singapore code of Corporate Governance states: 'The Board should examine its size and, with a view to determining the impact of the number upon effectiveness, decide on what it considers an appropriate size for the Board, which facilitates effective decision-making.' In deciding what is a suitable size of board for a particular company, 'the Board should take into account the scope and nature of the operations of the company.'

2.2 Executive and non-executive directors

A unitary board in large companies consists of executive directors and non-executive directors. Non-executive directors are found on the boards of most stock market companies, but they are also appointed to the boards of subsidiary companies within a group and to the boards of private companies.

(*Note*: UK listed companies may be required to include non-executive directors on their board. Other companies are not required to appoint non-executive directors, but might do so voluntarily.)

© International Financial Publishing Limited

Executive directors are directors who also have executive management responsibilities in the company. They are normally full-time employees of the company. Examples of executive directors are the chief executive officer (CEO) and the finance director (chief finance officer or CFO).

Non-executive directors or NEDs are directors who do not have any executive management responsibilities in the company. (They might be an executive director in a different company.)

■ NEDs are not employees of the company.

■ They are not full-time. When they are appointed there should be a clear understanding about how much time (each month or each year) the NED will probably be required to give to the company's affairs.

However, the status of executive directors and non-executive directors, as directors, is exactly the same.

2.3 Independence

All directors should show independence of character. They should be able to reach their own views and judgements, and should be able to express their personal opinions with conviction. In this sense, 'independence' means reaching opinions, expressing them and not necessarily agreeing with everything that fellow directors say.

These characteristics of independent character are mentioned in the Principles for Corporate Governance in the Commonwealth (the CACG Principles). These state that: 'The board should be composed of people of integrity who can bring a blend of knowledge, skills, objectivity, experience and commitment to the board which should be led by a capable Chairman who brings out the best in each director. Crucial to this is having a proper director selection process to avoid the propensity for 'cronyism' and 'tokenism'.'

In corporate governance, however, 'independence' means something much more specific than having an independent mind.

2.4 Independent directors

It is argued that the board of directors should consist partly of independent directors. An **independent director** is an individual who:

■ has no link to a special interest group or stakeholder group, such as executive management, other employees of the company, a major shareholder, a supplier or a major supplier or customer of the company

■ has no significant personal interests in the company, such as a significant contractual relationship with the company.

Given this definition of an independent director, it is impossible for an executive director to be independent, because he or she has a direct link with executive management.

Only non-executive directors can be independent. However, not all NEDs are independent. A NED is not independent when there are relationships with the company or circumstances that would be likely to affect the director's judgement.

Independent directors are defined in various codes and principles of corporate governance. The UK Combined Code states that in most circumstances, a director is **not independent** when he or she:

■ has been an employee of the company within the past five years

■ has (or has had within the previous three years) a material business relationship with the company, either personally or as a partner, shareholder, director or senior employee of another entity

■ receives remuneration in addition to a fee as non-executive director, participates in the company's share incentive scheme or a performance-related pay scheme, or is a member of the company's pension scheme

■ has close family ties with a director, senior employee or professional adviser of the company

■ has significant links with other directors through involvement in other companies or entities

■ represents a major shareholder

■ has served on the board for more than nine years since the date of his/her election as director.

(The 'nine year rule' on independence for NEDs has been slightly controversial, and some UK listed companies have NEDs who have been in office for over nine years, but who, according to the company, remain independent.)

Definitions of 'independent director' vary between countries and codes. In Singapore, for example, the definition is less strict than in the UK. Its Code of Corporate Governance states that examples of relationships where a director is not deemed to be independent are as follows:

■ Where the director is employed by the company (or any related company) or has been employed by the company at any time during the past three years.

■ A close family relative of an individual who is a senior employee of the company, or who has been a senior employee at any time during the past three years.

■ A director receiving remuneration from the company in the current or previous financial year, in addition to his fee as non-executive director.

■ A director who has (or has had in the current or previous financial year) a material business relationship with the company, either personally or through a close family member, or as a partner, shareholder, director or senior employee of another for-profit entity.

© International Financial Publishing Limited

2.5 Board balance and independent directors

The status of directors as independent or 'not independent' is significant for companies that are required to comply with a code of corporate governance.
A general principle of good corporate governance is that there should be a suitable balance of individuals on the board.

A board should consist of directors with a suitable range of skills, experience and expertise. However, there should also be a 'balance of power' on the board, so that no individual or small group of individuals can dominate decision-making by the board.

Experience has shown that in the past, a feature of many large public companies that have collapsed dramatically has been a domination of the board's decision-making by an individual or a small group of individuals. In the UK, for example, a link between bad corporate governance and domination by a powerful individual was evident in the cases of the Maxwell Communications Corporation (headed by Robert Maxwell) and Polly Peck International (headed by Asil Nadir). Both these companies collapsed unexpectedly in the early 1990s.

Example

The case of Robert Maxwell is notorious in UK corporate history. During the 1980s, Maxwell built up a major publishing group, which included Mirror Group Newspapers, the US publisher Macmillan and the New York Daily News. Mirror Group Newspapers became a listed UK company, but the other companies in the group remained privately-owned. Maxwell was reported to have been a tyrannical leader of the company, who dominated the board of directors of the companies within the group.

In November 1991, Mr Maxwell died in mysterious circumstances, drowning during a cruise off the Canary Islands. After his death, it was found that he had misappropriated about £900 million from the pension funds of his companies, using the money to fund business expansion and to support group companies that were in financial difficulty. In 1992, the Maxwell companies in the UK and US were forced to file for bankruptcy/insolvency. A subsequent investigation found that 'there were no proper corporate or financial controls' to prevent Maxwell from doing what he had done.

This case was one of several corporate collapses that led to recognition of the need for a balance of power on the boards of major companies.

Definition of a suitable board balance

The UK Combined Code states: 'The board should include a balance of executive and non-executive directors (and in particular independent non-executive directors) such that no individual or small group of individuals can dominate the board's decision-taking.'

It goes on to state that: 'To ensure that power and information are not concentrated in one or two individuals, there should be a strong presence on the board of both executive and non-executive directors.'

The Combined Code then goes on to specify that:

■ Except for smaller listed companies, at least 50% of the board, **excluding** the chairman, should consist of independent non-executive directors. This requirement applies to listed companies in the FTSE 350 Index. (It is usual for the chairman of a UK listed company to be independent.)

■ In smaller listed companies, there should be at least two independent non-executive directors.

Codes of corporate governance in other countries differ. For example, the Singapore Code of Corporate Governance states that independent directors should make up at least one-third of the board.

© International Financial Publishing Limited

> ## The roles of chairman, chief executive officer and NEDs
>
> - Separation of the roles of chairman and chief executive officer
> - Role of the CEO
> - Role of the board chairman
> - The role of non-executive directors
> - The appointment of non-executive directors
> - Criticisms of NEDs

3 The roles of chairman, chief executive officer and NEDs

3.1 Separation of the roles of chairman and chief executive officer

The two most powerful positions on the board of directors are those of chairman and chief executive officer (CEO).

To avoid the risk that one individual might dominate decision-making by the board, the UK Combined Code states that:

- The roles of chairman and chief executive officer should not be held by the same person.
- In addition, a CEO should not go on to be the chairman of the company.

The Combined Code states as a principle that 'no one individual should have unfettered powers of decision'. For the same reason, the Singapore Code of Corporate Governance includes a provision that the chairman and CEO should 'in principle' be different individuals. Obviously, however, there should be a good working relationship between the chairman and the CEO.

In the UK, it is now unusual for the same person to be both chairman and CEO of a listed company. However, the provision in the Code that a CEO should not go on to become the company chairman has caused some controversy. The idea behind the provision in the Code is that a CEO who 'steps up' to become the company chairman might seek to dominate or influence his successor as CEO. However, some companies have argued that when a CEO decides that he wants to do something different, a company might be able to retain his experience and knowledge of the company's affairs by offering him a part-time role as chairman.

 Example: Marks and Spencer

In 2004, Marks and Spencer successfully resisted a takeover bid for the company from Philip Green. The successful takeover defence was organised by the company's new chairman (Paul Myners) and new chief executive (Stuart Rose).

During 2005 the senior independent director (a non-executive director) argued that the chairman and the chief executive were too close to each other, and that there was insufficient independence between them. After strong pressure from Lomax, Myners agreed to step down as chairman and his successor Sir Terry Burns was appointed (initially as deputy chairman in 2005) to take his place.

Critics argued that this change had broken up a highly successful working relationship between the company's chairman and CEO.

3.2 Role of the CEO

The CEO is responsible for the executive management of the company's operations. He or she is the leader of the management team, and all senior executive managers report to the CEO. If there is an executive management committee for the company, the CEO should be the chairman of this committee.

Other executive directors may sit on the board of directors, the CEO reports to the board on the activities of the entire management team, and is answerable to the board for the company's operational performance.

3.3 Role of the board chairman

In many public companies, the role of chairman is part-time. The UK Combined Code states that on appointment to the position, the chairman should be independent. If companies comply with the Combined Code, a chairman will therefore be both independent and non-executive.

The board chairman, or company chairman, is the leader of the board of directors. He or she is responsible for managing the board. Whereas codes of corporate governance have little to say about the responsibilities of the CEO, they have quite a lot to say about the role and functions of the chairman.

The UK Combined Code identifies the following responsibilities for the board chairman:

- As leader of the board, the chairman is responsible for its effectiveness in performing all aspects of its role. The chairman also sets the agenda for board discussions.

- The chairman is responsible for ensuring that all directors receive 'accurate, timely and clear information'. This is particularly important for non-executive directors, who rely for most of their information about the company on what the chairman provides. If they are not well-informed, NEDs are unable to contribute effectively to the discussions of the board or to decision-making.

- The chairman is also responsible for communications between the company and its shareholders.

- The chairman is responsible for ensuring that the NEDs contribute effectively to the work of the board, and for ensuring co-operative relationships between the NEDs and executive directors.

© International Financial Publishing Limited

In 2003, a report on non-executive directors was published in the UK. This was called the Higgs Report (after its author) and some of the recommendations in the report were reproduced in the Higgs Suggestions for Good Practice which was issued as a supplement to the Combined Code.

The Higgs Suggestions include a slightly more detailed list of the functions of the board chairman. The role of the chairman, according to Higgs, should be to:

■ Run the board and set its agenda. The agenda should be mainly forward-looking, and should concentrate on strategic matters (not details of management).

■ Ensure that all members of the board receive accurate, timely and clear information 'to help them reach well-informed and well-considered decisions'.

■ Ensure effective communication with the shareholders. The chairman should make sure that the other directors are aware of the views of the major shareholders.

■ Manage the board, and make sure that enough time is allowed for the full discussion of complex or controversial issues.

■ With the assistance of the company secretary, arrange for the induction of new directors after their appointment, and the continuing training and development of all the board directors.

■ Organise the performance evaluation of the board, its main committees and its individual directors.

■ Encourage the active participation in the board's affairs by all the directors.

The chairman is responsible for the efficient functioning of the board, and its effectiveness. He (or she) calls board meetings, sets the agenda and leads the board meetings. He decides how much time should be given to each item on the agenda. He should make sure that the board spends its time dealing with strategic matters, and not matters that should be delegated to the executive management.

The chairman also represents the company in its dealings with shareholders and (usually) the media. He is the 'public face' of the company.

Comparison of the roles of CEO and chairman

The roles of CEO and chairman can be summarised as follows.

CEO	Chairman
Executive director. Full-time employee.	Part-time. Usually independent.
Reporting lines	*Reporting lines*
All executive managers report, directly or indirectly, to the CEO.	No executive responsibilities. Only the company secretary and the CEO report to the chairman directly, on matters relating to the board.
The CEO reports to the chairman (as leader of the board) and to the board generally.	The chairman reports to the company's shareholders, as leader of the board.
Main responsibilities	*Main responsibilities*
Leader of the board, with responsibility for its effectiveness.	Head of the executive management team.
To make sure that the board fulfils its role successfully.	To draft proposed plans, budgets and strategies for board approval.
To ensure that all directors contribute to the work of the board.	To implement decisions of the board.

3.4 The role of non-executive directors

One of the reasons for having independent non-executive directors on a board is to give the board a better balance, and to reduce the possibility that the board may be dominated by one individual or a small group of individuals.

The Singapore Code of Corporate Governance identifies two main roles for NEDs:

- To challenge 'constructively' and to help to develop proposals on strategy.
- To review the performance of management in meeting their targets.

The **Higgs Suggestions for Good Practice** states that NEDs contribute to the board in four ways. Two of these are similar to the roles identified in the Singapore Code of Corporate Governance. The other two point even more strongly to the complex role of NEDs, in having responsibility for matters that should be kept away from the executive directors, due to the risk of a conflict of interests. The four roles identified in the Higgs Guidance are as follows:

- **Strategy**. NEDs should challenge constructively and help to develop proposals on strategy.
- **Performance**. NEDs should monitor the performance of executive management in meeting their agreed targets and goals.
- **Risk**. NEDs should satisfy themselves about the integrity of the financial information produced by the company, and should also satisfy themselves that the company's systems of risk management and internal control are robust.
- **People**. NEDs should be responsible for deciding the remuneration of executive directors and other senior managers, and should have a major role in the appointment of new directors and in the 'succession planning' for the next chairman and CEO of the company.

These roles suggest that NEDs on a unitary board have the complex task of acting partly as a colleague of the executive directors, and partly as a 'policeman'. They act as a colleague in discussing strategy and helping to develop strategy. However, they act as a 'policeman' in monitoring the performance of executive management, checking the integrity of financial reporting, evaluating the effectiveness of the risk management system and internal control system, and deciding the remuneration of their executive colleagues.

It can be argued that a function of independent NEDs is to reduce the agency costs arising from the conflict of interests between the shareholders and management, by acting as independent monitors of the company's management and also by negotiating remuneration.

Senior independent director

The UK Combined Code suggests that one of the independent NEDs should be appointed as senior independent director (SID).

One of the roles of the SID is to act as a leader for the other independent NEDs, for example by calling meetings of the NEDs to discuss matters away from the executive directors.

© International Financial Publishing Limited

The SID would also be expected to act in unusual circumstances, when the corporate governance of the board is not functioning properly. For example:

- A disagreement might occur between the major shareholders of the company and the chairman which cannot be resolved. The shareholders might be asked to intervene, for example by making sure that the views of the shareholders are conveyed to the rest of the board of directors. The UK Combined Code states that the SID 'should be available to shareholders if they have concerns which contact through the normal channels of chairman, chief executive or finance director has failed to resolve, or for which such contact is inappropriate.'

- The SID might be required to argue with the chairman or chief executive in a situation where the company is failing to apply proper standards of corporate governance. For example, a disagreement between the company chairman and SID was reported in the UK when the supermarket group Morrison's became a listed company. The chairman was apparently reluctant to appoint a sufficient number of independent NEDs to the board, and the SID argued strongly (and eventually successfully) that the company should comply with the provisions of Combined Code.

3.5 The appointment of non-executive directors

It is generally accepted that the board of directors should collectively possess a suitable combination of experience and skills.

However, in the UK it has been common practice to recruit NEDs to listed companies from a very small circle of possible candidates. The Higgs Report on non-executive directors (2003) found that in UK public companies, only 7% of NEDs were non-British nationals, 6% were women and 1% were from ethnic minority groups. In many cases, individuals appointed as NED of a listed company were already an executive director of another listed company.

Following the Higgs Report, the government (Department of Trade and Industry) set up a committee under the chairmanship of Laura Tyson, Dean of the London Business School, to carry out an investigation into the recruitment and development of NEDs. The **Tyson Report** (2003) reached several conclusions.

- The effectiveness of a board of directors would be improved by having a board consisting of directors with a range of experiences and backgrounds, rather than a board whose NEDs all come from the same type of background.

- Companies should have a formal system of appointing new NEDs to the board. As part of this formal system, the company should begin by identifying which particular skills were missing from the board, that the board would benefit from having. The company should then seek an individual who has the missing skills or experience that has been identified.

- NEDs should be recruited from a wider range of different backgrounds. Individuals who might make excellent NEDs include senior managers in the 'marzipan layer' of corporate management, just below board level but without yet having any board experience. Other sources of NEDs should be individuals in private sector companies, 'professionals' (accountants, solicitors) and business consultants, and individuals working on the public sector or the non-commercial private sector.

The Tyson Report attracted a large amount of publicity when it was published, but it is not yet clear that it has had much effect yet on the practice of appointing new NEDs in the UK.

Keeping the board refreshed

There is a need to keep a board 'refreshed' by appointing new directors regularly, to bring fresh experience and skills to the board.

■ As a company grows or changes, the skills and experience required from its directors might change. This means that some of the directors should probably be changed.

■ Over time, the independence of a non-executive director is likely to diminish. It is therefore appropriate to replace NEDs after a number of years.

A new NED might be appointed for a three-year term, and re-appointed for a further three years if the NED has contributed well to the work of the board in the first three years. After six years, a company should possibly consider whether a NED should be replaced.

Changes to the board, to keep it refreshed, affect NEDs rather than executive directors. This is because executive directors hold senior positions in the management structure of the company. Once appointed to the board, they are likely to retain their position as director as long as they retain their job.

3.6 Criticisms of NEDs

NEDs are often criticised for failing to perform effectively in their role. There are three main criticisms.

■ **Lack of knowledge** about the company and the industry or markets it operates in. NEDs often lack the information about the company that they need to make well-informed decisions. The chairman is responsible for ensuring that all directors are properly informed, but this is an 'ideal situation' that does not always exist in practice.

■ **Insufficient time with the company**. NEDs might not spend as much time with the company as they need to, in order to perform their role effectively. When a NED is appointed, there should be an understanding about how much time the NED will be expected to spend with the company. Even so, the agreed amount of time might not be sufficient.

■ **Accepting the views of executive directors**. The NEDs might be too willing at times to accept the views and opinions of executive directors, because the executives know more about the company's operations. When the NEDs are too willing to agree with the executive directors, they do not contribute as much as they should to discussions on strategy.

In spite of these criticisms of non-executive directors, it is now widely accepted in many countries that major companies should have a strong presence of independent NEDs on the board. When NEDs do not appear to be effective in their role, institutional shareholders might well take action.

© International Financial Publishing Limited

Example

PIRC (Pensions Investment Research Consultants Ltd), a company providing corporate governance advice to institutional clients, occasionally advises its clients to use their votes as shareholders against a company's board. For example in June 2002, PIRC described Telewest, a cable television company, as a 'corporate basket case'. It recommended to its clients that they should vote against the re-election of four non-executive directors because they were not independent and because the corporate governance of the company was poor. PIRC argued that the four directors were not independent because one held share options in the company, two represented the interests of a major shareholder and the fourth had been a NED with the company for over nine years. PIRC also commented that the board, including these NEDs, had allowed large bonus payments to be made to executive directors that were not justified in view of the company's performance. (Telewest was subsequently taken over.)

> ## Directors and the law
>
> - The powers and rights of directors
> - Appointment, election and removal of directors
> - Duties and legal obligations of directors
> - Share dealings by directors
> - Disqualification of directors

4 Directors and the law

Corporate law varies between countries. However in all countries, directors act within a legal and regulatory framework. They have certain rights as directors, but also certain duties and responsibilities. If they fail to carry out their duties or responsibilities properly, they could become personally liable for their failure.

Various aspects of company law are described in this section. In different ways, each aspect of the law has implications for corporate governance.

4.1 The powers and rights of directors

The powers of the company are given to the board of directors as a whole, although many of these powers are delegated to executive management. Individual directors should normally have the authority to enter into contracts in the company's name. In UK law, individual company directors have an implied power to make legally-binding contracts for the company, even if they have not been given the specific actual authority to do so.

Service contracts

Executive directors are full-time employees of the company. As employees, they have a service contract with the company. A service contract for an executive director is a legally-binding contract of employment. A service contract includes terms such as entitlement to remuneration including pension rights, and a minimum notice period for termination of office.

An executive director, like any other employee of the company, should be protected by the same legal rights that are given to all employees by the employment law of the country.

The service contract of an executive director should specify his role as an executive manager of the company, but might not include any reference to his role as a company director. However, if he is subsequently asked to resign from the board, it is generally-accepted practice that the company is also dismissing him as an executive manager. The director then has all the rights given to him in his service contract in the event of dismissal, as well as rights provided by law relating to unfair or wrongful dismissal by the company.

© International Financial Publishing Limited

Fixed-term contracts

Non-executive directors are usually appointed for a fixed term. In the UK, normal practice is to appoint an NED for a three-year term. At the end of this term, the appointment might be renewed (subject to shareholder approval) for a further three years. This cycle of three-year appointments continues until the NED eventually retires or is asked to retire.

4.2 Appointment, election and removal of directors

An aspect of corporate governance is the power of the shareholders to appoint directors and remove them from office. Practice in the UK is fairly typical of other countries.

- When a vacancy occurs in the board of directors during the course of a year, the vacancy is filled by an individual who is nominated and then appointed by the board of directors.

- However, at the next meeting of the company's shareholders (the next annual general meeting), the director stands for election. In the UK, the director is proposed for election, and is elected if he or she obtains a simple majority (over 50%) of the votes of the shareholders.

- Existing directors are required to stand for re-election at regular intervals. In the UK, most companies include in their constitution (articles of association) a requirement that one-third of directors should retire each year by rotation and stand for re-election. This means that each director stands for re-election every three years. (This is why appointments of NEDs are for periods of three years.)

- It is usual for directors who retire by rotation and stand for re-election to be re-elected by a very large majority. However, when shareholders are concerned about the corporate governance of a company, or about its financial performance, there might be a substantial vote against the re-election of particular directors.

- When a director performs badly, it should be expected that he or she will be asked by the board or the company chairman to resign. This is the most common method by which directors who have 'failed' are removed from office.

- Occasionally, a director might have the support of the board, when the shareholders want to get rid of him. UK company law allows shareholders (with at least a specified minimum holding of shares in the company) to call a meeting of the company to vote on a proposal to remove the director. A director can be removed by a simple majority vote of the shareholders.

When a director is removed from office, he retains his contractual rights, as specified in his contract of employment. This could involve a very large payment.

4.3 Duties and legal obligations of directors

Directors have certain legal duties to their company. If they fail in these duties, they could become personally liable for the consequences of their breach of duty.

In the UK, the Companies Act 2006 has introduced statutory duties for directors. These are duties to:

- act within their powers
- promote the success of the company for the benefit of its shareholders
- exercise independent judgement
- exercise reasonable skill, care and diligence
- avoid conflicts of interest
- not to accept benefits from a third party
- declare any interest in a proposed transaction with the company.

Prior to the Companies Act 2006, the legal duties of UK company directors to their company have been:

- a **duty of skill and care**
- a **'fiduciary duty'**: this is a duty to act in the utmost good faith in the interests of the company.

Two examples of a breach of fiduciary duty are putting personal interests ahead of the interests of the company (when there is a conflict of interest) and failure to disclose a personal interest in a contract with the company. Both of these breaches of duty are agency problems, identified in agency theory.

Conflicts of interest

A director would be in breach of his fiduciary duty to the company, for example, if he puts his own interests first, ahead of the interests of the company.

One example from UK law is the case of an individual who was the managing director of a company that provided consultancy services. One client decided that it would not use the company for planned consultancy services, but indicated that if the managing director applied for the contract personally, it might be willing to give the consultancy work to him. The managing director informed his fellow directors that he was ill, and persuaded the company to release him from his contract of employment. On ceasing to be a director of the company, he applied for the consultancy work with the client, and was given the work. His former company successfully sued him to recover the profits from the contract.

The court decided that the former managing director was in breach of his fiduciary duty to the company, because he had put his own interests first, ahead of the interests of the company in obtaining the contract work for himself.

Disclosure of interests

A breach of fiduciary duty would also occur if a director has an **interest in a contract** with the company but fails to disclose this interest to the rest of the board and obtain their approval.

Typically, a company director might be a major shareholder in another company which is about to enter into a supply contract with the company. When this

© International Financial Publishing Limited

situation occurs, the director must disclose his interest as soon as possible to the rest of the board, and obtain their approval. Failure to disclose the interest would make the director liable to hand over to the company all his secret profits from the contract.

In the UK, it is also a criminal offence for a director to fail to disclose an interest, and the punishment for a breach of this law is a fine.

4.4 Share dealings by directors

It is common for directors of stock market companies to own some shares in their company.

Because they work inside the company, directors will occasionally obtain information about the company (or another company) that:

■ has not yet been made public, and is still confidential, and

■ when it is eventually made public, it is likely to have a significant effect on the price of the company's shares (or the price of the other company's shares).

An example is obtaining information about a planned takeover bid involving the company. When one company wants to take over another, it will make a private approach to the board of the other company, indicating its wish to buy the shares in that company. If the board of the target company is willing to negotiate terms, there is a period during which secret discussions take place. Inevitably, the directors of both companies will be aware of the discussions. During this period, the information about the probable takeover bid remains confidential, but when the information becomes public (after the terms of the takeover are agreed and announced to the stock market) the share price of the target company normally rises substantially, up to the price of the takeover bid.

It should be apparent that a director could use the confidential price-sensitive information about the takeover bid to buy shares in the target company, before the takeover is announced. By purchasing the shares, the director would expect to make a substantial profit by selling the shares in the takeover. The profit of the director, however, would be obtained at the expense of the shareholder who sold him the shares.

Taking advantage of price-sensitive information about a company to buy or sell shares, or to encourage anyone else to buy or sell shares, is a criminal offence, known as insider dealing.

When an individual such as a director is found to have carried out insider dealing (or insider trading):

■ he might be found to have committed a criminal offence, and face a fine and imprisonment, and/or

■ he might be found liable in civil law to the individuals at whose expense he made his profit.

Example

At the end of its financial year, a major stock market company (not named here) found that its profits would be much lower than stock market investors were expecting. In addition, it was probable that news of an anti-competitive arrangement with a major supplier might be made public in the near future.

Most of the directors and many senior executives in the company sold substantial quantities of shares in the company that they owned, before these items of news were released to the stock market. In doing so, they avoided losses that they would otherwise have suffered; when the information was released to the public, the company's share price fell.

The directors and senior managers of the company made themselves liable to a charge of insider dealing, avoiding losses at the expense of the investors who bought their shares. In addition, the directors who sold their shares in the company were in breach of their fiduciary duty, because they put their interests first, ahead of the interests of the other shareholders.

Stock market restrictions on share dealings by directors

Insider dealing is an offence. However, directors of a company will often be in a position to judge how well or badly the company is performing when other investors are not in a position to make the same judgement. If they buy or sell shares in their company, they might be suspected of insider dealing and putting their own interests first.

In the UK, the law on insider dealing has been supplemented by a code of conduct for directors and other senior employees of listed companies. This code is known as the Model Code. All listed companies are required to apply this code of conduct, or a code that is no less strict.

Applying the Model Code will help to maintain investor confidence in the activities of company directors. The main requirements of the Model Code are as follows.

- Directors must not deal in shares of their company during a 'close period'. A close period is the period before the announcement to the stock market of the company's interim and final financial results.

- A director must not deal in shares of the company at any time that he has price-sensitive information.

- Before dealing in the company's shares at any other time, a director must obtain the prior permission of the chairman.

4.5 Disqualification of directors

The corporate law of a country might provide for the disqualification of any individual from acting as a director of any company, where the individual is guilty of behaviour that is totally unacceptable from a director.

© International Financial Publishing Limited

To some extent, laws on the disqualification of directors might possibly provide some protection to the shareholders of a company. However, disqualification only occurs after the unacceptable behaviour has occurred.

In the UK, for example, the law allows a court to disqualify an individual from acting as a director of any company in a variety of circumstances. These include:

- when a director is bankrupt

- when a director is suffering from a mental disorder

- when a director has been found guilty of a crime in connection with the formation or management of a company (such as the misappropriation of company funds).

However, the disqualification of an individual from acting as a director is more likely after a company has become insolvent, rather than whilst the company is still operational and solvent.

Induction, training and performance evaluation of directors
■ Induction for new directors
■ Training and professional development for directors
■ Performance evaluation
■ Assessments of performance

5 Induction, training and performance evaluation of directors

5.1 Induction for new directors

Induction is a form of training. In a company, its purpose is to make a new person familiar with what the company does, how it operates, how it is organised, who the senior managers are and so on. New non-executive directors need induction training so that they can learn much more about the company that they are now helping to govern. Unless they know about the company in some detail, their views and opinions might be misinformed.

Executive managers who are appointed to a board of directors for the first time might also need induction training, to improve their familiarity with aspects of the company that they do not know much about. Executive managers should know more about the company than new non-executive directors, but this does not mean that they know everything that they should know about the company.

The UK Combined Code recognises the importance of induction, and states:

■ 'All directors should receive induction on joining the board', and

■ 'The chairman should ensure that new directors receive a full, formal and tailored induction on joining the board.' The company secretary should assist the chairman in ensuring that suitable induction is provided.

Induction to gain familiarity with the company

The Higgs Guidance suggests that the purpose of induction should be to help the new director to:

■ develop an understanding of the company, its business and the markets in which it operates

■ get to know the people who work for the company

■ develop an understanding of the company's main relationships, for example with key suppliers or customers.

© International Financial Publishing Limited

An induction programme might therefore include:

- visits to important sites/locations where the company carries out its operations
- demonstrations of the company's products
- meetings with senior managers and staff
- possibly, meetings with professional advisers of the company
- possibly, meetings with major shareholders (but only if the shareholder wishes to meet the new director).

Induction to gain familiarity with being a director of the company

Another aspect of induction is helping a new director to become familiar with the duties of being a director in the company. This can be particularly important for individuals who have never been a company director before.

A new director should be given:

- information about the matters that are reserved for the board (what the board does)
- guidance on the rules on share dealings by directors (including the law on insider dealing)
- copies of the minutes of recent board meetings
- a schedule of dates for future board meetings
- details of the committees of the board, and their responsibilities.

5.2 Training and professional development for directors

The UK Combined Code also states that:

- 'All directors should ... regularly update and refresh their skills and knowledge,' and
- 'The chairman should ensure that directors regularly update their skills and the knowledge and familiarity required to fulfil their role.... The company should provide the necessary resources for developing and updating its directors' knowledge and capabilities.'

The exact nature of the training and professional development that should be provided will vary with the company and the requirements of the individual director.

Deciding on the training or development that a director should receive might be discussed each year, as a part of the performance review of the director.

Subject areas for training and development might include formal training in business strategy, corporate governance issues or developments in financial reporting. Directors should also be given demonstrations of new products, services or processes that the company has developed.

The Higgs Report on non-executive directors (2003), commenting on development and training, stated that non-executive directors, on appointment, will already have some relevant knowledge, skills, abilities and experience. However, the non-executive director's effectiveness on the board will depend on far more than their existing skills; they need to have the ability to extend their skills further and refresh their knowledge. They therefore need to take some sort of 'training' – not formal, classroom training, but continued professional development tailored to the individual.

5.3 Performance evaluation

The board is expected to perform a particular role for the company. Effective corporate governance depends on having an effective board. It would therefore be appropriate to carry out regular reviews, to asses how well the board has performed.

The board is accountable to the shareholders, and it might therefore be argued that the performance of the board should be judged by the shareholders. However, in practice this would be difficult to achieve.

In some countries, codes of corporate governance include a requirement that the performance of the board and its individual directors should be reviewed regularly, and the review should be carried out by the board itself. The chairman should have the responsibility for the performance evaluation.

The purpose of the performance review should be to ensure that:

- the board is fulfilling its role and carrying out its responsibilities effectively
- the board committees are also fulfilling their roles effectively
- individual directors are contributing effectively to the work of the board and its committees
- the collective skills and experience of the board members remain appropriate for the needs of the company.

UK Combined Code on performance evaluation

The UK Combined Code states that the board should undertake a **formal** and **rigorous** annual evaluation of its own performance, the performance of the board committees, and the performance of each individual director.

The Code includes the following provision: 'Individual evaluation should aim to show whether each director continues to contribute effectively and demonstrate commitment to the role (including commitment of time…). The chairman should act on the results of the performance evaluation by recognising the strengths and weaknesses of the board and, where appropriate, proposing new members be appointed to the board or seeking the resignation of directors.'

The performance review of the chairman should be carried out by the NEDs, under the leadership of the senior independent director.

© International Financial Publishing Limited

The directors' report in the annual report and accounts should state how the performance evaluation of the board as a whole, its committees and its individual directors has been conducted.

Singapore Code of Corporate Governance on performance evaluation

The requirement for annual performance evaluation was introduced into the UK Code in 2003. The UK Code is not unique in requiring performance evaluation. The Singapore Code of Corporate Governance includes similar requirements, although the responsibility for carrying out the review is given to the Nominations Committee of the board, not the board chairman. The Code includes the following guidelines:

- The Nominations Committee should decide how the performance of the board should be evaluated and should suggest objective criteria for assessment.

- The performance evaluation of the board should also consider the changes in the company's share price over a five-year period.

- There should also be evaluation of the performance of individual directors.

The use of external consultants for performance evaluation

In most UK listed companies, the annual performance review is carried out by the chairman, with the assistance of the company secretary.

The chairman might use the services of specialist external consultants. The Higgs Guidance comments that 'the use of an external third party to conduct the evaluation will bring objectivity to the process.'

However, companies may combine performance evaluation by the chairman personally with the use of external consultants, for example by alternating the use of external consultants in one year with internal review by the chairman the next year.

5.4   Assessments of performance

Assessing the performance of the board as a whole

Questions that might be asked to assess the performance of the board as a whole include the following:

- How well has the board performed against specific objectives or performance targets that were set?

- What has been the contribution of the board to the development of strategy?

- What has been the contribution of the board to ensuring effective risk management?

- Is the composition of the board and its committees suitable? Is there a suitable balance of knowledge, experience and skills?

- How well (or badly) did the board respond to any crisis that occurred during the year?

There should also be an **evaluation of the procedures of the board** and its committees, to ensure that they use effective working practices. This should include an assessment of the length and frequency of board meetings, whether important issues were given the full amount of time and consideration that they needed, and what the meetings have achieved.

Assessing the performance of individual non-executive directors

Questions that might be asked to assess the performance of individual non-executive directors include the following:

- Has the attendance of the NED at meetings been satisfactory? Was he (or she) properly prepared for the meetings?
- Doe she show a willingness to spend time and effort with the company?
- What has been the quality and value of his contributions to meetings?
- What has he contributed to the development of (1) strategy and (2) risk management?
- How successfully have they brought their knowledge and skills to the discussions and decision-making of the board?
- How has he refreshed his knowledge and skills during the year?
- Does he give in too easily to the opinions of other directors?
- How good (or bad) are his relationships with other board members?
- Does he communicate effectively with anyone in management other than the executive directors on the board?

© International Financial Publishing Limited

CHAPTER

4

Board committees

Contents
1   The need for board committees
2   The audit committee
3   The remuneration committee
4   The nominations committee
5   The risk committee

The need for board committees

- The nature of a board committee
- The main board committees
- The reasons for having board committees

1 The need for board committees

1.1 The nature of a board committee

A board committee is a committee set up by the board, and consisting of selected directors, which is given responsibility for monitoring a particular aspect of the company's affairs for which the board has reserved the power of decision-making.

A committee is not given decision-making powers. Its role is to monitor an aspect of the company's affairs, and:

- report back to the board, and
- make recommendations to the board.

The full board of directors should make a decision based on the committee's recommendations. When the full board rejects a recommendation from a committee, it should be a very good reason for doing so.

A board committee will meet with sufficient frequency to enable it to carry out its responsibilities. It is important to remember, however, that **a board committee is not a substitute for executive management** and **a board committee does not have executive powers**. A committee might monitor activities of executive managers, but it does not take over the job of running the company from the management.

1.2 The main board committees

Within a system of corporate governance, a company might have at least three or possibly four major committees. These are:

- a remuneration committee, whose responsibility is to consider and negotiate the remuneration of executive directors and senior managers
- an audit committee, whose responsibility is to monitor financial reporting and auditing within the company
- a nominations committee, whose responsibility is to identify and recommend individuals for appointment to the board of directors
- a risk management committee, where the responsibility for the review of risk management has not been delegated to the audit committee.

© International Financial Publishing Limited

1.3   The reasons for having board committees

There are two main reasons for having board committees.

■ The board can use a committee to delegate time-consuming and detailed work to some of the board members. Committees can help the board to use its resources and the time of its members more efficiently.

■ The board can delegate to a committee aspects of its work where there is an actual or a possible conflict of interests between executive directors (management) and the interests of the company and its shareholders. However, to avoid a conflict of interests, board committees should consist wholly or largely of independent directors. This means independent non-executive directors.

     – A remuneration committee of independent non-executive directors negotiates and recommends remuneration packages for executive directors or senior managers. The committee members do not have a personal interest in the remuneration structure for senior executives, because they are not remunerated in the same way as executives. They receive a fixed annual fee.

     – An audit committee of indendent non-executive directors can monitor financial reporting and auditing, to satisfy themeselves that these are carried out to a satisfactory standard, and that executive management are not 'hiding' information or presenting a misleading picture of the company's financial affairs. The work of the audit committee therefore provides a check on the work of executive managers, such as the finance director. The committee can also monitor the effectiveness of the auditors, to satisfy themselves that the auditors carry out their work to a suitable standard.

     – Similarly, the work of a risk committee of the board should be to satisfy itself that executive management have a suitable system of risk management and internal control in place, and that these systems function effectively. This is another check on executive management.

     – A nominations committee makes recommendations about new appointments to the board. The views of executive directors are important in this aspect of the board's work, particularly when a vacancy for a new executive director occurs. However, independent non-executives should have some influence in the nominations process, to make sure that new appointments to the board will not be selected 'yes men' and supporters of the CEO or chairman.

Through the work of the board committees, independent non-executive directors therefore have a very important role to play in providing good corporate governance.

> ## The audit committee
>
> - Corporate governance and financial reporting: the responsibility of the board
> - The need for an audit committee
> - Independence of the external auditors
> - Role and functions of the audit committee
> - Composition of the audit committee

2 The audit committee

2.1 Corporate governance and financial reporting: the responsibility of the board

The board of directors of a company is accountable to the shareholders. An important aspect of accountability is the legal requirement to present an annual report and accounts.

Published financial statements should also be understandable to shareholders. The UK Combined Code states that the board should present 'a balanced and understandable assessment of the company's position and prospects.' In addition, it requires the directors to explain in their annual report their responsibility for the preparation of the financial statements.

Typically, the annual report of a UK listed company might include a statement from the directors as follows:

'The directors are required by law to prepare financial statements for each accounting period that give a true and fair view.

The directors confirm that appropriate accounting policies have been used and applied consistently, and reasonable and prudent judgements and estimates have been made in the preparation of the accounts. The directors also confirm that applicable accounting standards have been followed, any material departures being disclosed and explained, and that the financial statements have been prepared on the going concern basis.

The directors are responsible for ensuring proper accounting records are kept which disclose with reasonable accuracy at any time the financial position of the company and the group. They are also responsible for taking steps to safeguard the assets of the company and the group and to prevent and detect fraud and other irregularities.'

Having made such a statement of responsibilities, directors should expect to be liable for any failure in carrying out their responsibilities with due care.

© International Financial Publishing Limited

Example

The collapse of US corporation Enron has already been mentioned. However, it is also interesting for the attitude of the board to the financial reporting methods that were used.

■ In October 2000, about one year before the company collapsed, the finance committee of the board was informed that the company had about $60 billion of assets, of which nearly one half were held in 'unconsolidated affiliates' – in other words, 'off balance sheet'.

■ The board was informed in 2000 that one of these affiliates, LJM, had made $2 million profits in just six months. This was a huge amount of money, even for a company the size of Enron. The board apparently did not question the figure.

It could therefore be argued that the directors of Enron failed to fulfil their responsibility for ensuring the reliability of the financial statements.

2.2 The need for an audit committee

Many directors on company boards have only limited understanding of accounting and financial reporting, but the board is nevertheless responsible for the reliability of the financial statements.

In the past, the board has relied on the advice and assurances that it receives from:

■ executive management, and in particular the CEO and finance director, and

■ the external auditors.

The history of corporate governance has shown that when a corporate scandal occurs:

■ misleading financial statements have been used to disguise the wrongdoing and misdemeanours

■ senior executives (the CEO and/or finance director) are to blame for the misleading accounts, and

■ the company's auditors failed to spot the problem:

  – possibly because they were misled by the company's executives, or

  – possibly because the quality of the audit was not as good as it should have been, or

  – possibly because the auditors were willing to accept assurances from executive management when they should perhaps have asked more questions.

An audit committee can provide a check on the risks of misleading reporting, by providing an additional line of communication to the auditors and by ensuring that the auditors remain independent from executive managers and perform the audit effectively.

2.3 Independence of the external auditors

This text does not explore in detail the role of the external auditors. However, a critical aspect of good corporate governance is the need for the board to ensure that the external auditors carry out their audit work properly, so that the board of directors is able to rely on the conclusions and recommendations they provide at the end of the audit.

One of the requirements for the auditors is that they should perform their audit work with independence. In this sense, independence means freedom from the influence of the company's executive management.

There are at least two ways in which the independence of the auditors might be at risk.

- **Familiarity of the audit firm or audit partner** with the company. When the same audit partner is responsible for the audit of a particular client company every year for a long period of time, he or she is likely to become very familiar with the company and its management. As this familiarity grows, the audit partner will probably become more willing to accept assurances from management and rely on the accuracy of the information they provide. This obviously can be a very serious problem when the assurances given by management are false and the information is incorrect or incomplete.

- **Non-audit work** and a reliance of the audit firm on the company for a large amount of fee income. An audit firm receives an audit fee each year. In addition, it is common for the audit firm to obtain a substantial amount of fee income from non-audit work, such as providing tax advice and advice on information systems, and carrying out investigations for the company. If an audit firm obtains a large amount of its income from one corporate client, it will probably be reluctant to disagree with the company's management on issues relating to the preparation of the financial statements (such as the size of estimates and the application of accounting policies).

The audit firm Arthur Andersen collapsed in 2002 as a result of the Enron scandal. Andersens were the auditors of Enron, and it was found that the firm, in particular its office in Houston Texas, was not independent of the company. The publicity given to Andersens led to a general loss of confidence in the audit firm, which was dissolved.

The problem of familiarity of the auditors with an audit client can be reduced by either:

- **rotation of the audit firm**, so that the same audit firm does not carry out the audit of any company for more than a maximum number of years, or

- **rotation of the audit partner**, so that the same audit partner is not responsible for the audit of any company for more than a maximum number of years.

Rotation of audit partners has become a regulatory requirement in some countries (including the UK), as a means of dealing with this problem.

The task of monitoring the independence of the audit firm on the company for fee income should be the responsibility of the board of directors. It is generally-accepted good corporate governance practice that this responsibility should be delegated by the board to its audit committee.

 Example

In 2006 auditors PricewaterhouseCoopers were fined by the Accountants' Joint Disciplinary Scheme (JDS) for failures by Coopers & Lybrand in connection with the collapse of the engineering company TransTec in 1999.

The JDS found that Coopers & Lybrand had placed too much reliance on what they were told by the company's management, and as a result their audit procedures had been inadequate. Several senior executives of TransTec had colluded to conceal some key information from the company's board of directors and the auditors, about debit notes issued to the company by car manufacturers Ford. The auditors had not spotted the fraud, although they had been misled by management.

The JDS concluded that the audit firm had 'failed to carry out adequate audit procedures in relation to the debit notes, including investigating conflicting explanations as to what the debit notes were.... In the 1998 audit they did not clearly express their own concerns and so did not find fault with the management.'

2.4 Role and functions of the audit committee

Codes of corporate governance suggest what the role and functions of the audit committee should be. The UK Combined Code states as a principle of governance that the board should establish formal arrangements for:

- considering how they should apply the financial reporting and internal control principles, and
- maintaining an appropriate relationship with the company's auditors.

It should do this by establishing an audit committee. The Code states that the role and responsibilities of the audit committee should include:

- to monitor the integrity of the company's financial statements and any other formal statements relating to the company's financial performance
- to review the company's internal financial controls
- to review the company's internal control and risk management systems (unless this responsibility is given to a separate risk committee or retained by the full board itself)
- to monitor and review the effectiveness of the company's internal audit function
- to make recommendations to the board about the appointment, re-appointment or removal of the audit firm as auditors of the company (for the board to make a recommendation to the shareholders)
- approve the remuneration and terms of engagement of the external auditors
- to review and monitor the independence and objectivity of the company's external auditors

- to review and monitor the effectiveness of the audit process
- to develop and monitor a policy for the use of the external auditor to perform non-audit work for the company.

As a part of these responsibilities, the audit committee should: 'review arrangements by which staff of the company may, in confidence, raise concerns about possible improprieties in matters of financial reporting or other matters. The audit committee's objective should be to ensure that arrangements are in place for the proportionate and independent investigation of such matters and for appropriate follow-up action.' In other words, the audit committee is responsible for making sure that there is an effective system to allow 'whistleblowers' to report their concerns about possible wrongdoing without fear of retaliation from their bosses.

The audit committee should prepare a report to shareholders about its work, for inclusion in the annual report and accounts.

The Singapore Code of Corporate Governance contains similar guidelines about the role and responsibilities of the audit committee. However, in the following respects, it is more specific than the UK Code:

- The audit committee should review 'the scope and results of the audit and its cost-effectiveness'.

- When the auditors provide a large amount of non-audit services to the company, the audit committee should 'keep the nature and extent of such services under review, seeking to balance the maintenance of objectivity and value for money'.

- The audit committee should also review annually the independence of the external auditors.

Oversight, assessment and review

Recommendations about the role of the audit committee were first proposed in the UK in the **Smith Report**, a report on audit committees published at about the same time as the Higgs Report in 2003. The provisions in the UK Combined Code were based on the recommendations in the Smith Report.

Extracts from the Smith Report were subsequently included as an appendix to the Combined Code, called the **Smith** Guidance. Some of the comments in this Guidance were:

- The functions of the audit committee are concerned with 'oversight', 'assessment' and 'review' of functions performed by executive management and the external auditors. It is not the responsibility of the audit committee to perform those functions. For example, the finance director is responsible for preparing the financial statements, and the role of the audit committee is to oversee, assess and review this process. Similarly, the auditors perform the audit, but the audit committee is responsible for assessment and review.

- However, the oversight function of the committee might sometimes lead to more detailed work. For example, the audit committee might be dissatisfied with an explanation of management or the auditors about a particular matter. To resolve the problem, the committee might then need to seek other professional advice.

© International Financial Publishing Limited

- The audit committee reports to the board, and the board reaches decisions based on the recommendations of the audit committee. However, if the board and the audit committee disagree about a particular matter, the audit committee should have the right to report the disagreement to the shareholders.

Example

The Smith Guidance went into some detail about the role of the audit committee in the annual audit cycle. It is useful to look at some of the suggestions in the Guidance, to get an idea of what the audit committee might actually do.

- At the beginning of the annual audit, the audit committee should check that appropriate plans for the audit are in place. It should check that the work plan for the audit is consistent with the size and scope of the audit engagement. It should also check that the audit team will be of the right size and will have a suitable range of skills and experience for the work.

- At some stage in the audit cycle, the audit committee should meet with the external auditors to discuss the results of the audit and the findings of the auditors. As a part of this review, the committee should discuss any particular problems or disagreements that occurred during the audit (and whether these have been resolved). The committee should also ask about any important accounting judgements that have been made in preparing the financial statements. They should also ask the auditors about the errors that they found during the audit.

- There should be a review of the audit after it has been completed. The audit committee should consider the audit plan and whether the auditors met the requirements of the plan. The committee should also consider whether the auditors were strong-minded in their dealings with the company's management. It should also obtain the views of the finance director about the conduct of the audit by the auditors.

2.5 Composition of the audit committee

An audit committee should make its judgements and recommendations independent of influence from executive management. However, the opinion about the composition of the audit committee varies between countries.

- The UK Combined Code states that the audit committee should consist **entirely** of independent non-executive directors. In large listed companies there should be at least three members of the committee (and in smaller listed companies at least two).

- The Singapore Code of Corporate Governance states that the audit committee should consist of at least three members, all of them non-executive directors. However, only a majority of the committee, including the committee chairman, needs to be **independent**.

In order to perform their functions properly, the members of the audit committee should have some understanding of finance and accounting. However, it would be unreasonable to expect that all the audit committee members should be qualified accountants. There are differences of opinion about how much experience or understanding of finance and accounting the audit committee members should have.

- The UK Combined Code states that the board of directors should satisfy itself that 'at least **one** member of the audit committee has **recent and relevant** financial experience.' The Smith Guidance states that it is desirable that this person (who is likely to be the audit committee chairman) should have a professional accountancy qualification from one of the professional bodies. The amount of financial understanding required from the other audit committee members will depend on the nature of the company and its business.

- The guidelines in the Singapore Code of Corporate Governance state that the members of the audit committee should be 'appropriately qualified' to carry out their responsibilities, but **at least two** of the committee members should have 'accounting or related financial management expertise or experience'.

© International Financial Publishing Limited

The remuneration committee

- Remuneration as a corporate governance issue
- The need for a remuneration committee
- Main duties of a remuneration committee
- Composition of the remuneration committee
- Continuing problems with the remuneration of executive directors

3 The remuneration committee

3.1 Remuneration as a corporate governance issue

The remuneration of executive directors and senior managers is an important issue in corporate governance. It is at the heart of the conflict of interest between management and shareholders.

- It might be argued that executive directors and other senior managers, as full-time employees of their company, are primarily concerned about their personal remuneration. They will put concern for their personal remuneration ahead of concern for the wealth of the company's shareholders.

- Directors might attempt to increase their remuneration, without necessarily doing anything to justify the increase.

- Higher rewards for managers, without any improvements in the company's performance, mean lower profits for the company.

- However, the conflict of interest between management and shareholders might be resolved if the remuneration of directors could include incentives. If directors are rewarded for achieving performance targets that are consistent with the best interests of the company's shareholders, the conflict of interests could be reduced. Directors and shareholders would both benefit.

The issues involved in using incentives to reduce the conflict of interest, and link the remuneration of directors to performance targets that are in the best interests of shareholders, will be considered in more detail in a later chapter.

Origins of the controversy about directors' remuneration

The remuneration of executive directors is seen as a major corporate governance problem in some countries but not in others. The controversy began in the UK during the 1990s, when the government privatised state-owned businesses and a number of utility companies were created in energy production, and electricity, water and gas supply.

The senior directors appointed to the new companies were the same individuals who had managed the businesses when they were state-owned. For doing much the same job as before, these individuals were given a very large increase in remuneration. They were criticised by the press as 'fat cats', who were being paid far more than they were worth.

Directors' remuneration became a cause of anger in the press some years later when several high-profile directors of major companies were dismissed, or threatened with dismissal. Because of the terms of their employment contract, these directors were entitled on dismissal to very large termination payments. These termination payments were described in the press as **'rewards for failure'**.

Criticisms of excessive directors' remuneration have also been expressed by institutional investors, who consider that the remuneration of directors should be linked much more closely to company performance. There has been an increasing willingness by institutional shareholders to express their displeasure with remuneration for directors by voting against the board at general meetings of the company. In the UK, shareholders are able to use their votes by:

- voting against the re-election of directors, or

- voting against the directors remuneration report: quoted companies in the UK are required to include a directors remuneration report in their annual report and accounts, and shareholders are able to vote on the report, indicating their approval or disapproval.

Institutional investors have been concerned about the apparent lack of concern about directors' remuneration. There have been some reported cases where shareholder action appears to have had some effect.

 Example: United Business Media

At the annual general meeting of the media group United Business Media in 2005, the shareholders voted against the directors remuneration report. 76% of shareholders voted against the directors' remuneration report at the AGM and another 11% abstained. This was a remarkable majority.

The shareholders were objecting to the 'ex gratia' payment of a £250,000 bonus to Lord Hollick, the departing chief executive. There was some uncertainty about whether the payment was for helping to ensure a successful handover to the incoming chief executive, or for the role Lord Hollick had played in the sale of NOP World, a polling subsidiary. Shareholders felt that whatever the payment was for, it was not justified.

Following the vote, Lord Hollick agreed to waive the bonus. UBM announced that it would not make similar ex gratia payments to directors in the future.

© International Financial Publishing Limited

Example: Misys

In 2005, UK company Misys proposed to make a payment of shares to each of two senior executive directors. The reason for the payment was to persuade the two executives not to leave the company. The board considered that without the payment, they might otherwise leave the company unless they were appointed to the vacant role of chief executive. The board decided to hold a binding vote on the share award at the annual general meeting (AGM) of the company, to be held in September.

The proposed award met strong resistance from institutional investors, who argued that 'retention rewards' should have no part in succession planning.

The company, faced with the prospect of possible defeat at the AGM, withdrew the proposed share award in the week before the AGM.

3.2 The need for a remuneration committee

The remuneration of executive directors and senior management is such a contentious issue that it should be dealt with carefully.

The need for a remuneration committee was first recommended in the UK by the Greenbury Committee in 1995, which published a report into directors' remuneration. The Greenbury Report reached the following conclusions.

- Putting together a remuneration package for senior executives is a key issue in corporate governance.

- The system for negotiating and agreeing a remuneration package is open to abuse if executive directors can decide or influence their own remuneration arrangements.

- It is not practicable for shareholders to be involved in the negotiation of remuneration packages, and shareholders should not be able to make decisions about the remuneration of individual directors. However, they are entitled to extensive information about directors' remuneration.

- Remuneration for executive directors and other senior executives should therefore be decided by a remuneration committee of the board.

These recommendations were accepted. The UK Combined Code includes the following principles about remuneration.

- Levels of remuneration should be sufficient to attract, retain and motivate directors of the quality required to run the company successfully, but a company should not pay more than is necessary for this purpose.

- There should be a formal and transparent procedure for developing policy on executive remuneration and for fixing the remuneration packages of individual directors.

- No director should be involved in deciding his or her own remuneration.

The UK Code therefore states that a company should establish a remuneration committee. The committee should:

■ be given delegated responsibility by the board to set the remuneration levels for all executive directors and the chairman, and

■ recommend and monitor the level and structure of remuneration for senior management. (The board should decide the definition of 'senior management' but it will normally include the first layer of management below board level.)

3.3 Main duties of a remuneration committee

The duties of a remuneration committee should be decided by the board of directors. However, the Higgs Guidance suggested that the following duties should be included:

■ The committee should agree with the main board a policy for the remuneration of the chairman, CEO, other executive directors and any other designated senior management.

■ Where there is a performance-related pay scheme, the committee should decide the targets for performance.

■ The committee should decide the pension arrangements for each executive director.

■ The committee should approve the design of any new share incentive plan.

■ In negotiating service contracts with directors, the committee should ensure that severance payments in the event of dismissal are fair, but that 'failure' is not rewarded.

■ Within the framework of the agreed remuneration policy, the committee should negotiate and agree the remuneration of each individual executive director.

To provide advice and assistance, the remuneration committee should be able to hire the services of remuneration consultants. The committee should also make a report to the shareholders each year, for inclusion in the annual report and accounts.

Advice from executive colleagues

Although no one should be able to decide or influence their own remuneration, this does not prevent a remuneration committee from taking advice from executive colleagues on the board and other senior executives. Executives may be able to provide helpful information about what managers might expect to earn, and what specific performance targets might be appropriate for incentive schemes.

However, when it takes advice from executive colleagues, the remuneration committee should take care to recognise and avoid conflicts of interest (UK Combined Code).

The remuneration committee should also talk to the **finance director** about the potential impact of a proposed remuneration scheme on the company's reported profits. The committee needs to be aware that the company should not pay more in remuneration than it can sensibly afford, given its financial situation.

© International Financial Publishing Limited

3.4   Composition of the remuneration committee

As with the composition of the audit committee, views about the composition of the remuneration committee vary between countries. However, the general view is accepted that individuals should not be allowed to decide or influence their own remuneration.

- In the UK, the Combined Code states that in large companies, the remuneration committee should consist of at least three members, and all members should be independent non-executive directors. (In smaller listed companies, the remuneration committee should consist of at least two independent NEDs.)

- The Singapore Code of Corporate Governance does not specify the size of the remuneration committee. However, the committee should consist entirely of non-executive directors, the majority of whom should be independent. 'This is to minimise the risk of any potential conflict of interest.'

3.5   Continuing problems with the remuneration of executive directors

In the UK, since remuneration became a significant issue for corporate governance, the remuneration of executive directors in public companies has risen at a much faster rate than pay rises generally for the working population.

Remuneration committees have been criticised for making wrong judgements, or overlooking aspects of remuneration, and as a result remuneration has been higher than it should be.

The main reason for the problem appears to be 'benchmarking'. This is a method of deciding the level of remuneration by making comparisons with remuneration levels in other public companies.

Problems with using benchmarks

A problem with looking at what other companies are paying their directors is that when most companies do this, there is a tendency for remuneration levels to rise. Other companies are typically divided into four quarters (quartiles): companies paying the highest remuneration are placed in the upper quartile and companies paying the least are put in the lowest quartile.

The remuneration committee of a company in the FTSE 250 index might decide that its executive directors should be paid on a similar level to executives in companies in the second quartile, and negotiate remuneration on that basis. However, since very few companies will set a policy of being in the lowest quartile of companies in the benchmark group, there will be a tendency for remuneration levels to rise continuously as each company re-sets remuneration levels that put it in the middle level or in the upper quartile.

The UK Combined Code recognises that benchmarking is likely to result in higher remuneration. It therefore states that comparisons should be used with caution 'in view of the risk of an upward ratchet of remuneration levels with no corresponding improvement in performance.'

International benchmarks

For large companies, there is the additional problem of international comparisons. It may be argued in order to attract the best executive talent it is necessary to offer remuneration packages comparable to those paid to executives in global competitors. Global competitors will often include US corporations, where executive remuneration is high. For global companies in other countries, this could be an 'excuse' for increasing executive pay to very high levels.

 ### Example

Occasionally, a remuneration committee might overlook entirely an aspect of executive remuneration, and as a result executive rewards might be higher than they should be.

In August 2006, the Association of British Insurers (ABI) in the UK sent a letter to each of the FTSE 350 companies asking remuneration committees to look at the pension arrangements in the service contracts of senior executives.

The letter was prompted by the publication of details of the pension arrangements for four senior executives at the energy company Scottish Power, which the ABI criticised because it considered them excessive and they were not performance-based.

The four Scottish Power executives all retired (before their 'normal' retirement age) with very large increases in their pension funds. For example, the pension of the CEO doubled on termination of his contract, from £3.4 million to £6.8 million. In addition, his contract allowed him to retire early on exactly the same pension he would have received if he had stayed in his job until normal retirement age. The company argued in its own defence that it was contractually obliged to make the payments.

© International Financial Publishing Limited

> ## The nominations committee
>
> - Appointments to the board as a corporate governance issue
> - The need for a nominations committee
> - Main duties of a nominations committee
> - Composition of the nominations committee
> - The nominations committee and appointment of a new chairman

4 The nominations committee

4.1 Appointments to the board as a corporate governance issue

When new appointments are made to the board of directors, it is obviously important that the individual selected should be someone with suitable skills and experience. The board as a whole should also consist of individuals who collectively have an appropriate breadth of skills and experience to bring to the discussions and decision-making of the board.

To ensure that there is a suitable balance of power on the board, the system for nominating and selecting new directors should not put the choice into the hands of one individual or a small group of individuals.

However, executive directors should have a voice in new appointments to the board.

- When the appointment of a new executive director is considered, the executive directors are probably in a better position than NEDs to assess the qualities of internal and external candidates for the position.
- The executive directors should be aware of the skills and experience that they lack, and so can offer suggestions about the type of non-executive that they would like to add to the board.

Decisions about nominations to the board might occur quite frequently with non-executive directors. Whereas executive directors are normally expected to retain their position on the board as long as they have their job with the company, non-executives might be expected to retire when their current fixed term of appointment reaches an end. When a current NED retires, he or she will probably be replaced with someone else.

Succession planning

In addition to selecting new directors for the board, the process of nomination also involves succession planning. Succession planning means planning in advance for the eventual replacement of key members of the board when they eventually retire (or in the event that they are dismissed).

Succession planning applies in particular to:

■ the board chairman

■ the CEO, and

■ possibly, the finance director.

Institutional investors want reassurance that a company has plans for the eventual replacement of a successful chairman or CEO, so that the financial performance of the company will not be damaged when that individual retires or resigns.

4.2   The need for a nominations committee

There are two main reasons for having a nominations committee:

■ When a vacancy on the board has to be filled, or when succession planning is considered, the process of identifying and evaluating suitable candidates takes time. The board should delegate the task to a committee to save time and resources. The committee should then make recommendations to the board, so that the full board takes the final decision about any appointment.

■ The appointment of directors to the board, and the succession for top positions on the board, should be a carefully organised process. The UK Combined Code states that 'there should be a formal, rigorous and transparent procedure for the appointment of new directors to the board'. Such a formal procedure can be established by setting up a nominations committee. Transparency can be achieved by requiring the nominations committee to present an annual report on its activities to the shareholders.

4.3   Main duties of a nominations committee

The UK Combined Code states that the nominations committee should 'lead the process for board appointments and make recommendations to the board'. The board should decide what the exact duties of the nominations committee should be. The Higgs Guidance suggests that the committee's duties should include the following.

■ To identify candidates to fill vacancies on the board, when these arise.

■ To select a preferred candidate for nomination, and recommend this individual to the board for appointment.

■ Before recommending any person for appointment to the board, the committee should evaluate the balance of skills, knowledge and experience of board members, and on the basis of this evaluation identify the skills, knowledge and experience that the new director should have.

■ To consider succession planning.

■ To review regularly the size and composition of the board, and make recommendations for change if this is considered appropriate.

The Singapore Code of Corporate Governance suggests that the nominations committee should be responsible for the annual performance review of the board and its individual directors.

© International Financial Publishing Limited

4.4   Composition of the nominations committee

Views may differ between countries about what the composition of the nominations committee should be. The UK Combined Code makes the following recommendations:

- A majority of members of the nomination committee should be independent non-executive directors. A minority of members may therefore be executive directors.

- The chairman of the committee should be either the board chairman or an independent non-executive director. However, the board chairman should not chair the nomination committee when it is dealing with the appointment of a successor to the chairmanship.

The guidelines in the Singapore Code of Corporate Governance are slightly different. This Code states that the nominations committee (NC) should consist of at least three members, and the majority of members (including the committee chairman) should be independent.

4.5   The nominations committee and appointment of a new chairman

The UK Combined Code recognises that the appointment of a new chairman for the company requires particular care, to make sure that a suitable candidate is identified who will be able to give the company an appropriate amount of his (or her) time.

- For the appointment of a chairman, the nomination committee should prepare a job specification, including an assessment of the time commitment expected.

- A chairman's other significant commitments should be disclosed to the board before appointment and these should be included in the annual report. Changes to these commitments should be reported to the board as they arise, and included in the next annual report.

- No individual should be appointed to a second chairmanship of a FTSE 100 company. (It is assumed that one individual would not have the time to perform the role of chairman in two such important companies.)

The risk committee

- Risk management as a corporate governance issue
- The role of the board and board committees on risk

5 The risk committee

5.1 Risk management as a corporate governance issue

The board of directors is responsible for the performance of their company, and is accountable to the shareholders. Responsibility for financial performance is not simply a matter of trying to maximise profits. There is a need to manage the risks that the company faces. Risks include:

- the business risks and strategic risks that the company faces in its operations, and also
- risks of errors, fraud, losses through mistakes and breakdowns, and other failings in systems and processes.

Responsibility of the board for risk management and risk control

The board of directors is responsible for safeguarding the assets of the company and protecting the value of the shareholders' investment.

- The board has a duty to make sure that systems, procedures and checks are in place to prevent losses through errors, omissions, fraud and dishonesty. Control measures to prevent or detect such losses are internal controls. The board has the ultimate responsibility for the effectiveness of the internal control system.
- The board is responsible for protecting the company and its resources from the risks of adverse external events, such as damage to assets from fire or flooding, losses through theft, disruption caused by natural disasters or terrorist attacks, and so on.

The board is also responsible for developing the strategy for the company. All business strategies involve some business risk (or strategic risk) – for example, a risk that customers will not buy enough of the company's products or services, or that competitors will be more successful, or that costs will be higher than anticipated and profits lower. In developing strategy, the board should consider both the expected returns and the business risk, and assess whether a particular strategy is justified (whether the expected returns justify the risk).

Risk management as a task for management

Although the board has responsibility for risk management and internal control, management has the operational responsibility for planning and implementing risk management and control systems. Managing risk is a day-to-day requirement.

© International Financial Publishing Limited

Risk management and internal control should therefore be:

- planned and implemented by management, and
- monitored by the board, to ensure that effective systems of risk management and control are in place.

The Cadbury Committee, which produced the **Cadbury Report** on corporate governance in the UK in 1992, described risk management as 'the process by which executive management, under board supervision, identifies the risk arising from business ... and establishes the priorities for control and particular objectives.'

The Cadbury Report also suggested that risk management should be:

- systematic, and
- embedded in the company's procedures, rather than applied occasionally and by means of external review.

The Cadbury Report recommended that there should be:

- a sound system of financial control, and also
- a broader system of risk management.

It also suggested that the board should be responsible to the shareholders for making sure that appropriate systems of internal control and risk management are in place. This recommendation was not implemented at the time. However, board responsibility for the review of internal control and risk management was eventually introduced into corporate governance 'best practice' in the UK with the publication of the original Combined Code in 1998.

5.2   The role of the board and board committees on risk

Executive management is responsible for designing and implementing systems of internal control and risk management, and management should be accountable to the board of directors. The board in turn should be accountable to the shareholders.

The UK Combined Code suggests what the responsibilities of the board should be within the overall system of risk management. The Code states that the board should maintain a sound system of internal control to safeguard shareholders' investment and the company's assets.

In order to do this, the board should:

- conduct a review, at least once a year, of the effectiveness of the company's (or group's) system of internal controls, and
- report to the shareholders that they have carried out a review.

This annual review by the board should cover:

- all material controls, including financial, operational and compliance controls, and
- risk management systems.

Responsibilities of the audit committee for financial controls

The UK Combined Code also states that a responsibility of the audit committee should include the review of the company's internal financial controls.

The audit committee is in a good position to carry out a review of these controls, because of the discussions it has with the company's external auditors and internal auditors. For example, the external auditors produce a 'management letter' at the end of the audit, making recommendations for improvements in financial controls. The audit committee should discuss these recommendations with the auditors and management, to establish whether the recommendations have been implemented (and if not, why not).

Board responsibilities for the internal control system and risk management

However, the internal control system extends beyond financial controls. It includes not only financial controls, but also operational controls and compliance controls. In addition to internal control, there is also the system of risk management – how the company identifies, analyses and deals with business and strategic risks, environmental risks, and so on.

The UK Combined Code states that there should be a board responsibility to review the company's internal control and risk management systems. This responsibility for review should be carried out by:

- the audit committee, or
- the full board, or
- a risk committee consisting entirely of independent non-executive directors.

The Combined Code does not suggest how the board, the audit committee and the risk committee (if there is one) should carry out their responsibilities for the review of internal controls and risk management.

The need for a review of internal control and risk management by the board is also recognised in the Singapore Code of Corporate Governance. Its guidelines are similar to the provisions in the UK Code:

- The audit committee should review the adequacy of the company's internal financial controls, operational and compliance controls, and also the risk management policies and systems that have been established by management (collectively, all internal controls).

- The audit committee should ensure that a review of the effectiveness of the internal controls is carried out at least annually. This review should be carried out by the company's internal auditors, public accountants or a combination of internal auditors and public accountants. (If public accountants are used, and these are the company's external auditors, the audit committee must be satisfied that the independence of the public accountants will not be compromised by any other relationship they have with the company.

- The board should include a comment on the adequacy of internal controls and the risk management system in its annual report and accounts.

Internal control and risk management, and the responsibilities of the board and management, are dealt with in more detail later in this text.

© International Financial Publishing Limited

CHAPTER

5

Directors' remuneration

Contents
1   Principles of directors' remuneration
2   Remuneration package structures
3   Performance-related incentive schemes
4   Other remuneration issues

Principles of directors' remuneration
■ Remuneration: executive and non-executive directors
■ Components of a remuneration package
■ The purpose of a remuneration package

1 Principles of directors' remuneration

1.1 Remuneration: executive and non-executive directors

A previous chapter explained the importance of directors' remuneration in corporate governance and the role of the remuneration committee. This chapter considers in more detail what the remuneration package of a director should be, and the reasons for the different component elements of a remuneration package.

In some countries, for example the US, it is common for most senior executives to be excluded from the board of directors. References in this chapter to 'directors' remuneration' mean the remuneration of executive directors and other senior managers. The term 'directors' pay' will be used as a convenient general term.

Non-executive directors are paid an annual fee for their services. This is usually a fixed amount, based on the estimated number of days that the director will spend with the company during the year, for example attending board meetings and meetings of board committees.

A general principle of corporate governance is that the non-executives probably cannot be considered properly independent if they receive any additional remuneration from the company other than a basic fee. Additional remuneration could take the form of:

■ fees for additional consultancy services

■ membership of the company's share incentive scheme

■ membership of the company's pension scheme.

1.2 Components of a remuneration package

The remuneration package for an executive director is a part of the director's contract of service. Remuneration is reviewed regularly, typically each year. The broad framework of a remuneration package is agreed through negotiation between the individual director and the remuneration committee. The package is negotiated when the director first joins the company, and might be re-structured at any subsequent time.

The components of a remuneration package are commonly:

■ a basic salary

■ one or more annual cash bonuses, linked to the achievement of specific performance targets

---

　　　　　　　　　　　　　　　　© International Financial Publishing Limited

- free shares in the company or share options
- pension rights or a contribution to a pension fund for the director.

A director will often receive additional benefits such as free medical insurance, a company car, use of a company aeroplane or helicopter, and so on. Occasionally, a director might be paid a 'joining fee' to persuade him to join the company.

1.3 The purpose of a remuneration package

A remuneration package should attract individuals to a company, and persuade them to work for the company. The size of the remuneration package that is needed to attract 'top quality' individuals depends largely on conditions in the labour market. In other words, the amount that a company must offer its directors depends on:

- what other companies are paying, and
- how many suitable candidates are available.

The UK Combined Code states that levels of remuneration should be sufficient to retain and motivate directors of the quality required to run the company successfully, but the company should avoid paying more than is necessary for this purpose.

A second purpose of a remuneration package is to provide incentives for the director. Directors should be rewarded with incentives, so that they are motivated to achieve performance targets.

- A generally-accepted view is that unless a director is rewarded for achieving targets, he or she has no incentive to improve the company's performance. (This view is based on the conflict of interest between management and shareholders.)
- It can also be argued that companies have to offer incentives to their directors because other companies do so. Directors usually expect cash bonuses and equity awards.
- If suitable performance targets are selected, and the targets are made sufficiently challenging, the rewards for directors will be made dependent on achieving performance targets for the company that are in the best interests of the shareholders.

Both the UK Combined Code and the Singapore Code on Corporate Governance contain the identical principle that: 'A significant proportion of executive directors' remuneration should be structured so as to link rewards to corporate and individual performance.' The Singapore Code adds: 'There should be appropriate and meaningful measures for the purpose of assessing individual directors' performance', but does not go into further detail.

The specific purpose of cash bonuses, shares and share options will be considered in more detail later. However, a major difficulty in practice is finding suitable performance measures and performance targets as a basis for the payment of incentives.

Remuneration package structures

- Finding a balance between the different components of remuneration
- Basic salary
- Short-term incentives: bonus
- Long-term incentives: share plans
- Pensions
- The purpose of each component of a remuneration package

2 Remuneration package structures

2.1 Finding a balance between the different components of remuneration

When a remuneration committee designs a remuneration package for a director or senior manager, it should consider:

- each separate element in the package, and also
- all the elements in the package as a whole.

There are two issues to consider: the total size of the package and how it should be divided into its different components, between short-term and long-term incentives, between cash and equity and between current pay and pension rights. For example, a director may be paid an average basic salary, but may receive a generous pension entitlement and an attractive long-term incentive scheme. Another director may receive a low basic salary but a very attractive short-term cash bonus incentive scheme.

The relative proportions can vary significantly between companies, although the incentive element should be high.

2.2 Basic salary

The purpose of a basic salary is to give the director a guaranteed minimum amount of pay. If a director does not receive a basic salary, he will depend entirely on incentive payments. It could be argued that this would not be fair on the director, and would put him or her under stress.

The size of basic salaries varies between companies, and depends to some extent on the salaries paid to similar directors in comparable companies. However, salaries are also dependant on the extent to which directors and senior executives have an opportunity to boost their earnings through incentive schemes. A lower basic salary might be acceptable to a director who expects to receive large cash bonuses or equity awards.

© International Financial Publishing Limited

2.3   Short-term incentives: bonus

Many companies have an incentive scheme for its senior executives that offers directors and other senior managers in the scheme an annual cash bonus for meeting or exceeding target performance levels. The bonus scheme may be on a sliding scale, with a bonus for meeting target and higher bonuses for exceeding targets by a certain amount.

It is widely believed that the nature and potential size of annual bonuses can drive the behaviour of senior executives. Executives will possibly be much more concerned about short-term targets and annual cash bonuses than about longer-term share incentives and bonuses.

There may be a cap on the maximum bonus that any individual may earn. For example, an incentive scheme may provide for a bonus equal to 25% of basic salary for meeting performance targets, with a maximum bonus of 50% of salary for exceeding targets.

The bonus payments will be linked to one or more key performance indicators, possibly using a balanced scorecard approach. The targets may include:

- performance indicators for the business as a whole (such as a target for earnings per share) and/or
- personal targets for the individual executive. These might be financial targets, but might also be non-financial targets.

For example a sales director might receive a cash bonus of 15% of his basic salary if the company achieves its target profit for the year, and an additional 15% cash bonus if annual sales increase by at least 5% above the previous year.

2.4   Long-term incentives: share plans

Long-term incentive schemes usually take the form of awards of either:

- share options or
- fully-paid shares in the company.

A company might have several different share schemes, and individuals may participate in several or all of them. For example, there may be a share scheme or share option scheme for all employees, and a separate (additional) equity reward scheme for top executives.

Share options

A share option gives its holder the right, at a future date, to buy shares in the company at a fixed price. For example, a director might be given 20,000 share options, giving him the right to buy 20,000 new shares in the company at a fixed 'exercise price' of, say, £6.40 on or after a specified date in the future.

If the company's share price increases, the director will be able to exercise the share options and buy new shares in the company at a price below their current market price. If he wishes to do so, he can sell his new shares, and make an immediate profit.

A company will appoint a committee to decide how many share options should be granted to each individual. In the case of share option schemes for senior executives, this might be a responsibility of the remuneration committee.

■ In the UK, the earliest time that share options can be exercised is three years after they have been awarded. The option holder will make a profit if the share price rises above the exercise price during that time. The individual therefore has an incentive to want the share price to rise over the period. This is why share options are a long-term incentive.

■ The exercise price for the share options should not be lower than the market price of the shares at the time the share options were awarded. For example, if the share price is £6.00, a company should not issue share options with an exercise price of, say, £5.50. (In the US, several companies were accused in 2006 of back-dating share options for executives and awarding options at an exercise price equal to the market price at an earlier date, when the share price was lower.)

Under-water share options

A problem with share options as a long-term incentive for directors is that the share price can go down as well as up. If the share price falls below the exercise price for a directors' share options, the share options are said to be 'out-of-the-money' or 'under water'. Unless there is a reasonable chance that the share price will recover strongly, the share options will therefore have no value. If they have no value, or very little value, they cannot provide an incentive to the option holder.

Companies faced with this problem in the past have tried to maintain the incentive for a director, after the share price has fallen, by:

■ cancelling the existing share options, and

■ awarding new share options to the executive, at a lower exercise price.

The executive will then be rewarded if the share price rises above its new, lower level.

However, there are critics of this practice of cancelling share options that are under water and replacing them with new options. They argue that share options are awarded as a long-term incentive to executives, to link their personal interests more closely to the interests of the shareholders. If the share price goes up, the executive and the shareholders benefit. If the share price goes down, the executive and the shareholders should suffer together. However, if share options are replaced when they are under water, the executive benefits from a rise in the share price but does not suffer when the share price falls. This means that the interests of the executive and the shareholders are not the same – the executive is protected against bad results.

The award of fully-paid shares

An alternative to share options is the award of fully-paid shares in the company. This avoids much of the problem of a fall in the share price. Whereas share options under water have no value at all, fully-paid shares retain some value, even when the share price falls. The award of fully-paid shares might therefore be more successful in linking the personal interests of the executive with the interests of the shareholders.

In order to award free fully-paid shares to executives, the company will buy its own shares. It can do this either by making purchases of shares in the stock market, or by giving existing shareholders an opportunity to sell some of their shares to the company, in a tender or auction process.

Share plans and performance targets

The award of shares or share options should be conditional on the director or senior executive meeting certain performance targets. For example, a scheme might award free shares to executive directors for achieving Total Shareholder Return (TSR) targets over a three-year period, relative to comparator companies. Each director may be awarded up to 40% of the awards available to him if the company meets the TSR average for comparator companies, and 100% of the available awards for being in the top 25% ('top quartile') of comparator companies.

2.5 Pensions

Executive directors will also receive certain pension benefits. They may be members of a company pension scheme. In addition, there may be 'unfunded' pension arrangements for individual directors.

2.6 The purpose of each component of a remuneration package

Each element in a remuneration package has a purpose. In its 2006 directors' remuneration report, Tesco set out the elements of executive director remuneration and their purpose as follows:

Component of remuneration	Performance measure	Purpose
Base salary	Individual contribution to the business success	To attract and retain talented people
Annual cash bonus (up to 100% of salary)	Earnings per share and specified corporate objectives	Motivates year-on-year earnings growth and the delivery of business priorities
Annual deferred share element of bonus (up to 100% of salary)	Total shareholder return, earnings per shares and specified corporate objectives	Generates focus on medium-term targets. By incentivising share price and dividend growth, it ensures alignment with shareholder interests
Performance Share Plan (up to 150% of salary)	Return on capital employed over a three-year period	Assures a focus on long-term business success and shareholder returns
Share options	Earnings per share relative to retail prices index	Incentivises earnings growth and shareholdings by directors
Reproduced by kind permission. © Tesco plc, 2006		

Performance-related incentive schemes	

- Linking rewards to performance
- The UK Combined Code on performance-related schemes
- Performance targets
- Share option schemes and restricted stock awards
- Equity incentive schemes: a financial reporting problem

3 Performance-related incentive schemes

3.1 Linking rewards to performance

When a remuneration package contains an incentive element, the potential rewards for the executive should be linked to company performance, so that executives are rewarded for achieving or exceeding agreed targets. In principle, this gives an incentive to the executive to ensure that the targets are achieved.

If the performance targets are properly selected, incentive schemes should link rewards for executives with benefits for the company and its shareholders. In this way the directors share an interest with the shareholders in the financial success (long-term or short-term) of the company.

Problems with linking rewards to performance

In practice, however, linking the interest of directors and shareholders through remuneration incentives has not worked out well. In many cases the remuneration of directors and the best interests of the company and its shareholders have not been linked properly. There are several reasons why this might happen.

- There may be disagreement about what the performance targets should be. Should the executive have a performance target for company performance, or should he be rewarded for achieving personal targets? Should there be financial targets only, or should there be non-financial targets? Should there be just one target or several different targets? How can incentives and rewards for short-term targets be reconciled with incentives and rewards for longer-term targets?

- Executives may be rewarded with a large bonus for meeting an annual profit target. This will almost certainly motivate the director to achieve the target. However, a consequence of maximising the current year's profit might be that long-term profits will be lower. For example, profits in the current year might be improved by deferring much-needed capital expenditure, or by deciding not to invest in new research or development work. An executive might have much less concern for the longer-term performance of the company, partly because short-term incentives are usually paid in cash and partly because the director might not expect to remain with the company for the long term.

- Executives may have expectations that they will receive rewards, even when the company does not perform particularly well. The effect of an incentive scheme

© International Financial Publishing Limited

might therefore be to annoy a director when the bonus is less than expected, rather than give him an incentive to improve performance.

■ Executives are often protected against the 'downside'. Like the shareholders, they benefit when company performance is good. However they do not suffer significantly when performance is poor. The example of replacing under water share options was referred to earlier.

■ There may be a 'legacy effect' for new senior executives. For some time after a new senior executive is appointed, the financial performance and competitive performance of the company might be affected by decisions taken in the past by the executive's predecessor. Rewards for the new executive may therefore be the result of past actions by another person.

■ On the other hand, a new executive might find that he (or she) has inherited a range of problems from his predecessor, which the predecessor had managed to keep hidden. The new executive might therefore receive low bonuses even though he has the task of sorting out the problems.

■ Occasionally, incentive schemes are criticised for rewarding an executive for doing something that ought to be a part of his normal responsibilities. There have been cases, for example, where an executive has been rewarded for finding a successor and recommending the successor to the nominations committee. It could be argued that finding a successor is a part of the executive's normal job.

3.2   The UK Combined Code on performance-related schemes

The UK Combined Code has an appendix containing recommended provisions for the design of performance-related remuneration.

■ **Short-term incentives**. The remuneration committee should consider whether directors should be eligible for annual bonuses. If it decides that a director should be eligible, the performance targets should be 'relevant, stretching and designed to enhance shareholder value'. There should be an upper limit to bonuses each year. There may also be a case for paying a part of the annual bonus in shares of the company, and requiring the individual to hold them for a 'significant period' after receiving them.

■ **Long-term incentives**. The remuneration committee should also consider whether directors should be eligible for rewards under long-term equity incentive schemes. If share options are granted, the earliest exercise date should normally be not less than three years from the date of the grant. Directors should be encouraged to hold their shares for a further period after they have been granted or after the share options have been exercised, except to the extent that the director might need to sell some of the shares to finance the costs of buying them, or to meet any tax liabilities in connection with receiving the shares.

■ Any proposed new long-term incentive scheme **should be submitted to the shareholders for approval**. Any new scheme should form part of a well-considered overall remuneration plan that incorporate all other existing incentive schemes (and may replace an 'old' existing scheme). The total rewards that are potentially available to directors should not be excessive.

■ Grants under executive share options schemes and other long-term incentive schemes should normally be phased rather than awarded in a single large block.

- **Performance criteria**. Payments or grants under all incentive schemes should be subject to 'challenging performance criteria' that reflect the company's objectives. The committee should give consideration to performance criteria that reflect the company's performance relative to a group of other, similar companies in some key variables such as Total Shareholder Return (TSR).

- The remuneration committee should consider the consequences for the company's pension costs of awarding any basic salary increase to directors, especially directors who are approaching their retirement.

3.3 Performance targets

Annual bonuses

An annual bonus scheme may base the award of a bonus on achieving or exceeding an annual profit target. This target might a target for:

- profit after taxation

- profit before interest and taxation (PBIT), or

- earnings before interest, taxation, depreciation and amortisation (EBITDA).

The target might be a specific money value, or it might possibly be expressed in growth in profit relative to other similar companies. However, there a several problems with using profit targets as a basis for the payment of bonuses.

- Annual profits might be manipulated in order to increase the current year's profits. As stated earlier, a major capital expenditure or other large planned expenditure might be deferred to the next year.

- Achieving a profit target does not necessarily mean that the company's shareholders will benefit. Higher profits do not necessarily mean higher dividends or a higher share price. If higher profits are obtained, but investors consider the company to face much higher risks, the share price might fall.

A remuneration committee might recommend that bonuses should be based on the benefits obtained by shareholders during the period, measured perhaps as Total Shareholder Return (TSR). TSR is simply the sum of the dividends to shareholders plus the increase in the share price during the period (or minus the fall in the share price). This might be expressed as a percentage of the share price at the beginning of the year.

However, a problem with schemes that link bonus payments in TSR is that share prices are often volatile, so that the measurement of TSR for any year may be affected by relatively short-term movements in the share price that do not reflect underlying performance.

Personal targets

Within an incentive scheme for senior executives, each individual may be given 'personal' non-financial targets for achievement.

- A range of non-financial targets might be used, depending on the area of operations for which the executive is responsible. For example, a sales or marketing executive might have personal performance targets for customer satisfaction (provided that customer satisfaction can be measured objectively).

■ Personal targets might also be linked to a longer-term plan, such as a five-year business plan for the company. The executive might be rewarded for achieving specified targets within this longer-term plan.

Long-term incentives

Long-term incentive schemes for executives may set a target for profitability, possibly over a period of three years. Alternatively, they may set:

■ a non-financial target

■ a strategic objective

■ several different targets, with the total reward based on the extent to which each different target is achieved.

3.4 Share option schemes and restricted stock awards

Share incentive schemes can be used to link the long-term interests of individual directors with the long-term interests of shareholders, because both the director and the shareholders will benefit from a rising share price.

However, a remuneration committee needs to be aware of the potential problems with such schemes.

■ With share option schemes, options should not be granted occasionally, in large amounts. They should be granted regularly, in smaller amounts. If options are granted in large blocks, the director might have an incentive to do his best to ensure that the share price is as high as possible at the earliest date that the options can be exercised. What happens to the share price later is of much less importance to the director, who is able to take his profit at the earliest exercise date. If the director is not then given new share options, his incentive to remain with the company is reduced.

■ Some companies place a restriction on sales of shares by directors or executives after they have been awarded free shares or have exercised share options. These are commonly specified in Share Ownership Guidelines, which are the terms and conditions of the equity incentive scheme. The restriction may be in the form of a **minimum retention ratio**. This requires the director to retain a minimum percentage of the shares he has acquired, and not to sell them before the end of a specified minimum period. For example, a share option scheme might require an individual to retain at least 25% of the shares acquired by exercising share options, for at least three years after the shares have been acquired. The purpose of a minimum retention ratio is to ensure that the director continues to have a personal interest in the share price.

■ This same argument applies to the award of shares to executives. When executives are given shares in their company, they may be required to retain them for a minimum number of years before they are able to sell them or dispose of them in any other way.

- **The size of option awards**. There should be a limit to the quantity of share options granted. Share options 'dilute' the interest of existing shareholders in the company when the options are exercised.

3.5 Equity incentive schemes: a financial reporting problem

The board of directors (and the remuneration committee) needs to recognise the possible effect of equity incentive schemes on the company's financial statements. The award of shares and share options affects the company's reported profits each year. This might have affect the share price.

The problem arises because International Financial Reporting Standard 2 (IFRS 2) requires companies to recognise the award of share options as an expense in the company's annual income statements, from the time that the share options are granted.

Why are share options an expense?

The award of fully-paid shares in the company is an expense because the company pays money to buy the shares, and this spending is for the benefit of its executive directors. It is therefore an employment cost, and as such should be included as a cost in the income statement.

It might not be so clear why share options are an expense, because the option holder pays cash to buy new shares in the company.

IFRS 2 is based on the view that when a company issues share options, it incurs an expense. It gives employees the right to subscribe for new shares at a future date, at a price that is expected to be lower than the market price of the shares when the options are exercised.

Share options therefore have a value. When share options are awarded to an employee, the employee is therefore given something of value (a cost) in return for the benefit. This is an employment cost. Employment costs should be reported as an expense in the income statement.

Accounting for equity-settled share-based payment transactions

The method of accounting for equity incentives is not explained here, because it is not in the syllabus. It is sufficient to be aware of the consequences for these schemes on reported profits.

© International Financial Publishing Limited

> **Other remuneration issues**
>
> - Legal and regulatory issues: reporting on directors' remuneration
> - Legal issues: service contracts and compensation for loss of office
> - Ethical issues about remuneration
> - Remuneration and competition issues
> - Remuneration and shareholder attitudes

4 Other remuneration issues

4.1 Legal and regulatory issues: reporting on directors' remuneration

It should be a principle of corporate governance that the shareholders of a company should be given full information about the remuneration of the company's directors. This information should help shareholders and other investors to understand the link between directors' remuneration and company performance.

The requirement to publish remuneration details varies between countries. You do not need to know the details of disclosure requirements in each country. The following examples are provided to show:

- how disclosure requirements might vary
- the sort of information that might be provided by companies, and
- whether the disclosure requirements might be voluntary or compulsory.

The Singapore Code of Corporate Governance and remuneration disclosures

The Singapore Code of Corporate Governance, which does not have the force of law, requires companies to disclose details of their remuneration policy and the procedure they use to set remuneration for directors and senior executives. The specific guidelines in the Singapore Code are as follows:

- In its annual directors' report, a company should report to its shareholders on the remuneration of directors and at least the top five key executives who are not directors.

- The report should give the names of the directors and at least the top five key executives earning remuneration within bands of S$250,000. The remuneration of each should be analysed, in percentage terms into the amount earned as (1) base salary, (2) performance-related bonuses, (3) benefits in kind and (4) stock options and other long-term incentives. As best practice, companies are encouraged to disclose fully the remuneration of each individual director, but this is not a requirement of the Code.

- The same details should be provided (on a no-name basis) for immediate family members of a director or the CEO.

- The report should give details of employee share schemes, so that shareholders can assess the cost and potential benefit of these schemes to the company. These details should include details of the number of options issued and not yet exercised, and their exercise price(s).

UK law on disclosure of directors' remuneration

In the UK, quoted companies are required by law (the Companies Act) to prepare a directors' remuneration report each year. The report must contain extensive disclosures about directors' remuneration. It is normal practice to include this remuneration report in the annual report and accounts.

Some of the information in the remuneration report must be audited by the company's auditors. Other parts of the report are not subject to audit.

Shareholders must vote at the company's annual general meeting on a resolution to approve the report. This is an advisory vote only, and the shareholders do not have the power to reject the report or amend the remuneration of any director or senior executive.

Information not subject to audit

Information in the directors' remuneration report that is not subject to audit is as follows:

- The names of the members of the remuneration committee, and details about any remuneration consultants that were used by the committee.

- The company's policy on directors' remuneration. (This should be a forward-looking policy statement, not an explanation of policy in the past.)

- A graph showing the Total Shareholder Return (TSR) on the company's shares over a five-year period, and the TSR over the same period on a portfolio of shares representing a named broad equity market index. This graph can be used to compare shareholder returns on the company's shares with those of a market index.

- Information about the service contract for each director: the date of the contract, its unexpired term and details of any notice periods; any compensation payable for early termination of the contract and any other provisions in the contract affecting the liability of the company in the event of early termination.

Information subject to audit

The remuneration report must contain the following information which is subject to audit.

- The total remuneration for the year for each director, analysed into salary and fees, bonuses, expenses received, compensation for loss of office and other severance payments, and non-cash benefits.

- For each director, details of interests in share options, including details of options awarded or exercised during the year, options that expired during the year without being exercised, and any variations to the terms and conditions relating to the award or exercise of options.

- For options exercised during the year, the market price of the shares when the options were exercised should also be shown.

© International Financial Publishing Limited

- For options not yet expired, the report should show the exercise price, the date from which the options may be exercised and the date they expire. To allow shareholders to assess the value of the options to the directors, the report should also show the market price of the company's shares at the end of the year, and the highest and lowest market prices reached during the year.

- For each director, details should be given of any long-term incentive schemes other than share options.

- For each director, details should be given of pension contributions or entitlements.

- Details should also be provided of any large payments made during the year to former directors of the company.

Additional requirements recommended by the UK Combined Code

The statutory regulations for quoted companies on directors' remuneration are now quite extensive. The significant elements are:

- the shareholders' right to vote on the directors' remuneration report, which includes a statement on remuneration policy, and

- the extensive disclosures of remuneration details.

The Combined Code, however, makes further recommendations:

- Shareholders should be asked to approve all new long-term incentive schemes

- If grants under a share option scheme or long-term incentive scheme are made in one block, rather than phased over time, this should be explained and justified.

4.2   Legal issues: service contracts and compensation for loss of office

Service contracts

The point has been made in an earlier chapter that executive directors and other senior managers are full-time employees with a service contract. As full-time employees they have the rights given to all employees by the country's employment law.

One of the major concerns of shareholders about service contracts, other than the remuneration package itself, is the notice period. This is the minimum period of time that an employer must give between dismissing an employee and the employee actually leaving employment.

In the UK in the 1980s, it was standard practice for directors to have a notice period of three years in their contract of employment. As a result, if a company wished to dismiss one of its directors, it had to give three years' notice. More usually, the company would pay the director three years of remuneration to leave the company immediately.

Three-year notice periods are now rare in the UK. Pressure was exerted on listed companies by the UK codes of corporate governance. The current UK Combined Code specifies that notice periods should be set at one year or less.

Even so, when a director is dismissed the payment on termination of employment can be very high, since it might include one year's base salary, pension entitlements, shares and bonuses that the director might be entitled to under the terms of his various incentive schemes.

Compensation on loss of office

In the UK, institutional investors have stated their expectation that companies will seek limit payments of compensation on loss of office of a director or senior executive. Since a director is protected legally by the terms of his (or her) service contract, it is therefore essential that the remuneration committee should negotiate contract terms with a new director that will limit the potential size of compensation payments.

The UK Combined Code states that when a remuneration committee negotiates the terms of a service contract with a new director, it should consider what the compensation payments might be in the event that the individual is dismissed. The committee should seek to avoid agreeing terms of employment that would reward a director for poor performance and dismissal. The committee should therefore take a 'robust line on reducing compensation to reflect departing directors' obligations to mitigate loss'.

A director dismissed by a company should be required, by the terms of his service contract, to try to mitigate the losses he suffers as a result of the dismissal. He can do this, for example, by finding new employment as soon as possible. A service contract may therefore provide for the total compensation on loss of office to be payable in several stages (instead of in full at the time of dismissal) and for these payments to be stopped if the individual finds a new job.

4.3 Ethical issues about remuneration

There is an ethical aspect to directors' remuneration, which has attracted some publicity as the rate of increase in directors' pay has been much greater than the rate of increase in the pay of other employees.

- A Survey of Directors' Compensation 2005 in the UK by KPMG found that bonus payments to senior executives had risen at a fast rate, but were hardly ever linked to the long term strategy of the company and the shareholder value. This meant that executives were not adding to the value of the company but were being paid large bonuses. Executives in too many companies are being paid for achievements meeting targets with very little relevance to corporate strategy and the value proposition it puts to shareholders.

- Research by Income Data Services in the UK in 2006 stated that directors were now earning almost 100 times as much in annual remuneration than other full-time workers, compared with about 40 times as much in 2000. The gap between the remuneration of the most highly-paid and the remuneration of the least well paid, in percentage terms, was continuing to increase.

A trade union spokesman (the Trades Union Congress general secretary) is reported to have commented: 'It is hard not to conclude that this further huge rise in executive pay is more about greed than performance…. The stratospheric levels of directors' pay compared to average wages mean that executives now live in a class apart, even from employees in their own companies. It is not just socially divisive, but bad for the economy.'

4.4 Remuneration and competition issues

Although there might be ethical reasons for arguing that directors' remuneration is too high, there are competitive reasons for explaining the increase.

Directors' remuneration has risen because there appears to be a shortage of individuals who are considered to have the ability to lead major stock market companies. Given a shortage in the supply of talented individuals, general levels of remuneration for top executives have risen.

4.5 Remuneration and shareholder attitudes

Shareholders, particularly institutional investors, have shown a strong interest in remuneration as an issue in corporate governance. The views of insurance companies and pension funds are most often expressed by their trade associations, the Association of British Insurers (ABI) and the National Association of Pension Funds (NAPF), which provide guidance to their members and may sometimes co-ordinate their activities.

The Association of British Insurers has issued guidelines for its members on executive remuneration. These are consistent with the principles and provisions of the Combined Code, but are more specific in detail. The guidelines are directed at both:

- remuneration committees, because they indicate the aspects of remuneration that their shareholders will consider

- their members, by indicating what they should consider when deciding whether or not to show their approval of the remuneration policy of any company in which they invest.

Institutional investors do not argue in favour of lower remuneration. They believe that:

- directors should be paid a fair remuneration, but not excessive amounts

- a large part of a directors' remuneration package should consist of incentives

- performance targets for incentives should be relevant and challenging.

The ABI's guidelines on executive remuneration are about 10 pages long. A few guidelines are shown below, to illustrate the approach that institutional investors take to the assessment of remuneration policy.

- Remuneration committees should communicate their policy on base salaries to shareholders. If it seeks to pay salaries at the median (average) level or above, the committee should provide a justification.

- When a director is paid a bonus for achieving a performance target, the directors' remuneration report should give a full analysis of which performance targets were met.

- If performance is subsequently found to have been over-stated by management, the remuneration committee should have the right to reduce or reclaim the bonus payments to executives.

- When preparing the contract for a director, the remuneration committee should calculate the likely cost of any severance payment on dismissal, and whether this is acceptable.

- Where companies have share-based incentive schemes, executives should be encouraged to build up 'meaningful' holdings of shares in the company.

The significance of shareholder attitudes

Shareholder views on remuneration packages can be important. Institutional investors might act together and use their votes at general meetings.

The power of individual shareholders in large companies is usually restricted. Even the largest shareholders usually do not own a large proportion of the shares in their company, and it can be very difficult for shareholders to act together to obtain a majority of votes at any general meeting of the company.

However, institutional investors are increasingly active, and remuneration committees need to be aware that proposed incentive schemes, or the remuneration package of a senior executive such as the CEO, may arouse strong opposition.

Shareholders can express their displeasure with remuneration policy and remuneration packages by voting collectively in any of the following ways:

- to vote against a proposed new incentive scheme

- to vote their disapproval of the directors' remuneration report

- to vote against the re-election of a director who is retiring by rotation, particularly if the director is a member of the remuneration committee or is a beneficiary of a generous remuneration package.

© International Financial Publishing Limited

CHAPTER

6

Different approaches to corporate governance

Contents
1   Rules-based and principles-based approaches
2   Brief history of corporate governance in the UK
3   International codes and principles of corporate governance

> ## Rules-based and principles-based approaches
>
> - Reasons for the development of corporate governance codes
> - Corporate governance codes and different models of corporate ownership
> - Rules-based approach to corporate governance
> - The rules-based approach in the US: Sarbanes-Oxley Act 2002
> - Main governance aspects of Sarbanes-Oxley
> - Principles-based approach to corporate governance

1 Rules-based and principles-based approaches

1.1 Reasons for the development of corporate governance codes

Codes of corporate governance, in different forms, have been developed in most countries where there is a stock exchange. The main reason for codes of good corporate governance is to help and protect investors.

- Investors need reliable information about companies, to decide whether to invest in shares or (if they already hold shares) whether to sell them. Financial reporting by companies and external auditing should therefore be reliable. Investors should also be given other information to help them make their investment decisions, such as information about future prospects of the company, internal control and risk management and directors' remuneration.

- Investors need to be protected against unethical or dishonest behaviour by company management. For example, there must be strict laws against insider dealing, to prevent managers from making personal profits at the expense of other investors.

Many investment institutions invest in the stock markets of many different countries. They can choose which markets to invest in, and can choose to avoid stock markets where they believe that governance practices are poor and investors are treated badly.

Countries have developed corporate governance codes and practices because they want to attract and keep investment capital, especially from global institutional investors. This is because investment capital helps the country's economy to develop and its companies to prosper. Pressure for better corporate governance has come mainly for two reasons:

- The collapse of major stock market companies in a major financial centre, where investors have lost substantial amounts of money and the cause of the collapse has been largely attributable to bad corporate governance.

- Pressure from institutional investors in countries with well-developed corporate governance codes or rules.

The International Corporate Governance Network (ICGN) is an entity formed in 1995, whose members consist of major institutional investors, companies, banks and other interested groups. Its aim is to encourage the development of good corporate

© International Financial Publishing Limited

practices worldwide. It has published a statement on global corporate governance principles (revised 2005), which gives an indication of why corporate governance matters so much to institutional investors.

The statement commented that the governance of a corporation is one of the key factors that investors consider when they decide where to allocate their investment capital. ICGN members considering making investment decisions also consider the market's governance profile.

Ethics and company performance

Other reasons for encouraging the development of good corporate governance are that:

■ Good corporate governance practices are an application of good business ethics.

■ It might be argued that good corporate governance contributes to the efficiency and effectiveness of a company's leadership and management. If this view is correct, well-governed companies will be more successful in the long term than badly-governed companies. However, this has not yet been proved, one way or the other.

1.2 Corporate governance codes and different models of corporate ownership

Codes of corporate governance are applied to major stock market companies. Laws and regulations on corporate governance issues are also mainly applied to stock market companies. This is not surprising, as the main reason for codes of governance is to help and protect investors.

Other companies can normally decide what system of corporate governance they want, and they are not required to comply with any established principles or rules. However, these companies might decide to apply these principles or rules because they think that:

■ it is ethically correct to do so, or

■ it will improve the performance of the company.

 Examples

In the UK, the London Stock Exchange has a stock market for smaller companies, the Alternative Investment Market (AIM). There are fewer regulations for companies in this market, and AIM companies are not required to comply with the Combined Code of corporate governance. However, an unofficial code of governance for AIM companies has been developed, and AIM companies are encouraged to adopt this code.

The board of a family-owned company might be dominated by some of the family members who are also the company's senior executives. The company might decide to appoint a non-executive director to represent the interests of family shareholders or other shareholders who are not on the board. (The director would not be independent, but the appointment of a NED to represent the interests of smaller shareholders might help to ensure that the company is governed in the interests of all the shareholders, not just the owner-directors.)

1.3 Rules-based approach to corporate governance

A rules-based approach to corporate governance is based on the view that companies must be required by law (or by some other form of compulsory regulation) to comply with established principles of good corporate governance.

The rules might apply only to some types of company, such as major stock market companies. However, for the companies to which they apply, the rules must be obeyed and few (if any) exceptions to the rules are allowed.

There are some **advantages** with a rules-based approach:

■ Companies do not have the choice of ignoring the rules.

■ All companies are required to meet the same minimum standards of corporate governance.

■ Investor confidence in the stock market might be improved if all the stock market companies are required to comply with recognised corporate governance rules.

There are **disadvantages** with a rules-based approach.

■ The same rules might not be suitable for every company, because the circumstances of each company are different. A system of corporate governance is too rigid if the same rules are applied to all companies.

■ There are some aspects of corporate governance that cannot be regulated easily, such as negotiating the remuneration of directors, deciding the most suitable range of skills and experience for the board of directors, and assessing the performance of the board and its directors.

Corporate governance rules: practical applications

Every country with a stock market should have some rules of corporate governance. The UK for example, which is associated with a principles-based approach to corporate governance, has some statutory rules.

Examples of statutory rules in the UK are as follows.

■ With some exemptions, mainly for small and medium-sized companies, companies are required to submit a directors' report and financial statements to the shareholders each year. This is a key aspect of accountability of the directors to the company's owners.

■ The financial statements should be audited.

■ Quoted companies (companies whose shares are traded on a stock exchange) must prepare a directors' remuneration report each year, and present this to the shareholders.

■ The Companies Act 2006 specifies duties that the directors owe to their company.

© International Financial Publishing Limited

The difference between countries that take a rules-based approach and those that take a principles-based approach to corporate governance is mainly one of emphasis. Some countries have more rules than others, and rely more on the enforcement of rules to achieve the required standard of governance.

The country most associated with a rules-based approach is the USA.

1.4 The rules-based approach in the US: Sarbanes-Oxley Act 2002

In the US, corporate governance was not regarded as important until the collapse of several major companies in 2001 and 2002, and large falls in the stock market prices of shares of all companies. This major setback for the US stock exchanges damaged investor confidence.

It was recognised fairly quickly that one of the reasons for the unexpected collapse of several companies ('corporations') was poor corporate governance. Enron and WorldCom were the two most notorious examples, but there were others too. There were several well-publicised cases where:

■ A company in serious financial difficulties was dominated by a chief executive and a small number of other senior executives, who appeared to be running the company in their own interests, without concern for the interests of shareholders (other than themselves).

■ Financial reporting was misleading.

■ Financial controls were weak and inadequate to prevent the misleading reporting, and to prevent fraudulent activities by some executives.

Politicians soon became involved in analysing the problems in the stock market and the collapse of companies such as Enron and WorldCom. This involvement of politicians soon led to new legislation to improve standards of corporate governance. This was the Sarbanes-Oxley Act 2002, which was named after its two main sponsors in the US Congress.

1.5 Main governance aspects of Sarbanes-Oxley

The Sarbanes-Oxley Act introduced **corporate accountability legislation**. It includes some specific requirements. In addition, it required the financial markets regulator, the Securities and Exchange Commission (SEC) to issue rules to implement some parts of the legislation. The Act is very long. Some of its provisions are described below.

CEO/CFO certifications (section 302 of the Act)

The Act requires all companies in the US with a stock market listing (both US companies and foreign companies) to include in their annual and quarterly accounts a certificate to the SEC. This certificate should be signed by the chief executive officer and the chief financial officer (finance director) and should confirm the accuracy of the financial statements. The CEO and CFO are therefore required to take direct personal responsibility for the accuracy of the company accounts.

Assessment of internal controls (section 404 of the Act)

Section 404 is possibly the most notorious part of the Sarbanes-Oxley Act. The Act required the SEC to establish rules that require companies to include an internal control report in each annual statement. This internal control report must:

- 'state the responsibility of management for establishing and maintaining an adequate internal control structure and procedures for financial reporting; and

- contain an assessment ... of the effectiveness of the internal control structure and procedures of the [company] for financial reporting.'

The SEC issued rules to implement this requirement of the Act. The management of companies registered with the SEC (stock market companies in the US), with the CEO and CFO, must evaluate the effectiveness of the company's internal control over financial reporting. The rule states that: 'The framework on which management's evaluation of the ... internal control over financial reporting is based must be a suitable, recognised control framework.'

Companies are required to maintain evidence, including documentary evidence, to provide reasonable support for management's evaluation of the internal control system. (One of the criticisms of section 404 has been the large amount of work necessary to collect and maintain all this evidence.)

Companies must disclose any material weakness in their internal control system. If more than one material weakness exists, a company is not allowed to conclude that its internal control system is adequate.

A report on internal control must be included in the company's annual report to shareholders.

In addition, the external auditors are required to prepare an 'attestation report' on the company's assessment of its internal control system.

The consequence of section 404 is that companies in the US or foreign companies whose shares are traded on a US stock market must undertake a review of their internal control system for financial reporting every year, and to maintain evidence to support the assessment of the control system that management gives in its annual report to the shareholders. The criticism of section 404 has been mainly that the requirements create a very large amount of work, that it costly in terms of management time and other resources, as well as auditors' costs.

Loans to executives

The Act prohibits companies (other than banks) from lending money to any directors or senior executives.

Forfeit of bonuses

Another requirement of the Act is that if a company's financial statements have to be re-stated due to non-compliance with accounting standards and rules, any bonuses paid to the CEO and CFO in the previous 12 months must be paid back to the company.

Insider dealing

The Act introduced stricter rules to prevent insider dealing by directors and senior executives. They are not allowed to trade in shares of their company during any 'black-out period'.

Audit committees

Companies with a stock market listing must have an audit committee consisting entirely of members who are independent of the company. (There was a debate in 2007 about a member of the audit committee who used the company's corporate membership of an expensive country club to play golf at the club. Did this mean that he was not properly independent?)

Non-audit work by auditors

The Act restricted the types of non-audit work that the company's auditors can perform for the company. Auditors are not allowed, for example, to do book-keeping work for an audit client, or provide valuation services or perform any management functions for the company.

Protection for whistleblowers

A whistleblower is an employee of the company who reports, through a channel of communication other than his or her direct supervising managers) suspected fraud or illegal activities in the company. The Act provides protection for any employee who 'blows the whistle' on activities in the company, and prevents the company from taking action against the employee, such as terminating his or her employment. (This was what Enron did to an employee who acted as a whistleblower when she suspected fraudulent activities in the company.)

1.6 Principles-based approach to corporate governance

A principles-based approach to corporate governance is an alternative to a rules-based approach. It is based on the view that a single set of rules is inappropriate for every company. Circumstances and situations differ between companies. The circumstances of the same company can change over time. This means that:

■ the most suitable corporate governance practices can differ between companies, and

■ the best corporate governance practices for a company might change over time, as its circumstances change.

It is therefore argued that a corporate governance code should be applied to all major companies, but this code should consist of principles, not rules.

- The principles should be applied by all companies.

- Guidelines or provisions should be issued with the code, to suggest how the principles should be applied in practice.

- As a general rule, companies should be expected to comply with the guidelines or provisions.

- However, the way in which the principles are applied in practice might differ for some companies, at least for some of the time. Companies should be allowed to ignore the guidelines if this is appropriate for their situation and circumstances.

- When a company does not comply with the guidelines or provisions of a code, it should report this fact to the shareholders, and explain its reasons for non-compliance.

Comply or explain

This approach is sometimes called **comply or explain**. It applies in the UK, for example. With a comply or explain approach, stock market companies should be required to present a corporate governance statement to their shareholders in which they state that:

- they apply the principles in the code of corporate governance (the code that applies to companies in that stock market), and

- either the company has:

    - complied with all the provisions or guidelines in the code for applying the principles in practice, or

    - explain their non-compliance with any specific provision or guideline.

In the UK, the Combined Code is the relevant code of corporate governance for listed companies. All UK listed companies must comply with rules known as the **Listing Rules**, which are issued and enforced by the financial markets regulator (the Financial Services Authority or FSA). One of the Listing Rules is that companies must comply with al the detailed provisions of the Combined Code, or explain their non-compliance, in an annual corporate governance statement to shareholders. This statement is included in the annual report and accounts.

Which is more effective: a rules-based approach or a principles-based approach?

The advantages and disadvantages of a principles-based approach to corporate governance are the opposite of those for a rules-based approach. There is no conclusive evidence to suggest that one approach is better than the other.

It has been suggested that the burden of the detailed rules in the US, especially the requirements of section 404, has made the US an unattractive country for foreign companies to trade their shares. As a result, many foreign companies have chosen to

© International Financial Publishing Limited

list their shares in countries outside the US, such as the UK (London Stock Exchange).

However, the relative success or failure of New York and London as centres for listing shares by foreign companies is not the only relevant argument about which method of corporate governance is better. The relative advantages of a rules-based approach and a principles-based approach might become clear only when more corporate governance scandals occur - at some time in the future.

Brief history of corporate governance in the UK
■ The Cadbury Code (1992)
■ The Greenbury Report (1995)
■ The Hampel Report (1998)
■ The Combined Code (1998)
■ The Turnbull Report (1999)
■ The Higgs Report (2003)
■ The Smith Report (2003)
■ The revised Combined Code (2003)

2 Brief history of corporate governance in the UK

The UK was the first country to develop a detailed code of corporate governance for its listed companies. The example set by the UK has been followed in some other countries, which now have their own principles-based system and code of corporate governance. (One such example is Singapore. The Singapore Code has been mentioned in previous chapters.)

The principles-based approach was also adopted for 'international' codes of corporate governance such as the OECD Principles, which are described later.

The development of corporate governance practices in the UK is interesting because it helps to show how different aspects of corporate governance emerged at different times as issues of some importance.

2.1 The Cadbury Code (1992)

The Cadbury Code was the first corporate governance code for the UK. During the 1980s there were several financial scandals involving listed UK companies. Investors questioned whether the London Stock Exchange was a safe place to invest, and expressed doubts about the quality and reliability of financial reporting.

The London Stock Exchange led an initiative to investigate financial aspects of corporate governance. A committee was set up, under the chairmanship of Sir Adrian Cadbury. Members of the Cadbury Committee represented the major financial institutions in the UK.

The stated aim of the Cadbury Committee was to raise standards of corporate governance in the UK, and investor confidence in financial reporting and auditing, by setting out the responsibilities of the people and entities involved. However, the investigations by the committee were extended from financial reporting to include other aspects of corporate governance.

The committee issued a report on corporate governance and a Code of Best Practice for corporate governance. This was known as the Cadbury Code. The aim of the Code was to encourage companies to improve their corporate governance by

© International Financial Publishing Limited

complying with its provisions, if they did not do so already. The Cadbury Committee recommended that:

■ companies should be required to comply with the best practice as specified in the Code

■ the Code should be voluntary, but if companies did not comply, they should be required to explain in their annual report and accounts why they had not done so. (This was the origin of 'comply or explain'.)

In 1992, the London Stock Exchange had responsibility for the UK Listing Rules. In response to the Cadbury Report, it amended the Listing Rules so that all listed companies were required to include a statement of compliance in their annual report, stating that they had complied with all the best practice recommended in the Cadbury Code, or giving an explanation for any non-compliance.

Main provisions of the Cadbury Code

The main provisions of the Cadbury Code contain many aspects of 'best practice' in corporate governance that are still recognised today.

■ **Board of directors**. The Cadbury Committee recognised that it was impractical to give significant extra powers to shareholders and that the directors should have most of the essential powers. However, the board of directors should be effective, and should be properly accountable to the shareholders. Governance of the company should be the responsibility of the board as a whole: the board should meet regularly. At its meetings, it should monitor the performance of executive management. The board should reserve some matters for its own decision-making and should not delegate authority for these decisions to management. There had been a history in the UK of some public companies being dominated by a single individual holding the position of both chairman and chief executive officer. To avoid the risk of domination of a company by one person, the same individuals should not be chairman and CEO at the same time.

■ **Non-executive directors**. At the time of the Cadbury Report, the board of directors in most UK public companies consisted mainly of executive directors. The Cadbury code introduced a requirement for the board of directors to contain a minimum number of non-executive directors, and most of these NEDs should be independent.

■ **Remuneration and service contracts of executive directors**. At the time of the Cadbury Report, directors' remuneration was not seen as a major problem for corporate governance, although the Code recommended that a remuneration committee should be set up to decide (subject to board approval) the remuneration of executive directors, and most of this committee should consist of independent NEDs. However, a concern of investors was the lengthy notice periods given to many executives in their service contracts. The Code recommended that the maximum notice period in the contract of an executive director should be three years. (Under pressure from institutional investors, most UK listed companies quickly complied with this requirement, and many executives were asked by their company to agree to an amendment of the notice period in their service contract.)

■ **Financial statements**. At the time of the Cadbury Report, many companies did not have an audit committee. The Cadbury Committee saw an audit committee as an important board committee and recommended that every company should have such a committee of NEDs. Its role should be to communicate with internal and external auditors for the discussion of matters relating to financial reporting and auditing.

2.2 The Greenbury Report (1995)

After the Cadbury Code was implemented, directors' remuneration became more important as a corporate governance problem. The high pay awarded to directors in many large companies was criticised, both in the press and by institutional investors. More important, the remuneration packages of executive directors were badly designed, and many packages did not contain adequate or appropriate incentives to executives to improve company performance in the best interests of shareholders. It was widely believed that directors were being well paid regardless of whether the company performed well or badly.

A committee was set up under the chairmanship of Sir Richard Greenbury to investigate directors' remuneration. The Greenbury Report was published in 1995, with a code of best practice on directors' remuneration.

The Report also suggested that listed companies should provide much more information in their annual report and accounts about the remuneration of individual directors. The London Stock Exchange accepted this recommendation, and the Listing Rules were amended to include a (compulsory) rule about disclosure of information about directors' remuneration.

The Greenbury Report was not entirely successful. Some critics argued that it had not dealt properly with the problems for corporate governance of directors remuneration.

2.3 The Hampel Report (1998)

The Hampel Committee was set up in 1996 to continue the review into corporate governance in the UK. It was recognised (and continues to be recognised today) that corporate governance practice should be reviewed regularly, to make sure that the code of best practice is still relevant and appropriate.

The Hampel Report made a variety of recommendations. Some of the main recommendations were as follows.

- The Cadbury Code and the recommendations of the Greenbury and Hampel Committees should be combined into a single code of corporate governance for UK listed companies.

- The code of corporate governance should adopt a principles-based approach, not a rules-based approach. Detailed rules on corporate governance would be a form of 'box-ticking' and 'Box-ticking takes no account of the diversity of circumstances and experiences among companies and within the same company over time.' The Report added: 'We do not think there are universally valid answers' to all aspects of corporate governance.

© International Financial Publishing Limited

- The Hampel Report went further than the Cadbury Code and Greenbury Report on directors' remuneration. No director should be involved in deciding his own remuneration. The remuneration committee should develop the company policy on remuneration and should develop remuneration packages for executive directors that contained significant incentives to improve company performance. The notice period in the service contracts of directors should not exceed one year.

- The Hampel Report also recommended that institutional investors should be much more actively engaged in corporate governance. They should use their votes at general meetings of the company, and there should be regular constructive dialogue between a company and its major institutional investors.

- The Hampel Report also made recommendations about the responsibility of the board of directors for internal control and risk management. This was the first time that the importance of a sound system of internal control and risk management was formally recognised as a key issue in corporate governance.

2.4   The Combined Code (1998)

The Cadbury Code and recommendations of the Greenbury and Hampel Committees were combined into a single code of corporate governance, known as the Combined Code. The first edition of the Code was published soon after the Hampel Report in 1998.

The Combined Code was (and is) a principles-based code of practice. It specified general principles of corporate governance, and provided guidelines as to how these should be applied in practice. This was a continuation of the practice first established by the Cadbury Code.

The Combined Code is now the responsibility of the Financial Reporting Council (FRC) and regular reviews will be carried out (and minor revisions made as necessary) to ensure that the Code continues to recommend 'best practice' in corporate governance.

2.5   The Turnbull Report (1999)

The original Combined Code in 1998 included provisions relating to the responsibility of the board for the effectiveness of the system of internal control and risk management. The Code did not contain many details to explain what was required, or how the principles in the Code should be applied in practice.

The Turnbull Committee was established by the Institute of Chartered Accountants in England and Wales, and was given the task of providing guidelines to companies about this aspect of the Combined Code. The Turnbull Report was published in 1999. It was subsequently attached to the 2003 Combined Code (as the Turnbull Guidelines). It has since been updated (in 2005, by the Flint Committee), but the changes were not extensive.

The Combined Code made the board of directors recognise their responsibility for the effectiveness of the system of internal control and risk management within the company. The Code recognises that the objective of a company is not simply to maximise profits, because shareholders expect their investment to be protected against unacceptable risks. Risks cannot be eliminated from business, but shareholders have a right to expect that business risks (strategic risks) will be managed properly and unnecessary risks will be prevented or controlled.

The Turnbull Report was notable for several reasons.

- It required the board of directors to look forward, and consider the system used by the company for anticipating new and significant risks in the future, and taking measures to deal with them.

- It required directors to think in strategic terms about risk control and risk management, and to understand that risk control and risk management had to adapt to changes in the company's environment.

- Risks and controls should be reviewed regularly.

- Shareholders should be kept informed about risks and the systems for managing risk.

The Turnbull recommendations are described in detail in later chapters on internal control.

2.6   The Higgs Report (2003)

After the original Combined Code was introduced, it was recognised that some aspects of 'best practice' in the Code were not working as well as they should. One problem was the role of the non-executive directors, who did not appear to have as much influence as they should on decision-making by the board of directors.

The Higgs Report was published in 2003. Its title was 'Review of the role and effectiveness of non-executive directors'. It contained guidelines for making NEDs more effective. Some of these guidelines, which have been mentioned in earlier chapters, were as follows.

- At least one half of the board of directors should consist of independent non-executive directors. This should give independent NEDs greater influence over decision-making by the board. (This recommendation was included in the revised Combined Code in 2003.)

- The chairman should be independent at the time of his appointment. A CEO should not go on to become the chairman of the company. The Report also suggested in some detail what the role of the chairman should be.

- The Report also suggested in some detail what the role of other non-executive directors should be.

- It recommended that one independent NED should be appointed as senior independent director (whose role has been described in an earlier chapter).

- Before accepting an appointment as NED, an individual should question whether he or she has suitable skills or experience that would provide a valuable addition to the board of the company.

- NEDs should confirm, before they are appointed, that they will have sufficient time to carry out their duties properly.

© International Financial Publishing Limited

- To improve their ability to contribute effectively to the board, all new NEDs should be given induction after their appointment.

2.7 The Smith Report (2003)

The Smith Committee was established by the Financial Reporting Council to develop guidelines for companies on how to make their audit committees effective. The Committee published a report in 2003, entitled 'Audit Committees: Combined Code Guidance.'

The purpose of the report was to provide guidance to companies on how audit committees and their members should carry out their roles effectively.

The Smith Report recommendations were partly included in a revised version of the Combined Code, and partly attached to the new Combined Code as the Smith Guidelines.

2.8 The revised Combined Code (2003)

Following the Higgs Report and Smith Report early in 2003, a revised version of the Combined Code was published later in the same year.

The Code now consists of:

- **main principles**
- **supporting principles**, and
- detailed **provisions**, stating how the principles should be applied in practice.

When listed companies state in their corporate governance report whether they have complied with the Code, or explain their failure to comply, compliance refers to the provisions.

The Code is now reviewed regularly by the Financial Reporting Council, and minor changes have been made in the Code since 2003. A copy of the 2006 Combined Code is included as an appendix to this text.

> ## International codes and principles of corporate governance
>
> - The nature of international codes or statements of principle
> - The objectives of international statements of principle
> - Content of the OECD Principles
> - Content of the ICGN Principles
> - Limitations of international codes or statements of principles

3 International codes and principles of corporate governance

3.1 The nature of international codes or statements of principle

Some codes or statements of principles on corporate governance have been issued. The intention of these codes is to provide guidelines that should be adopted in all countries. They are therefore common standards of governance that should be applied internationally.

International statements of corporate governance principles include:

- the OECD Principles of Corporate Governance
- the ICGN Statement on Global Corporate Governance Principles
- the Principles for Corporate Governance in the Commonwealth (the CAGC Guidelines).

3.2 The objectives of international statements of principle

An international statement of principles seeks to establish minimum standards of corporate governance that should apply in all countries. Its main aim is therefore to raise standards in the 'worst' countries towards the standards that already exist in the 'best' countries.

The result of encouraging better standards of corporate governance should be that:

- better governance will attract more investment from global investors
- companies will benefit from more investment finance, to increase their profits
- national economies will benefit from having strong and profitable companies.

Objectives of the OECD Principles

The OECD Principles are published by the Organisation for Economic Co-operation and Development, and they are intended to:

- assist governments of countries to improve the legal, regulatory and institutional framework for corporate governance in their countries, and
- provide guidance to stock exchanges, investors and companies on how to implement best practice in corporate governance.

The members of the OECD are governments of about 30 economically-developed countries, and its objective is to encourage the development of the world economy. The OECD has recognised that a key to economic development in any country is an efficient market economy in which investors have confidence to invest their money.

The introduction to the OECD Principles makes a link between corporate governance and economic growth:
'Corporate governance is one key element in improving economic efficiency and growth as well as enhancing investor confidence.... The presence of an effective corporate governance system, within an individual company and across an economy as a whole, helps to provide a degree of confidence that is necessary for the proper functioning of a market economy. As a result the cost of capital is lower and firms are encouraged to use resources efficiently, thereby underpinning growth.'

Objectives of the ICGN Principles

The ICGN is the International Corporate Governance Network. It is a voluntary association of major institutional investors, companies, financial intermediaries and other organisations and its aim is to improve corporate governance practices around the world, in all countries where institutional investors seek to invest.

The ICGN Principles are consistent with the OECD Principles, but have the more specific objective of providing information to stock markets and companies around the world about the issues that investors will take into account in deciding how (and where) to invest. The ICGN gives greater emphasis than the OECD to **the right of investors to participate actively** in corporate governance in the companies in which they invest.

The ICGN says that one of its objectives is to aid international discussions about issues that investors are concerned about. ICGN believes that this process enables economies to prosper and companies to be more effective in their competition. According to the ICGN, encouraging and enabling company owners to participate in their governance is in the public interest.

3.3   Content of the OECD Principles

There are six main principles, but each of the main principles has a number of supporting principles.

(OECD *Principles of Corporate Governance* – 2004 Edition, © OECD 2004)

Principle I: Ensuring the basis for an effective corporate governance framework

'The corporate governance framework should promote transparent and efficient markets, be consistent with the rule of law and clearly articulate the division of responsibilities among different supervisory, regulatory and enforcement authorities.'

This principle is concerned with the framework for good corporate governance that is provided by the stock market and financial intermediaries, the regulation of the markets and the information that is available to investors about companies ('transparency' in the markets). It is useful to think about this principle in terms of countries that fail to provide transparency in markets, or stock markets that function efficiently, or markets in which the rule of law is fair and properly applied.

Principle II: The rights of shareholders and key ownership functions

'The corporate governance framework should protect and facilitate the exercise of shareholders' rights. This principle is concerned with the basic rights of shareholders, which should include the right to transfer the ownership of their shares, the right to receive regular and relevant information about the company, the right to vote at general meetings of company shareholders, the right to share in the company's profits and the right to remove directors from the board.'

These basic shareholder rights might seem 'obvious'. However, there are countries in which these rights do not properly exist, especially for foreign shareholders. For example the laws of a country may permit a company to insist that shareholders wishing to vote at a general meeting of the company must attend the meeting and cannot be represented by a proxy. This requirement in effect would remove the right to vote of most foreign investors, who do not have the time to attend general meetings in person in countries around the world.

Principle III: The equitable treatment of shareholders

'The corporate governance framework should ensure the equitable treatment of all shareholders, including minority and foreign shareholders. All shareholders should have the opportunity to obtain effective redress for violation of their rights.'

Within the same class of shares, all shares should carry the same rights. Minority investors should be protected against unfair actions by the majority shareholders. Restrictions on cross-border voting should be eliminated. Insider trading should be illegal. Directors should be required to notify their company of material personal interests they have in transactions with the company.

These rights might also seem 'obvious'. However, it is not uncommon in some countries for majority shareholders negotiating the takeover of their company by a buyer to arrange a higher price for their shares than the price that will later be offered to the minority shareholders.

Principle IV: The role of stakeholders in corporate governance

The corporate governance framework should recognise the rights of stakeholders that are established by law, or through mutual agreements. This will include, for example, employment rights and agreements negotiated for employees with trade union representatives.

There should also be active co-operation between companies and their stakeholders 'in creating wealth, jobs and the sustainability of financially sound enterprises.'

© International Financial Publishing Limited

Principle V: Disclosure and transparency

'The corporate governance framework should ensure that timely and accurate disclosure is made on all material matters regarding the [company], including the financial situation, performance, ownership and governance of the company.'

The disclosure of information to shareholders and investors is a critically important aspect of corporate governance. This issue will be considered in more detail in a later chapter.

Principle VI: The responsibilities of the board

'The corporate governance framework should ensure the strategic guidance of the company, the effective monitoring of management by the board and the board's accountability to the company and the shareholders.'

This principle relates to many of the functions of the board described in an earlier chapter. It includes the requirement that 'board members should act on a fully informed basis, in good faith with due diligence and care, and in the best interests of the company and the shareholders.' The board should also apply high ethical standards and take into account the interests of the company's stakeholders.

3.4   Content of the ICGN Principles

The ICGN Principles are consistent with the OECD Principles, and deal with issues such as disclosure and transparency, the rights and responsibilities of shareholders, and the role and structure of boards of directors.

An important objective of the Principles is to encourage the removal of bad corporate governance practices in countries where these still exist. Some of the Principles are listed below. It is useful to remember that the purpose of stating a principle is often to discourage different practices that are currently found in some countries.

- The **objective of a company**. The ICGN Principles begin with a statement that the main objective of a company should be to 'optimise' over time the return to its shareholders and that to achieve this, the board needs to develop a long-term strategy that will improve the equity value.

- **Shareholder rights**. The rights of all shareholders should be protected, including the rights of minority shareholders and foreign shareholders. If a company diverges from a 'one share one vote' standard of voting, so that some shareholders have voting power that is disproportionate to the amount of shares they hold, this should be explained and justified by the company. The voting system should enable all shareholders to exercise their votes: the ICGN therefore encourages initiatives to allow voting by telecommunications or other electronic channels.

- **The board of directors**. All directors must act in the best interests of the company and should be accountable to the shareholders as a whole. A well-governed company has independent-minded directors and there should be a strong presence of independent non-executive directors on the board.

■ **Corporate citizenship and the ethical conduct of business**. The ICGN Principles support the concept of 'corporate citizenship' and also the ethical conduct of business by companies. Companies should comply with the law and the board of directors is responsible for maintaining a culture of **integrity**.

3.5 Limitations of international codes or statements of principles

International statements of principle about corporate governance establish minimum acceptable standards of corporate governance, but they have several limitations.

■ Because they apply to all countries, they can only state general principles. They cannot give detailed guidelines, and so are not specific. Since they are not specific, they are possibly of limited practical value.

■ Their main objective is to raise standards of corporate governance in the 'worst' countries. They have less relevance for countries where corporate governance standards are above the minimum standard.

■ Unlike national laws and codes of corporate governance, there is no regulatory authority for international statements of principle. The principles therefore lack any 'force'. In specific countries, by contrast, there may be a supervisory body or regulatory body with specific responsibility for encouraging or enforcing corporate governance practices.

© International Financial Publishing Limited

CHAPTER

7

Governance: reporting and disclosure

Contents
1　General principles of disclosure
2　'Best practice' disclosures about corporate governance
3　Dialogue with shareholders: general meetings

> ## General principles of disclosure
>
> - The meaning of transparency and disclosure
> - Corporate governance: the need for transparency and disclosure
> - Principles of disclosure and communication

1 General principles of disclosure

1.1 The meaning of transparency and disclosure

Transparency in stock markets and other financial markets means that information about conditions in the markets is clear and well understood. For example, transparency exists when investors understand about the financial situation of companies, and the future plans and prospects for those companies, so that they can make well-informed investment decisions.

Investors need information about companies to make their investment decisions. Shareholders need information about the companies they have invested in, to assess the financial performance of the company and its future prospects, and to decide whether to hold on to their shares, sell them or buy more shares. Other investors need information about companies in order to decide which companies they should invest in, and how much to invest.

Disclosure means making information available, so that there is transparency. Companies have the main responsibility for disclosure in the stock markets. They provide regular reports to shareholders and other investors, and it is from these reports that investors obtain most of their information.

Transparency and disclosure are key issues in corporate governance.

1.2 Corporate governance: the need for transparency and disclosure

The need for transparency and disclosures in the financial markets is recognised in codes and statement of principles on corporate governance.

- The UK Combined Code includes a principle about the disclosure of financial information by companies, stating that the board has a responsibility to present 'a balanced and understandable assessment' of the company's position and prospects in its financial reporting.

- The OECD Principles state the requirement with greater force. They state that companies should provide 'timely and accurate disclosure' about their financial performance and position, and also about the ownership of shares in the company and also about other corporate governance issues.

- The ICGN Principles emphasise the need for information so that investors can make investment decisions, and state that companies should, on a timely basis, disclose the relevant information about the company to enable informed

© International Financial Publishing Limited

decisions about the acquisition obligations and rights, ownership and sale of shares to be made by investors.

What information should be disclosed?

There are three main categories of information that investors need from a company:

- Financial information about the past performance of the company, its financial position and its future prospects.

- Information about the ownership of shares in the company, and voting rights associated with the shares. This is important for global investors, who may have problems with investing in companies where there is a majority shareholder, or where there is a complex structure of share ownership, or where some shareholders have more voting rights than other shareholders (for the same class of shares).

- Corporate governance information. This is explained in more detail later.

1.3   Principles of disclosure and communication

There are several basic principles for disclosure and communication of information.

- The information should be **reliable**. Reliable information is information that is sufficiently accurate for investors to trust it when making their investment decisions. The OECD Principles, for example, state that information should be prepared and disclosed with high quality standards of accounting and high standards for both financial and non-financial disclosures.

- Information should be **understandable**. One of the criticisms of international financial standards (IFRSs) is that financial reporting in accordance with IFRSs can be very complex, and some investors might not properly understand the information that they provide. Many investors support the idea that companies should provide information about themselves in a narrative form, in addition to providing financial statements. **Narrative statements** are explained in more detail later.

- Information should be **timely**. In the financial markets, 'timely' often means 'communicated as soon as possible'. Information should be made available to all investors as soon as possible after it becomes 'public'. Efficient stock markets should ensure that information announced by companies is made available to everyone quickly after the announcement. In the European Union, for example, one of the aims of the **Transparency Directive** (introduced in 2007) is to communicate information available quickly to investors as soon as companies make announcements to the stock market.

- When information is disclosed by companies, it should be equally available to all investors. The OECD Principles state that the way information is distributed should enable users to access relevant information in an **equal**, timely and cost-efficient manner.

- Information should be made available by **convenient channels of communication**. Companies should be encouraged to make it available in electronic form to investors who want to receive it in that form. For example, companies should use their web sites for making disclosures.

■ The opportunities for exploiting confidential information to make a personal profit should be minimised. By making information available to investors quickly, **opportunities for insider dealing** should be reduced.

© International Financial Publishing Limited

> ### 'Best practice' disclosures about corporate governance
>
> - Requirements for disclosures about corporate governance
> - The content of 'best practice' disclosures
> - Mandatory and voluntary disclosures
> - Narrative reports: business reviews and interim management statements

2 'Best practice' disclosures about corporate governance

2.1 Requirements for disclosures about corporate governance

Institutional investors expect to be given information about corporate governance by companies, because this information helps them to make their investment decisions.

In the European Union and in other countries, the principle of 'comply or explain' is applied. Major companies are required to comply with a recognised code of corporate governance, or explain their non-compliance. However, this on its own does not provide all the corporate governance information that investors want.

- In countries of the European Union, major companies are required to prepare a corporate governance statement each year. This is included in their annual report and accounts. In the UK for example, the Listing Rules require a statement in the annual report and accounts (of listed companies) relating to compliance with the Combined Code.

- Similarly, the Singapore Exchange Listing Rules require similar disclosures from listed companies, in relation to the Singapore Code of Corporate Governance.

- The OECD Principles call for disclosures by companies about governance issues.

2.2 The content of 'best practice' disclosures

Corporate governance statements by listed companies are often quite long. Typically, they fill five or six pages in the annual report and accounts. (In addition, UK listed companies include a lengthy directors' remuneration report, in addition to their corporate governance report.)

The specific content of a corporate governance statement may vary. In the UK, statements by listed companies are required to contain the following information.

- A statement of how the board operates, including a high level statement about which matters are reserved for the board and which decisions are delegated to management. For example, a report might state: 'The Board has set out clearly the Schedule of Matters Reserved for Board Decision in order to ensure overall control of the Group's affairs. These include the approval of financial statements, major acquisitions and disposals, authority levels for expenditure, treasury policies, risk management, Group governance policies and succession plans for senior executives.'

■ Names of the chairman, CEO, senior independent director and chairmen of the nominations, audit and remuneration committees.

■ The number of board meetings and board committees during the year, and the attendance record of each director at those meetings. This information might be presented in a table, as follows.

	Board meetings	Nominations committee	Remuneration committee	Audit committee
Number of meetings held	8	1	4	4
Attendance				
Non-executive directors				
Mr S Lee (Chairman)	8	1	n/a	n/a
Mr J Glover	6	1	4	n/a
Mrs T Potter	8	1	4	4
Mr R Robinson	7	n/a	4	3
Mr A Timms	7	1	n/a	4
Executive directors				
Mr D Watts (CEO)	8	1	n/a	n/a
Ms G Hobbs	8	n/a	n/a	n/a
Mr B Lam	8	n/a	n/a	n/a
n/a = not applicable				

■ The names of the non-executive directors that the board considers to be independent. Reasons should be given where this is appropriate.

■ The other significant commitments of the chairman, and changes in these commitments during the year.

■ A statement about the performance evaluation of the board, and how this has been conducted.

■ A statement about the steps the board has taken to ensure that the directors (especially the non-executive directors) are informed about the opinions of the company's major shareholders. This statement might be quite brief. For example: 'Shareholders are offered the opportunity to meet with the Senior Independent Non-Executive Director. The Board is kept informed of the view of major shareholders through regular updates.'

Somewhere within the annual report and accounts, the following information should also be provided.

■ A separate section describing the work of the nominations committee.

■ A description of the work of the remuneration committee. (In the UK this is required as part of the Directors Remuneration Report Regulations, and is likely to be contained within the Directors Remuneration Report.)

■ An explanation of the directors' responsibility for preparing the financial statements.

■ A statement by the directors that the company is a going concern.

■ A report that the board has carried out a review of the company's system (and group's system) of internal controls.

© International Financial Publishing Limited

- A separate section describing the work of the audit committee.

- If the company does not have an internal audit department, the reasons why it does not.

- If the company's auditors provide non-audit services to the company, an explanation of how the auditors' objectivity and independence are safeguarded.

Other information that should be provided by companies includes:

- The terms of reference for the nominations committee, remuneration committee and audit committee. These can be made available on the company's website.

- The terms and conditions of appointment of NEDs (which can also be made available on the website).

- When papers are sent to shareholders for a general meeting where there will be a proposal to elect or re-elect a non-executive director, a statement by the board of why the individual should be elected. When a NED is proposed for re-election, the chairman should also confirm that the performance of the NED continues to be effective and the individual continues to commit the necessary amount of time to the company.

2.3   Mandatory and voluntary disclosures

Disclosures about corporate governance may be a mandatory requirement of the law or other regulations, or they may be provided as voluntary disclosures by a company. In practice, the disclosures by a company are likely to be a mixture of mandatory and voluntary items.

The nature and amount of **mandatory disclosures** depends on the laws and regulations of the country.

- Some disclosures are required by law. For example, companies are required to prepare an annual report and accounts, and present these to the shareholders. Company law specifies what the directors' report and the accounts must contain, and in addition other regulations about content apply such as the requirements of financial reporting standards. In the UK, there is a legal requirement for quoted companies to include a directors' remuneration report in their annual report and accounts.

- Some disclosures are required by stock market rules. For example, as mentioned earlier, the UK Listing Rules require listed companies to provide information relating to corporate governance in their annual report and accounts. There are also stock market rules about other announcements by the company, such as profit warnings and announcements of proposed takeovers.

In addition to the mandatory disclosures required by law or regulation, many companies provide additional information, as part of their normal reporting cycle. Typically, these include:

- a chairman's report describing the activities of the company and its different operating divisions: alternatively, an operating and financial review by the CEO

- a social and environmental report, or a corporate social responsibility report: these reports are described later.

The reasons for voluntary disclosures

Companies are not required to provide voluntary disclosures, but there are several reasons why they choose to do so.

- Some voluntary information might be provided as a **public relations** or **marketing** exercise, to present 'good news' about the company to investors and other users of the company's published reports. For example, this might be the purpose of a chairman's report. It could be argued that social and environmental reporting has been used by some companies to promote their 'green' image and strengthen their reputation with customers.

- Providing information on a voluntary basis might persuade the government or financial service regulator that compulsory disclosures and regulation are not necessary.

- Companies might publish social and environmental reports out of a genuine **ethical and cultural belief** in the responsibilities of the company to society and the environment. If a company believes that it has social and environmental responsibilities, publishing a report on these issues is a way of making itself accountable.

- A company might use voluntary disclosures as a way of **improving communications with its shareholders**. By giving more disclosures to shareholders, companies might encourage shareholders to respond, and enter into a dialogue with the company about its strategies and plans for the future.

2.4 Narrative reports: business reviews and interim management statements

As mentioned earlier, there is a view that companies should provide information in a narrative form about their financial performance and prospects for the future, in addition to providing financial statements. This view is based on the belief that narrative reports can be much easier to understand than financial statements and notes to the financial statements.

There is also a demand from investors for non-financial information, in addition to financial information.

Many major companies have provided **narrative reports on a voluntary basis**, usually in a chairman's report or an operating and financial review. However, these voluntary statements have limitations. The main limitations are that:

- the company can decide what to include in the report and what to leave out

- the information is often presented in a very positive form, as public relations for investors, and might not be entirely reliable.

Business review

The demand for narrative reporting and the limitations of voluntary narrative reporting have led to **mandatory narrative reporting** in some countries. In the European Union, the Accounts Modernisation Directive introduced a requirement for companies to include a **business review** in their annual report and accounts.

Example: UK requirement for a business review

The legal requirement for a business review was introduced in the UK by the Companies Act 2006 (section 417). The Act states that the purpose of the business review is to inform shareholders and help them to assess how the directors have performed their legal duty to promote the success of the company.

- The business review should contain:
    - a fair review of the company's business, and
    - a description of the main risks and uncertainties facing the company.
- The review should provide a 'balanced and comprehensive analysis' of:
    - the development and performance of the company's business during the year and
    - the position of the company's business at the end of the year.

With the exception of small companies (which are not required to prepare a business review at all) and medium-sized companies, the business review must include:

- an analysis of key **financial** performance indicators (KPIs), and
- where appropriate, other key performance indicators including KPIs relating to environmental matters and employee matters.

In addition, quoted companies are required to include in their business review, information about:

- the main trends and factors likely to affect the future development and performance of the company's business
- environmental matters (including the impact of the company's business on the environment), the company's employees and social and community issues
- 'persons with whom the company has contractual or other arrangements which are essential to the business of the company' – unless disclosure of this information would, in the opinion of the directors, be seriously prejudicial to that person or against the public interest.

The Act gives some exemption from the requirement to provide this information. Disclosures of 'impending developments or matters in the course of negotiation' do not have to be disclosed if this would be prejudicial to the interests of the company.

Interim management statements (IMSs)

The demand for more and better transparency and disclosures by listed companies has also led to a requirement in the European Union for major stock market companies to issue an interim management statement (IMS) each year. This is a requirement of the EU Transparency Directive, which came into force from January 2007.

An IMS is required in addition to the company's interim financial statements for the first six months of the financial year. The purpose of an IMS is to explain material events and transactions that have taken place in the (six-month) period, and their financial effect. It must also include a description of the principal risks and uncertainties that the company will face for the remaining six months of the year.

In the UK, the Financial Services Authority issued guidance to companies about the new rules, which stated that they believe that companies will meet the IMS requirements based on the content of performance reports, trading statements and other such similar formats with no extra information, if those reports or statements include the required information under the Disclosure and Transparency Rules. This means that the IMS must outline the material events and transactions for the IMS's relevant period and their impact on the financial position of the company and provide a general description of the financial position of the company.

(*Note*: The Disclosure and Transparency Rules, like the Listing Rules, are rules that all UK listed companies must comply with.)

© International Financial Publishing Limited

> ### Dialogue with shareholders: general meetings
>
> - The need for dialogue between companies and their shareholders
> - Shareholder activism
> - General meetings of the company and voting by shareholders
> - Problems with the use of voting rights

3 Dialogue with shareholders: general meetings

3.1 The need for dialogue between companies and their shareholders

Constructive dialogue between the board of directors and the main shareholders of the company should help to improve the quality of corporate governance. Dialogue between the directors and the main shareholders should reduce the problems in the principal-agent relationship between them.

- Through dialogue, the shareholders can tell the directors what they are hoping the company will achieve or any concerns they might have (for example, about the risks faced by the company, about the dividends they hope to receive or about the succession for the position of chairman or CEO, and so on).
- Similarly, the directors can explain their plans and intentions in more detail than through formal reports.

The need for dialogue is recognised in various codes of corporate governance and statements of corporate governance principles. For example, the UK Combined Code includes the following principles.

- The board is responsible for having a satisfactory dialogue with shareholders 'based on the mutual understanding of objectives'.
- In addition, institutional shareholders have a responsibility to enter into a dialogue with companies, also 'based on the mutual understanding of objectives'.

For a company, most of the dialogue with its shareholders is conducted by the chairman, the CEO and the finance director. These are the individuals, for example, who normally make presentations about the company to institutional investors. The UK Combined Code states that in his discussions with major shareholders, the chairman should discuss, amongst other things, governance and strategy.

It is the responsibility of the chairman to make sure that other members of the board are informed about the views and concerns of the major shareholders.

The UK Combined Code states that major shareholders should be given the opportunity to meet with the company's non-executive directors, if they wish to do so. However, with the exception of the senior independent director, it is unlikely that institutional investors will want to meet a company's NEDs, simply because their time can be used better in other ways.

Senior independent director (SID)

A role of the senior independent non-executive director is to listen to the concerns of shareholders, when shareholders have concerns that have not been resolved through their normal channel of communication with the chairman, CEO or finance director. The senior independent director might then be asked to discuss the concerns of the shareholders with the rest of the board – in effect, to challenge the views of the chairman and CEO.

In order to perform this role, the senior executive director must be known to the major shareholders. Some meetings between the SID and shareholders is therefore desirable.

3.2 Shareholder activism

When a shareholder is dissatisfied with the performance of a company, he can sell his shares. There is no requirement for a shareholder to continue investing in a company. This is probably a reasonable description of the 'traditional' approach of institutional investors to the companies in which they invested.

An alternative approach to selling shares in under-performing companies is to:

- monitor companies closely
- enter into a dialogue with a company when it is under-performing, and express the concerns that the shareholder has about the company
- use voting rights to put pressure on a company's management.

This approach is called **shareholder activism** or **shareholder engagement**.

Purpose of shareholder activism

The purpose of shareholder activism is to try to improve the performance of under-performing companies. This purpose is explained in a Statement of Principles of the Institutional Shareholders Committee (ISC), a joint body in the UK representing all institutional investor associations. The ISC Principles state:

'The policies of activism … do not constitute an obligation to micro-manage the affairs of … companies, but rather relate to procedures designed to ensure that shareholders derive value from their investments by dealing effectively with concerns about under-performance.'

The Principles also state that although institutional investors are encouraged to become 'active' investors, they should still use their right to sell their shares, if this is what they would prefer to do in the case of some companies.

The nature of shareholder activism

Shareholder activism consists of the following activities.

- Shareholders should monitor the companies in which they invest. Effective monitoring requires an active dialogue between the shareholder and the company. The ISC Principles state that institutional shareholders should 'endeavour to identify problems at an early stage to minimise any loss in shareholder value. If they have any concerns and do not propose to sell [their shares], they will seek to ensure that the ... company's board are made aware of them.'

- Shareholders should have a policy about when they will intervene in a company by expressing their concerns. Concerns may relate to the company's strategy, operational performance, ineffectiveness of the company's independent NEDs, failures in the company's internal controls, directors' remuneration packages or the company's social and environmental policies.

- Shareholders should then assess the effectiveness of their intervention.

- If the company is still concerned, and dissatisfied with the company's response to the concerns, the shareholder should consider using his vote against the board of directors on selected matters at the company's next general meeting. Institutional investors are encouraged to practice 'responsible voting'. **Responsible voting** can be defined as taking informed decisions about how to vote at company general meetings, within the framework of a well-considered corporate governance policy.

3.3 General meetings of the company and voting by shareholders

A general meeting of the company is a meeting of the company's owners (shareholders) to discuss and vote on certain items. The company's board also attends general meetings, and the auditors and company advisers might also attend. There are two types of general meeting:

- The annual general meeting (AGM) which is held each year to vote on 'routine' proposals.

- An extraordinary general meeting (EGM) is any general meeting that is not an AGM. An EGM might be called to consider specific issues, such as a proposal to approve a major takeover of another company.

The voting rights of shareholders

In a well-governed company all ordinary shareholders should have equal voting rights. In principle, this means one share, one vote.

The matters that shareholders have the right to vote on are fairly limited. They include votes on:

- the election or re-election of directors
- the re-appointment of the company's auditors for another year
- approving a dividend proposed by the directors
- in the UK, approval of the directors remuneration report
- approval of new share incentive schemes
- approval of proposed major transactions, such as a takeover.

Shareholder activism and voting rights

In principle, shareholders can use their votes against the board of directors when they have concerns about the company and they are not satisfied with the response from the board of directors. Shareholders might therefore:

- vote against the re-election of a director whose conduct or opinions they dislike

- vote against the proposal to approve the directors remuneration report, for example when they have concerns about the remuneration policy of the company or about the remuneration packages of directors..

Votes against the board of directors at a general meeting will attract press comment and adverse opinion from investors. The company's board of directors, after suffering defeat in a vote at a general meeting, or wishing to avoid the risk of defeat, might make concessions and do something to deal with the concerns that the shareholders have expressed.

3.4 Problems with the use of voting rights

Although shareholders can use their voting rights, or threaten to use their voting rights, to put pressure on a board of directors, there are limitations and problems with the use of voting.

- Individual shareholders, even major shareholders, might own only a small proportion of the company's shares. In the UK for example, the stock market considers any shareholder to be 'significant' if it owns more than 3% of the shares in a company. To win a vote at a general meeting requires a majority of the votes (and sometimes even more). Many shareholders need to organise themselves to use their votes in concert to have any chance of obtaining a majority of the votes.

- Some institutional shareholders might fail to use their votes in a responsible way. There are several reasons for this:

  - An institutional investor might own shares, but hand the management of the shares to a different organisation (a fund manager). It might be difficult for the institutional shareholder to give instructions to a fund manager on how to vote at a general meeting of each company in which it holds shares.

  - Institutional shareholders might engage in stock lending. Stock lending involves lending shares to another entity for an agreed period of time, in return for a fee. The benefit of stock lending is that it increases income from shares. A disadvantage of stock lending is that during the time that stock is being lent, the borrower has the voting rights, not the lender. The practice of stock lending makes it more difficult for institutional investors to vote, because they do not always know how many shares they currently hold.

  - Many shareholders, including some institutional shareholders, might arrange for the company chairman to vote on their behalf at the general meeting, as a 'proxy'. A shareholder can instruct a proxy on how to cast its votes on each specific proposal at the meeting. However, many shareholders give the chairman their proxy votes, and allow the chairman to decide how to use the votes. Giving proxy votes to the chairman can therefore make the chairman – and so the board as a whole – a very powerful voting force in a

© International Financial Publishing Limited

general meeting. It is then very difficult to vote successfully against any proposal from the board of directors.

- In some countries, there are restrictions on the ability of foreign shareholders to vote at general meetings of the company. Global investors are often unable to use their shares to vote on proposals at general meetings, for example because of restrictions on proxy voting.

These problems with voting are well recognised, and some measures have been taken to reduce them.

■ Institutional investors might be advised on voting by their association. In the UK for example the Association of British Insurers issues advice to its members to vote against a particular proposal by a company at a general meeting to be held in the near future. These warnings, known as **red tops**, are normally issued when the institutional investors have concerns about specific governance matters, such as the remuneration of the company's executives.

■ Associations such as the ICGN (the International Corporate Governance Network) continue to argue in favour of more voting rights for foreign shareholders, and the removal of laws or rules in a company's constitution that make it difficult for foreign shareholders to exercise their voting rights.

■ In some countries, including the UK, there have been initiatives to remove some of the inefficiencies and difficulties in voting for institutional investors.

The Myners Report

In the UK, the institutional investor organisations established a Shareholder Voting Working Party. In 2004, a report was prepared for the Working Party entitled: 'Review of the Impediments to Voting UK Shares'. It is more commonly known as the Myners Report, after the name of its author.

The Myners Report identified the problems faced by institutional investors in using their voting rights in UK companies, and it made several recommendations, including the following.

■ The institutions that own shares should give proper attention to using their voting rights and the responsible use of their votes. Since it is impractical for many institutional shareholders to attend all general meetings of companies in which they invest, they should use **proxy voting**.

■ Institutions that put their shares into the hands of a fund manager should make sure that the fund manager votes is accountable for the use of the voting rights and uses the votes as instructed.

■ Institutional investors should be careful about lending their shares and voting on contentious issues at a general meeting. 'The Report commented: 'When a resolution is contentious, I start from the position that the lender should automatically recall the [lent shares], unless there are good economic reasons for not doing so.'

■ The voting system at the time was largely paper-based. Myners recommended the use of **electronic voting**. With electronic voting, a shareholder submits his voting instructions to the company by electronic means. This is a form of **proxy**

voting, and the company will include the electronic proxy votes in any poll vote at the general meeting.

■ A feature of voting at general meetings in UK companies is that the chairman can decide whether a vote should be taken by a show of hands of the shareholders present at the meeting, or by a 'poll vote'. With a show of hands, a majority vote means the vote of more than one half of the shareholders present at the meeting, regardless of how may shareholders attend the meeting and how few shares they hold between them. A poll vote is a count of all votes submitted, including proxy votes, on the basis of one share, one vote. Myners argued that in order to encourage proxy voting, **all decisions at general meetings should be made by a poll vote**, not a shown of hands. Companies should also disclose in their website the results of all the poll votes at general meetings.

■ Proxy voting forms allowed a shareholder to indicate how to vote his shares, for or against a proposed resolution. Myners recommended that a third option should be added to proxy voting forms – the option to '**consciously withhold the votes**'. In other words, shareholders should be allowed to abstain from voting, and indicate to the company that this is a conscious decision, not a failure to vote at all. Abstaining from voting is a sensible option where a shareholder disapproves of a proposal but the disapproval is not strong enough for the shareholder to want to vote against the board of directors.

Progress has been made in the UK towards adoption of the Myners proposals. Nearly all large companies now permit electronic voting. Company chairman are much more conscious of the need to take proxy votes into consideration: although most decisions are still taken by a show of hands (for convenience and to save time at the meeting), the chairman usually announces the total numbers of votes submitted as proxy votes, for and against the proposal and as abstentions. The option to make a conscious decision to withhold a vote has been adopted.

© International Financial Publishing Limited

> ## Corporate social responsibility
>
> - Definition of corporate social responsibility (CSR)
> - Principles of CSR
> - CSR and stakeholders in the company
> - The effect of CSR on company strategy
> - CSR reporting
> - CSR and institutional investors

4 Corporate social responsibility

4.1 Definition of corporate social responsibility (CSR)

Corporate social responsibility refers to the responsibilities that a company has towards society. CSR can be described decision-making by a business that is linked to ethical values and respect for individuals, society and the environment, as well as compliance with legal requirements.

CSR is based on the concept that a company is a citizen of the society in which it exists and operates.

- As a corporate citizen of society, it owes the same sort of responsibilities to society at large that other citizens should owe.
- There is a social contract between a company and the society in which it operates. As the owner or user of large amounts of property and other resources, companies as corporate citizens also owe a duty to society to use its property and resources in a responsible way. In return, society allows the company to operate and remain in existence.

Corporate Social Responsibility is related to the idea that as well as their responsibilities to shareholders, boards of companies are also responsible to the general public and other stakeholder groups. There are two key areas of responsibility:

(i) general responsibilities that are a key part of the board's duties which need to be completed in order to succeed in their industry and/or are regulatory/legal requirements that are imposed on them

(ii) duties that are seen by some people feel go beyond these general responsibilities.

4.2 Principles of CSR

Corporate social responsibility has five main aspects. For any company, some of these aspects might be more significant than others.

- A company should operate in an ethical way, and with integrity. A company should have a recognised code of ethical behaviour and should expect everyone in the company to act in accordance with the ethical guidelines in that code.

- A company should treat its employees fairly and with respect. The fair treatment of employees can be assessed by the company's employment policies, such as providing good working conditions and providing education and training to employees.

- A company should demonstrate respect for basic human rights. For example, it should not tolerate child labour.

- A company should be a responsible citizen in its community. Responsibility to the community might be shown in the form of investing in local communities, such as local schools or hospitals. This can be an important aspect of CSR for companies that operate in under-developed countries or regions of the world.

- A company should do what it can to sustain the environment for future generations. This could take the form of:

  - reducing pollution of the air, land or rivers and seas

  - developing a sustainable business, whereby all the resources used by the company are replaced

  - cutting down the use of non-renewable (and polluting) energy resources such as oil and coal and increasing the use of renewable energy sources (water, wind)

  - re-cycling of waste materials.

4.3 CSR and stakeholders in the company

The concept of corporate citizenship and corporate social responsibility is consistent with a stakeholder view of how a company should be governed. A company has responsibilities not only to its shareholders, but also to its employees, all its customers and suppliers, and to society as a whole.

In developing strategies for the future, a company should recognise these responsibilities. The objective of profit maximisation without regard for social and environmental responsibilities should not be acceptable.

 Example

When a company promotes itself as a company with strong ethical views and a considered policy on CSR, it exposes itself to reputation risk. This is the risk that its reputation with the general public and customers will be damaged by an unexpected event or disclosure.

For example, an ethical company might find that one or more of its major suppliers, based in a foreign country, is using forced labour or child labour in the production of goods that the company buys.

© International Financial Publishing Limited

4.4   The effect of CSR on company strategy

The awareness of CSR will vary between different countries. To remain successful in business, companies must respond to changes in the expectations of its customers. In many countries, there has been a significant increase in public awareness of environmental problems, such as global warming (pollution and energy consumption) and the potential for natural disasters that this creates. There is also concern about the irreplaceable loss of many natural resources and the failure to re-cycle many raw materials that could be used again in products or services.

If companies fail to respond to growing public concern about social and environmental issues, they will suffer a damage to their reputation and the possible loss (long term) of sales and profits. This is the problem for companies of **reputation risk**.

Unfortunately, although there is genuine concern by some companies for CSR issues, other companies express concerns about CSR issues in order to improve their public relations image with the public, and as a way of marketing their products.

Formulating a CSR policy

The following steps might be taken by a company to implement a CSR policy:
- It should decide its code of ethical values, and possibly publish these as a Code of Ethics.
- It should establish the company's current position with regard to its CSR values, and decide the position it would like to reach in the future. The gap between the current position and the target position provides a basis for developing CSR strategies.
- The company should develop realistic targets and strategies for its CSR policies.
- These strategies should be implemented.
- Key stakeholders in the company should be identified, whose views the company wishes to influence (employees, pressure groups, customers).
- The company's CSR achievements should be communicated to the key stakeholders. This is the main purpose of **CSR reporting**.
- The company's CSR achievements should be monitored, and actual achievements compared with (1) the targets and (2) the CSR achievements of similar companies (including business competitors).

4.5   CSR reporting

In some countries, stock market companies have published annual reports on their corporate social responsibility. These reports have been voluntary, and have usually been published separately from the annual report and accounts.

CSR reports are also called **social and environmental reports**, and CSR reporting is sometimes called **sustainability reporting**, when its main focus is on environmental issues.

The purpose of CSR reports is to inform key stakeholders about the CSR policy objectives of the company and how successful it has been in achieving them.

- CSR reports in the UK originally developed out of Health, Safety and Environmental Reports, which reported on health and safety at work, accident rates, volumes of waste and pollution, and so on, and actions taken by the company to deal with problems.

- CSR reporting is broader in scope than health, safety and environmental reporting, because it includes social issues and more employee issues, such as ethical employment practices, education and training and investments by the company in community projects.

- A weakness with many CSR reports was their lack of structure, and (in many cases) a lack of facts and figures.

Global Reporting Initiative (GRI)

The Global Reporting Initiative is a US-based initiative that encourages companies world-wide to publish **sustainability reports** that are prepared using a common reporting framework.

The GRI defines sustainability reporting as 'the practice of measuring, disclosing and being accountable to internal and external stakeholders for performance towards the goal of sustainable development. Sustainable development is a broad term [meaning the same as other terms used] to describe economic, environmental and social impacts (such as triple bottom line, corporate responsibility reporting, etc).

The GRI promotes the view that to be a sustainable business in the long-term, companies will benefit by giving attention to environmental and social issues, as well as financial issues. Sustainability reporting within the GRI guidelines is based on measuring three areas of performance, sometimes called the 'triple bottom line'. These are:

- financial performance
- impacts on the environment and natural resources
- social benefits and costs.

Adverse effects and costs should be reported, as well as financial and non-financial benefits.

The GRI approach is also based on quantifiable measurements of performance, in preference to qualitative statements, so that progress towards 'sustainability' can be measured. There are GRI 'technical protocols' explaining the methods for measuring social and environmental (as well as financial) performance. There are also sector supplements, which deal with measurement problems in specific industry sectors, such as mining, car manufacture, financial services and telecommunications.

© International Financial Publishing Limited

Mandatory reporting on CSR issues

In some countries, such as the countries of the European Union, some reporting on CSR issues is required by companies in their annual business review. Business reviews were explained earlier in this chapter. It is not yet clear whether mandatory reporting in business reviews will replace voluntary sustainability reports.

4.6 CSR and institutional investors

Pressure on companies to show greater CSR awareness has come from institutional investors, as well as the general public and consumers. There are some '**ethical investors**', including some investment institutions, that choose to invest only in companies that meet certain minimum standards of social and environmental behaviour.

In the UK, the National Association of Pension Funds (NAPF) published a policy document on CSR in 2005. This stated that it did not consider CSR to be a corporate governance issue, since corporate governance is concerned mainly with how to handle the potential conflicts of interest between shareholders and management. The NAPF suggested that CSR issues are an issue for the management of a company rather than its governance.

However, the NAPF policy document stated that the board and managers should remember the company's wider role in society; the longer-tern prospects of a company can be damaged by maximising short-term gain in a manner that society finds unacceptable and this can lead to shareholders suffering real financial losses. These losses could be due to consumer preferences changing or new legislation adding more costs to the company.

 ## Example UN initiative

In 2005, the UN Global Compact launched the UNEP Finance Initiative. (UNEP is the United Nations Environment Program.) The aim of this initiative is to promote a set of principles that define best practice for responsible investment by institutional investors that have the full support of the UN and also of leading institutional investors worldwide.

The initiative is based on the view that institutional investors should consider sustainable development when making their decisions on investment in companies.

In 2006, the UN published six 'Principles for Responsible Investment', which provide a framework for institutional investors to use when considering CSR issues. These principles, which are 'voluntary and aspirational' are as follows.

1   CSR issues should be considered in investment analysis and decision-making processes by investment institutions.

2   Institutional investors will include CSR issues into its policies and practices on share ownership.

3   Institutional investors will seek appropriate disclosure on CSR issues by the companies in which they invest.

4   Investment institutions that subscribe to the Principles will promote their acceptance and implementation within the investment industry.

5   Investment institutions will work together to increase their effectiveness in implementing the Principles.

6   Investment institutions will each report on their activities and progress towards implementing the Principles.

© International Financial Publishing Limited

CHAPTER

8

Internal control systems

Contents
1   Risk management and corporate governance
2   Internal control
3   Elements of a sound system of internal control

> ## Risk management and corporate governance
>
> - Internal control risk and business risk
> - The importance of internal control and risk management
> - Responsibility for risk management and internal control
> - The governance responsibility of the board of directors for internal control and risk management

1 Risk management and corporate governance

1.1 Internal control risk and business risk

There are two broad types of risk that companies face.

- **Internal control risks** or **operational risk**. These are risks of losses that might arise due to failures or weaknesses in systems or due to errors (or fraud) by individuals. Internal controls are established to eliminate some of these risks, or to reduce the risks, or to identify an error or fault when it occurs. Internal control is defined in more detail later.

  A helpful definition of operational risk is given by the Basel Committee for banking supervision. Although this definition applies to risks in the banking industry, it has a wider application. Operational risk is 'the risk of losses resulting from inadequate or failed internal processes, people and systems, or external events.'

- **Business risk** or **strategic risk**. All business entities face risks in their business environment. Business entities take risks to make a profit, and profit is the reward for risk. When a company decides on its business strategies, management cannot be certain that they have made the right choices. Conditions in the company's markets might turn out differently from what management expect.

  The business environment is continually changing – competition in the market, customer demand, economic conditions, government regulation, the state of technology and many other factors. Business risk has to be managed. Companies have to respond to changes in their environment. Chosen strategies should not be excessively risky in relation to the size of profits that the company expects to make from its investments.

1.2 The importance of internal control and risk management

Internal control and the management of business risk are important matters for all companies.

In the UK, guidance on internal control for directors was published by the Institute of Chartered Accountants in England and Wales. This guidance was known as the **Turnbull Report**. The Turnbull Report set out four connected reasons why internal control and business risk management are important.

© International Financial Publishing Limited

(1) **A company's system of internal control is important for managing risks** to the achievement of the company's business objectives. A strong system of internal control helps to safeguard (a) the investment of the company's shareholders and (b) the company's assets. Protecting the investment of the shareholders and safeguarding the company's assets are duties of the board of directors towards their shareholders.

(2) **Internal control can achieve three things**: (a) control can improve the efficiency and effectiveness of operations (b) control helps to ensure the reliability of the company's financial reporting to shareholders and (c) controls can help the company to ensure compliance with laws and other regulations.

(3) **Effective financial controls are important**. These include controls to ensure that proper accounting records are maintained, that unnecessary financial risks (for example from fraud) are avoided and financial reporting is reliable.

(4) A company's strategic objectives and conditions in its business environment are continually changing. As a result the risks faced by the company are also continually changing. **A strong system of internal control depends on the ability of the company to identify the changing risks in its business environment** and the extent of the risk that it faces. Profits are (in part) the reward for successful risk-taking in business, and internal control helps management to manage and control the business risks (rather than eliminate them).

1.3 Responsibility for risk management and internal control

The responsibility for risk management and internal control is shared between the board of directors and management.

- The board of directors is responsible for safeguarding the company's assets, and for protecting the value of the shareholders' investment in the company. It should fulfil these duties with care, and should be accountable to shareholders for what they have done. **It is therefore a corporate governance responsibility of the board of directors to ensure that adequate systems for internal control and risk management are in place**.

- The board of directors are not responsible for running the operations of the company. Although the directors should monitor internal control and risk management systems, **management has the responsibility for designing and implementing these systems**.

1.4 The governance responsibility of the board of directors for internal control and risk management

The management of risk, and the internal control system for managing risk, are aspects of corporate governance. However, there are differing views about the extent to which risk management and internal control should be a governance issue.

- One view is that the directors have a governance responsibility for the strength of the financial controls in their company. They should therefore be responsible for ensuring that the **system of financial control** is adequate and should account to the shareholders for this responsibility. This view is accepted in the US, and is applied by the Sarbanes-Oxley Act.

- Another view is that the board of directors has a broader governance responsibility for ensuring the soundness of the entire internal control system and also for the business risk management system of the company. This view is applied in countries such as the UK, Singapore and South Africa.

UK Combined Code requirements

The UK Combined Code makes only a brief reference to the internal control system.

- A principle of the Code is that: 'The board should maintain a sound system of internal control to safeguard shareholders' investment and the company's assets.'

- A provision of the Code, linked to this principle, is that: 'The directors should, at least annually, conduct a review of the effectiveness of the [company's] system of internal control and should report to shareholders that they have done so. The review should cover all material controls, including financial, operational and compliance controls and risk management systems.'

UK listed companies are required to comply with all requirements of the Combined Code, or explain their non-compliance. This 'comply or explain' rule is contained in the Listing Rules of the UK financial services regulator. It would be very difficult for a board of directors to explain convincingly why they have not reviewed the system of internal control, which means that the requirement to conduct an annual review of the internal control and risk management systems is an obligation that listed companies cannot avoid.

US requirements: Sarbanes-Oxley Act

In the US, the Sarbanes-Oxley Act limits the governance responsibility to controls over financial reporting. Section 404 of the Act, which has been explained in an earlier chapter, requires the annual report of companies to:

- state the responsibility of management for establishing and maintaining an adequate internal control structure and procedures for financial reporting, and

- contain an assessment of the effectiveness of the company's internal control structure and procedures for financial reporting.

This assessment should be based on an evaluation by management (including the CEO and chief financial officer) of the effectiveness of the internal control over financial reporting.

© International Financial Publishing Limited

> ## Internal control
>
> - Definition of internal control
> - Internal control: financial, operational and compliance controls
> - The nature of internal controls

2 Internal control

2.1 Definition of internal control

The term 'internal control' is frequently used by accountants, but there is no generally-accepted definition. This point was made by the Securities and Exchange Commission (SEC) in the US, in a paper explaining its rules to implement section 404 of the Sarbanes-Oxley Act.

'There has been some confusion over the exact meaning and scope of the term "internal control" because the definition of the term has evolved over time.'

Historically, the term 'internal control' was used by the accountancy profession in auditing. When auditing practice changed from a process of detailed testing of all transactions and account balances towards a process of testing just a sample of transactions and balances, the auditors had to give more consideration to internal controls and their effectiveness.

If an internal control was well designed and appeared to be effective, the detailed checking task could be limited to making sure that the control was properly applied in practice. Assessing the design of internal controls and their implementation allowed the auditors to reduce the amount of detailed checks on transactions and account balances.

In this historical sense, internal control is associated with financial controls.

However, it is also recognised that internal control extends beyond financial controls, and includes operational controls and compliance controls, in addition to financial controls.

2.2 Internal control: financial, operational and compliance controls

The Turnbull Report in the UK defined an internal control system as 'the policies, processes, tasks, behaviours and other aspects of a company' that, taken together:

- Help it to operate effectively and efficiently. These **operational controls** should allow the company to respond in an appropriate way to significant risks to achieving the company's objectives. 'This includes the safeguarding of assets from inappropriate use or from loss and fraud and ensuring that liabilities are identified and managed.'
- Help it to ensure the quality of external and internal financial reporting (**financial controls**).

- Help ensure compliance with applicable laws and regulations, and also with internal policies for the conduct of business (**compliance controls**).

Financial controls

Financial controls have been explained as internal accounting controls that are sufficient to provide reasonable assurance that:

- transactions are made only in accordance with the general or specific authorisation of management

- transactions are recorded so that financial statements can be prepared in accordance with accounting standards and generally-accepted accounting principles

- transactions are recorded so that assets can be accounted for

- access to assets is only allowed in accordance with the general or specific authorisation of management

- the accounting records for assets are compared with actual assets at reasonable intervals of time, and appropriate action is taken whenever there are found to be differences.

Operational controls

Operational controls are controls that help to reduce operational risks, or identify failures in operational systems when these occur. The nature of operational risks varies between companies, because their operations differ widely.

In general terms, operational risks are risks of failures in operations due to factors such as human error, a failure in processes, a failure in systems, and so on.

One example of operational risk is the risk of a failure in health and safety systems and system controls. A well-publicised example was the series of apparent safety failures (and failures in safety controls) that led to an explosion at the Texas oil refinery of oil company BP in 2005, where 15 people were killed and about 500 injured. In addition to the direct losses suffered by BP, the incident also led to over 1,000 civil legal actions against the company and a federal grand jury investigation into whether criminal charges should be brought against the company.

Compliance controls

Compliance controls are concerned with making sure that an entity complies with all the requirements of relevant legislation and regulations.

The potential consequences of failure to comply with laws and regulations vary according to the nature of the industry and the regulations. For a manufacturer of food products, for example, food hygiene regulations are important. For a bank, regulations to protect consumers against mis-selling and other unfair practices are important.

When regulations are specific, compliance controls often involve detailed procedures for checking that every regulation has been properly complied with, and

© International Financial Publishing Limited

that there is documentary evidence that the checks have been made. This is often called a **box-ticking approach** to compliance.

A box-ticking approach to compliance control is more usually associated with a rules-based approach to regulation rather than a principles-based approach.

2.3   The nature of internal controls

If you have already studies auditing, you should be familiar with the nature of internal financial controls. If you are not sure what internal controls are, a brief reminder is given here.

Some years ago, a guideline of the UK Auditing Practices Board identified eight categories of internal (financial) controls, which can be remembered by the mnemonic SPAMSOAP.

	Type of control	Explanation
S	Segregation of duties	Where possible, duties should be divided between two or more people, so that the work done by one person automatically acts as a check on the work done by the other person. This should reduce the risk of accidental mistakes or deliberate fraud.
P	Physical controls	These are measures to protect assets against theft, loss or physical damage.
A	Authorisation and approval controls	These are controls over spending decisions and decisions to enter into transactions. These decisions must be taken or approved by a person with specific authority.
M	Management controls	Controls over systems are applied by management. In accounting, one example of a management control system is the system of budgeting and budgetary control.
S	Supervision	Controls can be applied by supervising the work done by employees.
O	Organisation controls	Everyone in the company should understand what his or her responsibilities are, and there should be lines of reporting from junior to senior staff.
A	Arithmetical and accounting controls	In accounting systems, there are many controls of this type, such as control total checks and bank reconciliation checks.
P	Personnel controls	There should be controls over the selection and training of employees, to ensure that they are suitably qualified and skilled for the work that they do.

This brief list should help you to understand the range of controls that might be applied and that together make up the controls in an internal control system.

Elements of a sound system of internal control

- COSO Framework
- The Turnbull Report: elements of an internal control system
- Control environment
- Risk assessment
- Information and communication
- Monitoring the internal control system
- Establishing and maintaining a system of internal control
- Internal control: transparency and disclosure

3 Elements of a sound system of internal control

3.1 COSO Framework

In 1992 a report was published on internal control by the Committee of Sponsoring Organizations of the Treadway Commission, or COSO. The report, entitled 'Internal Control – Integrated Framework' provided a broad framework that companies could use to assess the effectiveness of their system of internal control.

The COSO Framework identified five integrated elements in a system of internal control:

- The control environment
- Risk assessment
- Control activities (internal controls)
- Information and communication
- Monitoring.

3.2 The Turnbull Report: elements of an internal control system

A similar framework for internal control was identified by the Turnbull Report in the UK (1999, revised 2005). This guidance on internal control states that: 'A company's system of internal control will reflect its **control environment** which encompasses its organisational structure.' The system includes:

- **control activities**
- **information and communication processes**, and
- processes for **monitoring** the continuing effectiveness of the system of internal control.

The Report goes on to state that the internal control system should:

- 'be embedded in the operations of the company and should form part of its culture'

© International Financial Publishing Limited

- should be able to respond quickly to changing risks to the business from factors within the company and its business environment, and

- should include procedures for reporting to management any significant failures or weaknesses in control that have been identified and details of the action that is being taken to correct the problem.

A sound system of internal control should keep risks within a tolerable level, provided that they are applied properly. However, an internal control system cannot protect a company against losses from factors that the system is not designed prevent. The Turnbull Report explains this by stating that a sound system of internal control reduces, but cannot eliminate, the possibility of:

- poor judgement in decision-making

- human error

- control processes being deliberately circumvented by employees and others

- management overriding controls

- unforeseen events and circumstances.

This means that a sound system of internal control provides reasonable assurance that a company will not be delayed in reaching its business objectives by situations which can reasonably be predicted. However, a system of internal control cannot protect against a company not meeting its business objectives or against material losses, errors, fraud or breach of laws/regulations.

3.3   Control environment

The control environment describes the ethical and cultural attitudes towards risk and risk control within the company. The ethical standards and cultural attitudes to risk are set by top management, and the cultural environment has therefore been described as 'the tone at the top'.

A definition of the control environment, provided by the Institute of Internal Auditors, is as follows:
The control environment is 'the attitude and actions of the board and management regarding the significance of control within the organisation. The control environment provides the discipline and structure for the achievement of the ... objectives of the system of internal control.'

The control environment includes:

- the ethical values of the company and the integrity of its management and other employees

- the operating style and general philosophy of management towards control

- the organisation structure within the company

- the assignment of authority and responsibility

- the competence of employees and human resources (HR) practices and policies.

Senior management is responsible for setting the internal control policies. However, the control environment extends to all employees. The Turnbull Report comments that as part of their accountability for achieving objectives, all employees have some responsibility for internal control. Between them they should have the necessary skills, knowledge and authority to set-up, operate and keep an eye on the internal control system. To do this, they need an understanding of the company, the risks it faces and its overall objectives, industries and markets.

3.4 Risk assessment

Risk assessment is the process used by companies to identify and assess the risks that the company faces, and changes in those risks. The risk assessment process involves prioritising the risks, and (if possible) putting a quantitative measurement to them.

Companies may identify broad categories of risk within their operations, and establish a risk committee or risk task force for identifying and assessing risks within each category.

 Example

A manufacturing company might categorise its operational risks as: selling and markets, delivery, production, and purchasing and resources. Most of these risk categories involve more than one function or department within the company. Selling and markets is an aspect of operations that affects not just the marketing department, but also research and development, quality control and customer services, and so on.

The company might set up a risk committee for each category of operations, and each committee would be required to report back to senior management on risk identification and assessment.

Risk and risk assessment are described in more detail in a later chapter.

3.5 Information and communication

Within a system of internal control, there must be a system for reporting to management information about risks, the effectiveness of controls, failures in control and the success of action to remove weaknesses in controls and reduce risks. The information provided needs to be timely, relevant and reliable.

- Management need information about risks and their significance, in order to make decisions.

- Management also need information that allows them to review and assess the effectiveness of controls.

- The board of directors need information to enable them to monitor internal controls and risk management, and assess the effectiveness of the system.

© International Financial Publishing Limited

3.6   Monitoring the internal control system

The internal control system should contain processes for monitoring the application of internal control and risk management practices and policies. Monitoring processes might include:

- internal audit reviews and reports
- formal 'control self-assessments' by management
- confirmation by employees of compliance with policies and codes of conduct
- other management reviews.

Reports on the monitoring of internal control should be provided to management on a regular basis, and management should report to the board of directors.

The monitoring systems might identify the need for improvements or changes in controls, when existing controls are not sufficiently effective.

Example: Failure of an internal control system

A very well-known example of failure in a system of internal control is the collapse of Barings Bank in 1995 as a result of losses incurred in trading by a 'rogue trader', Nick Leeson.

Leeson was transferred to the Singapore office of the bank in 1992 as a general manager. He then took an examination that qualified him to trade on the Singapore exchange SIMEX. He soon became the general manager of the Singapore office, its head trader and (because of his previous experience with the work) the effective head of 'back office' operations, which included the settlement of market transactions by the bank.

Leeson took unauthorised speculative positions in his trading on the SIMEX exchange and also Japan's Osaka exchange, hiding the results of his trading in an unused error account, number 88888. By the end of 1992, losses hidden in this account were £2 million. By the end of 1993 the losses had risen to £23 million and by the end of 1994 they were £208 million. Barings senior management in London were not aware of what was happening. Leeson was able to pay for the losses by borrowing funds from other parts of the bank and from client accounts (by falsifying accounting records and other documentation).

While making heavy losses in account 88888, Leeson also reported some profits on trading in three other accounts, which he reported to Barings management. Some of the profits were made by cross-trading with account 88888, so that the profits were actually achieved by adding to the losses in account 88888. Leeson and the Barings staff in Singapore were paid bonuses on the basis of these reported profits.

In February 1995, Leeson left Singapore and boarded a plane for Kuala Lumpur, leaving behind losses of £827 million in the Singapore office. The bank could not afford to sustain losses of this size, and it collapsed soon after.

The collapse of Barings can be explained by severe weaknesses in the internal control system.

- The control environment was poor and the control culture was not strong enough. Senior management rewarded staff for making trading profits without regard for risk or controls.

- There were many weaknesses in internal controls. The segregation of duties was inadequate: Leeson was general manager, trader and in charge of the settlement of trading transactions. The organisation structure was weak: lines of reporting from Leeson to London were not clear, partly because the London office underwent a re-organisation. Leeson was inadequately supervised and reporting to management was inaccurate (falsified). Systems of authorisation and approval were inadequate: Leeson was able to obtain large amounts of money from other offices of Barings, which he could use to pay for his losses. The accounting controls did not work properly.

- Information about risk and control was not fed back to senior management in London or the board of directors of the bank.

- Monitoring of the internal control system was weak, or non-existent.

3.7 Establishing and maintaining a system of internal control

The board of directors is responsible for establishing and maintaining the systems of internal control and risk management.

Three ways in which they can do this are by means of:
- rigorous internal audit checks
- external audit of the financial statements
- regular evaluation of the internal control system and risk management system.

3.8 Internal control: transparency and disclosure

When a stock market company discovers a weakness in its system of internal control, the board should consider whether it has a duty to notify investors immediately. Regulations about transparency and reporting should require companies to make public any information about weaknesses in internal control or risk management that have had a material impact on the company's financial performance or financial position.

Example

In February 2007 Alfred McAlpine, a UK support services company, discovered accounting irregularities at one of its subsidiary companies following an internal investigation. The board was informed that incorrect reports of production volumes and sales had been provided by the subsidiary's management systematically over a period of about three years, and that the actions by management had been deliberate.

© International Financial Publishing Limited

The board of directors made an immediate announcement to the stock market information services, reporting the discovery of the accounting irregularities and 'the possibility of fraud'. It also reported that:

■ an initial estimate suggested that as a result of the irregularities, net assets of the group had been over-stated by about £11 million in the financial statements for the previous financial year

■ the company would be reducing its profit forecast for the current year

■ the managers at the subsidiary thought to be responsible for the false reporting had been suspended pending further investigation, and

■ independent forensic accountants had been appointed to investigate the accounts of the subsidiary in detail: this investigation would delay the publication of the company's financial statements for 2006.

The company's share price fell by over 20% on the day that this news was reported. However, the prompt reporting by the board of directors was a necessary part of good governance – even though the existence of the accounting regularities, undiscovered for several years, was an indication of weaknesses in internal control.

© International Financial Publishing Limited

CHAPTER

9

Internal control, audit and compliance

Contents

The function and importance of internal audit

- The function of internal audit
- Internal audit activities
- Internal auditors: independence, objectivity and status
- Internal audit and the role of the audit committee
- The audit committee, internal audit and the Combined Code

1 The function and importance of internal audit

1.1 The function of internal audit

Internal audit sections or departments are found in many large companies, in government organisations and other large entities. Their main role is to act as an **independent appraisal function within the** entity.

The function of internal audit can be explained as follows.

- 'Internal auditing is an independent, objective assurance and consulting activity designed to add value and improve an organisation's operations. It helps an organisation accomplish its objectives by bringing a systematic, disciplined approach to evaluate and improve the effectiveness of risk management, control and governance processes' (The Institute of Internal Auditors).

- 'The objective of internal auditing is to assist [management] in the effective discharge of their responsibilities. To this end, internal auditing furnishes them with analysis, appraisals, recommendations … and information concerning the activities reviewed' (The Institute of Internal Auditors).

- Internal audit is 'an independent appraisal activity established within an [entity] as a service to it. It is a control which functions by examining and evaluating the adequacy and effectiveness of other controls' (CIMA *Official Terminology*).

Internal audit may be described as a check or control over other controls. It is therefore a part of the internal control system, with a responsibility for monitoring the internal control system.

1.2 Internal audit activities

There is no legal requirement for an entity to have an internal audit department. There should be checks on the effectiveness of internal control. However, these checks could be made by operational managers or by managers in the accounts department, or possibly by an external firm of accountants/auditors.

When an entity does have an internal audit department, the tasks of the department may include the following.

© International Financial Publishing Limited

- **Reviewing parts of the internal control system**. Traditionally, internal auditors have carried out checks on financial controls. The work done by the internal auditors might reduce the need for the external auditors to carry out similar checks, when the internal auditors and external auditors co-operate closely. Weaknesses in financial controls should be reported to senior management and notified to the external auditors. Because internal auditors carry out checks on financial controls, it is usual for internal auditors to be professional accountants or trainee accountants.

- **Special investigations**. Internal auditors might be asked to carry out special investigations into particular departments or aspects of operations. These investigations may be at the request of the manager of the department.

- **VFM audits**. VFM stands for 'value for money' and VFM audits check whether an entity is obtaining value for money from particular activities or operations. Value for money means 'economy, efficiency and effectiveness'.

  - **Economy**. Economy means not spending more money than is necessary. A VFM audit searches for wasteful spending and recommends actions that should be taken to reduce spending without any loss of efficiency or effectiveness.

  - **Efficiency**. Efficiency (or productivity) means getting the most output from the resources that are used. It means, for example, using employees and equipment so that the output per employee or the output per item of equipment is improved.

  - **Effectiveness**. Effectiveness means success in achieving goals and objectives. An internal audit should check whether the operations subject to audit are successfully achieving their intended purpose.

- **Risk assessments**. Internal auditors may be involved in the identification and assessment of risks, for the purpose of risk management.

- **Compliance audits**. Internal auditors might carry out checks to confirm that there is proper compliance by the entity with particular rules and regulations, such as health and safety regulations, or regulations on pollution.

- **Stress tests**. Internal auditors might be involved in carrying out tests on what might happen to the entity, its business operations and financial position, in the event of a catastrophe or if extremely bad business conditions occur (a 'worst case scenario).

In carrying out these tasks, the internal auditors might be performing one or more of the following functions:

- **Supervision**, to check whether procedures and processes are being performed properly

- **Attestation**, to confirm that controls are functioning effectively

- **Evaluation**, to assess risks and the benefits of risk controls.

Internal auditors should help senior management to ensure that all the major risks facing the organisation, both internal and external, are identified and managed. To do this they need to have a good understanding of how the business functions.

1.3   Internal auditors: independence, objectivity and status

Independence

The internal auditors need to be independent, so that they are able to provide an objective analysis and objective recommendations, free from bias and conflicts of interest.

It is difficult for internal auditors to be independent, because they are full-time employees of the company. They rely on the company for their income, and possibly also for their future career. They must report to management, because they have to take their instructions from a person in the management structure. They are dependent on the goodwill of their manager they report to. Their manager, after all, decides what their remuneration should be.

Internal auditors might therefore have no problem with criticising managers in other departments, but they could have a major problem with criticising their own manager.

Objectivity

Internal auditors, like the external auditors, need to be independent because they are required to carry out checks on internal controls and evaluate how effective these controls are. It is important that their advice and recommendations should be free from the influence of other managers, and should be objective.

Status

The internal audit department should report to a senior person in management – the more senior, the better. This is because the internal auditors are expected to criticise 'line managers' and this is very difficult if the line manager is their superior in status and influence in the company. Internal auditors should therefore report to the highest level of executive manager possible.

In addition, to give even more protection to the internal auditors from pressure by senior management, the head of internal audit should also report directly to either:

■   the board of directors, or

■   the audit committee.

The Basel Committee for the supervision of banking, in a report on internal control systems (1998), commented that the internal audit function, because it provides an independent assessment of the compliance with the already established policies and procedures (and the adequacy of them), it is an important part of assessing the internal control system. The internal auditors provide unbiased information about the company by reporting directly to the board, senior management and the audit committee.

© International Financial Publishing Limited

Example

The problems facing internal auditors whose status is too low, or who report to a manager who does not listen to their recommendations, are illustrated by an example from local government, which has been described by a former head of internal audit for Flintshire County Council. This example, from 2000, raises some interesting questions about the status and effectiveness of internal audit in local government.

The internal auditor had concerns about some transactions by the Council, including an illegal payment to a former manager, suspicious land and property deals, and very large salary and overtime payments to an administrative worker. He was unable to persuade management to take any action, and therefore expressed his concerns through the channel available for 'whistle blowers'.

As a result of the disclosures he made, he was dismissed, and an Employment Tribunal decided that this was constructive dismissal by his employer.

The former auditor's comment was that management will give their support to the work of the internal auditors, but only if it does not affect them and is unable to criticise them. Some of his comments, which are presumably affected by his own experiences, make useful reading. He suggested that senior management are happy to give their support to an independent internal audit function, but only in the following circumstances.

■ When 'quite junior, or rank and file, personnel are on the receiving end of the internal audit findings, usually resulting in disciplinary action and often dismissal (in this way it helps feed the macho management style - internal audit provides the bullets and the macho manager fires the gun).'

■ 'When internal audit is … used as, a tool to rid organisations of perceived problematic individuals. In this regard there is a quaint phrase that I have heard used to define what internal audit does: "They comb the battlefield and bayonet the wounded".'

■ When they can 'use critical reports to "get one over" on boardroom rivals'.

■ When the internal auditor 'is a low profile "tick and check" operator, who does not ask too many challenging questions.'

However, when senior management feel threatened by the work of internal auditors, they might well be very critical of the internal auditors, ignore their recommendations and (possibly) victimise troublesome auditors.

This example has been adapted from a page on the Freedom to Care website (www.freedomtocare.org) and is reproduced by kind permission.

1.4 Internal audit and the role of the audit committee

The independence and objectivity of the internal audit department can be protected if the head of internal audit is required to report to the audit committee as well as to a line manager (the finance director).

This was a recommendation of the Smith Report in the UK (2003) on audit committees. The Report recommended that:

■ The audit committee should approve the appointment of the head of internal audit or the termination of his employment. By removing the authority for appointing and dismissing the head of internal audit from line management (the finance director), the independence of the internal auditors should be strengthened. The head of internal audit would not rely on line management for his job; he might therefore feel more secure in his job when he has to criticize weaknesses in internal controls for which the finance director is responsible.

■ The audit committee should also monitor the work of the internal audit department, which should prepare regular reports for the audit committee (for example a report for each scheduled meeting of the audit committee, which might be three or four times each year).

The Smith Report recommended that the audit committee, in its review of the work of the internal audit function, should:

■ Ensure that the head of internal audit has direct access to the chairman of the board of directors and the audit committee, and is accountable to the audit committee.

■ Review and assess the work plan for the internal audit department, to check that the work plan is appropriate.

■ Receive reports on the work performed by the internal audit department 'on a periodic basis'.

■ Review the response of management to recommendations that have been made to them by the internal audit department. Have management acted on the recommendations, to deal with weaknesses in internal controls, or have management ignored the recommendations and done nothing?

■ Meet at least once each year with the head of internal audit, without the presence of management (for example, without the CEO or finance director being present). This should make it easier for the audit committee to obtain independent and objective opinions from the internal audit department.

■ Monitor and assess the effectiveness of the internal audit department, within the overall system of internal control and risk management. The audit committee should assess whether the internal audit department is effective.

 Example

A well-reported story of internal audit is the discovery of fraud in US telecommunications company WorldCom in 2001/2002 by Cynthia Cooper, the company's vice president of internal audit. The example shows how, in extreme circumstances, the independence of the internal auditor can be strengthened by the audit committee.

Ms Cooper was responsible for operational audits (auditing operational controls), but she secretly began to carry out investigations into irregularities in financial accounting when an unusual transaction was brought to her attention. The company's CFO (chief financial officer) had taken responsibility for a reserve

© International Financial Publishing Limited

account of $400 million in the balance sheet, without explaining what he was doing or giving a satisfactory reason for the unusual accounting treatment of the reserve.

Ms Cooper reported her concerns to external auditors, Arthur Andersen, who ignored her. She therefore went to the audit committee, who investigated the problem and ordered the CFO to reverse the action that he had taken. The CFO warned Ms Cooper to stay out of his affairs in the future and to stop her investigations.

She did not follow his instructions, and continued to investigate the financial transactions of the company in secret. She found a $2 billion entry in the accounting records for capital expenditure, when there was no supporting evidence that any non-current assets had been purchased. Further investigations subsequently found that the company was regularly reporting operating expenses as capital expenditure, in order to boost current profits. Most of the fraud was linked to accounting for takeovers.

- The company had written down assets acquired in a takeover, but had included in the write-down estimates of future operating costs. In this way, the company was able to record the future costs as costs arising on acquisition, instead of having to record them as costs in future years.

- When WorldCom acquired another company MCI, it reduced the value of MCI's assets and increased the goodwill on acquisition by a corresponding amount. This allowed the company to amortise the goodwill at a much slower rate than it would have had to charge depreciation on the tangible assets.

- The company also under-provided for bad debts.

The discovery by Ms Cooper led to the discovery of much wider accounting fraud. She reported her concerns to the audit committee, and the company's CFO was dismissed. (Its chairman was later jailed.) In July 2002 WorldCom filed for bankruptcy, having admitted the need to make a downward adjustment of $9 billion to profits between 1999 and the first quarter of 2002.

1.5 The audit committee, internal audit and the Combined Code

The UK Combined Code includes some specific provisions about internal audit and the governance role of the audit committee. It states that:

- The audit committee should monitor and review the effectiveness of internal audit activities in the company.

- If there is no internal audit function (department), the audit committee should consider **each year** whether the company ought to have an internal audit function. It should then make a recommendation to the board of directors.

- If there is no internal audit function, the reason for not having one should be explained in the relevant section of the company's annual report to shareholders.

The audit committee and the external auditors

- The audit committee and financial reporting
- Disagreements between the audit committee and management
- The audit committee and the external auditors
- The audit committee and the external audit process

2 The audit committee and the external auditors

2.1 The audit committee and financial reporting

As a committee of the board of directors, the audit committee's main responsibilities are to:

- ensure the integrity of financial reporting by the company, and
- ensure the integrity of external auditing. It should do this by making sure that the external auditors are independent and objective, and that they perform their auditing function properly.

The Smith Report suggested how this should be done.

- It is the responsibility of management to prepare complete and accurate financial statements. This is not a responsibility of the audit committee.

- However, the audit committee should monitor the preparation of the financial statements. It should consider the significant accounting policies used by the company (and any changes in policy that have been made) and also any significant estimates and judgements that have a material effect on the figures in the financial statements.

- When transactions can be accounted for in two or more different ways, management should explain to the audit committee which method of accounting they have selected.

- The audit committee should compare the information received from management with the views of the external auditor, and decide whether the accounting policies, estimates and judgements used in the financial statements are appropriate.

2.2 Disagreements between the audit committee and management

A problem will arise whenever the audit committee is not satisfied with any accounting policy, estimate or judgement. When it cannot reach a satisfactory agreement with the management (and external auditors) the audit committee should report the disagreement to the board.

The Smith Report suggested that the audit committee should be strong-minded if necessary. The audit committee has a role to ensure that if things go wrong, they are put right. Audit committees must be capable of tackling the worst situations, for

© International Financial Publishing Limited

example if an audit failure seems to lead to poor, or even deliberately misleading, financial reporting decisions.

The Report goes on to state that an adversarial relationship between the audit committee and the company's management 'is of course not typical'. When it happens, there has been a failure in corporate governance. When corporate governance is good, the relationship between the audit committee and the company's management should be based on openness and mutual respect.

Example

The management of a company propose to capitalise a large amount of development costs, instead of writing them off as current expenditure, and the external auditors have agreed with this accounting treatment of the costs. However, the three-man audit committee disagree with this judgement, even though the technical issue is fairly complex and the audit committee is opposing financial 'experts' (the finance director and external auditors).

The audit committee meets only three times each year, for two hours. The members have discussed the problem at one of these meetings, and in telephone calls to each other.

There are nine members of the board of directors, five independent non-executives and four executives. The four executive directors agree with the opinion of the finance director. The other two non-executives, including the chairman, are inclined to agree with the independent external auditors. The members of the audit committee are therefore in a minority of 3 – 6 on the board of directors. What should the audit committee members do?

Answer

There is no obvious answer to this problem.

■ The audit committee could accept the opinion of the finance director and external auditors. If they did not agree, but accepted defeat to avoid a crisis, they have possibly failed in their responsibility to the company's shareholders, by allowing the financial statements to be misleading.

■ The nuclear option would be to resign. Alternatively, the committee members could accept the majority decision of the board but insist on explaining their different point of view in the audit committee's report to the shareholders (in the annual report and accounts). If the committee members did either of these things, investor confidence in the company might be damaged and the share price might fall. Instead of protecting the interests of the shareholders, the audit committee might therefore harm them.

In commenting on a similar problem, the Smith Report concluded that lots depends on the audit committee members' personal qualities. They need to be strong, well-informed and independent of mind. However, we should be reasonable in our expectations. The job is very hard and some committees will find it difficult to meet the highest standards.

2.3 The audit committee and the external auditors

The audit committee should be responsible for monitoring the company's relations with its external auditors, including their appointment and remuneration. The operational relationship between a company and its external auditors is the responsibility of management, but the audit committee needs to ensure that:

■ the auditors remain independent, so that they can provide independent views to the company, and also

■ the auditors do their job properly.

Appointment of external auditors

The Smith Report stated that the audit committee should have the main responsibility for making a recommendation to appoint, re-appoint or remove the external auditors.

■ The recommendation should be made to the board of directors.

■ If the board does not agree with the recommendation of the audit committee, the committee should make a statement in the directors' report to shareholders, explaining its recommendations and why the board as a whole has disagreed.

■ In many countries, the board makes a recommendation about the appointment or re-appointment of the auditors to the shareholders. The final decision is taken by the shareholders, although they almost always agree with the recommendation of the board.

The Smith Report also recommended that each year the audit committee should assess the qualifications, expertise resources and independence of the external auditors, to satisfy itself that these remain adequate.

Terms of appointment and remuneration

When the external auditors are appointed or re-appointed each year, the company's management and the auditors discuss the terms of engagement for the auditors for the next annual audit cycle.

The Smith Report recommended that the audit committee should review and agree these terms of engagement at the start of each audit. The scope of the audit should be discussed by the committee with the auditor, and if the committee is not satisfied that the audit work is adequate, it should ask for additional work to be undertaken.

The audit fee is negotiated between management and the auditors. The audit committee should satisfy itself that this fee is appropriate, and that an effective audit can be performed for such a fee.

© International Financial Publishing Limited

Independence of the external auditors

The audit committee is responsible for monitoring the independence of the external auditors, and ensuring that the external auditors are independent of the company and its management.

An assessment of the auditors' independence should take into consideration the **non-audit work** performed for the company by the audit firm, as well as the audit work. The annual assessment by the audit committee should take into consideration any ethical standards or guidelines issued by the professional accounting body/bodies.

The independence of the external auditors should be assessed in several ways.

■ When auditors are appointed for the first time, the audit committee should ask for a statement from the audit firm that the auditors and their staff have no family, financial, employment, investment or business relationship with the company, other than in the normal course of business.

■ Each year the audit committee should obtain information from the audit firm about the policies and processes that it uses for ensuring the continued independence of the auditors. This should include information about any requirements or regulations relating to the rotation of audit partners and staff. (For example, if it is accepted practice that a senior audit partner should not be responsible for the audit of a client company for more than five years, the audit firm should state that it is complying with this requirement; it might also indicate how it intends to provide for the 'succession' of a new audit partner for the company at the appropriate time in the future.)

■ The audit committee should agree with the board the company's policy on the appointment to its full-time staff of individuals who were previously a part of the audit team and are now moving directly from the audit firm to the company. Recruiting former auditors could affect the relationship of the company with the audit firm, and damage the independence of the auditors. This policy on recruitment should take account of ethical guidelines to auditors from the accountancy bodies.

■ The audit committee should check periodically that the policy on the recruitment of former auditors is complied with by the company.

■ The audit committee should check that the audit firm complies with ethical guidelines issued by the accountancy bodies and regulatory issues, such as:

   - the rotation of audit partners

   - the amount of fee income that the audit firm receives from the company, in relation to the overall fee income of (1) the audit firm or (2) a regional office of the audit firm, or (3) an individual audit partner.

The risk that the external auditors might lose their independence from a company is sometimes called the hazards of **auditor capture**.

Example

Audit firm Arthur Andersen, one of the five largest audit firms in the world, collapsed in 2002 due to a big loss of audit clients. The loss of clients happened as a consequence of the collapse of energy company Enron, an audit client of Arthur Andersen.

A reason given to explain the failure of the audit firm to identify financial irregularities in Enron was the lack of independence of the audit firm, and in particular its office in Houston, Texas (where Enron had its headquarters).

The Houston office had grown too dependent on Enron as a source of fee income, and had lost its willingness to ask searching questions to Enron's management.

Example

The annual audit of GFH plc, a UK public limited company, has been conducted by the same firm of auditors for ten years. The company has recently appointed a member of the audit team to be its new head of internal control. During the year, the chief accountant of GFH plc married a senior partner in the audit firm.

In its annual assessment of the independence of the audit firm, how should the audit committee respond to these developments?

Answer

The audit committee should have agreed a policy with the board of directors about the appointment of audit team members to management positions in the company. The policy may set limits on the number of former auditors who should be employed, and the status in the management hierarchy to which they should be appointed. The audit committee should check the company's policy to find out whether the appointment of the new head of internal audit breaches the policy rules.

The chief accountant holds a senior position within the accounting department at GFH and the marriage of the chief accountant to a senior partner in the audit firm could have a serious effect on the independence of the audit firm. The audit team might be unwilling (or less inclined) to question statements made to them during the audit by the chief accountant.

The audit committee should consider whether this development means that it would be appropriate for the company to consider a change of audit firm.

Auditor independence and non-audit work

The independence of the external auditors might be affected by non-audit work that the firm performs for the company. There are two main reasons why independence might be affected.

- The total fee income for the audit firm from the company, from audit work and non-audit work, might be a large proportion of the firm's total annual income. When this situation occurs, the audit firm might be reluctant to annoy the

© International Financial Publishing Limited

company's management, because it does not want to lose any work – and income – from the company.

- The audit team might be required to audit the (non-audit) work done by other employees of the firm. The audit team might be reluctant to question or criticise their colleagues, because this might damage the reputation of the audit firm in the opinion of the company's management.

The Smith Report recommended that the audit committee should be responsible for developing and recommending to the board the company's policy on giving non-audit work to its external audit firm. The chosen policy should ensure that by giving non-audit work to the auditor, the auditor's independence will not be affected.

A part of this policy should specify three categories of non-audit work, and allocate each type of non-audit work to one of these categories:

- Non-audit work that should not be given to the audit firm. The general principle should be that the audit firm should not be given any non-audit work where:
    - employees of the audit firm have to make management decisions for the company, or
    - employees of the audit firm have to act as advocates for the company, or
    - the audit team will have to audit the work done by other employees of the audit firm (for example, book-keeping services).
- Non-audit work that can be given to the audit firm without the need to refer the matter to the audit committee.
- Non-audit work where a case-by-case decision is necessary, and the matter should be referred to the audit committee for a decision.

The UK Combined Code states that it is a **responsibility of the board** to ensure auditor independence and 'the annual report should explain to shareholders how, if the auditor provides non-audit services, auditor objectivity and independence is safeguarded.'

2.4   The audit committee and the external audit process

The audit committee should review the audit plans and audit work of the external auditor, to make sure that these are satisfactory.

Audit plan

At the start of the annual audit cycle, the audit committee should ensure that an appropriate audit plan has been prepared. It should also check whether the resources that the audit firm proposes to use for the audit are sufficient, and that the audit team will have the required seniority, experience and expertise.

Review of the findings of the auditors

At the end of the audit, the audit committee should carry out a review. As a part of this review, the audit committee should:

- discuss with the auditors any major issues that arose during the audit. These may be issues that have been resolved with management, or issues that still remain unresolved

- review the key accounting judgements and audit judgements that have been made

- review the level of errors identified by the auditors, and should obtain from management an explanation of why any of these errors remain unadjusted

- review the response of management to the recommendations made by the auditors (in the auditors' management letter).

Assess the effectiveness of the audit

Each year, the audit committee should assess the effectiveness of the audit, and assess whether the auditors did their work to a satisfactory standard. The committee should:

- review whether the auditor met the requirements of the agreed audit plan (and if there were any changes in the plan, the reasons for the changes)

- consider how 'robust' the auditors were in discussing accounting and audit issues with management, and how perceptive the auditors appear to have been in making their judgements

- obtain feedback about the conduct of the audit from key people inside the company, such as the finance director and the head of internal audit

- review the contents of the auditors' management letter (to management), in order to:

  - assess whether the recommendations in the letter are based on a good understanding of the company and its business, and

  - establish whether management has acted upon the recommendations of the auditors, and if not the reasons why management has taken no action.

© International Financial Publishing Limited

Evaluating the effectiveness of internal control
■ Requirement for annual review of internal control
■ Responsibilities for the review of internal control effectiveness
■ The review process

3 Evaluating the effectiveness of internal control

3.1 Requirement for annual review of internal control

The board of directors is responsible for the effectiveness of the system of internal control and risk management, and there should be regular reviews of internal control and risk management.

- The UK Combined Code states that the board of directors, at least once each year, should conduct a review of the effectiveness of the company's system of internal controls.

- The Singapore Code of Corporate Governance states that the audit committee should ensure that a review of the effectiveness of the company's internal controls should be conducted at least annually. It adds that the review can be conducted by either internal accountants or public accountants.

- The requirements of the Sarbanes-Oxley Act in the US, which are stricter, have been described earlier.

When the requirement for a review of the effectiveness of internal control was introduced by the UK Combined Code in 1998, there was uncertainty about what this meant in practice. How should a review of the effectiveness of internal control be conducted?

3.2 Responsibilities for the review of internal control effectiveness

The responsibility for the annual review of the effectiveness of the internal control system should be clearly identified.

- In Singapore, the audit committee has the responsibility, although the audit committee reports to the board of directors.

- In the US, management have the responsibility. Management includes the chief executive officer and chief finance officer.

- In the UK, the Turnbull Report (or Turnbull Guidelines, as they are also called) states that:

    - The board of directors has the responsibility for reviewing the effectiveness of internal control.

    - Management is responsible for monitoring the system of internal control and reporting to the board on this work.

    - The board should decide whether its own review process should be carried out by the board as a whole, or by a committee of the board (the audit committee, or a risk committee). If the review process is delegated to a committee, the committee must report to the board on its review.

3.3 The review process

The Turnbull Report (Turnbull Guidance) provides useful guidance to directors about the process for reviewing effectiveness. The nature of the board's review will depend on the nature of the company, such as its size and the nature and complexity of its operations.

- There should be a monitoring process within the system of internal control. For example, the company might have an internal audit department which regularly monitors internal controls and risk management processes. However, the board cannot rely entirely on 'embedded monitoring processes'.
- The board should receive and review regular reports from management on internal control.
- In addition, for the purpose of reporting to the shareholders on internal control in the annual report, the board should assess each year whether it has considered all significant aspects of internal control.

The board should specify the process that it will use to conduct its review of the effectiveness of internal control. This process should cover:

- the frequency and content of the reports it should receive from management on internal control, and
- the method it will use to make its annual assessment of the effectiveness of internal control.

The board must be able to justify any statements on internal control and risk management that it makes to the shareholders. The review process should therefore ensure that the board is provided with documentary evidence to support the statements on internal control that it makes.

Management reports to the board on internal control

Reports from management to the board on internal control should 'provide a balanced assessment of the significant risks and the effectiveness of the system of internal control in managing those risks' (Turnbull Guidance). The reports should:

- discuss any significant weaknesses or failings in internal control that management have identified
- the effect that these have had, and
- the actions taken by management to deal with the problem.

There must be open and honest communication between management and the board on these matters, so that the board is given reliable information. A culture of 'blame' for weaknesses in controls should be avoided. If managers are criticised for weaknesses they report, they will probably choose not to report weaknesses and leave the board members in ignorance about what is actually happening.

© International Financial Publishing Limited

The board should use the management reports on internal control to make an assessment of the effectiveness of the internal control system and risk management system. It should:

- consider the significant risks that are reported to them, and assess how they have been identified, evaluated and managed

- assess the effectiveness of the related internal controls for managing the significant risks, particularly when significant weaknesses in internal control are reported

- consider whether management have taken the appropriate measures to deal with the weaknesses in internal control that they have reported

- consider whether there is a need for more extensive monitoring of the system of internal control (for example, consider whether the internal audit department should be increased in size).

Annual assessment of the effectiveness of internal control

In addition to conducting reviews on the basis of management reports, the board should make an assessment each year, for the purpose of making its annual report to shareholders on internal control.

This annual assessment should be based on the management reports it has reviewed during the year together with any other relevant information it considers necessary for the assessment. The Turnbull Guidance suggests that the annual assessment should consider:

- changes since the board's previous annual assessment in the nature and size of the significant risks faced by the company

- the company's ability to respond to changes in its business and in its external environment

- the scope and quality of the system of monitoring risks by management and of the internal control system: this should include where appropriate an assessment of the scope and quality of the work of the internal auditors

- the scope and frequency of reports by management to the board on internal control and risk management, and the extent to which the board is able to use its reviews of these reports to cumulatively assess the state of control and effectiveness of risk management in the company.

- the significant weaknesses in control that have been identified and the failings in control that have occurred at any time during the year, and their impact on the financial performance and financial position of the company.

Whenever the board becomes aware of a significant weakness or failing in internal control, it should:

- find out the reason why the weakness or failure occurred, and

- re-assess the effectiveness of the processes used by management for designing, operating and monitoring the system of internal control.

The annual assessment by the board should consider all aspects of the internal control and risk management system. This should include an assessment of the control environment, risk identification and assessment, internal controls, information and communication and monitoring systems. The table below indicates the issues that the board might consider.

Control environment

1   Is there an appropriate control environment? Do codes of conduct, human resource policies and performance reward systems support the company's risk management system and internal control system?

2   Is there a clear definition of management responsibilities and accountability for control and risk management?

3   Does the company communicate to its employees their responsibilities for risk management and control?

4   Do the managers and other employees (and providers of outsourced services) have the knowledge, skills and resources to support the achievement of the company's objectives and to manage risks effectively?

Risk assessment

1   Does the company have clear objectives about risk? Have these objectives been communicated clearly to employees?

2   Are significant operational, financial, compliance and other risks (both internal and external to the company) identified and assessed? Are there established processes for risk assessment and evaluation?

3   Do management understand clearly what level of risks is acceptable to the board?

Control activities

1   How are processes and controls adjusted when new risks occur or when risks change in significance?

2   How are processes and controls adjusted when weaknesses or failings in processes and controls are discovered?

Information and communication

1.   Does management receive timely, relevant and reliable reports on performance in relation to business objectives and the related risks? These reports might include performance reports and qualitative information on issues such as customer satisfaction and employee attitudes.

2   Does the board receive timely, relevant and reliable reports on the same issues from management?

3   Are information needs and related information systems re-assessed as objectives and related risks change, or as deficiencies in reporting are identified?

4   Are there established channels of communication for employees (as whistle blowers) to report suspected breaches in the law or regulations, or other improper activities?

Monitoring

1   Are there processes, embedded in the company's operating systems, for monitoring the effective application of processes, policies and activities relating to internal control and risk management?

2   Do these processes monitor the company's ability to re-assess risks and adjust controls in response to changes in the company's objectives, its business and its external environment?

3   Are there effective processes and procedures for making changes to controls when weaknesses or failings in the control system are identified?

© International Financial Publishing Limited

4   Is there appropriate communication by management to the board (or board committees) on the effectiveness of the processes for monitoring risks and internal control?

5   Is there a recognised procedure for reporting exceptional events to the board, such as suspected fraud, and other illegal acts or matters that could seriously affect the company's reputation and financial position?

Reporting to shareholders on internal control
■ The requirement to report to the shareholders on internal control
■ The content of a board report on internal control
■ Summary: maintaining a sound system of internal control
■ Internal control: information systems and technology

4 Reporting to shareholders on internal control

4.1 The requirement to report to the shareholders on internal control

A system of good corporate governance should include a requirement for the board of directors to report to shareholders on internal control and the effectiveness of the internal control system. The board is responsible for ensuring that a sound system of internal control is maintained, and it should be required to account to the shareholders to explain how they have fulfilled this responsibility.

However, the specific requirements for reporting to shareholders vary between different countries.

■ In the US, the annual report of stock market companies must include a statement on internal control that includes an assessment of the effectiveness of the internal control system and procedures for financial reporting. The internal control report relates to financial controls only (not operational controls or non-financial compliance controls), but it must provide an evaluation of those controls. Any material weaknesses in financial controls must be disclosed.

■ In Singapore, the board is required to ensure that an annual review is conducted into the effectiveness of the internal control and risk management system, but the board is required to report to the shareholders on the **adequacy** of the control system (not its effectiveness or weaknesses).

■ In the UK, listed companies are required to conduct a review of the effectiveness of the system of internal controls and report to the shareholders that they have conducted such a review. The board is not required to provide detailed information about the review, and so is not required to provide shareholders with an assessment of its effectiveness.

There are several reasons why the reporting requirements in the UK and Singapore differ from the regulations in the US.

■ The main argument is cost. To comply with the requirements of section 404 of the Sarbanes-Oxley Act requires a large amount of management time, and the costs of compliance are high. It has been suggested that the requirements of section 404 help to explain the preference of many foreign companies for seeking a listing for their shares in London (where the principles-based requirements are much less strict) rather than listing in New York.

■ Supporters of the principles-based approach in the UK (and critics of the rules-based approach in the US) argue that the board of directors should have

© International Financial Publishing Limited

freedom to decide what it is appropriate to report to shareholders. The US approach is based on compliance with detailed procedures and a 'box-ticking' mentality.

- The Sarbanes-Oxley report on internal control relates to financial controls and financial reporting only, not to operational controls and compliance controls. It has been argued that it is difficult to assess the 'effectiveness' of operational controls, because there is no objective standard for what these controls should achieve.

- Critics of the US regulations argue that there is an expectations gap, which is the difference between the real situation and what investors expect. If the board of directors made a statement that it was satisfied with the effectiveness of internal controls, investors might expect that nothing can go wrong and there are no risks that have not been controlled. This expectation would be incorrect.

- It is also argued that if the board has to make a report to shareholders on the effectiveness of internal controls, the directors would want to avoid any personal liability for incorrect statements. As a consequence, board statements would be written in 'legal language' with the assistance of the company's lawyers, and would not contain any information of value to shareholders.

4.2 The content of a board report on internal control

The report by the board of directors to shareholders on internal control should be included in the company's annual report.

In the UK, guidance on the content of this statement is provided by the Turnbull Report.

- The report to shareholders should provide 'meaningful, high-level' information that the board considers necessary, so that shareholders are able to understand the main features of the company's risk management processes and system of internal control. The information provided should not give a misleading impression.

- In its report, the board should disclose that:
    - there is an ongoing process for identifying, evaluating and managing significant risks faced by the company
    - the system has been in place for the entire year under review and up to the date that the annual report and accounts were approved by the board
    - the system is regularly reviewed by the board, and
    - the system is consistent with the guidance given in the Turnbull Report.

- The report should include a statement by the board that it is responsible or the company's system of control and for reviewing its effectiveness.

- The report should also state that the system of internal control is designed to manage risk rather than to eliminate the risk of failure to achieve business objectives. The internal control system can therefore only 'provide reasonable and not absolute assurance against material misstatement or loss.'

The information provided to shareholders does not need to go into details about controls and control processes. 'High-level' information is sufficient.

The Turnbull Report also states that in the report to shareholders, the board should:

- Summarise the process it has used, or board committees have used, to review the effectiveness of the system of internal control. (The board of directors is not required to provide detailed information about the processes it has used, only a summary.)

- Confirm that action has been taken to remedy any significant weaknesses or failings that were found in the system as a result of the review.

- Disclose the process it has used for dealing with the internal control aspects of any significant problems revealed in the annual report and accounts.

If the board has failed to conduct a review of the effectiveness of internal control and risk management, a UK listed company must disclose this fact in its annual report. (This regulation exists because of the 'comply or explain' requirement in the UK Listing Rules.)

Example: Risk management and internal control report to shareholders

It would be a useful exercise for you to read one or two internal control reports in company accounts. You can find these by visiting company web sites on the internet and looking for the most recent annual report and accounts.

A good example of a report, and the level of detail provided, is shown below. It comes from the 2006 report and accounts of Tesco plc (reproduced with kind permission). The level of detail in this report is fairly typical of similar reports by other large listed companies.

'Risk management and internal control

Accountabilities. Accepting that risk is an inherent part of doing business, our risk management system is designed to both encourage entrepreneurial spirit whilst also providing assurance that risk is understood and managed. In terms of broad accountabilities, the Board has overall responsibility for risk management and internal control within the context of achieving the Group's objectives. Executive management is responsible for defining and maintaining the necessary control systems. The role of Internal Audit is to monitor the overall system and report on its effectiveness.

Background. The Group has a five-year rolling business plan to support the delivery of the Company's strategy of long-term growth in returns for shareholders.

Every business units and support function derives its objectives from the five-year plan and these are cascaded to managers and staff by way of personal objectives. Key to delivering effective risk management is ensuring that our people have a good understanding of the Group's strategy and our policies, procedures, values and expected performance. We have a structured internal communications programme that provides employees with a clear definition of the Group's purpose, goals and accountabilities, and the scope of permitted activities for each unit, line managers and individuals. This ensures that all our people understand what is expected of them and that decision-making takes place at the appropriate level....

© International Financial Publishing Limited

Risk management. The Board maintains a Key Risk Register which we review formally twice a year. The register is populated with risks identified through discussions principally between the Head of Internal Audit and the Board of Directors although the views of senior management are also invited. Collectively, the Board conducts an assessment of risk severity, considering impact and likelihood and the adequacy of mitigating measures taken by the business....

Our key risks are set out [in the operating review]....

Internal controls. Accountability for managing risk at an operational level sits with management. We have a Group-wide process for establishing clearly the risks and responsibilities assigned to each level of management and the expected controls required to be operated and monitored....

Monitoring. The Board oversees the monitoring system and has set specific responsibilities for itself and Board or Executive Committees.... The Audit, Finance, Compliance and Corporate Responsibility Committees' reports are distributed to the Board and a formal discussion on each is held at least once a year. These all provide assurance that the Group is operating legally, ethically and in accordance with approved financial and operational policies. We continue to review how the Turnbull Guidance has been applied. In addition, internal and external audit play key roles in the monitoring process.

- **Audit Committee**. Annually, the Audit Committee reports to the Board on its review of the effectiveness of the internal control systems for the accounting year.... Throughout the year, the Committee also receives regular reports from the internal and external auditors and has dialogue with senior managers on their control responsibilities.

  It should be understood that such systems are designed to provide reasonable, but not absolute, assurance against material misstatement or loss.

- **Internal Audit**. The Internal Audit department is fully independent of business operations and has a Group-wide mandate. It operates a risk-based methodology ensuring that the Group's key risks receive appropriate regular examination. Its responsibilities also include maintaining the Key Risk Register and facilitating risk management and internal control with the Board, Audit Committee and senior management throughout the Group. Internal Audit facilitates oversight of risk and control systems of Group companies though a number of risk committees established on either a geographic or business basis. The Head of Internal Audit also attends all Audit Committee meetings....'

4.3   Summary: maintaining a sound system of internal control

The responsibility of the board of directors for maintaining a sound system of internal control, as suggested by the Turnbull Guidance, can be summarised as follows.

Internal control activities	
Responsibilities: the board, management and other employees	**The Board** sets policies on internal control. It should obtain regular assurance from management that the system is effective. **Management** should implement board policies on risk and control. Management should identify and evaluate risks, and report these to the board for consideration by the board. Management should design, operate and monitor the system of internal control, and report regularly to the board. **Employees** should consider internal control as part of their responsibility for achieving business objectives.
Key elements ■ Control environment ■ Risk assessment ■ Internal controls ■ Information and communication ■ Monitoring (A sound system of internal control reduces risk, but cannot eliminate it - unavoidable risks occur from poor judgement, human error, management override and unforeseeable circumstances.)	**Internal control** consists of the policies, processes, tasks and behaviour that, taken together: ■ enable the company to respond to the risks business, operational, financial and compliance risks (and other risks) to the achievement of its business objectives. These include business, operational, financial and compliance risks. ■ **safeguard assets** from misuse, loss and fraud ■ help to ensure the **quality of internal and external reporting** ■ help to **ensure compliance** with laws and regulations and with the company's internal policies for the conduct of business.
Reviewing effectiveness • Regular reports from management to the board. • Also an annual assessment should be made each year by the board.	Monitoring risks and controls on a **continuous basis** is essential for a sound system of internal control. The board should **receive and review reports on internal control regularly**. In addition, there should be an annual assessment. The board should define the process to be used. Management is accountable to the board for monitoring the control system.

© International Financial Publishing Limited

The Board statement to shareholders (in the annual report)	The board should state that there is an ongoing process for identifying, evaluating and managing significant risks, that this process is reviewed regularly by the board and accords with the Turnbull Guidance.

4.4   Internal control: information systems and technology

Providing information to management and the board of directors is an essential part of a system for monitoring internal control and risk management. The Turnbull Guidance states that management and the board should receive 'timely, relevant and reliable reports on progress against business objectives and the related risks'.

The Guidance does not specify in any detail how frequently reports should be obtained and what they should contain. The frequency and content of reports will differ according to the size, nature and complexity of the business.

- **Timeliness**. A company should have a policy about the timeliness of reports on risk and control. As a general rule, when significant weaknesses or failings on control are discovered, these should be reported to senior management and (by senior management) to the board as quickly as possible. Other reports on risk might be less urgent: for example, reports to management on risk might be provided after each meeting of a risk committee, which might meet every month. Reports to the board might be submitted by management every three months, or possibly more frequently (at every meeting of the board).

- **Reliability**. The information provided about risks should be reliable. The processes for identifying and monitoring risks should therefore be effective, so that management and the board of directors receive accurate assessments of risks and controls.

Reports on internal control and risk management should be **formal reports** to the managers responsible and the members of the board of directors. Unlike many management information systems, where information is made available on demand and online to management, internal control and risk management reports should be provided in a printed form as part of a regular and continuing process.

This is to make sure that relevant information about risks and internal control are brought to the attention of management, and the manager (or board director) responsible cannot claim that he (or she) does not know.

Whistle blowing

An effective system of internal control and risk management should provide a channel of communication for 'whistle blowers' to report their concerns about breaches of the law or other regulations. For example, a company might give employees to report their concerns to a board committee (such as the audit committee) or to the senior independent director.

The purpose of providing a channel of communication for whistle blowers is to allow information about failings in internal control to be reported when it might otherwise be suppressed by managers responsible for the failing (for example, a fraud).

A problem with providing a communication channel for whistle blowers to the board of directors is that some of the information provided might be unreliable. An employee might make false accusations against a manager.

The committee or individual responsible for dealing with information from whistle blowers should investigate the allegations with tact and care. It might be possible to establish the truth of the allegations quickly, and then take action. Alternatively, it might be necessary to suspend the individuals who are accused, 'pending further investigations'.

© International Financial Publishing Limited

CHAPTER

10

Identifying and assessing risk

Contents
1   Risk and risk management
2   Categories of risk
3   Concepts in risk management
4   Identification, assessment and measurement of risk

> ## Risk and risk management
>
> - The nature of risk
> - The nature of risk management
> - Responsibilities for risk management
> - Elements of a risk management system

1 Risk and risk management

1.1 The nature of risk

Risk is usually associated with the possibility that things might go wrong, that events might turn out worse than expected or that something bad might happen.

However, risk has a broader meaning. Risk exists whenever a future outcome or future event cannot be predicted with certainty, and a range of different possible outcomes or events might occur.

Risks can be divided into two categories:

- pure risks
- speculative risks.

Pure risk (downside risk)

Pure risk, also called downside risk, is a risk where there is a possibility that an adverse event will occur. Events might turn out to be worse than expected, but they cannot be better than expected.

For example, there might be a safety risk that employees could be injured by an item of machinery. This is a pure risk, because the expectation is that no-one will be injured but a possibility does exist.

Similarly, there might be a risk for a company that key workers will go on strike and the company will be unable to provide its goods or services to customers. This is a pure risk, because the expected outcome is 'no strike' but the possibility of a strike does exist.

Speculative risk (two-way risk)

Speculative risk, also called two-way risk, exists when the actual future event or outcome might be either better or worse than expected.

- An investor in shares is exposed to a speculative risk, because the market price of the shares might go up or down. The investor will gain if prices go up and suffer a loss if prices go down.

© International Financial Publishing Limited

- An individual might ask his bank for a loan to buy a house, and the bank might offer him a 10-year loan at a fixed rate of interest or at a rate of interest that varies with changes in the official bank rate. The individual takes a risk with his choice of loan. If he chooses a fixed interest loan, there is a risk that interest rates will go up in the next 10 years, in which case he will benefit from the fixed rate on his loan. On the other hand, interest rates might go down, and he might find that he is paying more in interest than he would have done if he had arranged a loan at a variable rate of interest.

- Companies face two-way risk whenever they make business investment decisions. For example, a company might invest in the development of a new product, on the basis of sales and profit forecasts. Actual sales and profits might turn out to be higher or lower than forecast, and the investment might provide a high return, moderate return or low return (or even a loss).

Companies face both pure risks and downside risks.

- Pure risks are risks that can often be controlled either by means of internal controls or by insurance. These risks might be called **internal control risks** or **operational risks**.

- Speculative risks cannot be avoided because risks must be taken in order to make profits. As a general rule, higher risks should be justified by the expectation of higher profits (although events might turn out worse than expected) and a company needs to decide what level of speculative risks are acceptable. Speculative risks are usually called **business risk**, and might also be called **strategic risk** or **enterprise risk**.

Business decisions taken by management could involve both business risk (strategic risk) and operational risk (downside risk).

Example

The following examples illustrate how there are both strategic risks and operational risks in many decisions taken by management. The examples relate to a large public company.

Management decision	Comment on the risk
The company has commissioned a software company to design a new information system. The system will be used for marketing analysis and to sell goods to customers on-line.	There are strategic risks with the new system. These include the risk that customers will not want to buy goods on-line, and the risk that a competitor will develop a more popular e-commerce web site.
	There are also operational risks. These include risks that the new system will fail to function properly, and might suffer from hardware or software faults. These risks can be managed by operational controls.

The company has a large customer service centre where its employees take telephone calls from customers and deal with customer complaints. On average, staff are on the telephone talking to customers for 75% of their working time. Management have decided that in order to increase profits, staff levels should be reduced by 10% at the centre. It is estimated that this will have only a small effect on average answering times for customer calls.

There is a strategic risk. The company might lose some customers if the level of service from the service centre deteriorates. Management must judge whether the risk of losing customers is justified by the expected reduction in operating costs.

There are also operational risks. If employees have to spend more time on the telephone the risks of making mistakes or providing an unsatisfactory service is likely to increase.

There might also be a risk that answering times will be much longer than expected, due to operational inefficiencies.

1.2 The nature of risk management

Risk management is the process of managing both downside risks and business risks. It can be defined as the culture, structures and processes that are focused on achieving possible opportunities yet at the same time control unwanted results.

This definition identifies the connection between risk and returns.

- The safest strategy is to take no risks at all. However, this is an unrealistic business strategy. All business activity involves some risk.

- Business decisions should be directed towards achieving the objectives of the company. The main objective is (usually) to increase value for shareholders over the long term.

- Strategies are devised for achieving this objective and performance targets are set. The strategies should be consistent with the amount of business risk that the company is willing to take, and the targets should be realistic for the chosen strategies.

- The strategies are implemented, and management should try to achieve the stated objectives and performance targets, but at the same time should manage the downside risks and try to limit the business risks.

A link between management of operational risk and management of strategic risk can be seen in the following statement from a bank in the UK:

'A priority for us is to maintain a strong control framework. This is the key for delivering effective risk management. We have further strengthened risk analysis and reporting so that risks and opportunities are identified, and have put timescales and straightforward responsibilities in place at both group and division level for risk mitigation strategies. Routine management information reporting still has risk at the heart and balanced scorecards are used to ensure this is in the staff objectives.'

© International Financial Publishing Limited

1.3 Responsibilities for risk management

Risk management is a corporate governance issue. The board of directors have a responsibility to safeguard the assets of the company and to protect the investment of the shareholders from loss of value. The board should therefore keep strategic risks within limits that shareholders would expect, and to avoid or control operational risks.

The responsibilities of the board of directors and management for risk management are the same as their responsibilities for the system of internal control. Many of the comments in the previous chapter on internal control apply to risk management generally.

For example, the Turnbull Guidance stated that in deciding the company's policies with regard to internal control, the board should consider:

■ the nature and extent of the risks facing the company

■ the extent and categories of risk which it considers as acceptable for the company to bear

■ the likelihood that the risks will materialise (and events will turn out worse than expected)

■ the company's ability to reduce the probability of an adverse event occurring, or reducing the impact of an adverse event when it does occur

■ the cost of operating the controls relative to the benefits that the company expects to obtain from the control.

These considerations should apply to strategic risks as well as to operational risk and internal control systems.

In the same way, the UK Combined Code requires the board of directors to maintain a sound system of risk management, and to carry out a review of effectiveness of the risk management system at least once each year.

1.4 Elements of a risk management system

The elements of a risk management system should be similar to the elements of an internal control system:

■ There should be a culture of risk awareness within the company. Managers and employees should understand the 'risk appetite' of the company, and that excessive risks are not justified in the search for higher profits.

■ There should be a system and processes for identifying, assessing and measuring risks. When risks have been measured, they can be prioritised, and measures for controlling or containing the risk can be made.

■ There should be an efficient system of communicating information about risk and risk management to managers and the board of directors.

■ Strategies and risks should be monitored, to ensure that strategic objectives are being achieved within acceptable levels of risk.

> ## Categories of risk
>
> - The need to categorise business/strategic risks
> - Categories of risk common to many types of business
> - Business risks in different business sectors

2 Categories of risk

2.1 The need to categorise business/strategic risks

A risk management system might be based on a categorisation of risks. There are no standard risk classifications, because the nature of business risks varies between different types of business.

The reason for categorising risks is to **give some structure to the risk management process**. In many large companies, **risk committees** are established, and each committee is responsible for identifying, assessing and measuring business risks in a particular category. The risk committee then provides information on risk to managers in a position of responsibility for taking decisions to control the risk, for example by introducing new risk control measures.

The board of directors might use the same risk categories to provide their report on internal control and risk management, or to discuss risk in their annual business review (narrative report).

2.2 Categories of risk common to many types of business

Some types of business risk are common to many different industries. The Turnbull Report mentioned the following risks that might be significant:

- market risk
- credit risk
- liquidity risk
- technological risk
- legal risk
- health, safety and environmental risk
- reputation risk
- business probity risk.

Each of these risks is explained below, with examples. The examples are illustrations of cases where events turned out badly for companies. It is important to remember, however, that risk management is not concerned about adverse events that have happened in the past. It is about managing risks that exist now that could affect events (and profits) in the future.

© International Financial Publishing Limited

Market risk

Market risk is the risk from changes in the market price of key items, such as the price of key commodities. Market prices can go up or down, and a company can benefit from a fall in raw material prices or incur a loss from a rise in prices.

A company might be able to pass on higher prices of raw materials to the customer, by raising the prices for its own goods or services. However, if it puts its price sup, there might be a fall in total demand from customers. Higher prices, leading to falling sales volume could result in lower profits (= 'losses').

Example

An oil company described one of its major risks as the risk of rising and falling oil and chemical prices due to factors such as conflicts, political instability and natural disasters.

Credit risk

Credit risk is the risk of losses from bad debts or delays by customers in the settlement of their debts. All companies that give credit to customers are exposed to credit risk. The size of the credit risk depends on the amount of receivables owed to the company, and the 'credit quality' of the customers.

Credit risk is a major risk for commercial banks, because lending is a major part of their business operations.

Liquidity risk

Liquidity risk is the risk that the company will be unable to make payments to settle liabilities when payment is due. It can occur when a company has no money in the bank, is unable to borrow more money quickly, and has no assets that it can sell quickly in the market to obtain cash.

Companies can be profitable but still at risk from a liquidity shortage.

Example

Long-Term Capital Management (LTCM) was a hedge fund set up in 1994 by a group of traders and academics. It was funded by many large investment banks. The company ran into difficulties in 1998 when it found that it was unable to sell securities that it held in some small financial markets, because there was insufficient demand from investors. This led to a liquidity shortage. As the hedge fund became desperate to obtain cash, it had to sell its assets at whatever prices it could obtain, and market prices fell. The fall in market prices resulted in big losses, and LTCM was on the verge of collapse. Fearing that the US banking system would suffer severe damage in LTCM did collapse, the US Federal Reserve Bank organised a $3.5 billion rescue package.

This major crisis happened because of the liquidity risk and market risk that the hedge fund faced and was unable to manage successfully.

Technological risk

Technological risk is the risk that could arise from changes in technology (or inadequacy of technological systems in use). When a major technological change occurs, companies might have to make a decision about whether or not to adopt the new technology.

- If they adopt the new technology too soon, they might incur higher costs than if they waited until later.
- If they delay adopting the new technology, there is the risk that a competitor will take advantage, and use the technology to gain market share.

Example

There are various examples of technological risk. The development of the internet, for example, created a risk for many companies. Traditional banks were faced with the risk that if they did not develop online banking (at a high cost), non-bank companies might enter the market and take customers away from them.

The internet has also created risks for many retailing companies, which have had to decide whether to sell their goods on the internet, and if so whether to shut down their traditional retail outlets.

A technological risk currently facing manufacturers of televisions and media companies is which format of high definition (HD) television they should support. There are two competing formats, and only one seems likely to succeed in the longer term.

Legal risk

Legal risk, which includes **regulatory risk**, is the risk of losses arising from failure to comply with laws and regulations, and also the risk of losses from legal actions and lawsuits.

Example

An example in 2006 was the decision by the US government to enforce laws against online gambling. US customers were the main customers for on-line gambling companies based in other countries. As a result of the legal action, the on-line gambling companies lost a large proportion of their customer base, and their profits – and share prices – fell sharply.

Health, safety and environmental risk

Health and safety risks are risks to the health and safety of employees, customers and the general public. Environment risks are risks of losses arising, in the short

© International Financial Publishing Limited

term or long term, from damage to the environment - such as pollution or the destruction of non-renewable raw materials.

The risks faced by companies vary according to the nature of the business.

■ Companies are required to comply with health and safety regulations. This has a cost. If they fail to comply with regulations, they could be liable to a fine if government inspectors discover the failure to comply. If there is an incident in which employees or customers suffer injury or ill health as a consequence of a failing in health and safety control measures, the company could be exposed to large fines from government and lawsuits from the individuals affected.

■ If a company fails to deal with environmental risks in a satisfactory way, it could suffer losses in various ways. For example:
  - It might be fined for a breach of anti-pollution regulations.
  - It might suffer a loss of customers, for example if its reputation suffers as a result of an incident in which severe damage is done to the environment, such as a major oil spillage.

Reputation risk

Reputation risk is difficult to measure (quantify). It is the risk that a company's reputation with the general public (and customers), or the reputation of its product 'brand', will suffer damage. Damage to reputation can arise in many different ways: incidents that damage reputation are often reported by the media.

Companies that might suffer losses from damage to their reputation need to be vigilant and alert for any incident that could create adverse publicity. Public relations consultants might be used to assist with this task.

Example

Some years ago, the owner of a popular chain of jewellery shops in the UK criticised the quality of the goods that were sold in his shops. The bad publicity led to a sharp fall in sales and profits. The company had to change its name to end its association in the mind of the public with cheap, low-quality goods.

More recently, a manufacturer of branded leisure footwear suffered damage to its reputation when it was reported that one of its suppliers of manufactured footwear in the Far East used child labour and slave labour. Sales and profits (temporarily) fell.

Many other companies that source their supplies from developing countries have become alert to the risks to their reputation of using suppliers whose employment practices are below the standards that customers in the Western countries would regard as morally acceptable.

The manager of a well know group of hotels summarised the importance of reputation risk in general terms. He said that managing this type of risk is of top importance for any company that has a well known brand as the brand is one of the most important assets and reputation is a key issue.

Business probity risk

Probity means honesty and integrity. Business probity risk is the risk of losses from a failure to act in an honest way. Companies in some industries might be exposed to this type of risk.

■ For some products, there might be a large trade in smuggled goods, such as cigarettes and alcohol products. Companies might be tempted to deal with smugglers in order to increase sales of their products. The consequences if any dishonesty or crime is discovered could be criminal prosecution, fines by government or loss of reputation with the public.

■ In some countries and some industries, bribery is a problem. Companies might find that in order to win sales in some countries, they have to pay bribes ('commissions') to individuals. By failing to pay bribes, companies would not win sales contracts. By paying bribes, companies act dishonestly, and could be exposed to regulatory action or criminal action by the authorities of evidence of bribery is uncovered. This problem has been reported, for example, in the markets for the sale of military equipment.

■ In the UK, various banks and insurance companies have been fined heavily by the authorities for mis-selling products to customers that were not appropriate. Many banks and insurance companies in the UK mis-sold endowment policies (life assurance policies) to many customers during the 1980s and were required to pay large amounts of compensation for the losses that those customers suffered.

Derivatives risk

Derivatives risk is another type of risk included in the syllabus for the examination. They include commodity derivatives and financial derivatives.

■ Commodity derivatives are contracts on the price of certain commodities, such as oil, wheat, metals (gold, tin, copper etc) and coffee. Derivatives contracts are contracts to buy and sell a quantity of commodities at a future date at a fixed price agreed in the contract. In most cases, the buyer and seller of the derivative instrument do not intend to buy and sell the physical commodities. The contract is a contract for the price, and it is settled by the payment of the difference between the fixed price in the contract and the market price at settlement date for the contract.

■ Financial derivatives are contracts on the price of certain financial instruments or market rates, such as foreign exchange rates, interest rates, bond prices and share prices. Like commodity derivatives, the buyer and seller of financial derivatives do not usually exchange items they have bought or sold. The contract is simply a contract on the price or market rate. It is settled by a payment for the difference between the fixed price in the contract and the market rate at the settlement date.

© International Financial Publishing Limited

Derivative instruments include options, futures and swaps. They can be used to control risks by 'hedging' exposures to price risks (market risks). On the other hand, they can be used to speculate on changes in market prices.

There have been incidents where the treasury department of a company or government organisation has used derivatives to speculate on changes in market prices, and suffered heavy losses because market prices moved against its position in the derivative instruments. All companies with a treasury department could be exposed to derivatives risk from trading by its treasury staff in the commodities or financial markets. Risk management and control systems (internal controls) need to be implemented and enforced to control the risk.

Example

One type of derivative instrument is a credit default swap (CDS). A CDS can be described as a form of credit 'insurance' or credit protection. It relates to a specific amount of a debt of a 'credit subject' (a bank loan owed by a specific borrower or bonds issued by a specific company). One person can use a CDS to buy credit protection from another person. The seller of the credit protection will be required to make a payment to the buyer if the credit subject defaults on payment of the debt.

For example, Bank XYZ can sell credit protection to Company ABC in the form of a credit default swap. The swap might be for $10 million of government bonds issued by the government of Brazil. Company ABC is not required to hold any Brazilian government bonds in order to buy the CDS. It can speculate on the possibility that the Brazilian government will default, and hope to make a profit.

It seems probable that many organisations have traded credit default swaps, and have speculated on the credit risk of other entities. There are no reliable statistics about the volume and value of CDSs, and no information about who holds them. If there is a major credit crisis in the world – for example if the Brazilian government were to default on the payment of its bonds – the financial consequences for sellers of CDSs could possibly be very damaging.

For any company that trades in CDSs, there is an urgent need for risk management and suitable internal controls.

2.3 Business risks in different business sectors

The major risks facing companies vary over time, and manager might have different opinions about which risks are more significant than others. Risks differ between companies in different industries or markets.

- Companies in different industries might face the same risks, but in some industries the risk might be much greater than in other industries. For example, credit risk is a very significant risk in the banking industry, but less significant in the oil industry. In contrast, the risks of environmental regulation are much higher for oil companies than for banks.

- Risks vary in significance over time, as the business environment changes. Companies need to be alert not only for new risks, but for changes in the significance of existing risks. Are they giving too much attention to risks that are no longer significant? Or have they ignored the growth in significance of any risk that has existed for a long time, but is now much more significant than it used to be.

 Example

The table below compares the significant risks facing a commercial bank, an international oil company and a large retailing organisation. These are the significant risks identified by three major listed companies (in the UK) in their annual report and accounts. All three companies have extensive business interests both outside and inside the UK.

Commercial bank	Retailing organisation	Oil company
Strategy risk. The risk of choosing strategies that do not maximise shareholder value.	Business strategy risk. Risk that the business strategy might take the company in the wrong direction, or is not efficiently communicated.	Market risk, especially risk of changes in the price of oil and natural gas.
Product-service risk. The risk of developing products and services for customers that do not meet customer requirements and are worse than the products or services offered by competitors.	Financial strategy and group treasury risk. This covers the risk of not having available funds, credit risk, interest rate risk and currency risk.	Exploration risk. The risk of being unable to find sufficient new reserves of oil and natural gas.
Credit risk.	Risk of under-performance in the UK business. This is dependent largely on economic conditions in the UK.	Reputation risk
Market risk. This includes the risk from variations in interest rates (interest rate risk) and currency exchange rates (currency risk) as well as the risk of changes in market prices of financial products such as shares.	Competition risk. This is the risk of losses due to the activities and successes of competitors.	Security risk (risk from crime, civil wars and terrorism). Environmental risk. The risk from climate change. Economic risk. Risk from changes in the state of national economies and the world economy.
Operational risks. Risks of losses due to human error or fraud, failures in systems (such as IT systems) and unforeseen external events (terrorism attacks, natural disasters).	People capabilities risk. This is the risk of failing to attract 'the best people' to work for the company.	Competition risk. Political risk. This is the risk of doing business in politically unstable countries or politically sensitive countries.
People capabilities risk. This is the risk of failing to attract 'the best people' to work for the company.	Reputation risk. Failure to protect reputation could lead to a loss of trust and confidence by customers.	Natural disaster risk
Risk of inadequate liquidity and inadequate capital.	Environmental risk. Risks arise from issues such as energy savings, transport efficiency, waste management and the recycling of waste.	Currency risk. IT failures risk

© International Financial Publishing Limited

Regulatory risk.

Product safety risk

Ethical risks in the supply chain. This is the risk to reputation of dealing with suppliers who do not use ethical business practices.

Fraud and compliance risk

IT systems risk. This is the risk of a failure in the company's major IT systems.

Political risk and terrorism risk

Pensions risk. The risk to the company from the costs of meeting its liabilities to the company's pension scheme for its employees.

Regulatory risk

Shortage of skilled labour risk, especially a shortage of science graduates.

Concepts in risk management

- Exposure to risk
- Residual risk
- Risk appetite
- A risk-based approach

---

3 Concepts in risk management

To understand risk management, it is necessary to understand a few key concepts.

3.1 Exposure to risk

When a company is exposed to risk, this means that it will suffer a loss if there are unfavourable changes in conditions in the future or unfavourable events occur. For example, if a UK company holds US$2 million it is exposed to a risk of a fall in the value of the dollar against sterling, because the sterling value of the dollars will fall.

Companies need to assess the significance of their exposures to risk. If possible, exposures should be measured and quantified.

- If a UK company holds US$2 million, its exposure to a fall in the value of the dollar against sterling is $2 million.
- If an investor holds £100 million in shares of UK listed companies, it has a £100 million exposure to a fall in the UK stock market.
- If a company is owed £500,000 by its customers, its exposure to credit risk is £500,000.

An exposure is not necessarily the amount that the company will expect to lose if events or conditions turn out unfavourable. For example, an investor holding £100 million in shares of UK listed companies is exposed to a fall in the market price of the shares, but he would not expect to lose the entire £100 million. Similarly a company with receivables of £500,000 should not expect all its receivables to become bad debts (unless the money is owed by just one or two customers).

Having measured an exposure to risk, a company can estimate what the possible losses might be, realistically. This estimate of the possible losses should help management to assess the significance of the risk.

Some risk exposures cannot be measured, because they are 'qualitative risks'. It is very difficult, for example, to estimate the possible losses that could arise from damage to a company's reputation. Qualitative risks must also be assessed, but since the amount of the exposure and the possible losses that might occur cannot be quantified, an assessment of these risks depends on management judgement and opinion.

© International Financial Publishing Limited

3.2 Residual risk

Companies control the risks that they face. Controls cannot eliminate risks completely, and even after taking suitable control measures to control a risk, there is some remaining risk exposure.

The remaining exposure to a risk after control measures have been taken is called **residual risk**. If a residual risk is too high for a company to accept, it should implement additional control measures to reduce the residual risk to an acceptable level.

3.3 Risk appetite

A company must accept some risk in order to make profits. This means that a risk of making a loss must be accepted in order to create a chance to make profit. A company will take the risk if its management decides that the risk of loss is justified by the expectation of a gain.

Risk appetite is concerned with how much risk management are willing to take. Management might be willing to accept the risk of loss up to a certain maximum limit if the chance of making profits is sufficiently attractive to them. For a market trader in the financial markets, risk appetite has been defined as 'the amount of capital that a trader is willing to lose in order to generate a potential profit.'

Risk appetite is used to describe how willing a board is to take on risk – on a scale from willing to take on risk through willing to take some risks down to aversion to taking a risk.

A Board of directors might also have an appetite for one type of risk but an aversion to a different type of risk. The risk appetite of a Board or management in any particular situation will depend on:

■ the importance of the decision and the nature of the decision

■ the amount and nature of the potential gains or losses, and

■ the reliability of the information available to help the Board or management to make their decision.

Board policy on risk

The risk appetite of a company should be decided by the board of directors, and a policy on risk should be decided and communicated by the board to its management. Managers need guidance on the levels of risk that it would be 'legitimate' for them to take on with any decision that they make.

■ Managers should not be allowed to take whatever decisions they consider to be suitable, regardless of risk. This would lead to inconsistent decision-making and could expose the company to unacceptable risks. 'Erratic, inopportune risk-taking is an accident waiting to happen' (HM Treasury).

■ At the other extreme, a risk averse culture is undesirable, in which managers are discouraged from taking any risky decisions, so that business opportunities are not exploited.

3.4 A risk-based approach

The term 'risk-based approach' is often used to describe risk management processes. It is an approach to decision-making based on a detailed evaluation of risks and exposures, and policy guidelines on the level of risk that is acceptable (risk appetite).

The risk-based approach takes the view that some risk must be accepted, but risk exposures should be kept within acceptable limits. Decisions should therefore be based on a consideration of both expected benefit and the risk.

Example

A company might use discounted cash flow to evaluate capital expenditures. If risk is ignored, the company might have a standard rule that capital investment projects should be undertaken if they are expected to have a positive net present value (NPV) when the forecast cash flows are discounted at the company's cost of capital.

With a risk-based approach, capital investment projects should not be undertaken unless their NPV is positive and the level of risk is acceptable.

Example

A risk-based approach can also be compared with a 'box-ticking' approach. With a box-ticking approach, certain procedures must be carried out every time an item is processed. For example, the customs and immigration department at a country's airports might have a policy of checking the baggage of every passenger arriving in the country by aeroplane, because the policy objective is to eliminate smuggling of prohibited goods into the country by individuals. This would be a 'box-ticking' approach, with standard procedures for every passenger.

With a risk-based approach, the department will take the view that some risk of smuggled goods entering the country is unavoidable. The policy should therefore be to try to limit the risk to a certain level. Instead of checking the baggage of every passenger arriving in the country, customs officials should select passengers whose baggage they wish to search. Their selection of customers for searching should be based on a risk assessment – for example what type of customer is most likely to try to smuggle goods into the country?

© International Financial Publishing Limited

> ## Identification, assessment and measurement of risk
>
> - Risk identification
> - The impact of risk on stakeholders
> - Assessing risks: impact and probability
> - Measuring risks
> - Prioritising risks
> - Role of the board of directors in identifying and assessing risks

4 Identification, assessment and measurement of risk

4.1 Risk identification

Risk identification is the initial stage in a system of risk management. A company needs to understand what risks it faces, both in its environment and markets (strategic risks) and internally (operational risks).

There are no standard rules about how risks should be identified.

- In a large company, it might be appropriate to identify risks at different levels in the organisation – on a group-wide basis, and for each business division and for each department or function.
- Management might be responsible for identifying strategic risks/business risks for the company, but the internal auditors or external auditors might be more efficient at identifying operational risks (and suggesting suitable internal controls to control the risks).

Many large companies set up **risk committees** to identify risks. These are committees of managers from several departments or functions. Each committee is responsible for reporting on a particular category of risk or risks in a particular geographical area of the company's operations. A committee meets regularly to discuss risks and their potential significance, and changes in these risks.

Risks identified by a company will vary in importance. Some risks might be unimportant, or easily controlled. Some risks will be very significant. Having identified risks, it is therefore necessary to assess the importance of each risk, in order to:

- rank the risks in order of significance (order of priority), and
- identify the risks that are the most significant, and
- identify the significant the risks where control measures are urgently needed.

(Deciding on suitable control measures will depend on the significance of the risk, and the cost of taking control measures. Control measures are only justified if the cost of the control measures is less than the benefits obtained from reducing the risk.)

4.2 The impact of risk on stakeholders

The process of identifying risks should concentrate on risks to the company, both strategic risks and operational risks. However, the risks for a company also create risks for its stakeholders. Management should be aware of the impact of the company's risks on stakeholders, because the risks for stakeholders could affect the attitude and the behaviour of stakeholders towards to the company.

The impact of a company's risks on risks for stakeholders varies and depends on circumstances.

Employees

Employees are exposed to several risks in their job. These include the risk of a loss of job, and the threat to health or safety in the work that they do. Employment benefits might be threatened. These risks to employees can be affected by risks that face their company.

- Jobs may be threatened by the strategic choices taken by a company. If a company makes the wrong strategic decisions, and the company loses money, many employees could lose their jobs.

- Safety risks for a company might be measured in terms of the risk of serious injuries and minor injuries to employees over a given period of time. (For example, a company might assess its current safety measures in terms of the expected number of serious injuries per 1,000 employees per year.)

The risk appetite of some employees might differ from the risk appetite of the company and the board's policy on risk. For example, a 'rogue trader' working in the financial markets for a bank might be willing to take high risks for the company because the potential benefits for him personally (a large cash bonus for making large trading profits) exceeds the risk (the possible loss of his job).

Investors

When investors buy the shares of a company, they have some expectation of the sort of company it is and the returns they might expect from their investment. For example, an investor might buy shares in a company expecting it to be a high-risk company which could achieve a very high rate of growth in the share price. Or an investor might buy shares in a company because the company is stable and can be expected to pay a regular annual dividend.

The board of directors should try to ensure that the risk appetite of the company is consistent with the risk appetite of its shareholders (and other stock market investors). A company should not expose itself to strategic risks that expose the investors to a risk to their investment that the shareholders would consider excessive.

- When a company increases its exposures to strategic risk, many existing shareholders might decide to sell their shares and switch to investing in a lower-risk company. Investors with a larger risk appetite might buy the shares.

- The board of directors should keep shareholders informed about the significant risks that the company faces, so that investors can assess their own investment risk. (In the UK, for example, stock market companies are now required by law

© International Financial Publishing Limited

to include disclosures about risks in their annual narrative report to shareholders, the business review.)

Creditors

The main risks to a company's creditors and suppliers from the company's own risks are that:

■ the company will not pay what they owe, and

■ the company will stop buying goods and services from them.

A high-risk company is a high credit risk. The liquidity risk and insolvency risk facing a company has an impact on the credit risk for a supplier or lender. When a company asks a bank for a loan, the bank will assess the credit status of the company, and it will make its decision to lend on the basis of whether it thinks that the company will be able to pay back the loan with interest and on schedule.

Communities and the general public

Communities and the general public are exposed to risks from the actions of companies, and the failure by companies to control their risks.

■ Risks to the general public include:

- the consequences for the country of a decline in the business activities and profits of a company due to recession, especially when the company is a major employer

- health and safety risks from failures by a company to supply goods that meet with health and safety standards

- risks to the quality of life from environmental pollution, due to a failure by the company to control its environmental/pollution risks.

■ Risks to a local community also arise from economic risks faced by the company. If a company is forced to close down a production plant in an area where it is a major employer, the economy of the entire community would be affected.

Pressure groups and popular action groups come into existence because 'activist' members of the general public believe that their well-being is threatened. The cause of the perceived threat is often the activities of companies.

Some companies take risk-based decisions that expose them to considerable strategic risk without necessarily considering fully the risk impact on the general public or local communities. For example, an energy company planning to construct a new nuclear power station should consider the long-term risks to the community – and the general public – not just their own business risks relating to costs.

Governments

For governments, companies are a source of economic wealth for the country. They create additional economic activity which creates extra wealth, and they provide employment and tax revenues for the government.

A risk for government is that major companies will decide to invest in a different country, or move its operations from one country to another.

For example, manufacturing companies in the European Union have been faced with the risk of low-cost competition from suppliers in the Far East, where labour costs in some countries are much lower than in Europe. To overcome this threat, companies might consider relocating their manufacturing operations to the Far East. The strategic threat to these companies has an obvious impact on the governments of European Union countries, because the economies of those countries would be affected by a loss of manufacturing businesses.

Customers

Some risks facing companies also have an impact on their customers.

■ A company might face operational risks from human error or system breakdown in its operations. Errors and delays in providing goods and services have an impact on business customers. For example, if a company is late in supplying a key component to a business customer, the customer will be late in supplying its own customers. Errors and delays work their way through the entire supply chain.

■ Product safety risks for a company are also a risk for customers who use them. For example, manufacturers of foods products, drink products and medicines and drugs need to consider the potential risk to customers from weaknesses in their own safety controls.

Business partners

There are risks in joint ventures for all the joint venture partners. A company in a joint venture might try to dominate decision-making in order to reduce the risk that the joint venture will not operate in the way that they want it to.

However, by reducing its exposures to risk in a joint venture, a company will affect the risks for the other joint venture partners.

Risks in partnerships can be controlled for all the partners – to some extent – by clear terms in the contract agreement between the partners, and by monitoring performance of the partnership.

A UK public company (with several joint ventures in other countries) has commented on joint venture governance and partnerships as follows: 'As we continue to enter into new partnerships and grow existing joint ventures, the risk inherent in managing these partnerships increases. It is more difficult to guarantee the achievement of joint goals and we rely on partners' reputations. We choose partners with good reputations and set out joint goals and clear contractual arrangements from the outset. We monitor performance and governance of our joint ventures and partnerships.'

© International Financial Publishing Limited

4.3 Assessing risks: impact and probability

The assessment of risk is sometimes called 'risk profiling' or 'risk mapping'.
To assess each risk, it is necessary to consider the likelihood that losses will occur as a consequence of the risk, and the size or amount of the loss when this happens.

A simple approach to risk mapping involves taking each risk that has been identified and placing it on a map. The map is a 2 × 2 matrix, with:

- one side representing the **frequency** of adverse events or the **probability** that the risk will materialise and an adverse outcome will occur, and

- the other side representing the **impact (loss)** if an adverse event occurs or adverse circumstances arise.

The format of a simple risk map is shown below.

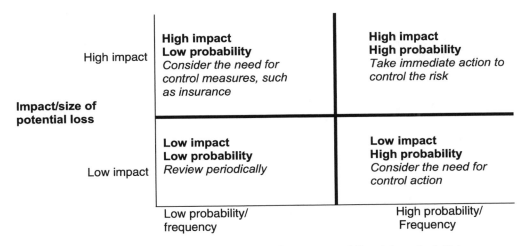

A risk map can help management to identify risks where immediate control measures are required, and where the need for control measures should be considered or reviewed periodically.

'High impact, low probability' risks might include the risks of damage to assets from fire or flooding, the risk of a terrorist attack or the risk of major legislation that will affect the company's business. Some of these risks, such as risks of fire, theft and criminal damage, can be insured. Insurance reduces the residual risk by the amount of the insurance cover obtained.

All key risks should be 'owned' by specific individual managers, who should be required to take the necessary control measures and report to their senior manager about what they have done.

4.4 Measuring risks

Whenever possible, risks should be measured. Measuring risk means quantifying the risk. When risks are quantified, the risk can be managed through setting targets for maximum risk tolerance and measuring actual performance against the target.

Risk measurements can be financial measurements (for example, a measurement of the expected loss) or non-financial (for example, a measurement of expected injuries to employees at work).

However, not all risks can be measured. Where risks are assessed in qualitative terms, risk management decisions become a matter of management judgement.

 Example

In the banking industry, banks use risk modelling to measure their main risks. A commonly-used model for measuring credit risk is called a Value at Risk model (VaR model). This can be used to estimate, at a given level of probability, the expected bad debts from the bank's current borrowers. For example, a VaR model could be used to predict at the 95% level of confidence that the bank's bad debt losses from its current borrowers will not exceed, say, £5 million in the next month.

Bank set targets for VaR limits, and monitor the actual credit risk by comparing actual value at risk against the maximum or target limit.

4.5 Prioritising risks

Within a system or risk management, companies need to establish a process for deciding which risks are tolerable and which might need more control measures to reduce the risk. (Sometimes, it might be decided that control measures are excessive, and that money can be saved by reducing the controls, without increasing risk above acceptable levels.)

Deciding on priorities for risk management might be a matter of management judgement.

Some companies and non-business entities use formal techniques to help them with the prioritisation of risk. One such technique is a risk dashboard.

Risk dashboard

A risk dashboard can be used to identify which risks need further control measures.

On a simple dashboard, each risk that has been identified is represented by a 'coloured light'. These are usually green, amber and red, representing the colours of traffic signals. When a risk has a red light, this indicates that further risk measures are needed. A green light indicates that the risk is under control. An amber light indicates that the risk needs to be kept under review.

A more complex risk dashboard can be used, for each risk, to show:

- the total amount of risk, assuming that no control measures are in place to contain the risk
- the residual risk, which is the remaining exposure to risk after allowing for the control measures that are in place

© International Financial Publishing Limited

■ the risk appetite of the company for that particular risk, which is the exposure to risk that the company is willing to accept in order to obtain the expected benefits from its activities.

Risk dashboard

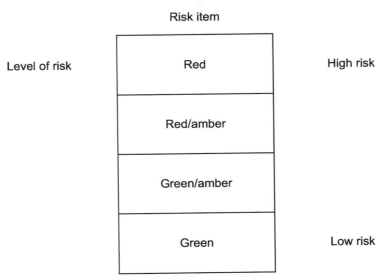

Risk item

Level of risk

High risk

Low risk

Risk appetite and residual risk can both be shown on the dashboard.

The company's risk appetite for a particular risk might be low, in which case it can be recorded in the 'green' section of the dashboard. If the risk appetite is higher, this can be shown in the green-amber or red-amber sections. It is unlikely that a company will have an appetite for a very high risk, so risk appetite is unlikely to be shown in the red section.

Residual risk can also be recorded, in the green, green-amber, red-amber or red sections of the dashboard.

■ When risk appetite and residual risk are in the same section of the dashboard, this means that current risk management/risk control measures are appropriate for the risk.

■ When the risk appetite is in a lower-risk section of the dashboard than the residual risk, this indicates that further control action is needed to reduce the residual risk to an acceptable level.

4.6   Role of the board of directors in identifying and assessing risks

Risk management is largely a responsibility for management. Management:

■ is normally responsible for identifying key risks (although the board of directors might take on responsibility, with advice from management and auditors)

■ is responsible for assessing risks and for designing and implementing risk controls

■ is responsible for monitoring the effectiveness of risk controls, and keeping risks under review

■ should report regularly to the board of directors on risks and risk management.

The board of directors has overall responsibility for risk management, just as it has overall responsibility for the system of internal control.

■ The board should set the company's policy for risk, and give clear guidance about the company's risk appetite.

■ In the UK, the Combined Code states that the board should conduct a review at least once a year of the effectiveness of internal controls, and this includes the effectiveness of risk management systems.

■ The UK Combined Code also requires the board to report to shareholders on its review of internal control.

The evaluation of risk management systems, and the board's responsibilities for reporting to shareholders, are the same as the board's responsibilities for internal controls. These responsibilities have been described in an earlier chapter, and are not repeated here.

© International Financial Publishing Limited

CHAPTER

11

Controlling risk

Contents

1	Monitoring risk
2	Embedding risk
3	Methods of controlling risk

Monitoring risk

- Role of the risk manager
- The role of risk committees
- The role of risk auditing

---

1 Monitoring risk

There is no widely-accepted approach to the management of risk. Each business and non-business entity develops its own risk management structure according to its own needs and perceptions. This chapter looks at some of the approaches that might be used.

1.1 Role of the risk manager

Companies and other entities might appoint one or more risk managers. A risk manager might be given responsibility for all aspects of risk. Alternatively, risk managers might be appointed to help with the management of specific risks, such as:

- Insurance
- Health and safety
- Information systems and information technology
- Human resources
- Financial risk or treasury risk
- Compliance (with specific aspects of the law or industry regulations).

A risk manager is not a 'line' manager and is not directly responsible for risk management. His role is to provide information, assistance and advice, and to improve risk awareness within the entity and encourage the adoption of sound risk management practice.

The role of a risk manager might therefore include:

- Helping with the identification of risks
- Establishing 'tools' to help with the identification of risks
- Establishing modelling methods for the assessment and measurement of risks
- Collecting risk incident reports (for example, health and safety incident reports)
- Assisting heads of departments and other line managers in the review of reports by the internal auditors
- Preparing regular risk management reports for senior managers or risk committees
- Monitoring 'best practice' in risk management and encouraging the adoption of best practice within the entity.

© International Financial Publishing Limited

How effective are risk managers?

The effectiveness of risk managers depends partly on the role of the risk manager and partly on the support that the risk manager receives from the board and senior management.

- The specific role of the risk manager might give him authority to instruct line managers what to do. For example, a health and safety manager can insist on compliance with health and safety regulations. Some risk managers have the authority to make decisions for the entity: the manager responsible for insurance, for example, might have the authority to buy insurance cover against certain risks.

- The status of the risk manager depends on the amount of support he receives from the board and senior management. A culture of risk awareness should be promoted by the board of directors.

1.2   The role of risk committees

Some entities establish one or more risk committees.

- A risk committee might be a committee of the board of directors. This committee should be responsible for fulfilling the corporate governance obligations of the board to review the effectiveness of the system of risk management.

- A risk committee might be an inter-departmental committee responsible for identifying and monitoring specific aspects of risk, such as:

    - strategic risks/business risks (or particular aspects of these risks)

    - operational risk (and internal controls)

    - financial risk

    - compliance risk

    - environmental risk.

Risk committees do not have management authority to make decisions about the control of risk. Their function is to identify risks, monitor risks and report on the effectiveness of risk management to the board or senior management.

Internal auditors might be included in the membership of risk committees. Alternatively, the internal auditors should report to the risk committees.

Similarly, risk managers might be included in the membership of risk committees, or might report to the committees.

The boards of directors should receive regular reports from these risk committees, as part of their governance function to monitor the effectiveness of risk management systems.

1.3 The role of risk auditing

Risks should be monitored. The purpose of risk monitoring is to ensure that:

- there are processes and procedures for identifying risk, and that these are effective
- there are internal controls and other risk management processes in place for managing the risks
- risk management systems appear to be effective
- the level of risk faced by the entity is consistent with the policies on risk that are set by the board of directors
- failures in the control of risk are identified and investigated
- weaknesses in risk management processes are identified and corrected.

Risks can be monitored through auditing. Risk auditing involves the investigation by an independent person (the auditor) of an area of risk management.

External auditors should monitor internal controls for financial risks as a part of their annual audit process. Internal auditors might also carry out checks on internal financial controls.

However, risk auditing can be extended to other aspects of risk, such as operational risks, compliance risks and environmental risks. The auditors might be a part of the internal audit function or risk management function within the entity. Alternatively, they might be external investigators and auditors from either an accountancy/consultancy firm or a firm that specialises in the audit of particular types of risk.

© International Financial Publishing Limited

Embedding risk

- The importance of risk awareness throughout an organisation
- Embedding risk awareness in the culture of an organisation
- Embedding risk awareness in systems and procedures
- The role of risk professionals and the need for embedded risk management

2 Embedding risk

2.1 The importance of risk awareness throughout an organisation

Risk managers, risk committees and risk audits can contribute to a culture of risk awareness, and can help to provide a sound system of risk management. It is important, however, that throughout the organisation managers and employees are aware of risk and the need for appropriate risk control.

Managers take decisions that expose the entity to risk. They need to understand the possible consequences of their decision-making, and should be satisfied that the risks they have 'created' are justified by the expected benefits.

Senior managers are responsible for the management of business risks/strategic risks. Every employee needs to be aware of the need to contain operational risks. For example:

- All employees must be aware of health and safety regulations, and should comply with them. A failure to comply with fire safety regulations could result in serious fire damage. For a manufacturer of food products, a failure in food hygiene regulations could have serious consequences for both public health and the company's reputation.

- All employees and managers should understand the need to report incidents where there have been excessive exposures to risk, and control measures have failed or have not worked properly.

- In some entities, there could be serious consequences of failure to comply with regulations and procedures. For example in banking, there must be a widespread understanding of anti money laundering regulations and the rules against mis-selling of banking products. The consequences for a bank of failures in compliance could be fines by the regulator and damage to the bank's reputation.

2.2 Embedding risk awareness in the culture of an organisation

It was stated in the earlier chapter on internal control that an essential aspect of risk management and control is the culture within the organisation. The culture within the organisation is set by the board of directors and senior management (the 'tone at the top'), but it should be shared by every manager and employee.

Risk awareness is 'embedded' in the culture of the organisation when thinking about risk and the control of risk is a natural and regular part of employee behaviour.

Creating a culture of risk awareness should be a responsibility of the board of directors and senior management, who should show their own commitment to the management of risk in the things that they say and do.

- There should be reporting systems in place for disclosing issues relating to risk. There should be a sharing of risk-related information.

- Managers and other employees should recognise the need to disclose information about risks and about failures in risk control.

- There should be a general recognition that problems should not be kept hidden. 'Bad news' should be reported as soon as it is identified. The sooner problems are identified, the sooner control measures can be taken (and the less the damage and loss).

- To create a culture in which problems are disclosed, there must be openness and transparency. Employees should be willing to admit to mistakes.

- Openness and transparency will not exist if there is a 'blame' culture. Individuals should not be criticised for making mistakes, provided that they own up to them promptly.

- The attitude should be that problems with risks will always occur. When they do happen, the objective should be to take measures to deal with the problem. Mistake should be analysed in order to find solutions and prevent a repetition of the problem. Risk management should be a constructive process.

2.3   Embedding risk awareness in systems and procedures

In addition to creating a culture of risk awareness within an entity, it is also important to establish systems and procedures in which the management of risk is 'embedded'.

'Embedding' risk in systems and procedures means that risk management should be an integral part of management practice. Risk management must be a core function which managers and other employees consider every day in the normal course of their activities. The concept of embedding risk can be compared with a situation where risk management is treated as an 'add-on' process, outside the normal procedures and systems of management.

There are no standard rules about how risk awareness and risk control can be embedded within systems and procedures. Each organisation needs to consider the most appropriate methods for its own purposes.

    © International Financial Publishing Limited

Example

One system for embedding risk awareness in the planning process is a two-stage process, as follows.

Stage 1. Managers responsible for preparing plans are required to identify the key risks that could prevent the achievement of their planning targets. This requirement makes managers consider risks and the measures that are required to control them, to ensure the achievement of planning targets.

Stage 2. Before plans are finally approved, managers must carry out sensitivity analysis or scenario analysis, to measure the effects of adverse events or circumstances. For example, a sales manager preparing a sales plan would be required to consider the consequences of weak sales demand, or a lack of success in a new product launch. Similarly a research and development director might be required to consider the consequences of a failure in a research project or a delay in the completion of a development project. They must then report the results of their testing.

Sensitivity analysis or scenario tests make managers consider risks and their consequences. In addition, they are made aware of the need to control risks, so that if future events are unfavourable, the risks are contained and the consequences are not worse than those predicted by their scenario testing.

2.4 The role of risk professionals and the need for embedded risk management

Risk managers and risk audits have a role in risk management, but they cannot be effective unless risk is embedded in the culture of the entity and in its systems and procedures.

The risk management team of an organisation can assist in the development of the risk management framework and policies. They can teach the team about risk management so as to ensure that strong reporting and examining structures exist.

However, there are two things that this risk management team cannot do. They cannot put a corporate culture in place that establishes risk awareness and transparency. The culture needs to be set and then passed on to all members of staff by the board of directors or the senior management team. They also cannot be the only risk managers. The people who created the risks originally – the business managers – need to be responsible. The risk management team's main aims should be to ensure that the right people are managing the right risks and that risk management is always considered.

Methods of controlling risk
■ Different approaches to controlling risk
■ Diversification
■ Risk transfer
■ Risk sharing
■ Hedging risks
■ Risk avoidance and risk retention

3 Methods of controlling risk

3.1 Different approaches to controlling risk

There are several different approaches to controlling risks. In a previous chapter, it was explained how internal controls can be used to control financial risks, operational risks and compliance risks.

Risk management methods are much more sophisticated in some industries (and in some countries) than in others. For example, the financial services and banking industry has developed products (financial derivatives) that can be used to manage financial risks.

Approaches to the management of business risks that are described in this section are:

■ diversification of risks

■ risk transfer

■ risk sharing

■ hedging risks

3.2 Diversification

Risks can be reduced through diversification. Diversification is also called 'spreading risks'.

The purpose of diversification in business is to invest in a range of different business activities, and build up a portfolio of different business activities. Each individual business activity is risky, but some businesses might perform better than expected just as some might perform worse than expected. Taking the entire portfolio of different businesses, the good performers will offset the bad performers, and the portfolio as a whole might provide, on average, the expected returns.

© International Financial Publishing Limited

Example

Investors in shares often diversify their investment risks by investing in a portfolio of shares of different companies in different industries and different countries.

Some investments will perform well and some will perform badly. The losses on poor-performing shares should be offset by higher-than-expected returns on others. Risk is also reduced because if an investor suffers a loss on some shares, the rest of the investment portfolio retains its value. The maximum loss in any single investment is limited to the amount that has been invested in the shares of that company.

When is diversification appropriate?

Diversification is appropriate in some situations, but not in others.

- A diversification strategy by a company might be appropriate provided that its management have the skills and experience to manage the portfolio of different business activities. For example, a film studio diversifies into films for the cinema, films for television and other home entertainment products. If there is a decline in the market for cinema films, the market for television programmes or downloading films from the internet might remain strong.

- A diversification strategy by a company is much more risky (and less appropriate) when it takes the company into unrelated business activities. For example, a company that diversifies into making tobacco products, selling insurance products and providing consultancy services could be exposed to very large risks, because its senior management might not have the skills or experience to manage all the different businesses. Each business is very different from the others. Investors in the company might also disapprove of such diversification: if investors want to diversify into different businesses, they can do so by buying shares in specialist companies rather than buying shares in a company that diversifies its activities.

- Risks are not reduced significantly by diversifying into different activities where the risks are similar, so that if there is an adverse change in one business activity, there is a strong probability that adverse changes will also occur in the other activities. For example, a company that diversifies into house-building, manufacturing windows and manufacturing bricks would be exposed in all three businesses to conditions in the housing market.

3.3 Risk transfer

Risk transfer involves passing some or all of a risk on to someone else, so that the other person has the exposure to the risk.

A common example of risk transfer is insurance. By purchasing insurance, risks are transferred to the insurance company, which will pay for any losses covered by the insurance policy.

Using insurance to manage risk is appropriate for risks where the potential losses are high, but the probability of a loss occurring is fairly low.

3.4 Risk sharing

Risk sharing involves collaborating with another person and sharing the risks jointly.

Common methods of risk sharing in business are partnerships and joint ventures. In a joint venture, all the joint venture partners share in the investment, the management, the cost of the investment, the risks and the rewards.

Companies pursuing a strategy of developing their business in other countries might use joint ventures as a way of entering the market in a different country. For the 'global' company, the joint venture partner would be a local business whose management have knowledge of the local market. For a local business, a joint venture with a foreign company reduces the financial risk, and also improves the opportunities for expansion and growth.

3.5 Hedging risks

The term 'hedging' risks is used extensively in the financial markets, and hedging is commonly associated with the management of financial risks such as currency risk.

Hedging risk means creating a position (making a transaction) that offsets an exposure to another risk. For example, if a company has an exposure to currency risk, and will lose money if the US dollar falls in value against the euro, a hedge can be created whereby the company will make a profit if the US dollar falls in value against the euro. The loss on the original risk exposure will be offset by a gain on the hedge position.

Risks can be hedged with a variety of derivative instruments, such as futures, options and swaps. A detailed knowledge of these instruments is outside the scope of the syllabus for this examination paper.

3.6 Risk avoidance and risk retention

Measures to control risk through diversification, risk transfer, risk sharing and hedging risks can help to reduce the risks. Similarly, internal controls can reduce risks to prevent problems from happening or identify them when they occur.

Control measures do not eliminate risk. They only reduce them. The risks that remain after risk control measures are implemented are the 'residual risks'.

An entity needs to develop a strategy towards these risks. The basic choice is between risk avoidance and risk retention.

- **Risk avoidance** means not having any exposure to a risk. A business risk can only be avoided by not investing in the business. Risk avoidance therefore means staying out of a business, or leaving a business and pulling out of the market.

- **Risk retention** means accepting the risk, in the expectation of making a return. When risks are retained, they should be managed, to ensure that unnecessary risks are not taken and that the total exposure to the risk is contained within acceptable limits.

© International Financial Publishing Limited

Risk appetite and risk retention

The choice between avoiding risks and accepting risk depends on risk appetite. This was described in an earlier chapter. Risk appetite is the amount of risk that an entity is willing to accept by investing in business activities, in order to obtain the expected returns from the business.

Risk appetite varies from one company to another. Some companies are willing to take fairly large risks whereas others are 'risk averse'. In general, companies expect higher returns by taking larger risks.

Risk appetite should be established by the board of directors, which should formulate a policy for strategic risk/business risk. Limits to strategic risks can be expressed in several ways.

■ The board of directors might indicate the risks that it is not prepared to accept, where risks should be avoided. For example, a water supply company might establish a policy of not investing water supply operations in any other country, because it considers the risks too great.

■ Risk limits can be established in terms of the maximum new investment that will be approved in each area of business activity.

■ As indicated in an earlier chapter, a risk dashboard might be used as a method of establishing appetite for particular risks and for monitoring residual risks.

It is easy to think of 'risk' as something undesirable, to be avoided. This attitude to risk focuses on downside risk. It is important to recognise that risk is unavoidable in business and that risks must be taken in order to make profits and a return on investment.

A key aspect of risk management is therefore managing the level of risk and:

■ deciding which risks are acceptable and which are not: setting risk limits

■ communicating the policy on risk, and

■ monitoring risks, and taking appropriate measures to prevent the risks from becoming excessive.

Variations in risk appetite between different companies

Risk appetite varies between different companies, and might vary according to the size, structure and development of the business.

■ Small companies are often more entrepreneurial than larger companies, and are willing to take bigger risks in order to succeed and grow. Entrepreneurial business leaders are associated with risk-taking. The leaders of small businesses might consider that they can take risks because:

- The directors of the company are also its owners; therefore they are not accountable to other investors for the risks that they take.

- In small companies, the risk of loss is limited by the size of the company. The worst that can happen is that the company will fail and go into liquidation. If the company is small and does not have large amounts of financing, this risk might be acceptable.

- In large companies with a high value, large risks will often be avoided if they threaten to reduce value significantly.

■ On the other hand, large companies can afford to take bigger risks than small companies when they are well-diversified. For example, a large bank can accept the credit risk from a major borrower, because if the loan turns into a bad debt, the bank's total profits might not be affected significantly.

■ As companies become larger, with a hierarchical management structure, they might become more bureaucratic. Bureaucracies are often the opposite of entrepreneurial businesses, because they are risk-averse. Managers are unwilling to take on risk, and because of the hierarchical nature of the management structure it might be difficult to promote a culture of risk awareness and embed risk within the management processes.

■ Business risk is often higher in markets where conditions are volatile and subject to continual and unpredictable change. When a new market emerges, risks are high. Companies investing in the new market must have an appetite for taking on the high risk because they expect the potential benefits to be large. As a market matures, it becomes more stable and more predictable. Volatility falls and there is less risk. As a consequence, the risk appetite of companies operating in a developed and mature market could be fairly low.

© International Financial Publishing Limited

CHAPTER

12

Ethical theories

Contents

Ethics and accountants

- Introduction
- Moral dilemmas
- Acting in an ethical way: moral philosophy

1 Ethics and accountants

1.1 Introduction

Ethics is about morality, and acting in a way that is morally justified. Most individuals develop a sense of morality, and act in accordance with what they consider 'right' and 'wrong'. However, opinions about what is 'right' and 'wrong' can differ enormously.

Ethics apply to organisations as well as to individuals and groups of people. Companies might be driven by the profit motive, and all their actions might be determined by doing whatever is necessary to maximise profits. On the other hand, companies might recognise the need – and the benefits – of acting in an ethical way.

Accountants – both students and qualified professionals – are expected to behave in accordance with professional codes of ethics, and to maintain standards of moral behaviour that are 'expected' from a professional body.

Personal ethics, business ethics and professional ethics are all relevant to how an accountant should behave.

1.2 Moral dilemmas

In practice, there are often pressures on an individual at work to 'bend the rules' and act in a way that is not ethical. Unethical behaviour might be illegal, but it is often 'legal but immoral'. Pressures to act unethically can create a moral dilemma – what is the right thing to do?

Sometimes it is not clear what the right course of action should be. When an individual thinks that something might be 'wrong', he could be faced with a decision about what to do. Making a moral or ethical decision might not be easy, especially when colleagues or bosses do not agree with you and will not listen to what you have to say.

Some individuals might take the view that when they are at work, they act according to a different set of rules and with a different moral outlook, compared to the way they think and behave in their private life. This view can be used to justify decisions or actions at work that are unethical, on the grounds that 'business is different'. This is not a view that accountants should take.

© International Financial Publishing Limited

Accountants are expected to act with professional ethics, and should be prepared to make difficult choices (if necessary) when faced with a moral dilemma.

 Example

You work as an accountant for a company that exports electronic equipment. You have been asked to prepare the export documents and invoice for an export order to a customer in Country X. You are aware that the customer in Country X is an agent for an organisation in Country Y. Because of a civil war in Country Y, your country's government has placed a complete ban on exports of goods to Country Y. What should you do?

The problem here is that you know, or have a strong suspicion, that your company is acting illegally. But the decision to sell the equipment was taken by someone else in your company, and the company's management presumably know what they are doing.

You are an employee of the company, so you might think that you should get on with your job and do what you have been ordered.

However, the action by your company in exporting goods to Country Y (through Country X) would probably be illegal, and would certainly be unethical. Whatever action is appropriate for you to take, the option of doing nothing, because it is 'none of your business', is unsuitable and inappropriate.

Accountants must deal with moral dilemmas when they arise, and doing nothing is not normally a satisfactory option.

1.3   Acting in an ethical way: moral philosophy

As an accountant, you need to recognise the need to behave in an ethical way. If you do not intend to act ethically in your work, you do not deserve to be an accountant!

To understand how to act ethically, it is necessary to have some understanding of ethics, how ethical codes of behaviour are established and maintained.

It is also useful to recognise a link between ethical behaviour and good corporate governance. Good corporate governance is associated with integrity, honesty and transparency. These are ethical qualities in business.

It is also important to recognise that individuals – and businesses – have differing views about 'right' and 'wrong'. We might think that we know what is right, but others might disagree strongly. Differences in ethical views can be very large between different communities and cultures.

- There is general agreement that some actions are 'wrong' and unethical. It is wrong to steal and wrong to commit murder.
- Many individuals take the view that war is 'wrong', but others might think that war is sometimes necessary to achieve a desirable and morally-worthwhile objective.

- There are strong differences of opinion on difficult moral issues such as abortion, euthanasia and medical research on animals.

- There are probably strong differences on opinion on many other issues. Is it wrong for a government to torture a 'terrorist' in order to obtain information that might reduce the risk of more terrorist attacks and deaths of civilians? Is it wrong to tell a lie to your boss at work in order to protect a colleague from dismissal for a minor disciplinary offence?

Moral philosophy

Moral philosophy is concerned with explaining the nature of ethics and morality, and with providing a justification for actions that are taken by individuals (and organisations). The remainder of this chapter describes briefly the differing views of some moral philosophers.

© International Financial Publishing Limited

Ethical theories of relativism and absolutism

- Absolutism
- Relativism

---

2   Ethical theories of relativism and absolutism

Moral philosophers do not agree on the nature of morality. Two opposing views are 'absolutism' and 'relativism'.

2.1   Absolutism

The ethical theory of absolutism, or moral absolutism, is that there are absolute moral standards against which the morality of actions can be judged. 'Right' and 'wrong' are recognised by objective standards that apply universally, to everyone. Plato was a philosopher who argued in favour of moral absolutism and in 'good' that always holds its value.

Absolutism might be associated with religious morality, but an individual can have an absolutist view of morality without being religious. For example, an individual might believe that slavery, war, child abuse and the death penalty are all morally wrong and cannot be justified under any circumstances.

2.2   Relativism

The ethical theory of relativism rejects the absolutist view. It states that there is no objective or absolute moral truth, and there are no universal standards of moral behaviour. There are two aspects to relativism:

- Descriptive ethical relativism. This is the view that different cultures and societies have different ethical systems and cultures. 'Right' and 'wrong' are concepts that relate to the particular culture. (There is no universal rule about right and wrong.)
- Normative ethical relativism. The beliefs or moral values within each culture are right within that culture. It is impossible to judge the values of another culture externally or objectively. Moral values of a culture can only be judged from within the culture.

Relativism accepts that ethical behaviour cannot be judged objectively. What is right and what is wrong can also vary according to circumstances.

J L Mackie is a fairly recent moral philosopher who supported the relativist view. He argued that ethical values and moral judgements are a human invention, which are imposed on society by 'institutions'.

Example

You might have your own view about which of these different approaches to making moral judgements is correct, absolutism or relativism.

Suppose that a manager is given confidential information by an employee which he promises to keep confidential and not to disclose to anyone else.

In your opinion, would there be any circumstances in which the manager might break his promise and disclose the confidential information to someone else, without the permission of the employee?

- The manager might take the view that having given a promise, he must keep it. A promise is given with the intention of keeping it, and there are no circumstances in which the manager would disclose the information to anyone else, without the prior permission of the employee. This would be an absolutist view of ethics.

- The manager might take the view that, having given his promise, there could be situations in which the information could be given to someone else, without permission from the employee. This would be unethical behaviour.

- The manager might give a promise not to disclose the confidential information to anyone else, but in giving his promise he might tell the employee that there are certain circumstances in which he might feel obliged to give the information to someone else (and give an indication of what those circumstances might be, such as legal reasons). In this situation, the manager would be saying that the right thing to do could depend on the circumstances and situation. This would be a relativist view of ethics.

It is therefore possible to take a moral position based on either an absolutist or a relativist view of morality. It is also possible to act unethically, from both an absolutist and a relativist point of view.

© International Financial Publishing Limited

Kohlberg's stages of moral development

- The six stages of moral reasoning and development
- Pre-conventional level of morality
- Conventional level of morality
- Post-conventional level of morality
- The Heinz dilemma
- Criticisms of Kohlberg's ideas

---

3 Kohlberg's stages of moral development

3.1 The six stages of moral reasoning and development

Kohlberg is an American moral philosopher who developed a theory of moral behaviour, which was first published 1958. His theory attempted to explain the reasoning that makes individual make their decisions when faced with a moral dilemma.

He argued that all individuals go through stages in their moral development. He identified six development stages that an individual might go through, although most individuals do not go through all six in their life.

- The six stages are progressive. Individuals start at Stage 1 and work upwards through higher stages as their life progresses.
- Each higher stage of moral reasoning is better at dealing with moral dilemmas than earlier stages.
- It is extremely rare for an individual, having reached one stage, to fall back to a lower stage of moral reasoning.
- However, individuals do not act at all times at the highest stage of moral development that they have reached.
- Individuals cannot 'jump' stages, or miss any stage of development. For example, an individual cannot go from Stage 3 to Stage 5 without first going through Stage 4.

Kohlberg argued that the moral response of an individual to any moral dilemma or decision can be identified with one of the six stages.

He divided the six stages of moral development into three levels, as follows.

Level of morality	Stage	
Pre-Conventional	1	Obedience and punishment
	2	Self-interest: individualism and exchange
Conventional	3	Inter-personal accord and conformity: good boy, nice girl attitude
	4	Maintaining social order
Post-conventional	5	Social contract
	6	Universal ethical principles

Each of these stages will be explained in more detail.

3.2 Pre-conventional level of morality

A pre-conventional level of moral reasoning is common in children, although it can also be found in adults. Kohlberg called this level of reasoning pre-conventional because individuals at Stages 1 and 2 do not yet see themselves as members of society, and their moral reasoning is based entirely on 'self'.

Stage 1: Obedience and punishment orientation

At Stage 1, individuals judge right and wrong on the basis of the direct consequences for them of the actions they take.

- An action is bad if the individual knows that he (or she) will be punished for it. The worse the punishment, the greater the moral wrong.

- An action is good if the individual knows that he will receive some benefit.

The individual believes that there are powerful authorities who are able to give rewards and punishments for behaviour.

Stage 2: Individualism and exchange

At Stage 2, the individual (often a child) recognises that there is no single view of what is right and what is wrong. Different individuals have different points of view. Each individual is also free to pursue his or her own personal interests, and will therefore want to do what is in his or her own **best interest**.

When faced with a moral dilemma, the individual's decision is based on: 'What's in it for me?'

The individual might show an interest in other people, but only to the extent that other people might help to further his own interests. A typical view in dealing with other people is; 'You help me and I will help you'. ('You scratch my back and I'll scratch yours.')

Concern for others has nothing to do with loyalty to the other person, respect or wanting to help them. It is based entirely on concern for oneself.

3.3 Conventional level of morality

The conventional level of moral reasoning is typical of adolescents and adults. When individuals think in a conventional way, they judge the morality of actions by comparing the actions with the conventional views and expectations of society.

Stage 3: Good interpersonal relationships

Individuals now enter society and see morality as more than making deals for personal benefit. They believe that they should live up to the expectations of family, friends and the community. They are aware of the approval or disapproval that they receive from other people, and try to live up to their expectations. They enjoy respect and gratitude, and their moral outlook is based on how this will be obtained. They want to be a 'good boy' or a 'nice girl'.

© International Financial Publishing Limited

Good behaviour means having good motives and feelings of love, trust and concern for others. The actions of another person are often judged by the reasoning: 'He means well....'

Stage 4: Maintaining social order

The moral reasoning at Stage 3 is based largely on interpersonal relationships and feelings, with family members and close friends, where it is possible to get to know the feelings and opinions of the other person very well, and try to help them.

At Stage 4, the individual is concerned with society as a whole, and the need to maintain social order. The focus is on respect for social conventions, authority and obeying the law, because these are important for maintaining society.

3.4 Post-conventional level of morality

The post-conventional level of morality is also called the 'principled' level. The individual now realises that he is a person with his own views, and not just a member of society. The individual does not accept that social conventions are necessarily correct. However, this is a higher level of moral development than the pre-conventional level, because the individual takes a principled view, not a purely selfish view of right and wrong.

Stage 5: Social contract orientation

At Stage 5, individuals think about society differently from the conventional way. They take the view that a good society is one in which there is a 'social contract' in which everyone works towards the common benefit of society. They recognise that people are different and have the right to their own views and opinions. However, all rational-minded people should agree about two things:

1   All people should have certain basic rights that society will protect, such as life and freedom.

2   There should be some form of democratic procedure for changing laws that are unfair and for improving society.

At Stage 5 people talk about 'morality' and 'rights' from their own individual perspective, recognising that other people might disagree (subject to the two points above). In contrast, individuals at Stage 4 might talk about 'morality' and 'rights' because they belong to a social group (such as a religious group) that supports these concepts. Stage 4 individuals believe in 'rights' because they are conforming to their group, not because they have reached their moral viewpoint individually.

Stage 6: Universal ethical principles

Kohlberg suggested that individuals **very rarely** reach Stage 6 of moral development. At this stage, moral reasoning is based on abstract 'universal' ethical principles. The individual queries the validity of laws, and considers that laws are only valid if they are based on justice. Individuals have an obligation to disobey unjust laws.

An individual makes moral decisions because they are right, not because they are a means to an end, or because the action is legal or expected.

There are universal principles of justice requiring that all people should be treated impartially, in an equal manner and with dignity. For example, it is morally wrong to vote for a law that helps some people but hurts others.

3.5 The Heinz dilemma

Kohlberg used a number of fictional case studies involving a moral dilemma, to establish the stage of moral development and reasoning that an individual had reached. One of these case studies, the Heinz dilemma, provides a good illustration of Kohlberg's analysis.

In this example, you should note that individuals at the same stage of moral development can reach differing views of 'right' and 'wrong'. Kohlberg was interested in the moral reasoning that individuals use to justify their opinions, rather than the actual decision that they reach through their reasoning.

The case study

The Heinz dilemma is based on the fictional case of a man, Heinz, whose wife is suffering from cancer and close to death. There is one drug that doctors think might save her. This is a drug that a scientist in the same town has recently discovered. The drug is expensive to produce, but the price charged for the drug by the scientist is ten times its production cost. The scientist paid $200 to make the drug and was charging $2,000 for a small dose.

Heinz wanted to buy the drug for his wife, but had very little money. He went to everyone he knew to obtain the money to buy the drug, but could raise only $1,000. He told the scientist about his wife's medical condition and that he could raise $1,000. He asked the scientist to let him buy the drug at that price, or let him pay the rest of the money later. The scientist refused, saying that he had discovered the drug and intended to make money from producing it. Heinz, in desperation, broke into the scientist's premises to steal the drug for his wife.

The questions asked by Kohlberg were:
(1)   Should Heinz have broken into the scientist's premises to steal the drug?
(2)   Why, or why not?

Analysis of the case study

For Kohlberg, it was not important what an individual would do in the situation faced by Heinz, but how he or she reached an opinion. The moral reasoning was more important than the decision or action that results from it.

Examples of some of the arguments that might be used by individuals at each stage of moral development are set out below.

     © International Financial Publishing Limited

Stage of moral development	Possible reasoning
1 Obedience and punishment	Heinz should not steal the drug because if he does he will be put in prison. This would be very bad. *Or* Heinz should steal the drug. It only cost $200 and he offered to pay a lot more. He was only stealing the drug, nothing else.
2 Self-interest	Heinz should not steal the drug, because if he does he will go to prison. Prison is a terrible place and he will suffer a lot if he goes there, more than if his wife dies. *Or* Heinz should steal the drug, because if he does he will be very happy, even if he has to spend some time in jail.
3 Interpersonal accord	Heinz should not steal the drug because stealing is bad and Heinz is not a criminal. *Or* You can't blame him. He did everything he could first without breaking the law. *Or* Heinz should steal the drug. He is a good husband and his wife will expect him to do it.
4 Maintaining social order	Heinz should not steal the drug because stealing is against the law. *Or* Heinz should steal the drug, but he should also face up to the consequences and take the punishment for the crime. You can see why he did it, but breaking the law has its consequences. You can't let criminals go around doing whatever they want.
5 Social contract	Heinz should not steal he drug because the scientist has a right to fair compensation. Even though his wife is near death, Heinz is not justified in stealing. *Or* Heinz should steal the drug, regardless of the law, because everyone has a right to life.
6 Universal ethical principles	Heinz should not steal the drug. If he does, this means that someone else will not be able to buy it and that person might need it just as much as Heinz's wife. Their lives are just as important. *Or* Heinz should steal the drug, because saving a human life is much more important than respect for someone's property rights.

3.6   Criticisms of Kohlberg's ideas

Some of the criticisms of Kohlberg's ideas are interesting, and have relevance to concepts of business ethics (especially for global companies) and professional ethics (especially for professional bodies with global membership).

■ Some critics have argued against the view that post-conventional morality exists or is at a higher level of moral development. At Stages 5 and 6, individuals put their own principles above society and the law, which is a dangerous moral stance to take.

■ Other critics have argued that Kohlberg's views have a cultural bias, because his ideas are based on Western philosophy. His views might not apply to non-Western philosophies and cultures.

■ Carol Gilligan (1982) argued that Kohlberg's views had a gender bias, and were based on a male view of the world. Kohlberg argued that moral thinking is based on reasoning linked to a sense of justice – rules, rights and abstract principles. Gilligan argued that for women, morality and ethical views are not based on these concepts of justice, but on concern for interpersonal relationships and the ethics of care and compassion.

© International Financial Publishing Limited

Ethics: deontological and teleological approaches

- Deontological approach: the ideas of Kant
- Teleological approach (consequentialist approach)

4 Ethics: deontological and teleological approaches

The absolutist and relativist views of ethics are concerned with moral reasoning and ethical opinions. These views lead on to the question of how should individuals apply their moral judgements in making decisions and taking action.

There are two differing approaches to ethical decisions:

- the deontological approach
- the teleological approach, also called the consequentialist approach.

4.1 Deontological approach: the ideas of Kant

A deontological approach to ethical decisions is based on an absolutist view of ethics. This approach is closely associated with the 18th Century German philosopher, Kant.

Deontology is a belief in a sense of duty. It is based on the view that there are universal moral laws, and individuals have a duty to obey them, in all the actions that they take and irrespective of what the consequences might be. These universal laws or principles are binding on everyone: the absolute set of moral standards applies to us all. Actions are right or wrong in themselves, and there should be no regard for the consequences. For example, it is always wrong for a government to torture a captured terrorist in order to obtain information, even if the consequence might be that there will be more terrorist attacks and more deaths of civilians.

Kant and the categorical imperative

Kant argued that an action is morally right only if the person taking the action is motivated by 'good will'. In other words, an action is morally right only if it is done from a sense of duty and for reasons of principle.

He developed the concept of the categorical imperative. He argued that we can judge whether an action is morally right by asking whether it would be consistent with the categorical imperative.

The categorical imperative can be expressed as follows:

- Act so that you can want the principle for your action to become a universal law. At a simple level, this means judging whether an action is moral by asking what would happen if everyone behaved in exactly the same way.

- Act so that you treat other people as an end in themselves, never as a means to an end.

For example, Kant argued that it is always morally wrong to tell a lie. Imagine what would happen if everyone told lies: trust between people would come to an end. You cannot argue that sometimes it is morally right to tell a 'white' lie in order to achieve a just result: this would mean that the person who has been told the lie has been used as a means to achieving the just result.

The same argument applies to torture. It can never be morally right to torture someone. What would happen if everyone used torture to get what they want. By torturing a person in order to save the lives of other people, the tortured person is used as a means to an end, not as an end in himself.

4.2 Teleological approach (consequentialist approach)

The teleological approach, also called the consequentialist approach, to moral action is based on the relativist view of ethics.

This approach takes the view that the morality of an action should be judged by its consequences. If the consequences are 'good', the act is morally correct. 'The end justifies the means.'

An example of the teleological approach is **utilitarianism**. This is a view of morality most closely associated with the 19th Century British philosopher John Stuart Mill. Mill argued that an act is 'right' if it brings the greatest amount of good to the greatest number of people.

The teleological approach to ethical decisions can therefore be explained as follows:

(1) Actions in themselves do not have an intrinsic moral value.

(2) The moral value of an action is determined by its consequences (not the act itself).

(3) Using reason, it is possible to calculate the costs and the benefits of an action, to determine whether or not it is morally correct.

Taking this approach, for example, it would be argued that telling a lie can be justified and would normally be acceptable provided that the consequences are 'good' or 'benevolent'.

Teleological ethics and the profit motive

Teleological ethics can be used to justify the profit motive in business. It can be argued that when a business is profitable, many people benefit. Shareholders benefit from higher returns and dividends; employees benefit from the employment that a profitable business provides; customers benefit from the goods and services that a profitable business is able to provide (that it would not be able to provide if it did not make a profit); the general public benefits from the benefits to the economy from profitable businesses and additional economic activity.

© International Financial Publishing Limited

Teleological ethics can also be used to justify actions in business that might otherwise seem morally 'dubious' or 'wrong', such as:

- cutting costs (including making employees redundant)
- down-sizing (which involves making people redundant)
- doing business in a country with a dubious political system, such as a tyrannical government.

Ethical decision-making models

- System development ethics
- The purpose of ethical decision-making models
- Tucker's 5 question model
- The American Accounting Association model

5 Ethical decision-making models

5.1 System development ethics

Business entities and non-business entities are exposed to ethical risk. This is the risk that some of its managers or employees will act in a way that is unethical, and the entity will suffer some loss or harm as a consequence. There is a risk to the entity itself from deception or fraud by employees. In addition, there is a risk of unethical action by some individuals causing harm to other – customers, other employees, suppliers, the community, and so on.

It might be argued that ethical risk can be minimised by recruiting and training individuals with strong moral character.

System development ethics, however, is based on the view that recruiting and training morally-strong individuals is not sufficient. In order to act in a moral way, individuals need support from the systems they work in, and the environment provided by their employer.

The employer should give clear guidance and moral support to its employees. 'Personal improvement and character-building can only occur in morally-supportive environments that are rationally-planned and maintained.'

Codes of corporate ethics and codes of professional conduct help to provide the environment that individuals need.

5.2 The purpose of ethical decision-making models

Guidance about ethical decision-making can also be provided by a decision-making model. The purpose of an ethical decision-making model is to help individuals to assess, before they make a decision, whether the decision is ethically correct.

These models do not deal with the problem of what is right or wrong. They assume that the basis for judging right and wrong is understood. This means that they could be used with either a deontological or a teleological approach to ethics, although a teleological approach is much more common in business.

© International Financial Publishing Limited

Several ethical decision-making models have been developed for use in a business context, and can also be applied to professional activities such as accounting. Two such models are:

■ Tucker's 5 question model

■ the American Accounting Association model.

5.3 Tucker's 5 question model

Tucker's 5 question model for ethical decision-making in business is based on the view that the profit motive is justified, and the purpose of decision-making in business should be to make a profit. However, profits should be made in an ethical way.

In order to be ethically correct, business decisions and actions should be legal. Activities outside the law by a business cannot be correct. Business should also be conducted in a fair way, without deception or other 'under-hand' acts. For example, competitors should be treated with respect, and customers and employees should be treated in a fair way. Tucker's model is also based on the view that decisions should not be taken in business if they do not support sustainable business or could be damaging to the environment.

The 5 question model involves asking five questions before making a business decision. If the answer to all five questions is 'Yes', the decision is ethically sound. The five questions about a decision are:

(1) Is it profitable?

(2) Is it legal?

(3) Is it fair?

(4) Is it right?

(5) Is it sustainable or environmentally sound?

5.4 The American Accounting Association model

The American Accounting Association developed a model for ethical decision-making in 1990. It is based on a teleological approach, and is consistent with professional ethical guidelines.

The AAA model is based on a seven-step approach to decision-making.

Step	Question to ask	Comment
1	What are the facts?	It is important to establish all the relevant facts. It is difficult to make a correct decision without having a clear understanding of the facts.
2	What are the ethical issues?	The decision-maker should identify what moral issues are involved (if any). What is the moral dilemma?

3	What moral principles, values or 'norms' are relevant to the decision?	The decision-maker should consider the ethical principles or values that ought to be considered in reaching the decision.
4	What are the alternative courses of action for the decision-maker?	
5	Which course of action (or courses of action) seems best, because it is consistent with the moral principles and values identified in Step 3?	Each course of action should be assessed according to whether it is morally correct. Each choice is judged against the principles and values that should be applied in the case.
6	What are the consequences of each possible course of action?	
7	What is the decision?	The decision-maker makes an ethical choice.

Example

A company makes and sells a range of products. One product, the mega-widget, has been produced for about ten years and has been very successful. It is still popular with customers, but profits have fallen to the point where the company is now losing money on the product.

The fall in profits has been due to rising costs. Due to competitive pressures in the market, increases in the selling price of the mega-widget have not kept pace with the increases in cost.

At a management meeting to discuss the problem, it was suggested that some technical alterations could be made to the mega-widget that would reduce costs substantially, but the expected useful life of the product would fall by over 25%. It would be necessary to prevent customers from finding out about any reduction in product quality, because they might switch to buying the products of competitors.

It was agreed that if the technical alterations are not made, the company would have to cease production and sales of the mega-widget. If the technical alterations are made, the product should become profitable again, at least for the next few years.

Required
What decision should management take: should the technical alterations be made to the product, or not? Management are expected to act in an ethical way by the company's board of directors. (You should ignore reputational risk in this example.)

© International Financial Publishing Limited

Answer

We could use an ethical decision-making model to help with making a decision.

Tucker's 5 question model

(1) Is the decision profitable? Making technical alterations to the product would improve profits, so the answer is: Yes.

(2) Is the decision legal? There is no law against making technical alterations to the product. As long as the company does not deceive customers with its advertising and marketing, making the technical alterations would be within the law.

(3) Is the decision fair? It is fair in the sense that all customers would be treated in the same way, and customers would have the choice to buy the products of competitors. However, it is not fair in the sense that customers would be encouraged to buy an inferior product, without knowing about the reduction in quality, at the same price as before when the product was better.

(4) Is the decision sustainable and environmentally sound? There are no indications to suggest that there is a problem with the environment or sustainable business.

(5) Is the decision right? The moral problem is that the company would be making changes to the product without informing customers. Managers might think that this wrong, but at the same time they would be under pressure to make profits for the company.

Using the Tucker model, the issue in this case might concern whether it is morally acceptable to withhold product information from customers. It would help managers in making their decision to know the ethical stance of the company towards its treatment of customers. If the company had a code of corporate ethics, this might help them to reach their decision.

American Accounting Association model

A similar conclusion might be reached using the American Accounting Association model.

(1) The facts are given in the question.

(2) The ethical issue is whether to reduce the quality of a product without informing customers.

(3) What are the ethical principles and values that are relevant to the moral dilemma? A key principle here relates to the treatment of customers.

(4) What are the alternative courses of action? These are to make the technical alterations to the product, or to stop making it. We do not know what the consequences of shutting down production might be (for example, whether it might lead to redundancies amongst employees).

(5) Which actions are consistent with the principles and values in (3)? Ceasing to produce the mega-widget would be consistent with the principle of fair dealing for the customer.

(6) The consequence of the decision to make the change is to increase profits. Ceasing production of the product should result in no further losses. However, it is more likely that in the long run the trust of customers in the company would be maintained. (There is a reputational risk to consider, in the

event that customers find out about the technical alteration, or find that the items that they buy have a shorter useful life than before.)

(7)   What is the decision? Management would be assisted by clear guidance from the company on its ethical stance. If the company has a code of ethics that insists on fair treatment and due consideration for customers, the technical alteration should not be made. Production of the product should be brought to an end.

This is just one example to illustrate how ethical decision-making models might be applied to reach an ethical business decision. You might find that it your examination, you are required to apply an ethical decision-making model to another case or problem in order to make a recommendation about what a particular decision should be.

© International Financial Publishing Limited

CHAPTER

13

Ethics and social responsibility

Contents
1   Ethics, governance and social responsibility
2   Seven positions on social responsibility
3   The cultural context of ethics

> ## Ethics, governance and social responsibility
>
> - Introduction
> - Shareholder theory
> - Stakeholder theory
> - Social contract theory
> - Johnson and Scholes: four possible ethical stances for a business entity
> - Ethical stance: personal and corporate

1 Ethics, governance and social responsibility

1.1 Introduction

Business entities operate within society. They interact with their local communities. Their employees, customers and suppliers are all members of the society in which the entity operates.

The responsibilities of a business entity towards society were considered in earlier chapters on corporate governance. There is a link between ethics, corporate governance and social responsibility.

1.2 Shareholder theory

The shareholder theory of corporate governance is based on the view that the objective of a company is to maximise value for its shareholders. It was suggested in the previous chapter that a teleological approach to ethics can be used to justify the profit motive in business, so that the objective of maximising shareholder wealth (within constraints of ethical behaviour) is perfectly legitimate.

Shareholders, especially shareholders of large stock market companies, often trade their shares. Some are investors in the company for the long term and others invest only for the short term, hoping to make a quick profit from a favourable movement in the share price.

- Long-term shareholders are likely to support the view that the company should invest for long-term growth. If necessary, short-term profits should be sacrificed in order to invest more retained profits in the business.
- Short-term shareholders are likely to support a policy of high dividend payments and measures to boost short term profits (in the hope that this will lead to a higher share price).

1.3 Stakeholder theory

The stakeholder theory of corporate governance is that a company's directors owe a duty to all major stakeholders in the company, including not just employees and customers, but also communities and society as a whole.

© International Financial Publishing Limited

This concept of governance can be linked to a deontological approach to business ethics. This would argue that all individuals have a basic moral right to be treated by business entities in a way that respects their interests and concerns. Employees should not be treated simply as a means to achieving the end of higher company profits.

The rights of stakeholders can be analysed in terms of stakeholder groups (employees, customers, shareholders and so on) rather than considering each stakeholder individually. The possession of intrinsic moral rights by stakeholders creates corresponding ethical duties for a company to respect to those rights.

1.4 Social contract theory

There is also a social contract theory of corporate governance. This is based on the view that members of society give legal recognition to a company. They allow the company to exist and act as a legal person within society. They also allow a company to use land and resources, and to hire members of society as employees.

The company therefore has an obligation to pursue the objective of making profits only in ways that will also enhance the material well-being of society as a whole. Profit-making must be ethical and a company must consider the interests of society in the decisions and actions that it takes.

1.5 Johnson and Scholes: four possible ethical stances for a business entity

Johnson and Scholes (2002) have suggested that companies can take any of four possible ethical stances. These are consistent with the differing views of corporate governance. The four ethical stances are to focus on:

- Maximising short-term shareholder interests (the 'least ethical' of the four stances)
- Maximising long-term shareholder interests
- Multiple stakeholder obligations: recognising obligations to different stakeholder groups
- Being a **shaper of society**.

Shaper of society

'Shaping society' means changing conditions in society and altering the way that society operates and perceives itself. In the past (and probably also the present), technology has been a significant shaper of society, affecting how and where we all live. Media companies have also been cited as important shapers of society in the past 100 years or so, because film has changed the way in which society viewed itself.

Companies control resources and make decisions about the future of technology. They are instrumental in shaping society.

Johnson and Scholes argued that ethical companies recognise this role that they have, and their decisions and actions are taken with a view to creating benefits for society and improving the well-being of society.

1.5 Ethical stance: personal and corporate

An ethical stance or posture is a position that someone takes on an ethical issue. Both individuals and organisations can develop a conscious ethical stance on certain issues, their decisions and actions are affected by it. For example, a company might take the view that it will not do business with certain types of customer or supplier. Here are just two examples.

■ Some retailers in the UK refuse to buy goods from suppliers in other countries that use slave labour or child labour. This ethical stance might be taken partly out of self-interest (reputation risk), but it might also be guided by ethical concerns.

■ In 2006, the British Jewellers Association took an ethical stance against the sourcing of diamonds from countries (such as the Congo and Sierra Leone) where fighting over diamonds has led to civil war and widespread killing. It calls these diamonds 'blood diamonds' and is attempting to eliminate the trade in these diamonds in the UK.

The ethical stance in a company comes from the moral values and ethical stance of key individuals who work within the company, and from the corporate culture. The ethical aspects of culture are discussed later.

The fictitious example below shows how personal ethics can influence the ethical stance of a company, which in turn might have an effect on its overall business and marketing strategies.

 Example

Rick and Tina used to be executives in a large company that made soft drinks. They have now set up their own company to make fruit drinks using a recipe devised by Tina.

They wanted to set up their own company so that they could do something that they enjoyed and believed in. During their time working for the large company, each of them accumulated substantial personal wealth; so from their own company all they wanted to do was avoid heavy losses after the initial set-up costs and earn a reasonable living. They were more interested in building the business than in making quick profits and returns.

Each of them had strong moral views about showing respect to other people and protecting the environment.

As owner-founders of the company, they had a vital role in establishing the general culture of the company, and its ethical stance on various issues.

© International Financial Publishing Limited

- They devised a mission statement for the company. This was to produce a healthy drink product that would contain only natural ingredients, and to operate as an ethical company with concern for its employees and the environment.

- The business strategies of the company were based on the production of a healthy food drink in a way that is 'friendly' to the environment.

    - The company invested in technology that enabled them to produce their own cartons and bottles from recycled plastic and glass. About 60% of the raw materials in the bottles and cartons for the drinks came from recycled materials.

    - The company uses a van for deliveries that can run on bio-fuel.

    - The company sources its energy from a renewable energy supplier.

- Employment policies were also driven by ethical concerns. Rick and Tina wanted their company to be a 'good employer to work for'. They have a small work force, but they promote teamwork, and provide generous pay, working conditions and holiday entitlements.

- The company also contributes in small ways to charity groups. For example, it provides drinks free of charge to local sports events run by different groups for handicapped people and young prison offenders.

A consequence of the strategies and policies of the company is that production costs are fairly high – higher than for the fruit drinks of competitors. However, the company is able to promote itself as a provider of healthy drinks with an ethical environmental policy. It was therefore able to position itself in a niche in the market as a 'high quality, high-price' brand.

Seven positions on social responsibility

- Responsibilities to society and to the environment
- 7-level classification by Gray, Owen and Adams

---

2   Seven positions on social responsibility

2.1   Responsibilities to society and to the environment

Traditional moral philosophy has been divided between the deontological and teleological approaches. A more recent philosophy is the environmental philosophy. This looks at the different ways in which different individuals and groups view society (and their responsibilities) and accept moral responsibility towards society.

Some individuals focus on ethical responsibilities towards other people. Others argue that individuals and entities have responsibilities not only towards other people in society, but also towards the earth and its environment.

2.2   7-level classification by Gray, Owen and Adams

Gray, Owen and Adams (1996) provided a framework for classifying different groups of people and their views of the relationship between business organisations and society. These can be used to analyse the ethical stance of business entities and their members (managers, employees, shareholders) towards society and social responsibility.

They identified seven levels or positions on social responsibility.

Level	Comment
1 Pristine capitalists	This position is dominant in the world of accounting and finance. The only responsibility of a company is to make money for its shareholders.
	This view is based on rational self-interest, and putting individual self-interest before the collective benefits of society as a whole. The market economy is a good thing. There are no environmental problems because human beings are inventive and adaptable: the market economy will find solutions to the world's environmental problems.
2 Expedients	This position is taken by people with a longer-term view, who recognise that economic success can only be achieved by companies by accepting certain social responsibilities.

   © International Financial Publishing Limited

3	**Proponents of the social contract**	These individuals believe that companies and other organisations exist at the will of society. They therefore have a responsibility and an obligation to respond to the needs of society.
		This is a right-based perspective in which the rights of all human beings are considered significant. Holders of this view would argue that government regulation might be necessary for the market economy, because free market prices do not properly reflect all the effects that companies have on society and its environment (for example, pollution and other environmental damage).
4	**Social ecologists**	Individuals taking this position are concerned for the social environment. They believe that companies and other large organisations have been responsible for creating social and environmental problems. They should therefore be held responsible for dealing with those problems and finding solutions to them.
5	**Socialists**	These individuals believe that there should be a significant re-adjustment in the ownership of assets and in the structure of society. They criticise all forms of domination, including the governments of a nation state, concentrated economic power (large companies) and authoritarianism.
6	**Radical feminists**	These individuals believe that society and social systems are dominated by an aggressive masculine view of the world. This is harmful and wrong. There is an urgent need for more feminine values to guide attitudes, such as care, compassion and co-operation.
7	**Deep ecologists/ deep greens**	These individuals are at the opposite extreme to pristine capitalists. They believe that human beings have no greater right to existence than any other form of life. Ethical decisions should be based on concerns for all forms of life.

To a greater or lesser extent, there is an acceptance of the views in positions 1 to 3 within business. Positions 4 to 7 are all based on a view that the world should be made into a better place, but to do this there must be a radical re-assessment of basic assumptions in society.

> ## The cultural context of ethics
>
> - Culture and ethics
> - Johnson and Scholes: the cultural web
> - Edgar Schein: three levels of culture
> - Culture, ethics and global companies

3 The cultural context of ethics

3.1 Culture and ethics

Culture has been defined as the 'shared beliefs, attitudes, norms, values and behaviour found among speakers of one language in one time period and in one geographical region.' This definition suggests that in order to share a common culture, people must speak a common language and live in the same geographical area. Culture might also change over time.

Companies (and other entities) also develop their own culture. The individuals who work in a company often develop cultural attitudes and habits that are unique to that company. Even global companies, in which employees do not share the same language or live in the same geographical area, can develop a culture of shared beliefs and attitudes.

There is a link between culture and ethics, because the culture in which people live shapes their ethical beliefs, attitudes and values.

Culture, ethics and corporate social responsibility

Corporate social responsibility (CSR) was described in an earlier chapter within the context of corporate governance, and the responsibilities of the board of directors (and a company) towards society. CSR is concerned with issues such as the interests and welfare of:

- employees
- customers
- communities in which the company operates
- the general public, and society as a whole.

Well-governed companies take a stand against crime and do not sanction criminal activities by their employees, in any country in which they operate.

In recent years there has been much greater awareness of environmental issues, and the role of companies in both damaging the environment and acting to protect the environment and create sustainable businesses.

© International Financial Publishing Limited

Attitudes to CSR are evident in the ethical stance that many companies now take on these issues, and ethical stance in turn is affected by the corporate culture.

3.2 Johnson and Scholes: the cultural web

Johnson and Scholes suggested that there is a cultural web within any organisation, which affects the way in which individuals understand the organisation in which they work. This understanding of their organisation called their 'paradigm' of the organisation. Employees find it difficult to think and act outside this paradigm.

The cultural web consists of six inter-related elements of culture within an organisation.

- **Routines and rituals**. Routines and rituals are 'the ways things are done around here'. Individuals get used to established ways of doing things.

- **Stories and myths**. Stories and myths are used to describe the history of an organisation, and to suggest the importance of certain individuals or events. They are passed by word of mouth. They help to create an impression of how the organisation got to where it is, and it can be difficult to challenge established myths and consider a need for a change of direction in the future.

- **Symbols**. Symbols can become a representation of the nature of the organisation. Examples of symbols might be a company car or helicopter, an office or building, a logo or a style of language.

- **Power structure**. Organisations are influenced by the individuals who are in a position of power. In many business organisations, power is obtained from management position. However, power can also come from personal influence, or experience and expertise.

- **Organisation structure**. The culture of an organisation is affected by its organisation and management structure. Hierarchical and bureaucratic organisations might find it particularly difficult to adapt to change and are often conservative in their outlook.

- **Control systems**. Performance measurement and reward systems within an organisation establish the views about what is important and what is not so important. Individuals will focus on performance that earns rewards. For example, it has been suggested that cash bonus systems help to create the profit-driven culture in investment banks.

The cultural web within a company shapes its corporate ethics.

3.3 Edgar Schein: three levels of culture

Schein had similar views about corporate culture. He suggested that employees working within a company have shared values, beliefs and ways of thinking: these interact with the policies, organisation structure and politics of the company's management system to create a corporate culture.

Schein also argued that organisation culture is strong because it is regarded as something that helps the company to succeed. An organisation culture is a set of assumptions that a group of people working together have invented or discovered by learning how to deal with problems that the organisation faces, internally and in its external environment. These assumptions work well enough to be considered valid; they are therefore 'taught' to individuals who join the organisation. New entrants therefore learn the culture of the organisation and become a part of that culture.

According to Schein, there are three levels of culture that members of an organisation acquire.

- **The outer skin**. At one level, the culture of a company is evident in what an observer can see by visiting the company, and in the values that it states. The facilities and surroundings in which employees work help to create culture. So too does the way that employees dress. Culture is also seen in the way that employees talk to each other and interact with each other. A company might have a formal code of ethical behaviour, which is intended to shape the attitudes of all its members. However, stated values and mission statements are often expressed in general terms, such as 'providing a service to the community' and 'providing the best quality of service to customers'.

- **An inner layer**. At this second level, the employees in a company share common views on specific issues. This layer of culture can be seen in the ethical stance that the company takes. Whereas the outer layer of culture is expressed in general terms, this inner layer is expressed in relation to specific issues, such as:

    - Should we trade with companies or governments in politically repressive countries?

    - Should we buy goods from suppliers who use slave labour or child labour?

- **The heart**. The third level of culture is the company's **paradigm**. This is a term for the shared assumptions and attitudes about what really matters, that are taken for granted and rarely discussed. These affect the way that the organisation sees itself and the environment in which it operates, and is the real 'core' culture of the organisation. Unlike mission statements and codes of ethics, a paradigm is not written down, and it is difficult to identify or explain. The 'paradigm' has also been described as the reason why the organisation exists. A police force exists to catch criminals, and a school exists as a place for learning.

Schein argued that changing corporate culture is very difficult. The 'outer skin' can be changed fairly easily, with a determined effort by management, but it is very difficult to change the paradigm.

The following example suggests that codes of corporate ethics cannot be made to work unless senior management enforces them and ensures that they are applied. The example can also be used as an illustration of how it is much more difficult to alter the paradigm of a company than the 'outer skin' of its culture.

© International Financial Publishing Limited

Example

In 2004 when James Young became CEO of a UK bank, the bank's reputation had been damaged by its associations with companies such as Enron and WorldCom, as a provider of both on-balance sheet and off-balance sheet finance.

Mr Young wanted to improve the image of the bank, which meant improving its cultural and ethical outlook. He introduced a code of conduct and the bank's executives world-wide were asked to adhere to this code. The code stated that the bank should aspire to be a company with the highest standards of ethical conduct and an organisation that people could trust.

In June 2005, there was a problem in Edinburgh on the bank's trading desk for European government bonds. The desk was under pressure to increase its profits, and the management decided to exploit a weakness in a Spanish-based electronic trading system for government bonds called PPQ. The trade involved selling a very large quantity of bonds early in the morning, sufficient to send bond prices falling sharply, then buying the bonds back at much lower prices later the same morning. The trade earned a profit of €23.7 million at the expense of other participants in the bond market.

Following this event, some banks refused to honour their commitment to make a market in the bonds on PPQ, and in the next three months, daily trading volumes on PPQ fell by 35%. This led to worries by European governments about whether they would be able to continue issuing bonds (to raise new finance) at a reasonable rate of interest.

Some governments reacted with anger against the bank and withdrew their business. In the UK, the Financial Services Authority fined the bank £12 million for failing to exercise due skill, care and diligence. The traders responsible for the trade were suspended.

In the bank, there had been a serious breach of its new code of conduct that customers, suppliers and competitors would be treated fairly. The change in culture that the code of conduct was intended to introduce had not reached the heart of the cultural thinking within the bank. The traders, after a brief suspension from work, returned to work. The bank admitted to bad ethical behaviour and poor professionalism, but top management did nothing, and no one within the bank was held responsible.

3.4 Culture, ethics and global companies

Global companies operate in many different countries and employ managers and other employees from diverse cultures.

It can be difficult for global companies to develop a single corporate culture. It is therefore difficult for the senior management of global companies to 'enforce' their view of business ethics on the entire organisation.

© International Financial Publishing Limited

Professional practice and codes of ethics

Contents	
1	Professions and the public interest
2	Corporate codes of ethics
3	Codes of ethics for accountants

Professions and the public interest
■ The nature of a profession
■ Acting professionally
■ Acting in the public interest
■ Influence of the accounting profession in business and government
■ Public expectations of the accountancy profession
■ Ethics and accountants: critical theory
■ Accountants and acting against the public interest

1 Professions and the public interest

1.1 The nature of a profession

The word 'professional' is associated with a highly-qualified group of individuals who carry out a particular type of highly-skilled work. Examples of professions are doctors and surgeons, dentists, lawyers, actuaries and accountants.

Each professional group is organised and regulated by a professional body. (In the UK, the professional bodies often have a royal charter. The accountancy profession has several different professional bodies.) The professional body has the power to:

■ admit new members to the profession

■ award qualifications to individuals who achieve a required standard of skill or competence

■ expel members from the profession, for unprofessional conduct.

It is often a legal requirement that certain aspects of the work of professionals must be performed by professionally-qualified people.

Professionals and their clients

The relationship between professionals and their clients is based on several perceptions of the nature of a professional person.

■ There is a **relationship of trust**. The client can trust the professional to act in a proper way, in accordance with a professional code of conduct. In return, the professional expects the client to place its trust in him (and her). For example, a client should not withhold relevant information from a professional that would affect his decisions or judgements.

■ There is an assurance that the professional has attained a minimum level of **expertise and competence**. This assurance is provided, in accountancy, by the requirements to (1) pass formal examinations in order to obtain a qualification, (2) have relevant work experience and (3) continue with professional development and training throughout the accountant's professional career.

© International Financial Publishing Limited

- There is also an implication in the professional-client relationship that the professional has more concern for the client than for his own self-interest. **The professional puts the client before himself**.

1.2 Acting professionally

Professionals are expected to act in a professional way. Professional behaviour means complying with relevant laws and obligations, including compliance with the code of conduct (including the code of ethics) of the relevant professional body.

Professional behaviour is commonly associated with:

- acting with integrity, and being honest and straight-dealing
- providing objective opinions and advice, free from bias, influence or conflicts of interest
- using specialist knowledge and skill at an appropriate level for the work
- confidentiality: respecting the confidentiality of information provided by clients
- avoiding any action that brings the reputation of the profession into disrepute
- compliance with all relevant laws and regulations.

The ACCA Code of Ethics and Conduct states that 'the principle of professional behaviour imposes an obligation on members to comply with relevant laws and regulations and avoid any action that may bring discredit to the profession.'

Example

Anton Rivers is the senior partner in a firm of accountants that specialises in preparing financial statements for clients, tax work and auditing. Mr Rivers has decided to advertise the services of his firm in the local newspaper.

The advertisement states that Rivers and Co is a highly experienced firm with numerous clients, including foreign and domestic companies. It adds that the services of the firm are of the highest standard, unrivalled by any other local firm of accountants.

His colleague challenges him by commenting that Rivers and Co does not have any foreign companies as a client. Mr Rivers replies that it is only an advertisement, and no one ever believes the marketing claims in advertisements.

Has Anton Rivers acted in a professional way? If not, why not?

Answer

Anton Rivers has breached the code of conduct of his profession, by:
- failing to act honestly (and with integrity), and
- by implication, criticising the work of other professionals.

The advertisement contains an untrue statement, that the firm has foreign companies as clients. This is dishonest.

The advertisement also states that the standards of service from the firm are better than those of any other firm in the area. This is a criticism of other accountancy professionals, and is not permitted by the professional codes of ethics.

1.3 Acting in the public interest

An aspect of professional bodies, which separates a profession from a trade, is that members of the profession are expected to act in the public interest. It is therefore a responsibility of the accountancy profession '**not to act exclusively to satisfy the needs of a particular client or employer**'.

When the demands or needs of a client or employer appear to be contrary to the public interest, accountants should consider the public interest.

So what is the public interest? Professional codes of ethics do not provide a clear definition, but it is usual to associate the public interest with matters such as:

- detecting and reporting any serious misdemeanour or crime
- protecting health and public safety
- preventing the public from being misled by a statement or action by an individual or an organisation
- exposing the misuse of public funds and corruption in government
- revealing the existence of any conflict of interests of those individuals who are in a position of power or influence.

1.4 Influence of the accounting profession in business and government

A function of the accounting profession is to record financial transactions and to report the financial performance and financial position of business entities and government organisations. Information about business and other organisations comes largely from accountants. Arguably, accountancy has an influence on business and government that is both:

- continuous and
- more extensive than any other profession.

Financial reporting

Accountants are involved in the preparation of financial statements, which are used by shareholders and other investors to assess companies and make their investment decisions. Financial reports are often used to prepare information about companies for other interested parties, such as the government (for tax purposes) and employees.

© International Financial Publishing Limited

Auditing

Accountants also check the financial statements of companies (and government organisations), and report on their 'accuracy' to shareholders or government. Shareholders rely on the opinion of the auditors to obtain reassurance that the financial statements give a true and fair view.

The need by investors for reliable financial reporting and auditing was discussed in an earlier chapter, in the context of corporate governance.

Management accounting

Management accountants provide information to management, to assist managers with decision-making. In many organisations, management accountants have extended their involvement with management information systems to the provision of strategic as well as shorter-term management information, and non-financial as well as financial information.

Tax

As tax advisers, accountants can help corporate clients to avoid payment of tax through tax avoidance schemes. A criticism of tax avoidance schemes is that they enable wealthy individuals and profitable companies to avoid paying tax, which means that the tax burden is shared by the poorer members of society.

Consultancy

Accountancy firms may provide consultancy services to a range of different clients. Major strategic decisions by government and companies might be influenced by the advice and recommendations from consultants. In the UK for example, the major accountancy firms have been involved in providing advice to the government on the privatisation of public services and the introduction of private capital into financing public investments.

Public sector accounting

Accountants within the public sector are responsible for recording financial transactions within government departments and government-owned organisations, and for financial reporting and auditing within the government sector.

1.5   Public expectations of the accountancy profession

The general public has high expectations of the accountancy profession.

■ Many non-accountants do not have much understanding of accounting issues, but they rely on accountants to ensure that financial reporting is reliable and 'fair', and that management is not 'cheating' by presenting misleading and inaccurate figures in their accounts.

■ Auditors are also seen, by many members of the public (rightly or wrongly), as a safeguard against fraud.

■ The public continues to believe that the accountancy profession is an ethical profession that offers some protection to society against the 'excesses' of capitalism.

A role of the accountancy bodies should be to reinforce this public perception of an ethical profession. They do this by issuing codes of conduct, including codes of ethics, and expecting all their members to comply.

1.6 Ethics and accountants: critical theory

The ethical codes of accountancy bodies are described in more detail later in this chapter.

First, however, it might be useful to consider some differing views about accountants, that accountants and the accountancy profession do not necessarily act in the public interest and in some ways they might act against it. The perception that the accountancy profession has of itself, that it is a defender of ethical principles in business and government, might not be correct.

The nature of critical theory

Critical theory is an approach to research and investigation used by many universities for many different academic disciplines, including accountancy. Critical theory originated with the Frankfurt School in the mid-20th Century. It is an approach to analysing aspects of society (such as accounting and the accountancy profession) based on an ethical view and a belief that there is a need for improvement and change. The original inspiration for critical theory was the work of Marx and Hegel. For example, some critical theorists argue that an organisation's culture can be seen as a tool for repression, and domination (by managers and owners), and for the maintenance and reproduction of a dominant group. One aim of critical theory is to make people think again about their perceptions and attitudes, and the ways in which they think.

Critical theory and accounting ('critical accounting')

Critical theory in accounting (sometimes called 'critical accounting') challenges the traditional view that accountants are objective individuals, free from bias and influence ('value-free') and with technical expertise, who are able to present reality in the information they provide.

Critical accountants would make the following arguments, in support of their view that accounting is not objective.

■ Accounting information is not objective and value-free. It was developed as a tool for government and business leaders, to help them maintain their position of power within society. Traditional financial reporting, for example, helps business leaders to retain control over the companies they run. Its main focus is on shareholders and profits. Different interest groups (such as shareholders and employees) are treated differently and some individuals have more and better access to accounting information than others.

■ Accounting is not objective because it is a social as well as a technical process. In any given situation or context, different accountants may have different views,

© International Financial Publishing Limited

arising from their cultural differences. All such social attitudes are based on historical conditioning and development of culture, and these attitudes cannot be changed easily because they are deep-rooted in the past.

■ The accountancy profession has created the concept of 'truth' in financial reporting, although the meaning of 'truth' (as in 'true and fair view') is uncertain and subject to different interpretations.

Example

The popular view of auditing is that it provides confirmation or reassurance that financial statements present a true and fair view. This might seem to provide an objective and value-free opinion, but the reality is very different.

(1) In an audit check, the auditors check only a sample of transactions or items, not every transaction.
(2) The auditors are concerned only with **significant** errors. Errors that are not significant do not matter.
(3) The auditors confirm that the financial statements present **a** true and fair view. This indicates that although the accounts present one true and fair view, there are other views that are equally true and fair.

Morgan (1986), a critical accountant, commented that accountants often believe that they represent reality as it really is, but in actual fact they present situations from a limited, one-sided viewpoint.

Accounting has shaped our perceptions of how performance should be reported.

■ Accountants make extensive use of numbers as a means of expression and presenting information. Numbers might seem to be 'correct', which makes it difficult to argue against them. However, numbers should not be confused with reality. They are a way of condensing, representing and summarising information, and need not be exact or complete.

■ Accounting processes de-humanise human beings and society, by reducing social relations to measurable numbers – or ignoring them and not measuring them at all.

■ There is bias in accounting, and accountancy helps to protect the interests of business and government leaders by providing only a restricted amount of information to the public, on selected topics.

The moral development of accountants: accountants as 'rule-followers'

The traditional view of accountancy is that it is a moral and ethical profession. Academic research in the US suggests that this might not be the case. Research has started from a four-step model of moral behaviour. If a person is moral and ethical, he will take moral decisions in the following ways:

■ Step 1. The individual must be able to recognise the moral issue or moral dilemma, whenever there is an ethical aspect to a situation. He or she must be able to recognise that a moral decision has to be taken.

- Step 2. The decision-maker must be able to recognise and select the course of action that is morally correct.

- Step 3. The decision-maker must give priority to the moral issue above all other considerations (for example, self-interest).

- Step 4. The decision-maker must have enough moral strength to implement the decision that he selects in Steps 2 and 3.

Some research has indicated that accountants, on the whole, are poor at taking ethical decisions. In many cases, they treat a problem as a technical accounting issue and fail to see any ethical implications at all.

Many accountants see their role in technical terms, without concern for values or moral issues. They are **rule-followers**, more concerned with identifying what the technical rules are and following them, rather than applying their own personal values to resolve moral dilemmas.

Critical theory and accounting: a summary

It has been argued that traditional accounting supports ethical reporting and decision-making, and promotes economic and social well-being through its provision of information to users.

The views of critical accountants can be summarised as follows:
'**If** all agents [groups] were equal and **if** markets were information-efficient and **if** this led to allocative efficiency and **if** this led, in turn, to economic growth and **if** this ensured maximum social welfare and **if** maximum social welfare were the aim of society, **then** accounting is morally, economically and socially justifiable and may lay claim to an intellectual framework. Of course, this is not the case' (Gray, Owen and Adams: 'Accounting and Accountability: Changes and Challenges in corporate Social and Environmental Reporting').

1.7   Accountants and acting against the public interest

As stated earlier, accountants may be rule-followers. Technical rules are provided by financial reporting standards and other reporting regulations.

A function of the professional accountancy bodies is to provide rules of conduct and ethical behaviour, with the expectation that all members should follow the rules. Accountants might not be moral by nature, but they can be taught to think and act ethically.

Occasional problems will inevitably arise when some accountants choose a different set of rules, or deliberately break the rules. The consequences depend on the nature of the rule-breaking. In an extreme case such as Enron, breaking the rules by accountants contributed significantly to the collapse of the company. Even in the Enron case, the accountants who were prosecuted and imprisoned did not necessarily understand what they had done wrong. They were simply doing the same as other people, and adopting the culture of the company.

                                    © International Financial Publishing Limited

Alvesson and Willmott (1996) have argued that employees come into a company bringing a notion of fairness and justice with them, which they expect to see within the company. However, different people have different views of right and wrong. Fairness and justice are abstract concepts and values that mean different things to different employees and in different work situations. This is how different cultures (and different sets of rules) arise.

So how do companies and accountancy firms apply ethical rules of conduct? One approach is to develop and implement business codes or professional codes of ethics. If forcefully applied, these can help to create a better understanding by accountants of what is right and wrong, how to identify moral dilemmas, and how to act whenever an ethical problem arises.

Corporate codes of ethics

- The nature and purpose of a corporate code of ethics
- The content of a corporate code of ethics
- Whistleblowing procedures

2 Corporate codes of ethics

2.1 The nature and purpose of a corporate code of ethics

A corporate code of ethics is a code of ethical behaviour, issued by the board of directors of a company. It is a formal written statement, and should be distributed or easily available to all employees. The decisions and actions of all employees in the company must be guided by the code.

The effectiveness of a code of ethics depends on the leadership of the company – its directors and senior managers. These individuals must be seen to comply themselves with the ethical code; otherwise other employees will see no purpose in complying with the code themselves. The culture of a company drives its ethical behaviour, and a code of ethics provides useful guidance.

It has been suggested that there are three reasons why companies might develop a code of ethics. These reasons are progressive, which means that companies might begin by having a code of ethics for the first reason, but then progress to the second and third reasons as they gain experience with implementing the code and appreciating its potential benefits.

- Reason 1: **Managing for compliance**. The company wants to ensure that all its employees comply with relevant laws and regulations, and conduct themselves in a way that the public expects. For example, companies providing a service to the general public need to ensure that their employees are polite and well-behaved in their dealings with customers.

- Reason 2: **Managing stakeholder relations**. A code of ethics can help to improve and develop the relations between the company and its shareholders, by improving the trust that shareholders have in the company. The code might therefore include the ethical stance of the company on disclosing information to shareholders and the investing public (openness and transparency) and on respecting the rights of shareholders.

- Reason 3: **Creating a value-based organisation**. A company might recognise the long-term benefits of creating an ethical culture, and encouraging employees to act and think in a way that is consistent with the values in its code of ethics. (It could be argued that an ethical company, like a well-governed company, is more likely to be successful in business in the long term. However, there is no firm evidence to prove this point, and it is therefore a matter of opinion.)

Note on global organisations. Global companies might have difficulty in developing and implementing a code of ethics for the entire organisation world-

© International Financial Publishing Limited

wide, because of differences in ethical values in different cultures in different parts of the world. A criticism of codes of ethics of global companies is that they often focus on the company's relationships with stakeholders in their 'home country' and do not give enough thought to their operations in other countries.

2.2   The content of a corporate code of ethics

A corporate code of ethics is normally quite short, dealing with each point in just a few sentences, and sometimes in just one sentence.

There is no standard format or content for a code of ethics, but a typical code contains:

- general statements about ethical conduct by employees
- specific reference to the company's dealings with each stakeholder group, such as employees, customers, shareholders and local communities.

General statements about ethical conduct

A code of conduct should specify that **compliance with local laws** is essential. In addition, employees should **comply with the policies and procedures** of the company. There might be a statement that any employee who fails to comply with the company's code of conduct will face disciplinary action.

The code might also include an **overview of business conduct**, and the need to protect the company's reputation and 'good name'.

It might also contain statements about the values of the company, such as:

- acting at all times with integrity
- protecting the environment
- the 'pursuit of excellence'
- respect for the individual.

Dealings with stakeholder groups

A code of conduct might address its main concerns about its dealings with stakeholder groups and its ethical treatment of each group.

- **Employees**. A code of ethics might include statements about:
  - human rights, including the right of all employees to join legally-authorised organisations such as a trade union or political party
  - equal opportunities for all employees, regardless of gender, race, ethnic origin, religion, age, disability or sexual orientation
  - refusal to tolerate harassment of employees by colleagues or managers
  - concern for the health and safety of employees
  - respect for the privacy of confidential information about each employee
  - company policy on giving or receiving entertainment or bribes.

- **Customers**. A code of ethics might include statements about:
  - fair dealing with customers
  - product safety and/or product quality
  - the truthfulness of advertisements
  - respect for the privacy of confidential information about each customer.
- **Competitors**. A code of ethics might include statements about:
  - fair dealing with competitors
  - the use of techniques for obtaining information about competitors (industrial spying)
- **Shareholders**. A code of ethics might not include much about shareholders, because the relationship between a company and its shareholders might be contained in a code of corporate governance that the company follows. The key issue with shareholders is to maintain and develop trust and confidence, which might be achieved through disclosure of information (openness and transparency).

 Example

The Institute of Business Ethics provides the following broad guidelines to the content of a code of corporate ethics.

1   Preface or Introduction
(to be signed by the Chairman, Chief Executive Officer or both)
Begin with the purpose of the statement. Include the values that the senior manage hold as important in the conduct of the business. These could include reputation, integrity and responsibility. Outline the company's leaders' commitment to keeping the standard high when dealing with others as well as within the company. Describe the company's role in the community. Finish up with an endorsement of the code by the chairman, CEO or both and the expectation that everyone in the company will uphold the standard laid out in it.

2   Key areas of the code should include:

(a)   The purpose and values of the business
  - The service that the company is providing.
  - The company's financial objectives.
  - The company's role in society (from the company's point of view).

(b)   Employees
  - How the business values its employees.
  - The company's policies on working conditions, recruitment, development and training, rewards, health, safety and security, equal opportunities, retirement, redundancy, discrimination and harassment.
  - Use of company assets by employees.

(c)   Customer relations
  - The importance of customer satisfaction and good faith in all agreements, quality, fair pricing and after-sales service.

© International Financial Publishing Limited

(d)   Shareholders and other providers of money

-   The protection of investment made in the company and proper 'return' on money lent.
-   A commitment to accurate and timely communication on achievements and prospects.

(e)   Suppliers

-   Prompt settling of bills.
-   Co-operation to achieve quality and efficiency.
-   No bribery or excess hospitality accepted or given.

(f)   Society or the wider community

-   Compliance with the spirit of laws as well as the letter of the law.
-   The company's obligations to protect and preserve the environment.
-   The involvement of the company and its staff in local affairs.
-   The corporate policy on giving to education and charities.

(g)   Implementation

-   The process by which the code is issued and used.
-   Means to obtain advice.
-   Code review procedures.
-   Training programme.

2.3   Whistleblowing procedures

'Whistleblowing' means reporting suspicions of illegal or improper behaviour to a person in authority.

In a normal situation, employees report to their supervisor or manager. If an employee has concerns about a transaction or a plan of action, and thinks that it might be unethical (illegal or against the company's code of ethical conduct) he or she should normally report the concern to the supervisor or manager.

A problem arises whenever:

■   the supervisor or manager is involved in the illegal or unethical activity, or

■   the employee has spoken to the supervisor or manager about the problem, but the supervisor or manager has taken no action and has ignored the matter, or dismissed it as something that is not important.

In these situations, the employee would have to report his or her concerns through a different reporting channel. In practice, this could mean reporting the matter to a director or a committee of the board of directors. Some companies have established procedures that allow employees to report their concerns ('blow the whistle').

Problems with whistle blowing

There are several problems with whistle blowing.

■   Experience in many organisations has shown that when an individual reports concerns about illegal or unethical conduct, the individual is often victimised, by colleagues and management. If the allegations by the individual are rejected, the individual might find that he (or she) does not receive the same salary increases

- as colleagues, and is overlooked for promotion. At work, colleagues and managers might treat the individual with hostility, making it difficult for the individual to continue in the job.

- On the other hand, some individuals make allegations about colleagues or managers that are unfounded. The allegations might be made for reasons of malice and dislike, or because there has been an argument at work. Malicious allegations about colleagues and managers should not be tolerated.

A problem facing companies is therefore:

- how to encourage reports of illegal or unethical behaviour, by protecting honest whistle blowers, but

- how to discourage malicious and unfounded allegations.

A company might state its policy on whistle blowing within its code of conduct. For example, a corporate code of ethics might include the following statements.

- Every employee should make known their concerns about illegal or unethical behaviour in the work place. If there are doubts, the employee should ask first, because incorrect behaviour might not be intentionally dishonest. It might be caused by a lack of information or by trying to get a job done too quickly. (This aspect of a code of ethics is to encourage employees to speak about their concerns, but to try to resolve them first by discussion with colleagues and managers.)

- An employee is **doing the right thing** if, **in good faith**, he seeks advice about improper behaviour or reports improper behaviour. (Whistle blowing is the correct thing to do, if the employee does it in good faith and is not being malicious.)

- The company will not tolerate any action taken by anyone in the company against an individual who has reported in good faith their concerns about illegal or unethical behaviour. (This is a statement that whistle blowers will be protected, if they have made their report in good faith.)

- Disciplinary action will be taken against any employee who **knowingly** makes a false report of illegal or improper behaviour by someone else. (Malicious reporting will not be tolerated.)

Unfortunately, in practice, it seems that in many cases whistle blowers are not given adequate protection by their employer.

> ## Codes of ethics for accountants
>
> - The need for a professional code of ethics for accountants
> - The IFAC Code (Code of Ethics for Professional Accountants) and ACCA Code
> - Fundamental principles

3 Codes of ethics for accountants

3.1 The need for a professional code of ethics for accountants

Every professional accountancy body has issued a code of conduct and code of ethics for its members and student members.

Even when an individual works for a company or a firm of accountants that has its own code of ethics, there is a need for a professional code of conduct. This is because accountants have a professional **duty to act in the public interest**, and this aspect of professional behaviour is not covered by corporate ethical codes.

3.2 The IFAC Code (Code of Ethics for Professional Accountants) and ACCA Code

Although each professional accountancy body has its own code of ethics, all codes are similar, because they are based on the IFAC Code. The IFAC Code (most recent version 2005) is issued by the Ethics Committee of the International Federation of Accountants, whose members include the professional accountancy bodies of most countries.

The IFAC Code sets our the ethical requirements for professional accountants and states that any member body of IFAC (such as the ACCA) or any individual firm of accountants may not apply ethical standards that are less strict than those in the IFAC Code.

The IFAC Code therefore establishes a minimum world-wide code of ethical conduct for accountants. The IFAC Code is divided into three parts:

- general principles and application of the code
- guidelines for accountants in public practice
- guidelines for accountants in business.

The same general ethical principles apply to all accountants. The circumstances in which ethical problems arise are different between accountants in practice and accountants in business. Accountants in practice have to deal in an ethical way with issues arising from the **client relationship**. Accountants in business have to deal with ethical issues where they are **employees** of the organisation in which the ethical problem has occurred.

The ACCA Code of Ethics and Conduct contains similar provisions to the IFAC Code, but is structured differently. It is contained in the ACCA Rulebook, which can be found on the ACCA website.

The description of professional ethics that follows is based on both the IFAC Code and ACCA Code.

Principles-based ethics codes and rules-based ethics codes

It would be possible for a regulatory body to issue a code of ethics for accountants that contains specific rules about how they should act in specific situations. This would be a rules-based code of ethics.

Rules-based codes have several weaknesses:

- There are many different situations that an accountant might face where an ethical decision must be made. Circumstances can be complex and varied, and it is impossible to plan for every type of ethical problem that will arise, and make a rule in advance – without knowing the exact details of the situation – of what course of action the accountant must take.

- Over time, the type of situations (ethical dilemmas) that an accountant might face could change, as the business environment changes. It might therefore be necessary to review and update the rule book regularly.

- Ethical views differ between countries and cultures. Behaviour that might be considered slightly unethical in one country might be perfectly normal and acceptable in another country. A rule book cannot easily make allowances for national and cultural differences in ethical viewpoint.

A principles-based code of ethics for accountants is a code that specifies general principles of ethical behaviour, and requires the professional accountant to act in accordance with the principles. The accountant is required to use judgement in deciding whether in each case a particular course of action is a 'proper' or 'ethical' one.

3.3 Fundamental principles

Professional accountants are required to comply with the following fundamental principles:

- integrity
- objectivity
- professional competence and due care
- confidentiality
- professional behaviour
- technical standards.

These have been mentioned in earlier chapters. The ACCA Code explains the fundamental principles as follows: 'Ethics is about the principles we use to judge the right and wrong of our actions.... It is about the fundamental principles that our

© International Financial Publishing Limited

members review and agree to each year when they renew their ACCA membership and submit their CPD (continuing professional development) return.'

Integrity

An accountant must be honest and straightforward in his professional and business dealings. This includes a requirement for 'fair dealing' and a requirement to be truthful.

Objectivity

An accountant must not allow his professional or business judgement to be affected by:

- bias (personal prejudice)
- conflicts of interest
- undue influence from others: for accountants in business, this includes undue pressure from the employer (senior management).

A very important aspect of integrity is that an accountant should not be associated with reports or any other provision of information where he or she believes that:

- the information contains a **materially** false or misleading statement
- the information contains a statement that has been prepared and provided recklessly, without proper care or consideration for its accuracy
- there are omissions or the information is presented in a way that makes the relevant information difficult to see, with the effect that the information could be seriously misleading.

For accountants in public practice, 'integrity' is often associated with independence of mind and judgement. For accountants in business, the concept of independence is not relevant: however, accountants in business should try to apply the principle of objectivity in all the work that they do.

For accountants in business, the concept of integrity also means observing the terms of his or her employment, but avoiding involvement in any activity that is illegal. If asked or encouraged to become involved in unlawful activity, the accountant must say no.

Professional competence and due care

An accountant has a duty to maintain his professional knowledge and skills at a level that enables him to provide a competent professional service to his clients or employer. This includes a requirement to keep up to date with developments in areas of accounting that are relevant to the work that he does.

Accountants should also act in accordance with relevant technical and professional standards when doing their work for clients or employer.

Confidentiality

Accountants must respect the confidentiality of information obtained in the course of their work. This applies to the confidentiality of information within the firm or employer's organisation, as well as to confidentiality of information about clients (for accountants in professional practice).

The requirement to keep information confidential applies:

- in a social environment as well as at work: for example, an accountant must be careful of what he says to a good friend who also happens to be a business associate, or to a wife or husband who is also a professional accountant
- after the accountant has moved to another job – confidentiality applies to information obtained when working for a former employer.

In addition, confidential information must never be used to obtain a personal benefit or a benefit for a third party.

There are some circumstances when the disclosure of confidential information is permitted or even required by law.

- Confidential information about a client (or employee) can be disclosed if the client (or employee) has given permission. Before disclosing the information, however, the accountant should consider whether the disclosure might harm a third party.
- Confidential information must be disclosed to the authorities in certain circumstances. These circumstances depend on the laws of the country. In the UK, for example, tax inspectors or the police might obtain a court order (warrant) to take away files relating to a client.
- The law might also require the disclosure of confidential information to the appropriate authorities. For example, firms of accountants are expected to disclose suspicions of money laundering by a client to the appropriate authorities. (The details of anti money laundering laws may very between countries). In addition, tax evasion is a crime and accountants are required to report tax evasion by clients to the authorities. However, accountants are not expected to disclose client information to the authorities where the work for the client is covered by legal professional privilege.
- Disclosure is also permitted when the accountant has a professional right or duty, and disclosure is not prohibited by law. An example is the right of ACCA members to respond to an enquiry by the ACCA.

Professional behaviour

Accountants are required to observe relevant laws and regulations, and to avoid any actions that would discredit the accountancy profession.
This requirement covers advertising by accountants, which must be truthful and must not disparage the services provided by 'rival' firms.

© International Financial Publishing Limited

Technical standards

A professional accountant should perform his professional tasks in accordance with the relevant technical and professional standards. Technical and professional standards include:

- standards issued by IFAC (such as International Standards on Auditing) or a similar national regulatory body
- financial reporting standards (IFRSs)
- standards and regulations of the member's professional accountancy body
- relevant legislation.

Professional accountants have a duty to carry out with care and skill the instructions of an employer or client, insofar as these are compatible with the ethical requirements for integrity, objectivity and (in the case of accountants in public practice) independence.

Example

You are an accountant working in public practice. You receive a visit from two police officers, who ask to see the files for one of your clients, a small import-export company. They show you a warrant that authorises them to take away the client files.

What should you do?

Answer

The requirement to maintain confidentiality of client information does not apply when authorities such as the police have a warrant to inspect or take files relating to the specific client.

You should be polite to the police in responding to their request, and you should check the details of the warrant before providing the files that are required. If there is any doubt about the details in the warrant, you might wish to ask for a legal opinion before handing over the files.

You should not tell the client what has happened.

Example

You are an accountant responsible for the audit of a business client. During the course of your audit work you discover that an employee of the client has probably been engaged in a fraudulent activity. You are not entirely certain that fraud has occurred.

What should you do?

Answer

The issue of confidentiality does not arise here, because the problem relates to an employee of the client. You should report your suspicions to a person of authority in the client organisation.

If the fraud appears to be minor, you might decide to leave the matter in the hands of the client. If the fraud appears to be a major crime, you should check what actions the client takes in reporting the matter to the police authorities, to satisfy yourself that appropriate action has been taken.

© International Financial Publishing Limited

CHAPTER

15

Conflicts of interest and ethical conflict resolution

Contents
1   Ethical threats and safeguards
2   A model for resolving ethical conflicts

Ethical threats and safeguards

- Rules-based and principles-based approaches to ethical dilemmas
- The nature of ethical threats
- The nature of ethical safeguards
- Threats to accountants in business

---

1 Ethical threats and safeguards

1.1 Rules-based and principles-based approaches to ethical dilemmas

When accountants are faced with an ethical problem, they need to know what to do. If there is a threat to their compliance with the fundamental principles of the ethical code, how should they ensure their compliance and deal with the threat?

There are two possible approaches that the professional accountancy bodies could take, a rules-based approach and a principles-based approach.

- A rules-based approach is to identify each possible ethical problem or ethical dilemma that could arise in the work of an accountant, and specify what the accountant must do in each situation.
- A principles-based approach is to specify the principles that should be applied when trying to resolve an ethical problem, offer some general guidelines, but leave it to the judgement of the accountant to apply the principles sensibly in each particular situation.

The IFAC Code (and other codes of accountancy ethics, including the ACCA Code) take a principles-based approach, with some guidelines.

The main reason for taking a principles-based approach is that it is impossible to identify every ethical dilemma that accountants might face, with differing circumstances in each case. Since it is impossible to identify every problem that might arise, rules could only be provided for some problems but not others.

The IFAC Code makes this point, saying that it is exceedingly difficult to predict all situations that create threats to compliant with the fundamental principles and the suitable course of action. Threats needing different safeguards may exist depending on the work assignment or engagement. It is in the public interest, therefore, to have a conceptual framework for the accountants to follow, rather than a set of strict rules.

It is interesting to note that IFAC considers the public interest when choosing a principles-based approach in preference to a rules-based approach.

　　　　　　　　　　　　　　© International Financial Publishing Limited

The nature of a principles-based approach

The recommended approach to resolving ethical problems, which will be considered in more detail later, is based on the following steps:

- **Identify threats** to compliance with the fundamental principles. Accountants have an obligation to identify any threat to their compliance with the fundamental principles, when it could reasonably be expected that they should be able to identify it.

- **Evaluate the threat.** Qualitative factors as well as quantitative factors should be considered in the assessment of a threat to compliance. Insignificant threats may be ignored but others should be dealt with.

- **Respond to the threat.** If it is 'not insignificant', the accountant should apply **appropriate safeguards**, if he can, to eliminate the threat or reduce the threat to an insignificant level.

- If suitable safeguards cannot be applied, more drastic action will be needed, such as refusing to carry out a professional service, ending the relationship with a client or resigning from the job.

1.2 The nature of ethical threats

Threats to compliance with the fundamental ethical principles are grouped into five broad categories:

- **Self-interest threats**, or **conflicts of interest**. These occur when the personal interests of the professional accountant, or a close family member, are (or could be) affected by the accountant's decisions or actions.

- **Self-review threats.** This type of threat occurs when a professional accountant is responsible for reviewing some work or a judgement that he was responsible for originally. An extreme example would be a situation where a professional accountant prepares the annual financial statements for a corporate client and then is appointed to do the audit.

- **Advocacy threats.** This type of threat can occur when an accountant promotes the point of view of a client, for example by acting as a professional witness in a legal dispute. Acting as an advocate for the client can reach the point where the objectivity of the accountant is compromised.

- **Familiarity threats.** A familiarity threat arises from knowing someone very well, possibly through a long association in business. The risk is that an accountant might become too familiar with a client and therefore becomes more sympathetic to the client and more willing to accept the client's point of view.

- **Intimidation threats.** A professional accountant might find that his objectivity and independence is threatened by intimidation, either real or imagined.

These threats to compliance with the fundamental ethical principles apply to firms of accountants, in their dealings with clients, as well as to individual accountants.

Example

Examples of ethical threats are listed below. Some apply to accountants in public practice, and some apply to accountants in business. Some apply to both types of accountancy work.

Threats from a conflict of interest	
Accountants in public practice	**Accountants in business**
The accountant has a financial interest in the client.	The accountant has a financial interest (for example, holds shares or share options in the employer company).
The accountant has a joint financial interest with the client in a business venture.	
The competence of the accountant to do the work is in question.	The competence of the accountant to do the work is in question.
The accountant is offered gifts or hospitality by a client.	The accountant is offered gifts or hospitality by a customer or a supplier.
There is a risk of losing the client, and the client taking his business somewhere else.	There is the risk that the accountant might lose his job.
Contingency fees. The client will pay a fee to the accountant only if a particular event occurs or a particular outcome is achieved. (The fee is dependent on the achievement of the desired outcome.) The accountant has a financial interest in achieving the outcome.	The accountant's basic pay or bonus might be affected.
There is a possibility that the client will offer a job to the accountant.	

Self-review threats	Familiarity threats
The accountant discovers a significant error on checking some work, and he was responsible for making the original error.	A member of the audit team has a close family relationship with a director or senior officer of the client company, or with an employee of the company who is in a position to influence significantly the subject matter of the audit
The accountant is asked to report on the operation of a system that he was responsible for designing and implementing.	Accepting gifts or hospitality from a client, customer or supplier. (This is both a self-interest threat and a familiarity threat).
A member of the audit team was recently an employee of the client and involved in the work subject to audit.	The senior personnel in an audit team have a long association with the client company.
The accountant is assigned to check any work that he did previously for the client as a professional service.	An accountant in business has along business association with another person, who might therefore be able to influence his judgement (integrity).

© International Financial Publishing Limited

Advocacy threats	Intimidation threats
The accountant is involved in providing a professional opinion in support of a client, in a case involving a dispute with a third party (possibly litigation).	The accountant is threatened with dismissal or a loss of benefits (pay, bonus, promotion) for failing to agree to the demands of management colleagues. The accountant has to deal with a dominant personality who expects everyone else to do what he tells them to. An accountant in public practice is threatened with litigation by a client. An accountant in public practice is under pressure from a client to reduce the amount of work in an audit, in order to reduce the audit fee. (This is a threat to the integrity of the audit work.)

There are some threats to compliance with the fundamental ethical principles, particularly a threat to integrity and professional conduct that are not easily categorised as one of the five threats listed above.

Threats to integrity and professional conduct can be classified as threats to self-interest.

Example

You are an accountant working in public practice. You are approached by a subsidiary company of a foreign parent company. This company would like you to provide a number of professional services. The parent company is based in a country where you have no professional contacts.

What are the ethical risks?

Answer

There are ethical risks in taking on an unknown new client. The new client might be involved in illegal activities, such as money laundering or drug trafficking.

As an accountant, you might become involved in providing services in support of criminal activities, which would threaten your integrity and professional conduct.

There must be ethical safeguards to ensure that you do not take on a new client without first 'getting to know' the client and satisfying yourself that there are no ethical concerns.

Example

You are an accountant working in public practice. A client has asked you to do some tax work, for which the fee would be quite high. You are keen to do the work in order to earn the fee, but you are aware that your knowledge of the relevant tax law is not up to date and there is no one else in the firm with suitable knowledge and experience in tax.

The same client has also asked your firm to perform a value for money audit on one of its operations. To do the work, you have estimated the amount of time and resource that would be needed and you have quoted a fee to the client. The client says that the fee is too high, and should be reduced by at least 50%.

What are the ethical risks?

Answer

In both cases, the risk is that you will not have sufficient competence to do the work. A lack of competence can be classified as a threat to self-interest.

You must not take on work for a client without having the competence to do the work to the required professional standard. You might be able to resolve the problem by going on a training course to update your tax knowledge, or you might apply to outsource the work to another accountant who has the appropriate tax knowledge.

If you cannot provide the service to the client to a suitable standard of competence, you should refuse to take on the work.

Providing a service with suitable competence is also the issue with the value for money audit (although you could argue that there is also the threat of not getting the work and the fee). By insisting that the fee should be reduced by 50%, the client is asking you to provide the service with only one half of the planned resources. You will probably be unable to provide the agreed service with sufficient competence with such limited resources.

You need to renegotiate the work with the client, who might agree to an audit that is less extensive. Alternatively you might try to explain to the client what the fee covers and why it is so high, in the hope that the client will agree to pay a higher amount. If the client refuses to agree to less work in the audit or a higher fee, you should refuse to accept the work.

Example

You are an accountant working in public practice and you have been assigned to the audit team to do the annual audit of Big Bank. You have a large mortgage loan from Big Bank that you obtained six months ago to buy your new house.

What is the ethical risk?

© International Financial Publishing Limited

Answer

The IFAC Code and ACCA Code are specific on this point. If an accountant has a loan from a client (or employer) the financial interest could in some cases create a conflict of interest.

However, if the loan from the bank has been provided on normal commercial terms, no conflict of interest exists. There is no ethical reason preventing you from working on the Big Bank audit.

1.3 The nature of ethical safeguards

When there are threats to compliance with the fundamental ethical principles, the accountant should assess the safeguards against the threat.

- There might already be safeguards in place that eliminate the possibility that the risk will ever materialise, or that reduce the risk to an acceptable level.
- If the safeguards that exist are not sufficient, the accountant should try to introduce new safeguards to eliminate or reduce the risk to an insignificant level.

Ethical safeguards can be grouped into two broad categories:

- safeguards created externally, by legislation, regulation or the accountancy profession
- safeguards established within the work environment.

Safeguards created by legislation, regulation or the accountancy profession

Safeguards that are created externally, by legislation, regulation or the profession, include the following.

- The requirements for individuals to have education and training and work experience, as a pre-condition for membership of the professional body.
- The continuing professional development (CPD) requirements for qualified members, to ensure that they maintain a suitable level of competence.
- Corporate governance regulations, particularly those relating to auditing, financial reporting and internal control.
- Professional standards, such as financial reporting standards and auditing standards.
- Monitoring procedures and disciplinary procedures.
- External review by a legally-empowered third party.

Safeguards in the work environment

A variety of safeguards can be applied within the work environment. These can be categorised into:

- safeguards that apply across the entire firm or company, and
- safeguards that are specific to a particular item of work.

Safeguards that apply across the entire firm or company might include the following:

- a code of ethics for the company or firm and suitable ethical leadership from senior management

- a sound system of internal control, with strong internal controls

- the application of appropriate policies and procedures for monitoring the quality of work done for clients

- policies that limit the reliance of the firm on the fee income from a single client

- procedures for identifying personal interests and family relationships between employees and partners of the firm and key staff in client organisations

- whistle blowing procedures for reporting illegal or unethical behaviour.

Safeguards that might be applied to particular jobs or work procedures include the following:

- keeping individuals away from work where there might be a threat to their compliance with the fundamental principles (for example where a conflict of interests or a conflict of familiarity might exist)

- in the case of audit firms, rotating the audit partner so that the same audit partner is not responsible for the audit of the same client company for more than a specified maximum number of years

- the application of strong internal controls

- using another accountant to review the work that has been done by a colleague

- discussing ethical issues with those people in the company who are responsible for governance issues, such as the audit committee, senior non-executive director, or board of directors.

 Example

A member of the audit team working on the audit of ABC Company has just received an inheritance that includes a large number of ABC Company shares.

What is the ethical risk and what safeguards against the risk might be appropriate?

 Answer

The risk is that the member of the audit team has a financial interest in the client, by owning a large number of the client company shares. There is a potential conflict of interest, which will threaten his or her integrity.

Suitable safeguards would be either:

- to persuade the individual to sell the shares, or

- to remove the individual from the audit of ABC Company.

© International Financial Publishing Limited

Example

A senior partner in an accountancy firm is also a director of XYZ Company. XYZ Company has approached the audit firm, and asked it to become the company's auditors.

What is the ethical risk and what safeguards against the risk might be appropriate?

Answer

The risk is that the senior partner has a financial interest in the client company, and presumably also has a familiarity risk.

The IFAC Code and ACCA Code state that in this situation, there are no safeguards that are strong enough to reduce the threat from the conflict of interest to an insignificant level. The firm must refuse to take on the audit work.

Example

You are an accountant working in public practice. You are approached by a subsidiary company of a foreign parent company. This company would like you to provide a number of professional services. The parent company is based in a country where you have no professional contacts. The ethical risks in taking on a new client were described in a previous example.

Required
What are the safeguards against the risk that should reduce the risk to an acceptable, insignificant level?

Answer

A key safeguard is to obtain information that verifies the ownership of the parent company and shows who has ultimate control over the group, including the UK subsidiary.

Before accepting the UK subsidiary as a client, enquiries should be made in the country of the parent company. The enquiry might be made through an ACCA member in that country, or an ACCA member might be asked to recommend a local lawyer who could do the work.

You would want to receive certified copies of original documentation relating to the structure of the parent company, evidence of its registration as a company (including the details registered on its incorporation), a list of the members of its board of directors and any other information about the company that is available to the public in that country.

If you are satisfied with the information you receive, you should feel able to take on the subsidiary company as a client. If you are not satisfied, and are unable to obtain any other information that provides the safeguards you are looking for, you should inform the company that you are not able to provide the services that the company requires.

1.4 Threats to accountants in business

You should be aware that accountants who work in business can be placed under serious pressure by an employer to act in an unethical way. A problem could arise when senior management want to 'bend the rules' in financial reporting and expect compliance from their accounting staff. Accountants might therefore be asked to:

- break a law or regulation: illegal activity is always unethical
- ignore technical standards, such as financial reporting standards or auditing standards
- lie to the external auditors or regulators
- issue a report that is misleading and misrepresents the facts.

When an accountant is put under pressure to act in this way, the threat comes from:

- self-interest threats: by doing what senior management expect, the accountant might expect to benefit from personal rewards, such as a bonus, a higher salary or promotion
- intimidation threats: there might also be a threat from senior management that the accountant might not receive a bonus or might be expected to resign unless he agrees to do what senior management ask
- familiarity threats: in some cases, an accountant might be expected to agree to what senior management ask because he has known them for a long time and should be expected to trust them to do 'what is right' for the company.

However, threats of this nature are very serious. Breaking a law, ignoring a technical standard, hiding information from the auditors or lying to them and providing misleading information could all have serious consequences. There is a threat to the accountant's compliance with the fundamental principles of:

- integrity
- objectivity
- professional competence and due care
- professional behaviour.

Finding a solution to ethical problems can be very difficult. The extreme option (or 'nuclear option') is resignation, but this is something that should be avoided where possible. A better solution can often be found.

A model for dealing with ethical problems is suggested in the next section.

© International Financial Publishing Limited

> ## A model for resolving ethical conflicts
>
> - A model based on threats and safeguards
> - The mirror test
> - Applying the model in practice

2 A model for resolving ethical conflicts

2.1 A model based on threats and safeguards

The ACCA has suggested a model for dealing with ethical dilemmas, and using judgement to decide how the dilemma should be resolved. It is based on recognising threats to compliance with the fundamental principles, and assessing safeguards to eliminate the threats.

The model is in several logical stages, as follows.

- Stage 1. Recognise and define the ethical issues.
- Stage 2. Identify the threats to compliance.
- Stage 3. Assess the significance of the threats.
- Stage 4. If the threats are 'not insignificant', consider the additional safeguards that could be used.
- Stage 5. Re-assess the threats to compliance after additional safeguards. Do the additional safeguards eliminate the risk or reduce it to an insignificant level?
- Stage 6. Make the decision about what to do.

Define the issues

Accountants are expected to identify potential threats to their compliance with the fundamental ethical principles. To do this, they must be able to recognise the ethical issues that exist, or might possibly exist, in a particular situation. The first step is therefore to define the issues.

In order to do this, it might be necessary to **establish the facts**. An accountant might suspect that an ethical issue exists, but cannot be sure because he does not have enough facts to inform him about the situation.

In addition, the accountant should ask whether he has considered all the possible alternative courses of action, and whether there are any courses of action that avoid the threats.

Yet another question the accountant should ask is whether the problem is his, or whether it is the problem of someone else. An accountant does not have a duty to take on the ethical responsibilities of another person. He must consider his own actions, and whether these are ethical and acceptable.

Identify the threats to compliance with ethical principles

Having established the facts and defined the ethical issues, the accountant must next think about his own involvement. The concern for the accountant should be whether his compliance with the fundamental ethical principles is under threat, and if so, what is the nature of the threat.

- Is there a self-interest threat, a self-review threat, an advocacy threat, a familiarity threat or a threat from intimidation?

- How does this threaten the accountant's ability to comply with the requirements for integrity, objectivity, professional competence and due care, confidentiality and professional behaviour?

Assess the significance of the threats

The next stage is to identify the significance of the threats to compliance with the fundamental ethical principles. If existing controls are sufficient to eliminate the risk of non-compliance, or if the existing controls are sufficient to reduce the risk to an insignificant level, no further action is needed.

If the threats to compliance with fundamental ethical principals are higher than insignificant, additional safeguards should be considered in order to eliminate or reduce the threats.

Introducing safeguards

Safeguards, or additional safeguards, can be introduced to reduce the threats to compliance with the fundamental ethical principles. These threats must be eliminated entirely or reduced to an insignificant level.

Taking action

Introducing additional safeguards might be sufficient to deal with the problem.

However, if the threats to compliance with the fundamental ethical principals cannot be eliminated or reduced to an insignificant level, more extreme measures are necessary.

- For accountants in public practice, an extreme measure is to decline to work for a particular client, or to cease working for a client.

- For accountants working in industry and commerce, an extreme measure would be to become a 'whistleblower', and to report concerns to an appropriate authority. In an extreme case, the appropriate action might be for the accountant to resign from his or her job.

Members of the ACCA are able to obtain confidential advice about the appropriate course of action from the Advisory Services Section of the ACCA.

© International Financial Publishing Limited

2.2 The mirror test

The ACCA has also suggested that when an ethical issue is involved, an accountant should carry out a mirror test.

To carry out a mirror test, you have to answer a basic question about the ethics of a course of action. If you choose a course of action, are you able to look yourself in the mirror and see a person who has acted in a moral and ethical way. Can you justify the decision you have taken from an ethical perspective?

Three questions that you can ask when carrying out the mirror test are as follows.

For the course of action you have chosen, the three questions are:

1   Is it legal? If it is not legal, you should not be doing it.

2   What will other people think? Think about the opinion of people whose views matter to you, such as close family members (a parent, spouse, or close friend) or the media. Are you satisfied with the effect of your action on these people?

3   Even if the action is legal, it is ethically correct? A problem for accountants is often that an action is legal (or not illegal) but is nevertheless unethical and should be avoided.

2.3 Applying the model in practice

You need to be able to identify ethical problems that could face an accountant, and suggest a way of resolving the problem in a way that is consistent with ethical principles. The model described above provides a useful framework for doing this.

Remember that the aim should be to find a sensible solution to each ethical problem. The solution can often be reached through agreement with other people, and through discussions. It is not always necessary to opt for an extreme solution, such as reporting a problem to an external authority, resigning from a job or declining to work for a client.

Here are a few examples to show how the model might be applied.

Example

Until recently you were a senior accountant working for the state hospital service and you have now left to work for a company that is applying to take over some aspects of the treatment of patients with eye problems. Until now this work has been performed by specialist state-owned hospitals. The government has a policy of transferring a considerable proportion of medical services to private sector companies, and it wants to transfer the responsibility for eye treatment to the private sector.

Your new employer has asked you to lead a team that will make the company's application to the government. Your boss is aware that when you were working for the state hospital service, you worked closely with the management responsible for the eye hospitals and you are familiar with many of the senior figures in both hospital management and the government department responsible for public health. From your experience in your previous job, you know a lot about the reasons why the government wants to transfer this work from the state-owned hospitals to a private sector company.

Your company pays large bonuses to employees in teams that successfully apply to take over work from hospitals in the state sector.

Required
Consider whether you are faced with an ethical problem, and if so how it might be resolved.

 Answer

Step 1
The first step is to identify the ethical issue. You are being asked to lead a team that will apply to provide medical services for the government. The reason why you have been selected is probably your knowledge and experience of the medical services for eye patients, and your familiarity with senior managers in the hospitals and government department.

Step 2
Consider the threat that this creates for your compliance with the fundamental ethical principles.

In this case, there is a threat to the ethical requirement to respect the confidentiality of information obtained from a previous employer. You should not use confidential information obtained in a previous job for the benefit of a new employer.

On the other hand, you have an ethical duty to assist your new employer in achieving its legitimate business aims.

Step 3
You need to consider the significance of the threat to your compliance with the fundamental principles.

The significance of the threat will depend on how much confidential information you would use in carrying out the work for your employer. If there is no threat to confidentiality, there is no problem. However in this case it seems likely that you would inevitably be using information that you acquired when you worked for your previous employer, and this information should be treated as confidential.

Step 4
You should therefore consider safeguards to the ethical threat and find a solution to your problem.

The first step should be to discuss your ethical problem with your boss. If your employer is sympathetic to ethical issues your boss is likely to agree that you should not be asked to lead the team that applies to do the work. Another colleague should be appointed to lead the team on this occasion.

© International Financial Publishing Limited

However, you might agree to be involved with the team, on work where you can use your experience and knowledge where there is no threat to confidentiality. If this is possible, you will be working to promote the legitimate interests of your employer without any threat to your compliance with the fundamental principles.

Example

You are an accountant working for a medium-sized public company. You report to the chief accountant, who is preparing the annual accounts.

You have been involved in preparing valuations for inventory, and you have identified a substantial amount of slow-moving inventory that, in your opinion, is should be written down in value, or even written off altogether.

The chief accountant has called you in for a meeting. He thanks you for the work you have done, and comments that he is hoping that you can expect to earn a bonus at the year end when the financial statements are approved and published. He then adds that before he discusses the accounts with the finance director and the auditors, he thinks that there is a problem with the write-down of the inventory. He thinks that it would be premature to write down the inventory this year, and he does not want to create a problem by drawing the matter to the attention of the auditors.

He goes on to say that he thinks the matter is important, but he is sure that you will shown good professional judgement by agreeing with his point of view, and that you will alter the figures for inventory valuation in your report. He hints that if you do not agree with his request, he will have to reconsider his recommendation to the finance director about your annual bonus and that he will find it difficult in the future to work with you on a constructive professional basis.

How should you deal with this situation?

Answer

Step 1
The first step here is to identify the issue. First, the valuation of inventory is your problem, because you have prepared a report on the subject and you are being asked to reconsider your professional opinion.

You might think that your initial opinion about the inventory valuation is too cautious. It would therefore be appropriate to ask for time to re-assess your valuation. However, this should not be an excuse for accepting the opinion of the chief accountant. You should re-assess your valuation objectively. There might be more up-to-date information that will help with your re-assessment.

Step 2

If you consider that there is an ethical problem, you need to identify the nature of the threats and assess show serious they are.

- There is a conflict of interest (self-interest) threat, because a suggestion has been put to you that your annual bonus depends on your willingness to accept the views of the chief accountant. There is also an intimidation threat, in the sense that your future career might be affected by hostility from the chief accountant. You might also think that there is pressure to accept the view of the chief accountant, because you are familiar with him and are willing to accept his opinion.

- These create threats to your integrity, if you believe that your assessment of the inventory valuation is correct. There are also threats to your objectivity and to the requirement for you to act with professional competence and due care.

Step 3

The next step is to assess how serious the threats are. The scale of the threat might depend to some extent on the significance of the write-down in inventory, and the effect this would have o n the reported profits for the year. A minor difference might be overlooked, but anything more serious should not be ignored.

Step 4

You need to consider safeguards to protect yourself against the ethical threat. As an initial course of action, after you have re-assessed the inventory valuation, should be able to discuss your concerns to the chief accountant. If the chief accountant has not changed his opinion, you can ask for some time to think about what you should do.

If you disagree with the chief accountant and you consider the problem to be serious, it would be inappropriate for you to decide that it is no longer your problem and you will simply do what you are told.

It would also be inappropriate to decide that you can wait and see what the auditors have to say about inventory valuation. This is shifting the responsibility to the auditors, when the responsibility is initially yours. You cannot be sure that the auditors will identify the problem during the course of their audit.

Safeguards to the ethical threats you are facing can possibly be obtained by informing other people within the company to the nature of the problem. You can consider arranging a meeting with the finance director or the chairman of the audit committee to discuss your concerns.

If you find that the finance director or audit committee are not willing to listen to your views, you might consider informing the auditors about your concern. However, before you do this you might wish to ask the ACCA for confidential advice on the matter.

If these measures fail to remove your concerns about the ethical risk, you might need to consider resignation from the company.

© International Financial Publishing Limited

Example

You are a senior accountant working for a public company that produces sophisticated telecommunications equipment.

For political reasons, the government has placed a total ban on exports of all goods to Country X, where there is a repressive dictatorship and a civil war in one region.

You have been asked to prepare the documentation for the sale of a large quantity of equipment to a customer in Country Y, and arrange the method of payment. There is no ban on exports to Country Y, but the customer has acted in the past as a buying agent for the government in Country X. You are therefore aware of the fact that the equipment exported to Country Y will soon find its way into Country X.

You have discussed your concern with the finance director, who told you that there was no ban on sales to Country Y, and what happened to the equipment after that was none of his concern and should be none of your concern either.

What should you do?

Answer

Step 1
The first step here is to identify the issue. The problem here is your involvement in an export transaction which is not strictly illegal, but is probably intended to have the same end result as an illegal action.

The export is not strictly illegal, so you are not under a legal obligation to report your concerns.

Step 2
You should assess the threat to your compliance with the fundamental ethical principles. The threat here is to your integrity. You are under pressure from the finance director to keep quiet and get on with your job, suggesting perhaps that action will be taken against you if you fail to comply. This is a form of intimidation threat.

Step 3
You should assess the significance of the ethical issue. In this case, it is probably sufficiently significant for you to consider an appropriate response to the problem.

Step 4
When problems arise of an ethical nature, the first course of action should be to find a way to resolve the matter through internal procedures. Since the finance director will not listen to your concerns, you might consider using the arrangements that the company has for internal 'whistle blowing'. If there are no formal arrangements for whistle blowing, you might consider reporting your concerns to the senior independent director.

If no-one in the company take up your concerns and tries to deal with the problem, you might consider, as a final resort, reporting the matter to someone in authority. However, before you become an external whistle blower, you should consider the following matters:

- What will be the effect on the public interest if the unethical transaction goes ahead? Is there a sufficiently strong public interest concern to justify informing an external authority?

- The answer to this question depends partly on the gravity or significance of the matter. Is a serious ethical problem involved, to justify you informing the authorities?

- Is there a probability of a repetition of the problem in the future? In this case, is it probable that there will be more export orders from the same customer in the future?

- What is the quality of the information that you have? In this case, how certain are you that the equipment will be transferred to Country X after it has been sold to the customer in Country Y?

- What is the reason for your employer's refusal to act?

All these matters could affect your decision on whether or not to report your suspicions to an external authority. If you decide that you must 'blow the whistle', you should keep documentary records to provide evidence of your concerns and of your attempts to resolve the problem internally.

This is a problem where different individuals might reach a different conclusion about the appropriate action to take.

© International Financial Publishing Limited

16

Social and environmental issues in ethics and business

Contents
1   Social and environmental footprints
2   Sustainability and accounting for sustainability
3   Environmental management systems, environmental management accounting and environmental audit

Social and environmental footprints
■ Introduction
■ Environmental footprint (ecological footprint)
■ Carbon neutrality
■ Social footprint
■ Social ecology
■ Towards the measurement of social and environmental effects

1 Social and environmental footprints

1.1 Introduction

The purpose of economic activity is to create economic wealth. It is now recognised, much more than in the past, that economic activity also has an environmental impact and a social effect. An organisation is said to create an 'environmental footprint' and a 'social footprint' - a visible mark on the environment and on society. (The word 'footprint' is intended to have the same meaning as in everyday use, when we speak of leaving a footprint in the sand, as a mark that we leave behind where we have been.)

The social footprint may be either beneficial or damaging. The environmental footprint is almost inevitably damaging.

1.2 Environmental footprint (ecological footprint)

An environmental footprint, also called an ecological footprint, is a term that means the impact that an entity has on the environment, in terms of:

■ the amount of raw materials that it uses to make its products or services, where the raw materials are subject to depletion (see note)

■ non-renewable resources that it uses to make its products or services

■ the quantity of wastes and emissions that it creates in the process.

Note: Raw materials subject to depletion are raw materials that can be renewed, but where the current total rate of consumption exceeds the total current rate of renewal. Fish stocks and hard wood timber are examples.

In the past, it was accepted that in order to grow, companies (and economic activity as a whole) had to increase their environmental footprint. With the recognition today that the world cannot go on increasing its environmental footprint, many leading companies are looking for ways to reduce the size of their own particular footprint and 'tread more softly'.

© International Financial Publishing Limited

Reducing an environmental footprint involves the development and implementation of policies for:

- better (more efficient) resource management, and using different resources
- 'green' procurement policies
- waste minimisation and waste management (for example, policies on reducing pollution and recycling waste).

The measurement of environmental footprint

There have been attempts to measure environmental footprint, using a common measure for all activities. It can be measured in terms of the area of productive land and aquatic ecosystems that have been used, from whatever global source. An environmental footprint for any economic activity or any company can therefore be measured in terms of hectares of productive land or aquatic ecosystems.

One widely-used method of footprint analysis for the economic activity of nation states is to identify four methods of environmental consumption:

- energy use
- the built environment (land covered by a human settlement and its connecting infrastructure, such as roadways)
- food products
- forestry products.

For each category, it is possible to measure the land area used for these activities within the country, in global hectares, to obtain a total environmental footprint for the country. This is then converted into an environmental footprint per head of the population.

Countries that consume most environmental resources and create most environmental damage relative to other countries are those with the highest environmental footprint per head of the population.

1.3   Carbon neutrality

The effect on the environment of economic activities by individual companies may be measured in terms of emissions of carbon-based pollutants, such as the release of carbon dioxide into the atmosphere.

Some environmentally-conscious companies already measure their impact on carbon pollution, and might have a stated environmental policy of being 'carbon neutral'.

Carbon neutrality exists when a company is able to counterbalance its use of carbon products, and particularly its carbon dioxide emissions, with activities that reduce the amount of carbon dioxide in the atmosphere such as growing trees or plants (which absorb carbon dioxide from the atmosphere). Some companies have also tried to reduce their impact on carbon dioxide pollution by switching to the use of fuel and energy that does not involve carbon consumption.

Example

There are many examples of large environmentally-conscious companies.

One company has listed some of the initiatives it has taken to create a sustainable business as:

■ Setting a target of zero waste generation and zero waste emissions

■ Conserving energy and resources such as oil, coal, natural gas, water and minerals

■ Recycling materials to reduce the need for disposals

■ Reducing packaging waste

■ Making, using, handling and transporting materials safely and in an environmentally-friendly way and in compliance with local regulations

■ Managing land efficiently to increase habitats for wild life

■ Developing new products and processes that reduce the environmental risks.

1.4 Social footprint

A social footprint is the effect of economic activity on society and people. In general, economic activity is seen as providing benefits for society, although some companies are much more 'people-friendly' than others. Some companies, for example, use child labour and/or pay subsistence-level wages to their workers.

Companies might seek to measure the contribution of their activities towards society in terms of:

■ Total numbers employed or increase in the total number of employees

■ The proportion of the total work force employed in different parts of the world

■ The proportion of the total work force that is female or from different ethnic groups

■ Health and safety at work (for example, numbers of employees injured each year per 1,000 of the work force).

1.5 Social ecology

There are critics of the Western capitalist approach to environmentalism. Social ecologists argue that the environmental crisis has been caused by companies seeking growth, profits and economic self-interest. Nothing fundamental has changed. Companies are still trying to get bigger and more profitable, even though they use environmental ideology to express their plans and ambitions. They argue that the environmental crisis cannot be averted without a radical change in human society.

The following comments are illustrative of the thinking of social ecologists.

■ Environmental problems are caused by companies that seek continued growth in size and profits.

© International Financial Publishing Limited

- Social ecologists also argue that the structure of society and the future of the environment are closely linked.

- They argue that most environmentalists focus, wrongly, on improving technology to improve the environment, or even on restricting population size. These environmentalists are focusing on symptoms of the environmental problems, not its root causes; so they will not find any lasting solution.

- A truly 'green' entrepreneur cannot possibly survive in today's capitalist culture, because by using ecologically/environmentally sound methods they would be at a disadvantage to more ruthless rivals who will produce at a lower cost.

1.6 Towards the measurement of social and environmental effects

So what is the relevance of social and environmental issues to the accountancy profession?

The answer to this question is that, setting the arguments of social ecologists to one side, many companies are becoming increasingly aware of environmental and social issues, and their responsibility for preserving the environment and developing society, as well as for making a profit.

In order to help companies to set targets for achievement and assess their actual performance, there should be measurement. Environmental and social effects should be quantified, because managers find it easier to plan and control using numbers than using more general qualitative assessments.

Some accountancy bodies, including the ACCA, are contributing towards efforts to establish measurement and reporting systems for social and environmental issues, to complement traditional financial reporting. As it is increasingly recognised that conventional financial accounting and financial reporting systems might contribute to non-sustainability, sustainability has become a key issue for accountants. There is now important progress in exploring how financial accounting and financial reporting can play a part in a more sustainable future.

These initiatives may become linked to the developments in corporate governance and reporting to shareholders. It was mentioned in an earlier chapter that in the European Union, companies are now required to provide information about social and environmental risks in an annual business review for shareholders.

Sustainability and accounting for sustainability

- Accounting, the economic model and sustainability reporting
- Sustainable development
- Reporting by companies on sustainable development
- 'Environmental footprint' for individual companies
- Triple bottom line reporting
- Balanced scorecard and sustainable balanced scorecard
- Sustainability Assessment Model (SAM) and full-cost accounting (FCA)
- Sustainability reporting: concluding remarks

---

2 Sustainability and accounting for sustainability

2.1 Accounting, the economic model and sustainability reporting

The capitalist system creates incentives for maximising wealth, and it is based on the assumption that wealth can only be increased through continual economic growth. This is the 'economic model' of society. As a result, growth-seeking economic activities continue, in spite of growing concerns for the environment, and recognition that continual growth in its current form cannot be sustained.

Accounting has developed in support of the economic model. Financial reporting measures the consequences of a company's activities in terms of the use of the assets that it owns and the liabilities for which it has the direct responsibility for payment. Current accounting practice does not allow companies to report the consequences of their actions on external assets that it does not own, and the creation of liabilities for which it does not have to pay directly.

Investment decisions by large companies are made using accounting techniques such as discounted cash flow analysis, which focuses exclusively on economic consequences of investment, and does not measure or evaluate the environmental and social impact.

In the past, companies ignored their consumption of natural resources such as air and water because they assumed that supplies of these items were both limitless and free. This is no longer the case. It can now be argued that whereas companies are increasing economic wealth through growth and the search for profit maximisation, society may well be getting poorer because of the damage that economic activity is having on the environment and society.

As companies have become increasingly aware of environmental issues, and begin to accept that economic growth might not be sustainable, they have become more interested in measuring sustainability and environmental impact.

Traditional accounting methods do not provide for this type of measurement, and to the extent that companies (and society) want environmental and social impacts to be

---

© International Financial Publishing Limited

measured, traditional accounting is inadequate. Alternative measurement and reporting systems that recognise the need for economic activity to be **sustainable** have therefore been considered, although there is as yet no widely-accepted standard measurement and reporting system.

It seems quite possible that as systems for reporting sustainability are developed, the accountancy profession will be closely involved, because of its long experience with measurement and performance reporting systems.

2.2 Sustainable development

A problem with accounting for sustainable development is to identify what 'sustainable development' actually means. A generally-accepted definition provided by the Brundtland Report (for the World Commission on Environment and Development, 1987) is: development that meets the needs of the present without compromising the ability of future generations to meet their own needs.'

However, there are practical difficulties with this definition:

- What are the needs of the present? Presumably, these are more than simply survival needs, because current levels of consumption are, in many parts of the world, well above survival level.

- What are the needs of future generations? Are these just survival needs? If so, there is presumably an assumption that economic wealth will decline.

- Over what time period should the needs of future generations be measured? In theory, future needs should be measured into the long-term future. However, companies and governments plan for the future over much shorter time frames.

- Do we mean the needs of all people in all societies, or is sustainability measured in terms of individual countries or regions of the world?

Since companies plan for the future and report their performance within fairly short time frames, reporting for sustainable development by companies is likely to focus on relatively short-term measures of sustainability.

Another definition of sustainable development is: 'a dynamic process which enables all people to realise their potential and improve their quality of life in ways which simultaneously protect and enhance the Earth's life support system' (Forum for the Future).

2.3 Reporting by companies on sustainable development

The previous section of this chapter suggested that the environmental footprint (or ecological footprint) can be measured for countries and governments in terms of geographical area per head of the population. Companies need something different. Several techniques have been used by companies to plan and report their sustainable development, or the impact of their activities on society and the environment. These include:

- measures of the 'environmental footprint' for individual companies

- triple bottom line reporting

- the balanced scorecard and sustainability balanced scorecard
- the sustainability assessment model (SAM) and full-cost accounting (FCA).

2.4 'Environmental footprint' for individual companies

It is possible to talk about an environmental footprint for individual companies rather than countries, although not as common. A company can measure its environmental footprint through a series of measurements. The measurements appropriate for each individual company might vary according to the nature of its operations, but should relate to the following environmental issues:

- the company's consumption of materials subject to depletion (such as quantities of livestock, timber or non-farmed fish) and non-renewable resources (such as oil, natural gas and coal): also the company's use of other key resources such as land

- the pollution created by the company's activities, measured for example in terms of emissions of carbon dioxide, chemical waste or spillages of oil

- an assessment, in either qualitative or quantitative terms, of the broader effect of the company's resource consumption and pollution on the environment.

2.5 Triple bottom line reporting

The term 'triple bottom line' was 'invented' in 1994 by J Elkington. Its aim is to encourage companies to recognise social and environmental issues in their business models and reporting systems. This method of reporting is encouraged by the Global Reporting Initiative (GRI), an internationally-recognised body that promotes sustainability reporting.

The 'triple bottom line' gets its name because companies report their performance not simple in terms of profit: they provide key measurements for three aspects of performance:

- economic indicators
- environmental indicators, and
- social indicators.

Triple bottom line reporting is therefore providing a quantitative summary of a company's economic environmental and social performance over the previous year.

Economic indicators will include measurements relating to:

- sales revenue
- profits, earnings and earnings per share
- dividends per share
- global market share (as a % of the total market)
- in some industries, such as car production, units of sale worldwide.

© International Financial Publishing Limited

Environmental indicators might include measurements relating to:

- reducing the 'intensity' of materials in products and services
- reducing energy intensity
- minimising the release of toxic materials/pollutants
- improving the ability to recycle material
- maximising the use of renewable resources
- extending the life of a product.

Example

One major global company using triple bottom line reporting reported its environmental performance in terms of:

- global energy use, measured in thousand of GWh
- global carbon dioxide emissions, measured in metric tons
- production of non-recycled waste, measured in metric tonnes
- the number of manufacturing sites that had been awarded an ISO 14000 certificate (which is explained later).

The same company reported, as social indicators:

- its donations to communities and sponsorships, measured in US dollars
- diversity: the percentage of its employees who were female and the percentage who came from minority groups
- the number of discrimination charges brought against the company during the year
- employee satisfaction, based on a census of employee opinion
- the recordable injury rate per 1,000 employees.

Weaknesses in triple bottom line reporting

There are several weaknesses with triple bottom line reporting.

- There are no widely-established standards for triple bottom line reporting, and no standard methods for measuring social and environmental impacts. It is therefore usual to compare the sustainability of one company with the sustainability of another. (The work of the Global Research Initiative or GRI is to standardise measurements for the triple bottom line. It has been publishing Sustainability Reporting Guidelines since 1999. These were updated and amended in 2002.)
- If the social and environmental measures are not subject to independent audit, there might be doubts about the reliability of the data presented in a company's report.

2.6 Balanced scorecard and sustainable balanced scorecard

The concept of the balanced scorecard was suggested by Kaplan and Norton in the 1990s, as a method of setting targets and measuring performance, for both entire companies and individual managers within a company.

The balanced scorecard is a 'strategy map' divided into four element or perspectives:

- a financial perspective
- a customer perspective
- an internal perspective (operations)
- an innovation and learning perspective.

For each perspective, goals, targets and tasks are established, with indicators of performance for comparing actual results against the target. The purpose of a balanced scorecard is to prevent management from directing all their attention to short-term financial considerations. The four perspectives give suitable importance to short-term profitability, but also provide for non-financial and longer-term strategic issues.

A sustainable balanced scorecard has been developed by Moller and Schaltegger. This adds a 'non-market' perspective to the balanced scorecard, for the environmental and social impacts of the company's operations or the manager's activities. This type of scorecard therefore includes an element of accounting for sustainability.

2.7 Sustainability Assessment Model (SAM) and full-cost accounting (FCA)

The Sustainability Assessment Model (SAM) measures the impacts on sustainability of a product over its full life cycle, from raw material extraction through the production process to its final consumption. These impacts:

- the direct economic cost of the product, but also
- the direct impact of the company's operations on society and the environment, and also
- the broader social costs and benefits.

The total impacts are measured as a cost, known as **full cost**, and the measurement system supporting the Sustainability Assessment Model is called full-cost accounting or FCA, because it includes environmental and social costs as well as economic costs.

The SAM is also used to measure the performance of a company on an index of sustainability (SAMi). This measures the percentage distance that the company is from achieving sustainability.

The SAM and FCA approach

The SAM is a four-step approach to measuring the impacts of a project or product over its entire life cycle, from cradle to grave.

© International Financial Publishing Limited

- Step 1. A SAM exercise is established. The object of the exercise is identified, that will be subjected to evaluation. This might be a product, a process, a part of an entity's operations or the whole of its operations.

- Step 2. The boundaries of the SAM evaluation are defined. All the costs and benefits to be included, including environmental and social costs or benefits, are identified over the full life cycle of the product (or other object of the exercise).

- Step 3. The impacts of the product are measured under four headings:

  - economic

  - resource use

  - environmental

  - social.

  Some of these measurements might be in money terms, but many of the costs and benefits will be non-monetary measures, including physical (environmental) measures.

  Typically, the economic impacts and social impacts should normally be positive (benefits), whereas the resource use and environmental impacts are negative.

- Step 4. These non-monetary measures are converted into a common basis of measurement: money. This total money measurement provides the full cost analysis of the product, process or operation.

'None of these steps is easy to do and a great deal of judgement will be exercised at each stage.... While at some levels FCA appears to be conceptually straightforward, it is not an easy technique to develop and use in practice. In particular, FCA requires substantial amounts of physical data about the object of the exercise and requires extensive modelling of complex real-world relationships. The data required for FCA is usually only available in organisations that are at the forefront in responding to the environmental agenda' (Bebbington, Gray, Hibbitt and Kirk, 2001). The main problem is deciding how to convert the physical measurements of environmental impacts into money measures.

Making use of FCA

Full-cost analysis might show the entire cost of a product or an activity, including its social and environmental impacts (or '**externalities**'). However, it might have benefits for strategic planning in companies where it might be expected that in future companies might be required to pay for its 'externalities', so that the 'externalities' become internal costs.

For example, companies might in the future be required to pay for their impact on the environment by:

- paying a carbon tax for their carbon emissions

- having to take back products from customers at the end of their useful life, for recycling or disposing of the materials

- having to comply with stricter environmental standards.

Companies that are aware of the full costs incurred by their products should be in a better position than other companies to plan reductions in those costs, by acting now to reduce carbon emissions, improve environmental standards and so on.

2.8 Sustainability reporting: concluding remarks

For various reasons, companies are increasingly producing sustainability reports in one form or another. The reasons that seem to be persuading companies to report on sustainability include competition, risk management, emerging markets, corporate reputation and, in some countries, mandatory minimum reporting requirements.

However, there is (as yet) no universal agreement about the meaning of sustainability, which acts as a restraint on the development of suitable reporting.

© International Financial Publishing Limited

> ### Environmental management systems, environmental management accounting and environmental audit
>
> - Environmental management systems: ISO 14000 and EMAS
> - Environmental management accounting (EMA)
> - EMA techniques
> - Social and environmental reporting
> - Social and environmental audit / environmental audit

3 Environmental management systems, environmental management accounting and environmental audit

3.1 Environmental management systems: ISO 14000 and EMAS

An environmental management system is a broad general term for any system used by an entity to monitor and manage the impact that its products and operations have on the environment. The aims of a management system might be to:

- minimise the negative impact of operations on the environment (damage to air, water or land)
- comply with environmental laws and regulations
- make continual improvements in either of the above areas.

An environmental management system includes an environmental information system. Information is needed to:

- monitor compliance with environmental laws and regulations, and/or
- monitor the implementation of the company's own environmental policies.

An information system may provide, for example, information about physical quantities of emissions of waste or toxic materials, resources in the environment, the environmental characteristics of the company's products or services, information about environmental 'incidents' such as spillages of waste or toxic materials.

Guidance for companies in the structuring and operating of an environment management system is provided by a number of international.

ISO 14000

The International Standards Organisation (ISO) has issued a series of standards on environmental management systems, known as the ISO 14000 series of standards. They are standards that specify a process for managing, controlling and improving an entity's environmental performance.

They specify an environmental management system, provide guidance for using the system and explain how a company's environmental management system can be audited and receive an ISO 14000 certification.

ISO 14001, one of the standards in the 14000 series, provides general guidance on:

- the general requirements for an environmental management system

- environmental policy: an entity must have an environmental policy in existence, as a condition of meeting ISO 14000 requirements

- planning: an entity should declare its main environmental objectives, which should be primary areas of planning the company's environmental programme and improvement process

- implementation and operation: a system must establish procedures, work instructions and controls to ensure that the environmental policy is implemented and the planning targets are achieved

- checking and corrective/control actions

- management review: there should be a regular review of the environmental management system to ensure that it is suitable (for the entity and its objectives) and effective in operation.

The standard can be applied by any company in any industry, any where in the world. Companies wishing to obtain ISO 14000 certification will be audited against the requirements of this standard. Having obtained the certificate, companies will be subject to regular audits to ensure that they are maintaining compliance with the requirements of ISO 14000.

Another standard in the series, ISO 14004, provides more detailed guidance, including guidance on how to take a structured approach to setting environmental targets and objectives and establishing and implementing a system for monitoring and control.

Companies that apply ISO 14000 and obtain ISO 14000 certification will therefore have a management system for:

- identifying the aspects of its business that have an impact on the environment

- monitoring changes in legislation and regulation on environmental issues

- producing objectives/targets for improvement

- planning to achieve these improvements, and

- conducting regular reviews for continual improvement.

ISO 14000 does not specify targets for achievement or standards of environmental performance. It provides guidance on a management system for the management of environmental issues.

The benefits of obtaining an ISO 14000 certificate

Companies must be 'audited' by an independent external expert before they are awarded an ISO 14000 certificate. Having obtained a certificate, they are therefore

© International Financial Publishing Limited

able to provide an assurance that the company has an active concern for environmental issues to:

■ employees, and

■ individuals and groups outside the company, such as the government, the public, customers and investors/shareholders.

Certification also allows companies to make validated claims about the environmental effect ('environmental-friendliness') of their products.

EMAS

EMAS is the Eco-Management and Audit Scheme. It is a scheme operated by the European Union which recognises companies that are continually improving their environmental performance. Organisations registered with EMAS comply with law, run an environment management system and publish environmental statements which are independently-verified.

EMAS is very similar in concept to ISO 14000.

3.2   Environmental management accounting (EMA)

Management accounting is concerned with the provision of information to management, to help management make decisions. Environmental management accounting has the same purpose, but it identifies environmental costs and benefits, which might be measured in either physical terms or money terms.

Environmental management accounting (EMA) provides information that supports the operation of an environmental management system. It provides managers with financial and non-financial information to support their environmental management decision-making. EMA complements other 'conventional' management accounting methods, and does not replace them.

The main applications of EMA are for:

■ estimating annual environmental costs (for example, costs of waste control)

■ budgeting and setting targets for improvements in environmental performance

■ product pricing

■ investment appraisal (for example, estimating clean-up costs at the end of a project life and assessing the environmental costs of a project)

■ identifying opportunities for cost savings

■ estimating savings from environmental projects.

Although environmental management accounting information is intended for use mainly by management, it is also included in reports that the entity publishes externally, such as sustainability reports/environment reports.

Example

Environmental management accounting can be used to identify opportunities for cost savings.

An example might be the assessment of a proposal to replace the use of toxic materials with a non-toxic alternative material that has a higher purchase cost from the supplier.

An analysis of environmental costs might show that the company would benefit from a switch to non-toxic materials in the form of:

■ removing the cost of having to make reports to the regulatory authorities on toxic materials, and

■ a reduction in materials handling costs.

The benefits might exceed the higher costs of the non-toxic materials.

Environmental management accounting is also used in the assessment of using recycled materials and making constructive use of 'waste' materials.

A framework for environmental management accounting

Burritt et al (2001) suggested a framework for EMA based on providing information to management:

■ that is gathered from internal or external sources

■ as monetary or physical measurements: physical measures of energy consumption, pollution and so on can be converted into a monetary measure

■ as historical or forward-looking information

■ where the focus is short-term or longer-term

■ that consists of routine reports or ad hoc information.

Four of these elements of EMA are shown in the following table.

© International Financial Publishing Limited

Environmental management accounting (EMA)		Monetary EMA		Physical EMA	
		Short-term focus	**Long-term focus**	**Short-term focus**	**Long-term focus**
Historical orientation	Routine reporting	Environmental cost accounting	Analysis of environmentally-induced capital expenditures	Material and energy flow accounting	Accounting for environmental capital impacts
	Ad hoc (one-off) information	Historical assessment of environmental decisions	Environmental life cycle costing, environmental target costing	Historical assessment of short-term environmental impacts, e.g. of a site or product	Post-investment assessment of environmental impacts of capital expenditures
Future orientation	Routine reporting	Environmental operational budgets and capital budgets (monetary reporting)	Environmental long-term financial planning		Environmental long-term physical planning
	Ad hoc (one-off) information	Relevant environmental costing (e.g. special orders)	Environmental life cycle budgeting and target costing	Assessment of environmental impacts	Physical environmental investment appraisal. Specific project life cycle analysis

3.3 EMA techniques

Environmental management accounting techniques include:

■ re-defining costs

■ input-output analysis

■ environmental activity-based accounting

■ environmental life cycle costing.

Re-defining costs

The US Environmental Protection Agency (1998) suggested terminology for environmental costing that distinguishes between:

■ conventional costs: these are environmental costs of materials and energy that have environmental relevance and that can be 'captured' in costing systems

■ potentially hidden costs: these are environmental costs that might get lost within the general heading of 'overheads'

■ contingent costs: these are costs that might be incurred at a future date, such as clean-up costs

■ image and relationship costs: these are costs associated with promoting an environmental image, such as the cost of producing environmental reports. There are also costs of behaving in an environmentally irresponsible way, such as the costs of lost sales as a result of causing a major environmental disaster.

In traditional management accounting systems, environmental costs (and benefits) are often hidden. EMA attempts to identify these costs and bring them to the attention of management.

Input-output analysis

Input-output analysis is a method of analysing what goes into a process and what comes out. It is based on the concept that what goes into a process must come out or be stored. Any difference is residual, which is regarded as waste.

Inputs and outputs are measured initially in physical quantities, including quantities of energy and water. They are then given a monetary value.

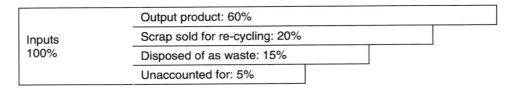

Inputs 100%	Output product: 60%
	Scrap sold for re-cycling: 20%
	Disposed of as waste: 15%
	Unaccounted for: 5%

Environmental activity-based accounting

Environmental activity-based accounting is the application of environmental costs to activity-based accounting. A distinction is made between:

- environmental-related costs: these are costs that are attributable to cost centres involved in environmental-related activities, such as an incinerator or a waste recycling plant
- environmental-driven costs: these are overhead costs resulting from environment-related factors, such as higher costs of labour or depreciation.

The cost drivers for environment-related costs may be:

- the volume of emissions or waste
- the toxicity of emissions or waste
- 'environmental impact added' (units multiplied by environmental impact per unit)
- the volume of emissions or waste treated.

Environmental life cycle costing

Life cycle costing is a method of costing that looks at the costs of a product over its entire life cycle. Life cycle costing can help a company to establish how costs are likely to change as a product goes through the stages of its life (introduction, growth, maturity, decline and withdrawal from the market). This analysis of costs should include environmental costs.

Xerox provides a good example of the environmental aspect of life cycle costing. Xerox manufactures photocopiers, which it leases rather than sells. At the end of a lease period, the photocopiers are returned from the customer to Xerox. At one time, photocopiers were delivered to customers in packaging that could not be re-used for sending the machines back at the end of the lease period. Customers disposed of the

© International Financial Publishing Limited

old packaging and had to provide their own new packaging to return the machines to Xerox. Xerox then disposed of this packaging. The company therefore incurred two costs: the cost of packaging to deliver machines and the cost of disposal of the packaging for returned machines.

By looking at the costs of photocopiers over their full life cycle, Xerox found that money could be saved by manufacturing standard re-usable packaging. The same packaging could be used to deliver and return machines, and could also be re-used. At the same time, the company created benefits for the environment by reducing disposals of packaging materials.

3.4   Social and environmental reporting

Reporting on social and environmental issues is a major feature of corporate social responsibility reporting (CSR reporting) which was described in an earlier chapter.

Some companies publish social and environment reports, often called sustainability reports, as a separate document each year. It is usually published at the same time as the annual report and accounts, but as a separate booklet.

These reports are entirely voluntary (although in the EU companies are now required to include some social and environmental information in their annual business review). Companies can therefore choose what to put in and what to leave out.

This, for example, is where companies that use triple line reporting might publish their triple line results.

There could be several reasons why a company chooses to publish a social and environmental report:

- The board of directors and senior management might have a genuine ethical wish to achieve a sustainable business, and consider that reporting on social and environmental issues is extremely important. For example, a company with an ISO 14000 certificate should want to provide information about its achievements.

- The company might want to publicise its 'green credentials' to investors. This is particularly important as institutional investors expect to see information about a company's social and environmental policies and achievements.

- There could be some element of competition. A company might see a competitive advantage in explaining its social and environmental achievements to customers, for comparison with rival companies.

3.5   Social and environmental audit/ environmental audit

A social and environmental audit, or simply an environmental audit, can have several meanings.

- It can mean a formal audit of an environmental management system, to check that the system operates effectively. Companies with an ISO 14000 certificate are required to have an audit each year of their system, undertaken by an independent external expert.

- It could be an internal check of a particular aspect of the company's environment management system, such as its system for measuring the environmental costs of waste, or the methods used to measure the cost of site contamination at a particular manufacturing site. This audit might be carried out by members of the company's own internal audit team (who might be an environmental expert rather than an accountant).

- There may be a check on the company's compliance with environmental and social legislation and regulations.

- It could involve a verification of social and environmental information that will be included in a published report, such as an environmental performance report.

- Similarly it might be a check on the accuracy of figures supplied by the company to the government authorities responsible for environment regulation.

- It could also refer to the checks that the company's external auditors need to carry out on the company's financial statements, insofar as they relate to environmental issues. For example the introduction of new environmental laws might have an impact on the impairment of non-current assets, and a failure by the company to carry out environmental improvements required by law might create a requirement to make an accrual for remedial costs or a provision for the payment of a fine.

Environmental audits are performed at the discretion of the company's management and can be performed by internal or external experts. An environmental audit is often carried out by a multi-disciplinary team and is used for internal use.

How can environmental audits contribute to environmental accounting?

At the moment there is no legal requirement in any country for environmental audits. This type of audit is voluntary.

Similarly there is no legal requirement for environmental accounting, although professional accounting bodies such as the ACCA are encouraging more research by academics and practice by companies.

It seems quite possible, however, that environmental audits and environmental accounting will both become more common, as companies become increasingly aware of the problems of sustainability and sustainable growth.

The development of environmental accounting and environmental auditing will depend to a large extent on the development of environmental management systems, and how soon more companies establish environmental management systems. When environmental management systems are established:

- management needs reliable environmental information

- in general, managers prefer information in a quantified/measured form rather than in qualitative and descriptive terms

© International Financial Publishing Limited

■ as environmental management systems develop, with measurement systems for setting targets and monitoring performance, it seems likely that the need for audits of the information system will be necessary, to reassure management that the information systems are sound.

However, there still seems a long way to go before social and environmental reporting rivals financial reporting (economic reporting) as the main method of reporting by companies.

© International Financial Publishing Limited

Practice questions

Contents		
		Page

© International Financial Publishing Limited

1 Transparency and independence

Explain the relevance of the following concepts for good corporate governance:

(a)   transparency

(b)   independence, in particular independence of non-executive directors.

2 Principles of public life

In the UK, The Nolan Committee identified seven principles that should be applied by individuals holding public office (in government or in a public organisation). The application of these principles should help to ensure good governance in public organisations and government, similar to good governance in companies.

The seven principles are listed below. You are required to suggest what each of these principles means and how they should be applied by a person holding a public office:

(1)   selflessness
(2)   integrity
(3)   objectivity
(4)   accountability
(5)   openness
(6)   honesty
(7)   leadership

3 Agency

Explain the following:
(a)   The nature of agency theory and its relevance to corporate governance
(b)   The fiduciary duties of agents
(c)   The importance of accountability in the agency relationship
(d)   Agency conflicts
(e)   Agency costs

4 Transaction costs

Explain the relevance of transaction cost theory to corporate governance.

5 Stakeholder theory

Explain the implications of stakeholder theory for:
(a)   corporate governance, and
(b)   reports published by companies.

© International Financial Publishing Limited

6 Composition of the board

Frontier Spirit plc (FS plc) is a UK public company that is planning a stock market flotation that will make it a listed company. You have been asked to give advice to the company chairman about corporate governance.

You have been given the following information about the company's board of directors.

(1) Ken Potter is the chairman and CEO. He founded the company over ten years ago, and even after the stock market flotation he will hold over 10% of the company's shares.

(2) There are three other executive directors: a finance director, a sales and marketing director and a director of operations.

(3) Wendy Potter is a non-executive director. She is the wife of Ken Potter.

(4) Jasper Back is also a non-executive director. Until 18 months ago, when he retired, he was the operations director of FS plc.

(5) Alan Todd is another non-executive director. He is a retired investment banker, and was appointed to the board of FS plc 7 years ago.

(6) Nancy O'Brien is a non-executive director. She is also the CEO of DRP plc. You learn that Ken Potter is a non-executive director of DRP plc.

Required

(a) Comment on the composition of the board of directors and suggest with reasons why the composition of the board does not meet the requirements of the UK Combined Code on corporate governance. You should assume that FS plc will not be a 'small' company, and the full provisions of the Combined Code should apply.

(b) Recommend changes, if any, that should be made to the membership of the board.

7 John Smith

John Smith has been the chief executive officer of Buttons plc for over 25 years. During that time the company has grown in size from a small stock market company to being one of the FTSE250 companies on the London Stock Exchange. The share price has grown substantially in those years, although in the past 12 months it has fallen by about 25%.

The company has just announced that John Smith will be retiring as CEO in three months' time, but he has agreed to become the company chairman then when the current chairman retires. A new CEO to replace John Smith has not yet been appointed.

Required

(a) Explain the risks to good corporate governance of the planned boardroom changes.

(b) Suggest how these risks might be kept under control.

8 Balance of power

(a) Why is it desirable to achieve a 'balance of power' on the board of directors of a major stock market company?

(b) What measures might be taken to achieve a suitable 'balance of power'?

9 Chairman

The Higgs Report (2003) commented: 'The chairman is pivotal in creating conditions for overall board and individual non-executive director effectiveness, both inside and outside the boardroom.'

Explain the role of the chairman of the board in a major stock market company.

10 Two-tier boards and unitary boards

In many countries, companies have a unitary board structure. In some countries, large companies have a two-tier board structure.

Explain the advantages and disadvantages of a unitary board structure, compared with a two-tier board structure, for large stock market companies.

11 Role of NEDs

(a) Explain the **four** roles of non-executive directors on the boards of stock market companies, and the contribution of each of these roles towards the achievement of good corporate governance.

(b) Explain the meaning of 'cross-directorships' and suggest how the existence of cross-directorships could reduce the effectiveness of NEDs in fulfilling their roles.

12 Induction, CPD and performance review

(a) Explain the relevance for corporate governance of induction and continuing professional development (CPD) for directors.

(b) Suggest how the chairman of a public company (with a unitary board) might conduct an annual performance review of the board, the board committees and individual directors.

13 Nominations committee

How does a nominations committee help to achieve good corporate governance within a large public (stock market) company?

© International Financial Publishing Limited

14 Remuneration committee

(a) Describe what you consider to be the **four main functions** of a remuneration committee.

(b) Explain the reasons why the remuneration of executive directors can be a major problem for good corporate governance.

(c) Colin Butt is an executive director of DEW plc, a large UK public company. Colin has a contract of employment that requires two years' notice of termination of employment. He receives a small basic salary and the rest of his remuneration is an annual cash bonus linked to the achievement of annual sales targets. In the past three years, his annual cash bonus has been five times the size of his basic salary.

He also receives an annual payment into a company-funded personal pension scheme. This pension contribution is equal to 10% of his annual basic salary plus cash bonus for the year.

Required
Explain the weaknesses in the remuneration arrangements for Colin Butt.

15 Risk committee

State briefly the purpose of a risk committee, when this committee is established as a sub-committee of the board of directors.

16 Share schemes

Explain the purpose of share incentive schemes and share option schemes for executive directors and other senior company executives, and explain the possible limitations of these schemes.

(Note: In a share incentive scheme, executives are rewarded with fully-paid shares in the company.)

17 Rules-based and principles-based

The practice of corporate governance might be based on voluntary guidelines: alternatively, it might be based on compulsory laws or rules. Guidelines or laws on corporate governance might be either principles-based or rules-based.

Required
(a) Giving examples as illustration, explain the difference in corporate governance between:
   (i) rules-based laws or regulations
   (ii) principles-based guidelines.

(b) Explain the advantages and disadvantages of a principles-based voluntary approach to corporate governance, compared with a rules-based regulatory approach.

18 Family-run company

Discuss briefly whether there are any advantages for a company that is 100% family-owned in applying generally-recognised principles and provisions of good corporate governance.

19 OECD and ICGN

Explain briefly the purpose and the limitations of the OECD Principles and ICGN Principles of corporate governance.

20 Activism

Describe the nature of shareholder activism and explain the effects that shareholder activism might have in improving the quality of corporate governance.

21 Corporate social responsibility

Explain (briefly) the nature of corporate social responsibility (CSR) and list the ways in which CSR should be demonstrated.

22 Internal control system

(a) Explain the objectives of an internal control system.
(b) Describe briefly the main elements of a system of internal control.

23 The Black Oil Corporation

The Black Oil Corporation operates three oil refineries in the United States. Six months ago, there was an explosion at one of the refineries, resulting in serious injury to over 20 employees. An investigation was carried out by a government agency, the Safety and Hazard Investigation Board. In the introduction to its report, the Board commented: 'The Black Oil Corporation has not provided effective process safety leadership and has not adequately established process safety as a core value across all its three refineries. The Board found instances of a lack of operating discipline, toleration for serious deviations from safe operating practices and apparent complacency towards serious process safety risks at each refinery.'

The previous year, an investigation of safety procedures had been conducted at two of the refineries by an independent company of safety experts. The report of the experts had expressed major concerns about weaknesses in safety practices. The report had been distributed to the refinery managers, but no action had been taken.

The Board's report went on to comment that none of the refineries had a printed safety manual and that the senior refinery managers themselves were responsible for breaches of safety procedures.

 © International Financial Publishing Limited

It mentioned a case of a whistle blower three weeks before the explosion, who had reported a serious safety risk. His report to his immediate superior had been ignored, and he had therefore made an urgent report direct to the refinery manager, who told him to speak to his immediate superior. Frustrated at his inability to get anyone to listen to his concerns, the employee had reported his concerns to a television news company. After the explosion, the television company used the concerns of the employee (and how they were ignored) as part of its coverage of the story.

Required

(a)   State the requirements for a 'sound' system of internal control, as suggested in the Turnbull Guidelines on internal control.

(b)   Explain how conditions at the refineries of the Black Oil Corporation indicate that it does not have a sound system of internal control in operation.

24   Auditor independence

Proud Company is a stock market company. Its annual report and accounts are audited by a firm of auditors called Tyre and Ballance. The senior audit partner, Martin Ballance, has been leading the audit team for the Proud Company audit for 10 years. He is a hard-working and serious-minded individual, but he is not assertive and will often give way in an argument. The CEO of Proud Company often has arguments with Martin about the preparation of the financial statements, and some of the judgements and estimates that are used.

Tyre and Ballance is not a large firm. It does non-audit work for clients as well as audit work. The non-audit work that it did for Proud Company last year included some tax advice and some book-keeping work. During the year, Tyre and Ballance earned 35% of its total fee income from audit and non-audit work for Proud Company.

Six months ago, Proud Company appointed a new Finance Director, Maisy Lee. Maisy had worked before for Tyre and Ballance and had been a member of the Proud Company audit team for four years.

Required

(a)   Explain the reasons why it is doubtful that Tyre and Ballance are sufficiently independent as auditors of Proud Company.

(b)   Recommend changes that should be made to improve this aspect of corporate governance.

25   Internal audit and risk management

(a)   Suggest ways in which an internal audit department can contribute to risk management in a large public company.

(b)   Explain how the objectivity of internal auditors can be protected against undue influence.

26   The need for an internal audit function

Flow plc is a UK listed company. It does not have an internal audit function. Its audit committee is carrying out a review to assess whether the company would benefit from having an internal audit function.

Explain the factors that the audit committee should consider in reaching a decision about the recommendation that it should make to the board of directors.

27   Audit committee

The CEO of Plotting plc, a public company whose shares are traded on the stock exchange, has just returned from a meeting with the chairman of the audit committee. He is angry about some of the things that the committee chairman said to him.

"The audit committee does nothing of value for this company," he said. "They are part-time workers who like to hear the sound of their own voice, but they waste my time and serve no useful purpose. We have a fully competent finance director. Why can't the audit committee just let him get on with his job and stop trying to do his job for him?"

Required
(a)   Explain, with reasons, whether an audit committee takes responsibilities away from the finance director.
(b)   Give reasons why an audit committee should improve the corporate governance in a company.

28   Reputation risk

(a)   Explain the meaning of reputation risk for a company, and the sources of this risk.
(b)   Suggest what effect reputation risk might have on a large global company.

29   Technology risk

Explain the nature of technology risk (or technological risk) for companies.

30   Liquidity risk

Explain the nature of liquidity risk and suggest what measures a non-bank company should take to keep liquidity risks under control.

© International Financial Publishing Limited

31   Market risk and derivatives risk

Sham Group is a large global group of companies. It has a treasury department based in the Netherlands. The role of the treasury department is to manage funding for all the companies in the group and to manage its cash. A part of its operations involves investing surplus funds in market instruments.

The department is a profit centre, and it is permitted to take speculative positions in financial and commodity markets, in order to make profits.

The newly-appointed head of the treasury department recognises the need for all treasury staff to be aware of the risks they face in their work, and to understand the need to monitor and control risks. He has called a meeting to speak to the staff about market risk and derivatives risk.

Required
Explain the nature of market risk and derivatives risk, and how these are relevant to the work of the treasury department.

32   Charity

Whitecoats is a charity that raises funds for investment in research into a major disease. There are four charities in the country that raise funds for similar causes. Whitecoats is the second largest, but it is much smaller than the largest charity, Medhelp.

Medical research into the major disease has made substantial progress in recent years, but the cost of investing in a new research projects is now much higher than it was ten years ago. One new three-year project could require funding equal to about 75% of the annual revenue collected by Whitecoats.

Whitecoats has been in existence for about 25 years. A new managing director has been appointed, who wants to introduce risk management systems. He believes that the risks facing the charity are not sufficiently recognised, and systems should be in place for identifying and assessing risks and devising policies and procedures for dealing with those risks.

Required
Suggest what might be the main risks facing Whitecoats, and the nature of risk management measures that might be taken to deal with them.

33   Risk appetite and other terms

The finance director of Basket Company is preparing a proposal to put to the board of directors. He believes that the company is much too cautious in its policy of giving credit to customers. At the moment all customers are given 30 days' credit.

He believes that by increasing its exposure to credit risk, and increasing credit terms to 60 days, the company will achieve an increase in annual sales of up to 20%. He also thinks that some improvements in debt collection procedures will reduce the level of bad debts, although some bad debts cannot be avoided. He thinks that the value of sales where there is a default will fall each year from 2% of sales to 1.8% of sales.

He believes that in order to increase annual sales and profits, the company should be willing to increase its risk appetite, and accept the risk of higher bad debts.

Required

Using this example of managing credit risk, explain and illustrate the meaning of:

(a) exposure to risk

(b) risk of losses

(c) residual risk

(d) risk appetite.

34 Risk map and risk dashboard

Explain briefly the nature and purpose of:

(a) a risk map, and

(b) a risk dashboard.

35 Approaches to risk management

Explain, with an example for each, the following approaches to risk management:

(a) risk reduction

(b) risk transfer

(c) risk avoidance

(d) risk sharing.

36 Risk management review

Robert Lam has just been elected to the board of directors of Global Widgets, a large manufacturing company, as an independent non-executive director. It is his first appointment as a non-executive director, and he is not yet familiar with his role and responsibilities.

At the next board meeting, an item on the agenda is a review of risk management within the company. The board are required by the country's code of corporate governance to review each year the adequacy of the system of risk management.

Robert Lam is preparing a list of questions to ask at the board meeting on this topic. He wants to obtain satisfactory answers to his questions before he will be prepared to agree that the risk management system is adequate.

© International Financial Publishing Limited

Required

Prepare a list of at least six questions that Robert Lam should ask, to help him assess the adequacy of the company's risk management system.

37 Risk model

Describe the features of a risk model and explain the purposes of using a risk model in business.

38 Embedded

Explain the meaning of 'embedding' risk in a company's culture, values and procedures.

39 Consequentialist

(a) Compare a consequentialist approach to ethics and ethical values with a deontological approach, using an example to illustrate the difference.

(b) Explain the strengths and weaknesses of applying a consequentialist approach to ethics in business.

40 Kohlberg

Describe briefly the levels of morality that were identified by Kohlberg and explain why Kohlberg's ideas might have relevance for business managers and professional accountants.

41 Social responsibility

Gray, Owen and Adams (1996) provided a framework for classifying different groups of people and their views of the relationship between business organisations and society. They identified seven different positions that might be taken on the responsibility of companies towards society and the environment.

Required

Explain briefly the nature of these seven different positions, and suggest how the analysis of Gray, Owen and Adams can contribute to an understanding of business ethics.

42 Integrity

Explain what is meant by 'integrity' and why integrity is a fundamental ethical principle, both in corporate governance and for a professional accountant.

43   Public interest

Explain what is meant by 'the public interest' and indicate ways in which professional accountants should be expected to show a concern for the public interest.

44   Business and professional ethics

(a)   Describe the main differences between a business code of ethics and a professional code of ethics for accountants.

(b)   List four situations in which an accountant might face a moral or ethical dilemma.

45   Two clients

You are a sole practitioner in public practice and you have taken on three new appointments. One is to prepare the annual accounts of a small business partnership with two partners, and the other two are to assist with the tax affairs of the two individual partners.

After taking on the appointments, you are told that the partners have now agreed to dissolve the partnership. One partner plans to retire and the other will take over the entire business and run it as a sole trader business. The partners have discussed how the assets of the business should be transferred to the partner who will remain as the owner.

You are informed that the partners have privately agreed an amount for the value of the goodwill of the business, and the retiring partner will receive 50% of this agreed goodwill value plus the return of his balance sheet capital.

You are aware that in the balance sheet, the main asset is a workshop, which is valued at cost, at £120,000. You do not have a current valuation, but you estimate that this workshop could have a current market value in excess of £250,000. You do not know whether the retiring partner is aware of this, and you are concerned that the agreed value for business goodwill might therefore be too low. It has also not escaped your notice that the book-keeper for the partnership business is the husband of the partner who is acquiring the entire business.

Required

Consider whether there is an ethical issue in this situation, and whether you have a duty to bring the value of the workshop to the attention of the retiring partner. Suggest what you should do, if anything.

© International Financial Publishing Limited

46   Errors in the numbers

The board of a company was about to make a decision about whether to make a very large investment to produce and market a new range of products. Tom, the senior management accountant, prepared figures for a board paper that analysed the financial implications of the investment. He used a spreadsheet model to prepare the figures, but did not ask anyone to check his figures. Judy, one of the team working for Tom, subsequently found some errors in the figures that Tom had prepared, which were caused by a small error in the spreadsheet model. Although the error in the model was small, it had a big effect on the figures. The original figures indicated that the new investment should be undertaken. The amended figures raised doubts about whether the investment would be financially viable.

Judy told Tom about the errors in the figures, but Tom decided not to inform the board. At the next board meeting, the directors decided that the investment was too risky, and decided not to proceed with it. Judy was relieved, but felt that she could not ignore the problem of the errors in the figures. She had a meeting with Tom, and Tom agreed that in future he would involve his team more closely in preparing and checking figures that were produced as management information.

Two months later Tom's boss, Will, spotted some errors in another set of figures that Tom had produced and he asked Judy to correct them. In making the corrections, Judy found even more errors that Will had not seen, and she brought the matter to the attention of Tom. Tom told her to correct the errors that Will had seen, but not the others. He didn't want to 'lose face' with his boss, and he didn't think that the errors mattered too much.

Required
(a)   Suggest, with reasons, whether Judy took appropriate action in relation to the incorrect figures produced by Tom for the board paper.
(b)   Suggest with reasons the action, if any, that Judy should take in the current problem about providing the corrected information for Will.

47   Discount

Peter is working on the audit of a company that operates a chain of jewellery shops. You mention to the finance director that you are looking for a special birthday for your mother and you are thinking of buying her a necklace.

Two days later, the finance director comes into the office where you are working and shows you a tray full of necklaces. He tells you that he is able to offer you any of the necklaces for a good discounted price.

Required
Explain the ethical issues involved in this situation, and recommend the action that Peter should take.

48   Principles and rules

What is the main difference between a rules-based and a principles-based code of professional ethics for accountants?

49   Imported meat

Ben Meakin is a senior accountant with Venal Foods, a company that imports and sells a range of meat products. A large quantity of meat was delivered from a supplier in Eastern Europe. This was checked by the company's hygiene and safety inspectors, who reported that some of the meat was contaminated with a virus that could be very harmful to anyone eating it.

Ben was at a meeting where the senior management decided that the risk to human health was probably low, and that the company should sell the meat to its customers in the normal way. However, Ben did not hear any convincing explanation about why the risk was low.

When Ben mentioned the hazards to public health, he was told that as an accountant he did not properly appreciate the risks and that he should leave the decisions to operational management. He should ignore the problem, as this was his duty as an employee of the company.

Required
(a)   Explain the ethical responsibilities of a professional accountant to his employer.
(b)   Explain the ethical responsibilities of a professional accountant as a 'professional.
(c)   Advise Ben Meakin what action he should take in this situation, giving reasons for your advice.

50   Footprint

Explain the meaning of the term 'environmental footprint' and suggest how a company might provide a report to shareholders and the public in general on its 'environmental footprint'.

51   Sustainability

(a)   Describe the nature and features of a sustainability report.
(b)   Explain why sustainability reports should be verified and suggest a way in which verification can be provided.
(c)   Explain the difference between sustainability reporting and social and environmental risk reporting.

© International Financial Publishing Limited

Answers to practice questions

Contents		
		Page
The scope of governance		
1	Transparency and independence	348
2	Principles of public life	348
Agency relationships and theories		
3	Agency	349
4	Transaction costs	351
5	Stakeholder theory	351
The board of directors		
6	Composition of the board	352
7	John Smith	353
8	Balance of power	354
9	Chairman	355
10	Two-tier boards and unitary boards	355
11	Role of NEDs	356
12	Induction, CPD and performance review	357

© International Financial Publishing Limited

1 Transparency and independence

(a) Transparency means making something clear to see and understand, without hiding or obscuring anything from view. Companies that are well governed should make transparent to shareholders and other stakeholder groups information relating to their financial and operating results, the company's objectives, major shareholdings in the company, the directors and senior executives (and their remuneration), significant foreseeable risks facing the company, other issues of significance to employees and other stakeholder groups, and governance structures and policies.

A requirement for companies to disclose information and be transparent is one of the OECD's principles of good corporate governance.

(b) Independence means reaching opinions and making decisions that are not subject to influence from other people. Independence is often linked to objectivity; an objective person reaches views rationally and without bias or prejudice.

The concept of independence is important for corporate governance because a company should be managed by independent-minded and objective leaders, who will reach opinions on the basis of objective judgement, and without influence from other people or other groups.

A well-governed company should have a substantial number of independent people on the board of directors. In the UK for example, a requirement of the Combined Code on corporate governance is that (except for smaller companies) at least one half of the members of the board of directors should be independent non-executive directors. In this way, the board will be more likely to reach decisions that are in the (objective) best interests of the shareholders, and will not be dominated by the opinions of other individuals or interest groups.

2 Principles of public life

(Tutorial note: You should be able to explain most of the seven principles of public life, by applying the qualities of good governance to people holding a public office. However, some concepts are not so easily identified from their 'name'. In particular 'integrity' and 'honesty' can mean in the same thing, and in corporate governance integrity means honest and 'straight dealing'. The Nolan Committee gave integrity and honesty different meanings, although both are related to 'straight dealing'.)

(1) **Selflessness**. Holders of public office should take decisions that they consider to be in the public interest, and should not make their decisions in order to benefit their own self-interest.

(2) **Integrity**. Holders of public office should not place themselves in a position where they are under any financial or other obligation to outside individuals that might influence them in the performance of their duties.

(3) **Objectivity**. When making appointments and awarding contracts, holders of public office should make their choices on merit.

© International Financial Publishing Limited

(4) **Accountability**. Holders of public office should be accountable for their decisions to the public. They should therefore be prepared to submit themselves to public scrutiny, in whatever form is appropriate.

(5) **Openness**. Holders of public office should be as open as possible about the decisions they have taken and the reasons for their decisions, and should only restrict the information they give when this is clearly in the public interest.

(6) **Honesty**. In their dealings and transactions, holders of public office should avoid conflicts of interest between the public interest and their own self-interest.

(7) **Leadership**. Holders of public office should promote and support the other principles through leadership and by setting an example to others.

3 Agency

(a) Agency theory is a theory of the relationship between a principal and an agent. In limited companies, the directors and senior management act as agents of the shareholders, who own the company. Agency theory is based on the view that when an agent represents a principal, the self-interests of the agent are different from the interests of the principal. Without suitable controls and incentives, the agent will take decisions and actions that are in his own interests rather than those of the principal.

Agency theory is relevant to corporate governance because many of the measures recommended for good corporate governance are concerned with controls and incentives that will persuade agents to act in the shareholders' best interests. For example, controls are applied though accountability and incentives are given in remuneration packages.

(b) A fiduciary duty is a duty to act in good faith, in the best interests of someone else. A person with a fiduciary duty is in a position of trust. In the laws of some countries, company directors have a fiduciary duty to their company (rather than to the shareholders), which means that they must act in good faith in the interests of the company and should not be in breach of that duty.

The existence of a fiduciary duty is not sufficient, however, to ensure good corporate governance.

(c) Agents can be encouraged to act in the best interests of their principal through a combination of controls and incentives. Accountability is a form of control. The agent should be required to account to the principal for their decisions and actions, and for how they have performed their duties. In companies, the directors are accountable to the shareholders and are required to submit an annual report and accounts. Accountability is more expensive in several countries, with statutory requirements for narrative reporting (such as the requirement in the EU for companies to provide an annual business review) and additional voluntary reporting (such as sustainability reports).

(d) Agency conflicts are differences in the interests of a company's owners and the self-interests of its managers. They arise in several ways.

- **Moral hazard**. A manager has an interest in receiving benefits from his or her position as a manager, including all the benefits that come from status. Larger benefits mean lower profits, and so are not consistent with shareholders' interests.

- **Effort level**. Managers may put less effort and care into their work than they would if they were the owners of the company. The effect of this could be lower profits and a lower share price.

- **Earnings retention**. The remuneration of directors and senior managers is often related to the size of the company, rather than its annual profits. The size of a company depends on the scale of its operations and volume of sales. Management might prefer to re-invest profits to make the company bigger, rather than pay out the profits as dividends – even if the investments provide a poor return.

- **Risk aversion**. Executive directors and senior managers are often more risk-averse than their shareholders. They do not like taking risks that could threaten the stability of the company, and their jobs and careers. Shareholders often invest in a portfolio of different companies; and risk-taking by individual companies in the portfolio is of less concern to them.

- **Time horizon**. Shareholders are concerned about the long-term financial prospects of their company, because the value of their shares depends on expectations for the long-term future. Managers might only be interested in the short-term, especially when the payment of bonuses is linked to achieving annual performance targets.

(e) Agency costs are the costs of having an agent to make decisions on behalf of a principal. Applying this to corporate governance, agency costs are the costs that the shareholders incur by having managers to run the company instead of running the company themselves.

There are three aspects to agency costs:
- **Costs of monitoring**. The owners of a company can establish systems for monitoring the actions and performance of management, to try to ensure that management are acting in their best interests. This includes financial reporting and auditing, which are expensive activities.

- **Bonding costs**. These costs might be incurred to provide incentives to managers to act in the best interests of the shareholders, and so reduce the size of the agency problem. The incentives are given in the director's remuneration package.

- **Residual loss**. Costs to the shareholder of management decisions that are not in the best interests of the shareholders (but are in the interests of the managers themselves).

Agency costs = Monitoring costs + Bonding costs + Residual loss

© International Financial Publishing Limited

4   Transaction costs

Transaction cost theory, as developed by Coase and Williamson, is an economic theory. It is concerned with how companies develop and take on their form and structure. The form a company takes depends on what activities it chooses to carry on 'in-house' and which goods and services it chooses to buy from external suppliers and leave to other entities. However, it also attempts to provide an explanation of the actions and decisions of managers that are not consistent with rationality and profit maximisation.

Williamson argued that the actions and decisions of managers are based on a combination of bounded rationality and opportunism. Opportunism will often mean that managers take decisions that are in their own personal interests.

A conclusion from this analysis is that the actions of managers should be controlled, to prevent them from acting in their own interests rather than in the best interests of shareholders. In this respect, transaction cost theory is consistent with agency theory, and provides a theoretical justification for the need for rules or principles of good corporate governance, that companies and their managers should apply.

5   Stakeholder theory

(a)   Stakeholder theory is based on the view that companies, especially large companies, have an enormous effect society and the environment. In addition to providing wealth for their shareholders, they provide jobs to a large number of employees, and contribute to national economies and the economies of local communities. They also affect the quality of living of customers and society as a whole.

Companies are 'corporate citizens' and like other citizens they should have responsibilities to society.

In addition to providing returns to their shareholders, companies should therefore consider the interests of its other stakeholders – employees, customers, governments, communities, suppliers, lenders and the general public. Directors and managers should manage their company in a way that serves the interests of all stakeholder groups.

There is a close link between stakeholder theory and the concept of corporate social responsibility (CSR).

(b)   Accountability is an important aspect of responsibility. The managers of companies should be accountable to all stakeholder groups for which they have responsibility.

If the objective of management is to maximise the wealth of shareholders, without regard for any other stakeholders, it might be sufficient for companies to restrict their reporting to the annual report and accounts. This is a document prepared for and directed towards shareholders, and its main concern is with financial performance and financial position.

When a stakeholder theory of corporate governance is applied, companies should be expected to report to all the relevant stakeholder groups. Companies should therefore either produce more reports for other stakeholders, or should include more information in their annual report and accounts and publish the report and accounts for the benefit of all major stakeholders, not just the shareholders.

This might explain the publication by some companies of an annual sustainability report (for circulation to interested readers, not necessarily shareholders) and employee reports for the benefit of the company's employees.

6 Composition of the board

(a) The composition of the board of directors fails to comply with the provisions of the Combined Code in two ways.

   (i) The same individual, Ken Potter, is both the company chairman and the CEO. The Combined Code states that the same individual should not hold both these positions.

   (ii) The Combined Code states that (except for small companies) at least one half of the board members should be independent non-executive directors. In FS plc, at least three of the NEDs are not independent, and on a board with 8 members, one at most is an independent NED.

- An NED cannot usually be independent if he or she (like Wendy Potter) has a close family tie with another director.

- An NED cannot usually be considered independent if he or she (like Jasper Back) was an employee of the company within the previous five years.

- An NED cannot usually be considered independent if he or she (like Nancy O'Brien) holds a cross-directorship with a member of the board. Nancy O'Brien has a cross-directorship with Ken Potter.

- The independence of an NED is also questionable if he or she has been a member of the board for over nine years. Alan Todd has been a NED for seven years. There is no other evidence suggesting that Alan Todd might not be considered independent.

(b) The composition of the board of directors should be changed.

Ken Potter should be persuaded to give up the position of chairman, so that he is only the CEO. An independent chairman should then be found for the company.

The size of the board should not be too large for the company, and it is doubtful whether a suitable solution is to appoint about six extra independent NEDs so that they make up at least 50% of the board. This would make the board too big.

The appropriate solution is to ask some directors to retire. It might be difficult to ask one or two of the executive directors to retire from the board, because the individuals affected might regard this as a 'demotion'. A more appropriate solution would be to ask the three NEDs who are not independent to retire.

If there is a new independent chairman, there would be four executive directors (including Ken Potter as CEO) and one independent NED (Alan Todd). Assuming that Alan Todd is a suitable individual to remain as NED, at least three independent NEDs should be appointed. This would mean that independent NEDs made up exactly one half of the board, excluding the chairman.

The individuals appointed as NEDs should have a suitable range of skills and experience, so that they can contribute effectively to the work of the board of FS plc.

7   John Smith

(a)   Codes of corporate governance vary between countries. However in the UK, the Combined Code states that a former CEO of a company should not move on to become the company chairman. This is to avoid the risk that a chairman who has been the CEO will have a strong and undesirable influence on the new CEO. For example a new CEO might want to make changes to the way the company is run, which the chairman (former CEO) might take as a criticism of the way he used to run the company. The chairman might therefore challenge the changes that the new CEO proposes to make.

A new CEO has not yet been appointed. The current CEO plans to become the chairman in three months' time, and it is not clear whether there will be time to find a successor. If the nominations committee has not already discussed succession planning and a replacement for the CEO, it has been failing in its responsibilities.

If a new CEO is not appointed in the next three months, and the former CEO becomes the chairman, he might also retain temporarily the role of CEO. The UK Combined Code argues that the powers of chairman and CEO should not be held by one individual, because it gives too much power on the board to that individual. A situation in which an individual is both CEO and chairman should normally be temporary and should not continue for longer than is necessary.

(b)   When a former CEO moves on to become the company chairman, the responsibility of the non-executive directors for maintaining a balance of power on the board becomes even more important than usual. The non-executive directors, possibly with the senior independent director acting as their spokesman, should be able to challenge attempts by the chairman/former CEO to exert undue influence over decision-making by the board.

8 Balance of power

(a) A board of directors in a major company should contain a suitable balance of power in order to prevent one person or one small group of individuals from dominating decision-making by the board. When a board is dominated by one individual, there is a risk that decisions by the board will be taken in the best interests of that individual personally, rather than in the interests of the shareholders.

When there are several independent-minded individuals on the board, it is more likely that the interests of the shareholders, and possibly also other stakeholders in the company, will be properly represented.

(b) There are several ways of trying to achieve a suitable balance of power on the board. The suggestions below are based on corporate governance practice in the UK.

- The same individual should not hold the position of both chief executive officer and chairman of the board of directors. The CEO is the head of the executive management team, and the chairman is the leader of the board of directors. They are both positions of substantial power or influence. If different individuals hold the positions, some 'balance' of power is achieved.

- The roles of the CEO and chairman should be specified formally (in writing) so that one of these individuals is not able to take responsibilities (and power) away from the other.

- There must be a strong presence of independent non-executive directors on the board. The UK Combined Code states that in large stock market companies, a majority of the board should be independent NEDs. The chairman should be responsible for making sure that each NED contributes to the discussions at board meetings and to decision-making by the board.

- There should be a senior independent director with sufficient strength of character to challenge both the chairman and the CEO if this seems necessary.

- The NEDs must be effective in their role. A suitable balance of power on the board cannot be achieved unless the NEDs are able to contribute sufficiently and effectively. When they are appointed, they must indicate that they will be able to give sufficient time to the company. The chairman is responsible for their induction, and for arranging an annual performance review.

- Some decision-making should be delegated to board committees, to remove decision-making from directors in cases where a conflict of interest might rise (for example the remuneration committee) or to act as a check on some of the activities of executive directors (for example the audit committee).

© International Financial Publishing Limited

9 Chairman

The board chairman is the leader of the board of directors, and is responsible for ensuring that the board as a whole and also individual directors contribute effectively to the work of the board. He is also a figurehead for the company, and represents the company in many of its dealings with external institutions.

As leader of the board of directors, the chairman:

- sets the agenda for board meetings, and leads board meetings
- provides all directors with suitable (and timely) information before each board meeting – the 'board papers'
- at board meetings, encourages contributions to the discussions from all directors
- at board meetings, allows sufficient time for discussion of complex issues
- helps non-executive directors to contribute effectively to the company.

The chairman is responsible for the effectiveness of the board. He is therefore responsible for:

- the induction of all new directors and
- the annual performance review of the board, board committees and individual directors.

The chairman should also set the values and standards for the company. The culture and ethical stance of a company is often expressed in public and to employees by the chairman, more than by any other member of the board.

The chairman is also responsible for creating a relationship of trust between the executive management and the non-executive directors. The relationship between the chairman and the CEO is also important in creating a sense of trust between the board and the executive management of the company.

The chairman has a key role in establishing and maintaining communications (and dialogue) with the company's shareholders. He also acts as chairman of general meetings of the company.

10 Two-tier boards and unitary boards

In a unitary board structure, there is a single board of directors. In a two-tier structure, there are two boards of directors: a management board of executive directors and a supervisory board of non-executive directors. The management board has the authority to take some business decisions and the supervisory board is responsible for other board-level decisions by the company.

The main advantages of a unitary board structure are as follows.

- The executive directors and non-executive directors meet together and are jointly responsible for all the decisions of the board. They can all contribute their skills and experience to decision-making.

- Non-executive directors can influence business strategy more directly than in companies with a two-tier structure, where many strategic decisions are taken by the management board. With a unitary board structure, non-executive directors can therefore be more effective in using their knowledge and experience to contribute to decision-making by the board.

- Since all board decisions are taken by a single board, all the directors are jointly accountable to the shareholders. Accountability of the directors to the shareholders is a key feature of good corporate governance.

- In a two-tier board structure, the chairman and CEO are very powerful individuals, even more so than in companies with a unitary board. With a unitary board. The NEDs are able to exert more influence, and so help to achieve a better balance of power.

The main disadvantages of a unitary board are as follows.

- It is usual for unitary boards to have a majority of independent NEDs. This is a requirement for large listed companies in the UK. If any NEDs represent a particular interest, such as a major shareholder or the employees of the company, they are not independent: the board will need be quite large if it is to have a majority of independent NEDs.

- Two-tier boards make it much easier to appoint directors who represent particular interests, such as the interests of employees. This has advantages as well as disadvantages. The advantage of having non-independent NEDs is that the supervisory board can represent more stakeholder groups. A stakeholder approach to corporate governance is a valid alternative to a shareholder-focused approach.

- On a unitary board, NEDs are both colleagues of their executive director colleagues, but also supervisors or 'policemen' with the task of preventing executive directors from running the company in their own interests rather than those of the shareholders. With a two-tier board, the supervisory board (as its name suggests) has a supervisory role over executive directors. Directors on the supervisory board are not required to mix the roles of 'colleague' and 'policeman'.

11   Role of NEDs

(a)   The Higgs Report (2003) commented that the role of the non-executive director is frequently described as having two main elements: (1) monitoring executive activity and (2) contributing to the development of strategy. There is a tension or conflict between these two roles.

Higgs drew different conclusions and his report identified four roles for non-executive directors, which do not contain any conflicts or tensions.

(1)   **Strategy**. NEDs should make a constructive contribution to the development of the company's business strategy.

(2)   **Performance**. NEDs should 'scrutinise' the performance of management in meeting agreed goals and objectives. They should also monitor the reporting of performance.

    © International Financial Publishing Limited

(3) **Risk**. NEDs should satisfy themselves that financial information produced by the company is accurate. They should also satisfy themselves that financial controls and systems of risk management are 'robust and defensible'.

(4) **People**. NEDs are responsible for deciding the level of remuneration of executive directors. They also have a prime role in appointing and (where necessary) removing senior management, and in succession planning.

In fulfilling these roles, NEDs help to ensure that the board of directors makes decisions in the best interests of its shareholders and is accountable to shareholders for the objectives that it sets for the company, the company's performance and the management of risk. With their responsibility for remuneration of executive directors, NEDs are also able to reduce the 'conflict of interests' between shareholders and executive directors, by devising remuneration schemes that create a unity of interests between the two groups.

(b) A cross-directorship occurs when an executive director of Company A also sit on the board of Company B as a non-executive director, and at the same time an executive director of Company B sits as a non-executive director on the board of Company A.

When cross-directorships exist, the non-executives involved might be reluctant to criticise each other. In the example above, the non-executive of Company B might be reluctant to criticise the executives of Company B, provided that the executive of Company B who is also a NED of Company A does not criticise him. There is a clear conflict of interests.

The conflict of interests can be even more extreme when each director is a member of the remuneration committee of the other company, helping to decide the remuneration package of the other. Each might be tempted to be generous to the other, for example in deciding cash bonuses and share option awards.

In practice, many companies do not allow cross-directorships. However, the problem is not eliminated entirely. Many non-executive directors who are also executives of major companies are familiar with each other. An executive of Company A may be a NED of Company B, an executive of Company B may be a NED of Company C and an executive of Company C may be a NED of Company A. In this way a circle of self-interest can still operate.

12 Induction, CPD and performance review

(a) When directors are appointed to the board of a company, they are expected to bring the benefits of their knowledge and experience to the discussions of the board. In order to contribute effectively, individuals need to have an understanding of the company, its markets and its operations. They also need to keep their relevant technical knowledge up-to-date, so that they are aware of developments that affect their own technical knowledge or their responsibilities as directors (for example by remaining up-to-date with changes in company law and other regulations).

Induction is important for non-executive directors when they first join the board of a company. The purpose of induction is to teach them about the company, its products, markets, operations, key personnel, key assets and so on. Induction can be provided by a combination of documents, site visits and meetings/interviews with managers and other employees.

Continuing professional development is necessary to make sure that directors remain up-to-date with their relevant professional knowledge.

(b) In some countries such as the UK, there is a requirement for an annual performance review in listed companies of the board of directors, the board committees and individual directors. The chairman is responsible for the performance review (except for his own review which is carried out by the independent NEDs).

There are no specific rules about how a performance review should be conducted, and a chairman might seek the advice of external specialists.

The general principles for a performance review are as follows.
(i) Performance targets should be established. These might be quantitative targets but are more likely to be qualitative targets. For example, qualitative targets might be set for individual directors (contributions to board or committee discussions) and for board committees (such as a requirement for the remuneration committee to negotiate successfully the annual remuneration review for executive directors and other senior executives).
(ii) Actual performance should be compared with the targets.

Another approach might be for the chairman to consider the answers to a list of questions about performance.

Questions for assessing the performance of the board as a whole might be as follows. (**Tutorial note**: These are based on the Higgs Guidance).
- If the board set any performance objectives for itself, how has it actually performed in comparison with those objectives?
- What has the board contributed to the development of strategy?
- What has the board contributed to ensuring risk management for the company that is 'robust and effective'?
- Is the composition of the board and its committees appropriate, in terms of the balance of skills and knowledge, to maximise performance in the light of future strategy?
- For any problems that occurred during the previous year, how well did the board respond to dealing with them?
- How well does the board communicate with management, the company's employees and others? How effectively does it use the AGM and the annual report for communicating?
- Is the board as a whole up-to-date with the latest developments in the regulatory environment for the company and in its markets?

© International Financial Publishing Limited

The performance of individual directors can be judged by answers to the following questions. Some of these questions are particularly relevant for NEDs.

- How well prepared and informed are they for meetings? Has their attendance at meetings been satisfactory?

- Have they shown a willingness to give their time and effort to understanding the company's business? Have they shown a willingness to take part in events outside board meetings, such as site visits?

- What has been the quality and value of their contributions to board meetings?

- What has been their contribution to the development of strategy and to risk management?

- How successfully have they brought their knowledge and experience to bear in the consideration of strategy?

- Where necessary, how resolute have they been in maintaining their own views and resisting pressure from others?

- How effectively have they followed up their areas of concern?

- How effective and successful are their relationships with other board members, the company secretary and senior managers?

- How well have they refreshed their knowledge and skills?

- How well do they communicate with fellow board members, senior managers and others (such as shareholders)? Are they able to present their views diplomatically? Do they listen to the views of other board members?

If the chairman considers performance to be unsatisfactory, he should consider ways of encouraging directors to improve their performance.

13 Nominations committee

A nominations committee can help to achieve good corporate governance in the following ways.

- It is responsible for ensuring that the board contains a suitable balance and spread of skills and experience.

- It monitors the current composition of the board and considers the ideal composition of the board, as change soccer in the business circumstances and environment of the company. The nominations committee is responsible for recommending changes in the balance and skills/experience of the board to meet the changing needs of the company.

- Although it is likely to consist of a mixture of executive and non-executive directors, it prevents the chairman or CEO from dominating of the process of appointing new directors.

- It is responsible for planning the succession to key positions on the board, particular the succession to the positions of chairman and CEO.

14 Remuneration committee

(a) The main functions of a remuneration committee are, in my opinion, as follows.

(1) The remuneration committee should formulate a remuneration policy for executive directors and other senior management. The policy should have the objective of offering remuneration packages that are sufficient to attract and retain talented individuals as directors, without being excessively generous. The policy should also have the aim of structuring remuneration packages so that individual directors (and executives) are rewarded when their performance or the performance of the company as a whole is in the best interests of the shareholders. The detailed remuneration policy formulated by the remuneration committee should be submitted to the board of directors for approval. It should also be reviewed regularly.

(2) The committee is also responsible for negotiating the individual remuneration package for each executive director, and possibly also individual senior executive managers. The remuneration committee should negotiate all aspects of remuneration with the individual: basic pay, pension contributions, short-term bonus arrangements, long-term bonus arrangements and other benefits.

(3) The committee should also review and agree actual bonuses for each individual executive director (and senior executive manager).

(4) The committee should be accountable to the shareholders for the remuneration of directors. In the UK, the remuneration committee (of quoted companies) is required to prepare a directors' remuneration report each year, and shareholders vote on a part of this report at the annual general meeting (in an advisory vote only).

(**Note**: You may have selected other functions of the remuneration committee that in your opinion are more important.)

(b) The remuneration of executive directors can be a major problem for good corporate governance.

(1) One aim of a remuneration package should be to offer a sufficiently good remuneration to attract talented individuals as directors, but to avoid paying too much. Experience has shown that remuneration committees are inclined to overpay.

(2) Remuneration packages can reduce the conflict of interest between individual directors (who want to maximise their own personal benefits) and the company's shareholders. This is done by offering a number of short-term bonuses and longer-term awards for the achievement of agreed performance targets. However, the conflict of interest is only reduced if the directors are rewarded for achieving targets that are actually in the best interests of the shareholders.

- Sometimes bonuses are paid for the achievement of performance targets that are not necessarily in the best interests of the shareholders.

© International Financial Publishing Limited

- It can be difficult to find a suitable balance between short-term targets and longer-term objectives. Sometimes, short-term profits have to be sacrificed for the longer-term gain, but remuneration schemes do not necessarily recognise this point.

(3) Directors might be tempted to 'manipulate' reported profit figures so as to maximise their personal cash bonuses or share awards.

(4) Unless arrangements are agreed about payments to a director in the event of his dismissal from the company, there is a risk that a remuneration package will provide for a very generous payment. High payments to a director who has been dismissed have been called 'rewards for failure'.

(5) There have been reported cases where a share option incentive scheme for directors has been amended after a fall in the share price, with new share options issued at a lower exercise price. For example, share options issued to executives at an exercise price of $6 per share might be replaced with share options at $5 per share if the share price falls. In this way, the shareholders suffer from the fall in the share price but the executives do not.

(c) There are several weaknesses in the remuneration package of Colin Butt.

(1) There are no long-term incentives, such as a share award scheme or a share option scheme. The remuneration package does not therefore attempt to bring the interests of Colin Butt into line with the long-term interests of the shareholders.

(2) The basic pay is a small proportion of the total annual pay. This means that Colin Butt relies heavily on bonus payments to make up his remuneration. It might be more appropriate to set the basic pay higher and make the cash bonus element smaller.

(3) The annual cash bonus is such a large part of the total remuneration of Colin Butt that the will almost certainly do whatever he can to maximise annual sales. It is not at all clear that maximising sales will be in the best interests of the company, either in the long-term or even in the short term. There is still a conflict of interest between him and the shareholders that this bonus payment does not reduce.

(4) It is generally considered undesirable to make pension contributions variable with bonus payments. Pension contributions should be linked to basic pay only.

(5) The two-year notice period in the employment contract of Colin Butt is undesirable. If he is dismissed from the company, the two-year notice period means that he might be entitled to a high 'severance' payment. This might be seen by shareholders as a 'reward for failure.'

15 Risk committee

(**Tutorial note**. This question asks about a risk committee that is a sub-committee of the board. Do not confuse this risk committee, when such a committee exists, with risk management committees. Risk management committees are committees of executives and advisers, such as internal auditors. They are not committees of the board.)

The board of directors of a company might establish a risk committee. The purpose of a risk committee would be to review the company's internal control and risk management systems.

In the UK, listed companies are required by the Combined Code to carry out a review of the effectiveness of the company's internal control system and risk management system. Internal controls consist of operational controls and compliance controls, as well as financial controls.

Membership of the risk committee should consist entirely of independent non-executive directors. As a sub-committee of the board, should report to the board on its findings and recommendations.

When a company does not establish a risk committee for this task, the work should be done instead by the audit committee.

16 Share schemes

Share incentive schemes and share option schemes are commonly included in the remuneration package for executive directors and other senior executives of a stock market company.

The purpose of these schemes is to provide a long-term incentive, which gives the executives a personal interest in the performance of the company's share price over a period of several years. Since the executives will gain personally from an increase in the share price, they have an incentive to do what they can to improve the company's financial performance and longer-term prospects. In this way, the self-interest of the executives is consistent with the interests of the company's shareholders.

These long-term incentive schemes are a part of the overall remuneration package for an executive, which normally includes a short-term incentive arrangement (often an annual cash bonus based on achieving short-term performance targets).

There can be some problems with share schemes, with the result that they are not always effective in giving a sufficient incentive to the executives.

- The executives might be motivated more by short-term targets and cash bonuses than by longer-term targets and share awards. When short-term considerations are not consistent with longer-term interests of the company, the executives might put short-term considerations first, in order to earn their cash bonus.

- A problem with share options is that if the market price of the shares falls, for example because of a general fall in stock market prices, the options may be 'under water' and worthless. When this happens, they will not provide much of an incentive.

- Share schemes are often a three-year arrangement. The executive receives an award of fully-paid shares, or is able to exercise share options, after three years. If the executive then sells the shares, his or her interest in the company's share price comes to an end, unless another share incentive or award of share options is granted.

© International Financial Publishing Limited

17   Rules-based and principles-based

(a)   **A system of corporate governance based on rules and regulations** requires companies to comply with specific governance requirements and failure to comply with the rules will result in action by the authorities responsible for the enforcement of the rules.

In the US for example, many aspects of corporate governance for stock market companies are enforced as laws or regulations. The Sarbanes-Oxley Act provides a legislative framework, and detailed rules have been implemented by the Securities and Exchange Commission, the US financial markets regulator.

An example of a corporate governance rule is the requirement in the US for senior management to conduct an annual review of the internal control system for financial controls, and to report to shareholders on any weaknesses in the system.

However, in all countries with a stock market, there are laws requiring stock market companies to prepare annual financial statements for the shareholders. This is a basic form of regulatory corporate governance, involving the accountability of a company's directors to the shareholders.

A system of corporate governance based on guidelines is a voluntary system, although there might be strong 'moral pressure' to comply. In the UK for example, the Combined Code is a voluntary code of governance, but UK listed companies are required to comply with the Code or explain any non-compliance in their annual report and accounts.

Listed companies that fail to comply with any aspect of the Combined Code often come under strong pressure, from institutional investors and investment banking advisers, to change their system of governance and start to comply.

Voluntary systems of corporate governance might be rules-based, with the guidelines specifying exactly what companies should do. In practice, however, voluntary codes are usually principles-based. In the UK, for example, the Combined Code is principles-based: the Code specifies certain principles of corporate governance that all companies should comply with and apply. It then specifies some guidelines, suggesting how the principles might be applied in practice. Listed companies are required to comply with these practical guidelines or provisions, or explain their non-compliance. There might be good reasons for non-compliance with specific provisions, but the principles should always be applied.

(b)   A voluntary principles-based system of corporate governance has the following advantages:
   (1)   It is flexible, and allows companies to adapt the detailed application of corporate governance to suit the requirements of their own particular situation. Variations from the general guidelines can be justified provided that the reasons for (principles supporting) the non-compliance are justified.

(2)   It is much cheaper and easier to operate than a rules-based legal system. A major criticism of the Sarbanes-Oxley Act has been the large amount of resources that companies have had to commit to ensuring compliance with the law, and the high costs of compliance. It has even been suggested that the high costs and effort needed to comply with Sarbanes-Oxley has led to a switch by some companies from listing in New York to listing in other financial centres that have only a voluntary corporate governance system, such as London.

(3)   A voluntary system is easier to alter, if the system is not working effectively. In contrast, it usually takes more time to change a law or set of regulations.

(4)   Many aspects of corporate governance are concerned with improving the relationship between shareholders of a company and the board of directors. It could be argued that it is difficult to specify rules on how to achieve a good relationship. There must be a large voluntary element.

A voluntary principles-based system of corporate governance has the following disadvantages:
(1)   If a company's directors intend to act in pursuit of their own personal interests and not in the best interests of the shareholders, rules are needed to govern their behaviour.
(2)   Some shareholder rights need to be protected by law. However, there is variation between different countries in the amount and extent of legal requirements on governance.
(3)   It might be argued that a system of laws or regulations will give investors more confidence in the system of corporate governance by companies.

18   Family-run company

In a family-run company, the directors of the company are usually also its owners. In these circumstances, the agency problem does not exist, because the self-interest of the directors is the same as the self-interest o f the shareholders.

When the agency problem does not exist, it is much less important to have provisions for corporate governance that make the directors more accountable to the shareholders and executive management more accountable to the directors.

It might be unnecessary, for example, to have a remuneration committee of independent NEDs, or a nominations committee to consider board appointments.

It might be useful to have an audit committee to perform a monitoring role over the preparation of the financial statements and the audit, but this committee need not consist of independent NEDs.

It might also be useful to have a risk committee (or an audit committee) to carry out regular reviews of the systems of internal control and risk management. The board should satisfy itself that these systems are effective.

    © International Financial Publishing Limited

In summary, some of the principles of good corporate governance might be applied in a family-run company, and independent NEDs might be appointed to the company's board. However, family-run companies do not need a code of corporate governance to the same extent as stock market companies, and the 'rules' or 'provisions' can be less strict.

19   OECD and ICGN

The OECD Principles are published by the Organisation for Economic Co-operation and Development, an organisation whose members are the governments of about 30 economically-developed countries. The objective of the OECD is to encourage development in the world's economy. The OECD recognises that a factor in the development of a national economy is the existence of a successful capital market in which investors have confidence and are willing to invest.

The OECD principles are minimum requirements for corporate governance, since the confidence of investors is dependent on the quality of corporate governance in companies whose shares are traded on the stock market.

The OECD has explained the purpose of its principles as being to:

■   assist governments of countries to improve the legal, regulatory and institutional framework for corporate governance in their countries, and

■   provide guidance to stock exchanges, investors and companies on how to implement best practice in corporate governance.

The International Corporate Governance Network (ICGN) is a voluntary association of major institutional investors, companies, financial intermediaries and other organisations. Its aim is to improve corporate governance practices around the world, in all countries where institutional investors seek to invest.

The ICGN Principles are consistent with the OECD Principles, but have the more specific objective of providing information to stock markets and companies about the issues that investors will take into account in deciding how (and where) to invest. The ICGN gives greater emphasis than the OECD to the right of investors to participate actively in corporate governance in the companies in which they invest.

Both the OECD Principles and ICGN Principles apply to all national jurisdictions. They have the advantage of identifying universal principles of corporate governance. This is also a limitation, because they are minimum standards that countries, stock markets and companies should be expected to achieve. They do not set higher targets. Consequently, they are of no practical value to countries, stock markets and companies that already practice corporate governance to a higher standard.

20   Activism

Shareholder activism describes actions that are taken by shareholders to influence decisions by the board of directors of their company, or to indicate their disapproval of directors and the decisions they have taken.

Activism is contrasted with a more passive approach. Shareholders taking a passive approach accept whatever decisions are taken by the board of directors, and if they disapprove of what a company and its directors are doing, they sell their shares.

Shareholder activism involves shareholders entering into a (constructive) dialogue with the board of directors of a company and making the directors aware of their opinions and views. It also involves making thoughtful use of voting rights at general meetings of the company, usually by appointing proxies to vote on their behalf and instructing the proxy how to vote on each proposal that is put to the meeting.

Shareholder disapproval of the actions of the board of directors can be shown by voting against certain proposals, such as proposals to re-elect certain directors or, in the UK, voting against approval of the directors' remuneration report.

In the UK, institutional investors are given guidance on how to vote at company meetings by advisory groups such as RREV and PIRC. Advice to vote against a particular proposal at the general meeting of a company is known as a 'red top'. If a sufficiently large number of shareholders vote in the same way, a substantial 'no' vote can be obtained. In some cases, a majority of votes might be obtained against a proposal by the board of directors in a general meeting, although this is a rare event.

In general, however, active shareholders are supportive of the board of directors, and seek to engage in constructive dialogue.

Shareholder activism can improve the quality of corporate governance in several ways.

■ It helps to make directors more accountable to the company's shareholders. Regular dialogue with major shareholders forces senior members of the board (the chairman or CEO) to justify their decisions and actions to shareholders. Accountability of the directors to the shareholders in an important aspect of good corporate governance.

■ The board of directors are more likely to consider the views of their shareholders before making important decisions. A company needs to maintain the goodwill of institutional investors, whose help and support they might need in the future in raising new finance. The directors will also want to avoid defeat in a vote at a general meeting of the company.

■ Shareholder activists encourage all shareholders to make well-considered use of their votes in general meetings. This contributes to better corporate governance, because when a larger proportion of shareholders vote, more shareholders are exercising their rights.

■ Bad corporate governance is discouraged because disagreements between the directors and shareholders are likely to be notified to the media. The company and its directors would then attract unfavourable media coverage.

© International Financial Publishing Limited

- Activist shareholders have contributed in the UK to the improvement in the range and quality of information that companies provide. For example, the increasing amount of disclosures by quoted companies about environmental and social issues (in an annual business review or sustainability report) has happened partly because of pressure from institutional investors.

21   Corporate social responsibility

Corporate social responsibility is the responsibility that each company has towards the society (or societies) in which it operates. It includes responsibilities for individuals, communities and the environment generally.

A justification for the view that companies have a social responsibility is that companies, like individuals, are a citizen of their society. Companies are a 'corporate citizen'. All citizens have an obligation to act responsibly and to deal fairly and properly with other citizens of society.

Good citizenship, and therefore corporate social responsibility, apply to the following aspects of corporate activity.

(1)   Ethical behaviour. Companies should behave ethically.

(2)   Human rights. Companies should respect the rights of people. For example, they should avoid dealing with suppliers who use child labour or slave labour.

(3)   Employee rights. They should respect the rights of employees and treat them fairly as an employer.

(4)   Dealings with communities. Companies should contribute to the welfare of the communities in which they operate, in all countries.

(5)   Environmental issues. Companies should shown concern for the environment and work towards the sustainability of their business.

It might also be argued that companies should be accountable to the rest of society for their social and environmental behaviour. This is the reason why some public companies publish annual CSR reports, social and environmental reports, or sustainability reports.

22   Internal control system

(a)   The risks facing a company can be divided into two broad categories: business risks (also called strategic risks or enterprise risk) and 'governance' risk. Business risk or strategic risk is the risk that must be taken when investing in business ventures. Some risk must be taken in order to earn a return.

Governance risk is the risk of losses from failures in systems, due to weaknesses in policies and procedures, technological breakdown or failures, human errors, fraudulent activity, and unforeseen events (such as natural disasters or terrorist attacks).

An internal control system is a system of policies, procedures, organisation structures, management, supervision and recruitment and training that provides some control over governance risks. A key element of a system of internal control is internal controls.

There are different definitions of internal control. In the UK, internal controls are defined as all the financial controls, operational controls and compliance controls that are in place to control risks.

An internal control system cannot eliminate these risks. Sometimes, the benefits from additional controls are not worth the cost of applying the control. Internal controls cannot prevent risks from human error in failing to apply controls, cannot prevent managers from deliberately ignoring controls, and cannot provide for all unforeseen events. However, the purpose of an internal control system should be to create an awareness of risk within the entity and an understanding of the need to control risk. It should also reduce the residual risks to an acceptable level.

The purpose of an internal control system is therefore to provide reasonable assurance that (1) the system of financial reporting provides reliable accounting information, (2) risks of fraud are limited, (3) the entity is complying with all relevant legal and regulatory requirements and (4) operational systems and procedures function effectively.

(b)   The COSO Framework is one way of describing the structure of an internal control system. This identifies five elements in the system.
   (1)   A control environment. This describes a culture of risk awareness, set by senior management. For an internal control system to function properly, risk awareness should be 'embedded' in the culture of the organisation.
   (2)   Risk assessment. There should be procedures for regular risk identification and assessment (evaluation). The entity should be able to identify new risks that emerge and changes in the significance of risks that have already been identified.
   (3)   Control activities (internal controls). Internal controls should be applied to reduce the exposures to risk.
   (4)   Information and communication. There should be a free flow of information about risks, risk control measures and problems with risks and controls.
   (5)   Monitoring. The effectiveness of the system of internal control should be continually monitored and reviewed. Weaknesses should be identified and dealt with.

23   The Black Oil Corporation

(a)   An internal control system consists of the policies, processes tasks and behaviours in a company that, taken together:
   ■   facilitates its efficient and effective operation by enabling it to respond to significant business, financial , operational, compliance and other risks

   ■   help to ensure the quality of internal and external reporting

   ■   help to ensure compliance with relevant laws and regulations and with internal policies relating to the conduct of business.

© International Financial Publishing Limited

The Turnbull Guidelines state that a 'sound' system of internal control should:

- be embedded in the operations of the company and form a part of its culture
- be capable of responding quickly to risks as they evolve
- include procedures for reporting significant weaknesses and failures of control to the appropriate level of management.

(b)   The internal control system for safety at Black Oil Corporation fails to meet these requirements. These are severe failings in operational controls (and probably with compliance controls, because it is highly probable that the company has failed to comply with safety regulations at its refineries).

- Control is not embedded in the culture of the company. The attitude of senior managers has a very strong influence on the culture of an entity. In Black Oil, executives ignored safety procedures themselves. This would encourage other employees to assume that safety is not important and that the 'correct' procedures can be ignored.

- It is not clear that control is embedded in the operations of the company. It is very surprising that the company does not even have a formal manual of safety procedures. The Board report stated that breaches of safety procedures were common.

- The procedures for reporting weaknesses or failings in internal control do not function properly. The report from the employee should have been investigated by senior management and acted on. Instead, the employee considered it necessary to report the problem to a television news company.

The control weaknesses go to the very top of the company. The report of the safety experts was not acted on by senior management in the Corporation. The reports were passed to the refinery managers, but head office management should have checked what actions, if any, were being taken in response to the recommendations in the experts' report.

24   Auditor independence

(a)   There are several reasons why it could be argued – strongly – that Tyre and Ballance are not sufficiently independent.

(1)   Martin Ballance, the senior audit partner, has been responsible for the audit of Proud Company for 10 years. This is a long time. A risk is that Martin Balance has become too familiar with Proud Company and the people responsible for its financial statements. He might be too willing to accept the assurances they give him, without asking appropriate questions and making suitable checks.

(2)   The CEO of Proud Company often has arguments with Martin Ballance about the financial statements, and it appears that Martin Ballance is an individual who will often give way in an argument. This might suggest that the CEO can influence (or even intimidate) him. This raises questions about the professional competence of Martin Ballance, who might not be demonstrating the independence that should be expected from an auditor.

(3)   The independence of Tyre and Ballance from Proud Company should also be questioned because of the large proportion of its total annual fee income that comes from the company. The firm might be reluctant to do anything that would put this fee income at risk, so it might be too wiling to go along with the views and opinions of the company's management.

(4)   It is inappropriate for an audit firm to carry out audits on work that has been done by its own staff. Although there is probably no problem with the tax advice work, there is clearly a problem with independence if auditors are required to check book-keeping work done by the firm's own staff.

(5)   The appointment of Maisy Lee to the position of Finance Director in Proud Company might also affect the firm's independence.

(b)   The most appropriate solution to the governance problem of the audit firm's independence might be to appoint new auditors for the company.

If the audit firm is not changed, corporate governance can be improved in several ways.

(1)   A new audit partner should be appointed by the firm, to replace Martin Ballance. It is perhaps surprising that a requirement for audit partner rotation is not a requirement of the country's professional auditing body.

(2)   The company should establish an audit committee, consisting of independent non-executive directors. This will provide an additional reporting line for the external auditors, and will help to reduce the problem of the domineering CEO. The auditors will be able to discuss problems relating to the financial statements with the audit committee, as well as 'arguing' with the CEO and Finance Director.

(3)   The audit committee should be given responsibility for deciding a policy on giving non-audit work to the audit firm. Again, it is surprising that the country's professional auditing body does not have some ethical guidelines on this matter. The audit firm should not be given any book-keeping work. As a more general guideline, the reliance of the audit firm on Proud Company for fee income should be monitored: the reliance is probably too great at the moment.

(4)   The company should establish a policy about recruiting senior accounting staff from the audit firm.

25   Internal audit and risk management

(a)   The internal audit department is a part of the system of internal control in a company. Internal auditors can carry out checks on internal controls, to ensure that they are working efficiently and effectively. Internal control audits can be carried out on financial controls, operational controls or compliance controls.

The internal auditors should identify and report on weaknesses in the internal control system, and recommend improvements.

The internal auditors might assist the board of directors in conducting its annual review of the system of internal control and risk management, where this is required by the system of corporate governance (for example in the UK).

In some companies (particularly those that do not have risk managers), internal auditors might be included in the membership of risk committees. These committees are responsible for identifying risks and assessing their significance.

However, internal auditors are not responsible for risk management. Their role is to provide advice to executive managers who are directly responsible for the management of the risks.

(b)   The objectivity of internal auditors is threatened whenever they are required to report to an executive manager or director whose decisions and responsibilities might be the subject of their audit investigations. For example, it will be difficult for internal auditors to criticise decisions by the finance director if the head of internal audit reports directly to the finance director.

The main problem is to prevent undue influence over the internal auditors by the finance director or CEO. Ways in which this influence might be kept under control are as follows.

(1)   The head of internal audit should have access to the audit committee, and should be able to report matters of concern to the committee. The audit committee may decide to invite the head of internal audit as a 'guest' to every audit committee meeting.

(2)   The audit committee should require the head of internal audit to present a report on the work of the internal audit department, possibly once each year.

(3)   The board of directors, as a part of their review of the effectiveness of the system of internal control and risk management, should investigate how many recommendations by the internal audit department have been implemented by the managers responsible, and how many have been ignored. Managers can be required to explain their reasons for ignoring recommendations from the internal auditors.

(4)   When internal auditors are professional accountants, they should remain aware of their professional ethical responsibilities, and the requirement for all accountants to show integrity and independence of mind.

26   The need for an internal audit function

The UK Combined Code states that where there is no internal audit function, the audit committee should consider annually whether there is a need for an internal audit function and make a recommendation to the board.

The work of an internal audit department is to carry out checks and audits, and to report on weaknesses in controls and recommend improvements. It is a form of internal control, acting as a check on other internal controls.

In some companies, an internal audit function might be used to investigate compliance with appropriate laws and regulations. Other companies might appoint specialists, such as health and safety officers to check compliance with health and safety regulations, and compliance officers to check on compliance with other major regulations. If the company uses specialist managers to check on compliance, there is no need for an internal audit function to do this work.

In some companies, an internal audit function might be used to assist with the identification and assessment of business risks and risks in the company's business environment. Other companies might appoint specialist risk managers. The need for an internal audit function to assist with risk management will depend partly on whether it has specialist risk managers. If it does not have specialist risk managers, the need for an internal audit function to assist with risk management will depend on a judgement about whether internal auditors could make an additional and effective contribution to the current risk management system.

Internal auditors might also carry out investigations into the economy, efficiency and effectiveness of operational systems (value for money audits). The audit committee should assess whether the company would benefit sufficiently from VFM audits to justify an internal audit function to perform this work.

Internal audit has traditionally been associated with investigations into financial controls and the reliability of accounting systems and financial reporting. Where an internal audit function does this work, the external auditors might be able to rely on work done by internal audit. This would reduce the amount of work – and cost – for the external audit. The audit committee should make an assessment of the strength of current financial controls, to decide whether an internal audit function would improve the quality of the control system (and if so whether the cost would be justified).

The need for an internal audit function depends on the scale and extent of weaknesses in the internal control system. If the audit committee considers that there seem to be extensive weaknesses in internal control, the introduction of an internal audit function should help to improve the control system and provide a benefit to the company. If the audit committee considers that current controls are sufficient, it will reach a view that an internal audit function is not (yet) required. However, it must be able to explain to the board the reasons for the recommendation that it makes.

27   Audit committee

(a)   An audit committee consists entirely of independent non-executive directors, and it meets on only a few occasions each year, possibly about four times a year. An audit committee has no executive responsibilities. So it cannot take away executive responsibilities from the finance director, a full-time executive of the company.

However, an audit committee does have some responsibilities that might once have belonged entirely to the finance director (or the CEO).
- The audit committee provides an extra line of reporting for the internal auditors and external auditors. As well as reporting to the finance director, the auditors must also report to the audit committee.

© International Financial Publishing Limited

- The audit committee has the responsibility for reporting on certain audit matters and financial reporting matters to the board.

- The committee should be responsible for developing the company's policy on giving non-audit work to the external auditors, and submitting this policy to the board for approval.

- The committee should also be involved in approving the re-appointment of the external auditors and recommending acceptance of the proposed audit fee for the next annual audit.

(b) There are several reasons why an audit committee should improve the quality of corporate governance, even though the committee consists of non-executive directors and meets on only a few occasions each year.

- **Independence of the external auditors**. The committee helps to ensure the independence and objectivity of the external auditors from influence and pressure that the executive management of the company might try to apply. The committee receives a report on audit issues from the external auditors, and looks at issues that were raised by the auditors with executive managers during the course of the audit. It also formulates policy on giving non-audit work to the external auditors and approves the audit fee.

- **Competence of the external auditors**. The audit committee also assess the competence of the external auditors and judges whether the external auditors have performed their job competently.

- **Providing an assessment of the financial statements and audit process**. The audit committee reports to the board on matters that they consider relevant, with regard to the financial statements and audit process. This is supplementary to reports by the finance director to the board. However, the work of the audit committee helps the board as a whole to fulfil its responsibility for ensuring that the financial statements are reliable.

- **Independence and effectiveness of the internal auditors**. The audit committee helps to ensure the objectivity of the internal auditors, and their independence from influence of senior executive managers, by requiring reports from the head of internal audit. The committee also reviews the effectiveness of the internal audit function, and its contribution to the system of internal control and risk management.

28   Reputation risk

(a) Reputation risk for a company is the risk that an event or item of information will damage the standing (reputation) of the company in the opinion of other people. Reputation risk is normally regarded as a 'downside risk', but a company might use its public relations department to try to improve its general reputation.

The main source of reputation risk is the activities of the company. A company might engage in activities that damage its reputation in the opinion of customers, a portion of the general public, the government and possibly investors, suppliers and employees. For example, companies that conduct scientific research using live animals attract the hostility of 'animal rights activists'.

Employees might also be a source of reputation risk, by behaving rudely to customers or the general public. Some companies, for example, have a poor reputation for dealing with requests to a call centre from customers asking for help.

Some companies have suffered damage to their reputation from the activities of suppliers, for example by purchasing supplies from manufacturers who use child labour.

The impact of an event on reputation risk can be substantial when the event is publicised in the media, such as television or the newspapers.

(b) The effect of reputation risk is difficult to predict, and adverse effects may be either short-term or long-term. In a large global company, the effect of reputation risk may also be localised, because an event that damages the company's reputation in one part of the world might not be considered so bad in other countries.

- A reputation for unethical selling or poor quality can have a lasting impact on customer demand. Some years ago, the owner of a chain of jewellery stores in the UK criticised the poor quality of the goods sold in his stores. The effect was a very large fall in sales for the group, and the company had to change its name as one measure for overcoming the reputational damage.

- Reputation can affect the choice of one producer's goods or services in preference to another. For example, a reputation for high prices or poor quality, compared with rival products, can be damaging for sales.

- A bad reputation can make a company a target for pressure groups and activists.

- In some cases, damage to reputation can lead to intervention by the government, which may introduce new laws or regulations.

29   Technology risk

There are several ways in which a company might be affected by technology risk.

- There is a risk that a company might fall behind in the use of new technology in its operations. If the new technology is successful, rival companies might gain a competitive advantage by making earlier use of the technology. There is also a risk that a company might decide to invest in a new technology, only to find that it is much less popular than expected with customers.

- There is also a risk that a company might fall behind its rivals in the development of an existing technology, such as the use of new versions of computer software.

© International Financial Publishing Limited

- Occasionally, there may be two different technologies to choose from, and there is a risk of choosing the technology that will prove inferior. This risk can affect companies that manufacture products (such as high definition digital televisions) and have to choose between the rival technologies for sin gin their products.

- The potential cost of investing in new technology can be a serious risk for profitability.

Technological risk is greater when the pace of technological change is faster. Many companies are facing greater technological risk than in the past, as the life cycle of products appears to get shorter.

30   Liquidity risk

Liquidity is cash or ready access to cash. Liquidity risk for a company is the risk that it will not have sufficient cash, or ready access to sources of cash, to settle liabilities when they fall due. Faced with a liquidity 'crisis', a company might be at risk from insolvency.

Sources of ready cash are near-cash assets, such as money market securities that can be sold quickly in the financial markets to obtain cash. Companies sometimes invest surplus cash in money market securities (rather than holding on to the cash) because securities earn interest.

Another source of liquidity is an available line of credit from a bank, such as an overdraft facility or a revolving credit facility. In the past, however, a problem for some companies has been that when they have been faced with a liquidity shortage, their bank has withdrawn an overdraft facility. When the companies needed the liquidity most, their banks took away the line of credit.

An essential requirement for liquidity risk control is careful cash budgeting or cash forecasting. Companies should keep expected cash inflows and payments under continual review. Forecasting cash flows will help a company to anticipate temporary cash shortages and to take measures in advance to deal with them, such as delaying non-essential expenditures or negotiating an overdraft with a bank.

Companies should also avoid taking actions that could create long-term liquidity problems, such as regularly paying for capital expenditures out of operating cash flows, when the company cannot afford this.

Efficient working capital management can also help to improve cash flows and reduce liquidity risk. In particular, companies should avoid investing in slow-moving inventory, and should have efficient procedures for collecting receivables.

31 Market risk and derivatives risk

Market risk is risk arising from unexpected changes in the market price of items or in market rates. The risk is higher when market prices are volatile, and subject to large and unexpected movements both up and down.

For the treasury department of Sham Group, there is an exposure to market risk for any assets or liabilities whose value fluctuates with changes in market prices. It might invest in shares of other companies or market instruments whose value is linked to the market price of commodities. If so, it has an exposure to market risk, because share prices and commodity prices might change unexpectedly, creating profits or losses.

The treasury department might also hold investments or have liabilities whose value is affected by changes in foreign exchange rates or interest rates. For example, it might hold bonds as investment, and the market price of bonds varies with changes in long-term interest rates. Similarly the department might hold investments denominated in a foreign currency, and the value of these investments will change (in the department's reporting currency) with changes the currency's exchange value.

The head of the treasury department is likely to insist that the department sets limits to its exposures to market risk, and the treasury team will not be allowed to deal in the financial or commodity markets in a way that exceeds the risk limits that have been set.

Derivatives risk is the risk of unexpected gains of losses on trading positions in derivatives. Derivative instruments, such as options, futures and swaps, can be used to hedge exposures to risk and reduce residual risks. In the case of Sham Group, it seems probable that the treasury team can trade in derivative instruments with the intention of making a profit.

Gains or losses on derivatives depend on changes in the market value of the underlying items to which the derivatives relate, such as share prices, commodity prices, interest rates, exchange rates and bad debts (credit default swaps). A significant risk with trading in derivatives is that a relatively small investment in derivatives can create an exposure to major losses if the underlying market prices move adversely.

There have been reported cases in the past where treasury departments of companies or government organisations have suffered severe losses through speculation in derivatives.

Trading positions in derivatives need to be monitored regularly, and trading limits should be set to restrict the exposure to losses to a level that the treasury department considers acceptable.

© International Financial Publishing Limited

32   Charity

(**Tutorial note**: There is no 'correct' answer to this question. A suggested solution is given here.)

From the limited amount of information available, it is difficult to identify in any detail the key risks facing the charity organisation.

The main function of a charity is to raise money for spending on the charitable cause. Key objectives should therefore be (1) to raise a sufficient amount of funds and (2) to spend the funds effectively.

A major risk must be that Whitecoats will have difficulty in raising enough funds to invest in the research projects that it would like to support. There are three other charity organisations that might, to some extent, be competing for funds from the same sources. One of these other charity organisations, Medhelp, is much larger and is presumably much more successful at raising funds, from private and government sources. The management of Whitecoats must therefore consider the risk that funding will possibly be less than expected, due to competition from other sources.

The ability to raise funds for the charity could also be exposed to the risk of a downturn in the general economy (which might reduce funding from private sources) or in the state of the government's finances (which might reduce funding from government sources).

Another major risk is that Whitecoats might invest its funds in unsuccessful projects. Each new research project uses up a large part of its annual funding income. Unsuccessful projects would mean that Whitecoats is not as successful as it would like to be in achieving its objectives. A lack of success could also damage the perception of Whitecoats as a worthwhile charity, and persuade individuals and organisations to give their money to Medhelp instead.

There will be some key risks affecting the operational effectiveness of Whitecoats. An important requirement will be the need to recruit and retain individuals who have the skills that are necessary to make Whitecoats successful. For example, it will need to attract and retain fund-raisers. It is not clear whether Whitecoats employs scientific or medical experts: if it does, recruiting and retaining these individuals will also be important. The risks are that Whitecoats will fail to attract high-quality individuals, or having recruited talented individuals, will fail to retain them.

Like any other organisation, Whitecoats will face a range of financial risks, operational risks and compliance risks. The proposal by the new managing director to improve risk management systems is a very good one.

33   Risk appetite and other terms

(a)   **Exposure to risk**. All business activities involve some risks and whenever a risk exists, there is an exposure to that risk. This means that the actual outcome might be worse (or better) than expected. For example if a company makes a strategic capital investment, there is a risk that the investment will make a loss, or will fail to provide an adequate return. With credit risk, there is a possibility that when a company gives credit to its customers, the customer might fail to pay what he owes, and there will be a bad debt. With credit risk, the total exposure to risk can be measured as the total amount of receivables.

(b) **Risk of losses**. When a business entity has exposures to risk, there is a risk that some unexpected losses will occur if adverse events occur. The amount of the loss that might occur is rarely the full amount of the exposure. For example, if a company has an exposure to bad debts, with receivables of $10 million, it is most unlikely that all the receivables will become bad debts. Even when a customer becomes a bad debt, some of the debt might be recovered in legal proceedings. The risk of losses is an estimate of what the losses might be from a given exposure to risk.

The risk of losses cannot always be measured, but with credit risk, it might be possible to estimate the risk of losses from an exposure to credit risk as:

Total exposure (= total receivables) × Probability of default × Loss in the event of a default

For example, if a company has $10 million of annual sales, there is a 2% probability of default and in the event of default by a customer only (on average) 25% of the debt will be recovered, the risk of losses is:

$10 million × 2% × 75% = $150,000.

(c) **Residual risk**. Residual risk is the risk of losses after allowing for all risk control measures to reduce or contain the risk. In the case of bad debt risk, the risk might be reduced through better credit-checking procedures, or more efficient debt collection procedures. The finance director of Basket Company thinks that the bad debt risk can be reduced by improving debt collection procedures. If the probability of default could be reduced to, say, 1.8%, and sales will increase by 20% each year to $12 million, the risk of losses would be reduced to $12 million × 1.8% × 75% = $162,000.

(d) **Risk appetite**. Risk appetite describes the amount of risk (losses) that an entity is prepared to accept in order to obtain the expected benefits. In this example, if the company is willing to increase the credit period allowed to customers from 30 days to 60 days, the risk of annual losses from bad debts will rise from $150,000 to $162,000.

The company must decide whether it has the 'appetite' to accept the risk of losses of $162,000 in order to obtain the benefits of higher annual sales ($2 million) and the additional profits from those sales.

34   Risk map and risk dashboard

A risk map and a risk dashboard are both simple visual aids to assist management with the understanding and assessment of risks.

© International Financial Publishing Limited

(a) A risk map in its simplest form is a 2 × 2 matrix, where one side of the matrix represents the probability that an adverse outcome or event will occur, and the other side of the matrix represents the amount of the loss that is likely to occur when there is an adverse outcome.

Loss given an adverse outcome (= Impact)

	Low	High
High		
Low		

Probability or frequency of adverse event

The concept of a risk matrix is based on the assessment of risk as:

Risk = Probability of adverse event × Loss when an adverse event occurs.

A risk map can be used to place individual risks on the map. This provides a visual aid to understanding the nature and severity of each risk. It can be useful for management when risks are prioritised and decisions are taken about how risks should be managed.

For example, priority for risk management and control should be given to risks with a high probability of occurring and a large loss when an adverse outcome occurs. Risks with a low impact and low probability might be considered acceptable. Measures such as insurance might be considered for risks with a low probability of happening but a high impact.

(b) A risk dashboard is another visual aid for risk management. There are different ways of constructing a dashboard, but the basic idea is that it indicates which risks are dangerously high (coloured red), which are relatively small (coloured green) and which are somewhere between (coloured amber). A dashboard can also be used to indicate the current exposures to the risk (residual risk) and the 'risk appetite' of the company for accepting exposures to the risk. Residual risk should not exceed the company's appetite for that risk.

35   Approaches to risk management

(a) **Risk reduction**. Risk reduction involves the application of control measures. A risk that exists before the control measures are applied is reduced to a residual risk. The aim of risk reduction should be to restrict residual risks to an acceptable level. Internal controls reduce the operational risks (risks from human error, fraud, technological failures, and so on). Financial risks can be reduced by means of forward contracts or derivative instruments: 'hedging' a financial risk reduces the residual risk.

(b) **Risk transfer**. Risk transfer involves moving the risk to another person. Usually, a payment has to be made for the risk transfer. The most common form of risk transfer is probably insurance. By paying the premium for an insurance agreement, a person can transfer all or most of the risk to an insurance company.

(c) **Risk avoidance**. Risk avoidance means having no exposure at all to a risk. In business, it is impossible to invest and operate without having some risk exposures. Avoiding risk therefore means not investing, or withdrawing from an investment.

(d) **Risk sharing**. With risk sharing, the risk is divided between two or more people/organisations, who are all exposed to the risk of losses or the ability to benefit from unexpected gains. Joint ventures or partnerships are examples.

36   Risk management review

(**Tutorial note**: There is no single 'correct' answer to this question. The list of questions below is indicative of the questions that Robert Lam should ask.)

Questions:

1   Does the company have a system for identifying risks (and if so, what is it)?
2   Does the company have a system for assessing risks and prioritising risks?
3   Does the company actively manage its risks?
4   Has the board of directors communicated to management what levels of risk are acceptable? (Or: Has the board formulated and communicated a clear policy on risk and risk management?)
5   Has the board of directors identified the limits of its 'risk appetite'?
6   Should certain risks be taken at all, or should they be avoided? (Or: Should the exposure to certain risks be increased/reduced?)
7   Do independent non-executive directors occasionally select and challenge operational risk reports and investment decisions by management?

37   Risk model

A risk model is usually a mathematical model. The model contains a number of variables, and the relationships between the variables are expressed in the form of mathematical formulae.

Models vary in complexity, and range from simple models with a small number of variables, to much larger models with a large number of different variables and complex relationships between the variables.

The variables in a model are either input variables or output variables. Input variables are items whose value is either known or estimated. Output variables are items whose value depends on the value of the input variables.

Mathematical models are used to predict what will happen, or what might happen. By giving values to all the input variables in the model, the model user can calculate values for the output variables. For example, a simple model for the total costs of

© International Financial Publishing Limited

production might be y = a + bx. By giving values to fixed costs, the variable cost per unit and the number of units (a, b and x respectively) we can calculate the total costs, y.

With risk models, there is some uncertainty about the value of the input variables in the model, or about the mathematical relationship between the input variables. This means that there is also some uncertainty about the value of the output variables. By altering the value of the input variables, different values for output variables are obtained.

Mathematical models can therefore be used to prepare forecasts, with some statistical analysis of the range of different possible outcomes. Models can also be used to assess risk, also be measuring and analysing different possible results under differing circumstances. The risk in any situation can often be quantified mathematically, in the form of a probability distribution.

Risk models can, in some cases, be used to control risk levels. For example in banking Value at Risk models are used to assess credit risk, and measure the possibilities of losses of differing amounts from bad debts. Value at Risk models can be used to control the total credit risk, by restricting the total credit that a bank gives to customers. The total bad debt risk can be kept within acceptable limits at a specified level of probability.

Risk models can also be used for **stress testing**. The purpose of stress testing is to predict how an operation or activity will perform under extreme conditions. If the model predicts that the operation or activity will not function adequately under extreme conditions, extra risk control measures can be planned and introduced, to make the operation or activity more 'robust'. For example, a company operating train services might use a risk model for stress testing, by predicting what might happen if the total volume of passenger traffic on the trains were to increase by, say, 20%.

In summary, mathematical risk models can be used to obtain quantified measurements of risk.

38 Embedded

'Embedding' means that risk awareness and risk control procedures and management practices should be an integral part of operational and management systems within an organisation.

It can be distinguished from risk control that is applied occasionally by an external agency. For example, the annual audit of a company's financial statements by the external auditors is a form of risk monitoring, but it is not embedded within the company's own systems. It is a risk control measure applied from outside the company. Similarly, inspections by external agencies, such as government inspectors, are not embedded risk control measures.

Controls that are applied internally might not be 'embedded' when they are carried out occasionally as a special initiative. For example, a company might carry out a risk review, but if this is a one-off exercise it is not an embedded feature of the risk management system.

Risk (or risk awareness) should be embedded in a company's culture. This means that an awareness and understanding of risk should be a part of the thinking of management and other employees. Decision-makers within a company should consider the risks when they make their decisions. Employees should be conscious of the need to control risks and apply risk controls in the work that they do.

Risk (or risk awareness) should also be embedded in a company's values. This means that the company should recognise the importance of risk management when setting targets for performance and when judging actual performance. Reward systems should not be based on profit maximisation: the payment of rewards should also be linked to successful risk management. A frequent criticism investment banks is that traders are rewarded for maximising profits on trading, without regard for the risks they take: as a result, risk management might not be given the status and recognition that it ought to have.

Risk should also be embedded within a company's procedures. There should be suitable internal controls within operating procedures, and employees should apply those controls at all times. For example, safety procedures should be taught to all employees and properly carried out at all times.

39   Consequentialist

(a)   A consequentialist approach to ethics (also called a teleological approach) is to take the view that the 'correctness' or 'rightness' of an action depends on its outcome. An example of this approach is utilitarianism, which is the view that the ethics of an action should be judged in terms of the good that it brings, and the best course of action is the one that brings the greatest good to the greatest number of people. The 'rightness' of an action therefore depends on the circumstances of the situation.

A deontological approach to ethics is associated with the ideas of the eighteenth century philosopher Kant. This approach takes the view that certain actions are ethically right and others are wrong. It is the action itself that makes it ethical or unethical, not the consequences of the action. This view can be simplified into a statement that it is the means that is more important than the result or 'ends' and if it is not ethical, 'the means' can never justify the 'ends'.

An example can illustrate the difference. There are differing views about whether it is ethical to conduct experiments on animals in order to conduct scientific research into developing new medicines for humans. A consequentialist approach might be that the means justifies the ends, and although experimentation on animals is unpleasant, it is necessary in order to develop new medicines to save more human lives. A deontological approach might be that experimentation on animals is wrong, and cannot be justified even for the purpose of medical research.

    © International Financial Publishing Limited

(**Tutorial note**: You might choose a different example for your answer, to compare the two approaches. A commonly-used example is whether it can be right to tell a lie. A consequentialist approach is that telling a lie can be justified if the end result is 'good' or beneficial. A deontological approach is that it can never be 'right' to tell a lie.)

(b)   A consequentialist approach to business ethics is common. Many businessmen who regard themselves as ethical individuals will take the view that the 'rightness' of an action can often be judged by the moral benefits that it will bring.

This approach is often essential, because situations occur in business where a deontological approach could have unacceptable consequences. Business is so complex that it forces individuals into compromises.

For example, a deontological approach to ethics might be that it is wrong to take away the job from an individual who has worked well and shown loyalty to the employer. It is difficult to take this approach in a situation where a company is losing money and will become insolvent unless it takes measures to cut costs, including making some employees redundant. A consequentialist approach would be that although it is unpleasant to make employees redundant, this might be the right thing to do in order to keep the business in existence, providing work to the employees who remain.

A major problem with a consequentialist approach, however, is that it is largely subjective in its evaluation of what is right. It can be used, for example, to justify the view that the purpose of a company is to maximise the wealth of shareholders, and all actions by a company can therefore be justified on ethical grounds if they add to profits. This approach would not be accepted by someone who argues that a company has obligations to its employees, society and the environment, as well as to its shareholders.

In an extreme form, a business man might argue that he always 'knows what is right' and so will always act in an ethical way. This would be a highly subjective view, which uses an ethical argument to justify selfishness and egotism.

Although ethical views vary between different cultures, it might be argued that business ethics ought to be determined to some extent by 'core values', and that a deontological approach is appropriate to deciding what is right and wrong, at least in certain situations.

40   Kohlberg

Kohlberg identified three levels of morality and six stages of moral development. He suggested that individuals progress through the stages of moral development during their life, one stage at a time. Many individuals do not progress to the higher stages, but cease to progress when they have reached a lower level. Although the ethical behaviour of individuals is sometimes at a lower stage of development than the one they have reached, they do not regress to a lower stage of development having reached a higher one.

At a pre-conventional level of morality, there are two stages of development. The first is an obedience and punishment orientation, where the 'rightness' or 'wrongness' of an action depends entirely on the reward or punishment that follows. The second level of development is an individualism and exchange morality, where individuals act in an entirely selfish way but recognise the benefit of mutual help. ('You scratch my back and I will scratch yours.')

The next level of morality is a conventional stage, which contains the third and fourth levels of moral development. The third level is based on the concept that good behaviour means having good motives and showing love, trust and concern for others. The actions of another person are often judged by the reasoning: 'He means well….' The fourth level is one where ethical judgements are based on a concern for maintaining the social order. Rules and regulations are there to be obeyed.

Kohlberg also identified a post-conventional level of morality, containing the fifth and sixth levels of moral development. The fifth level is a social contract orientation. Individuals at this level recognise that people are different and have the right to their own views and opinions. Society should protect certain basic rights for all individuals, such as the right to life and freedom. In addition laws might be morally wrong and there should be some form of democratic procedure for changing laws that are unfair.

The sixth and final level of morality is based on a belief in universal ethical principles. However, very few individuals reach this stage.

This framework of moral development can be used in all aspects of life, including business and accountancy, to evaluate ethical dilemmas and understand the different ethical views of individuals. For example, it can help to create an understanding of a dilemma in which an individual is faced with showing loyalty to a colleague or a boss (Level 3) and applying the rules and regulations because the rules exist for a reason and have to be obeyed (Level 4). It can also help to create an understanding of individuals who argue that the current rules are wrong and unfair, and ought to be changed (Level 5).

Ethics is not a simple matter of 'right' and 'wrong', and ethical problems and dilemmas are made even more complex by different perspectives and views.

Kohlberg's views might therefore have some relevance to business and accounting, by providing a framework for the formulation of ethics codes and for giving guidance when ethical dilemmas occur.

41 Social responsibility

The seven different positions on the social responsibility of business identified by Gray, Owen and Adams are as follows.

- **Pristine capitalists**. These individuals put self-interest before the collective benefits of society as a whole. They believe in 'free market' forces and argue that market forces will find solutions to major social problems such as the threat to the global environment.

© International Financial Publishing Limited

- **Expedients**. These individuals take the view that companies cannot succeed in the long term unless they accept certain social responsibilities.

- **Proponents of the social contract**. These individuals believe that companies exist only through the goodwill of society and they therefore have an obligation to act in the interests of society. Government regulation is needed to restrain the damaging effects on society and the environment of free market forces.

- **Social ecologists**. These individuals take the view that problems in society and the environment have been created by companies, and it is therefore the responsibility of companies to admit their liability and solve the problems.

- **Socialists**. These individuals argue for a re-distribution of assets between members of society and against the concentration of resources and power in the hands of large organisations (companies and governments)

- **Radical feminists**. These individuals believe that there is too much male domination of society and too much aggression. More feminine values are needed, such as care and compassion.

- **Deep ecologists/ deep greens**. These individuals argue that human beings have no more right to life than any other living species. Ethical decisions should be based on a concern for all forms of life.

Individuals who work in business take the first two or three positions in the list, whereas many opponents of business and critics of unethical business practices take one of the last four positions in the list.

The analysis by Gray, Owen and Adams can be useful in adding to an understanding of ethical differences, and differing views about the morality of business. A better understanding of different ethical views can help individuals (managers and professional accountants) for search for solutions to disagreements.

42   Integrity

Integrity means honesty. In business, it means 'straight dealing'. If you deal with a person of integrity, you know that he or she will tell you the truth and will not try to mislead you.

A person of integrity will behave in accordance with a set of ethical values, and so will always behave in an ethical way.

Integrity is important because it creates trust. Trust is an essential requirement for the creation and maintenance of constructive relationships.

It is important in corporate governance. Directors of companies should be individuals of integrity. If they are, the shareholders will believe what the directors tell them and will trust them to govern the company in the interests of the shareholders and not in the self-interest of the directors themselves.

Integrity is also important for professional accountants, and is one of the fundamental ethical values that accountants should demonstrate at all times. If accountants are able to show integrity, they will have the trust of their employer or clients and also the trust of the general public. (This is important, in view of the responsibility of accountants to consider the public interest.)

The behaviour of directors and professional accountants can be regulated to some extent, by rules and detailed codes of conduct. However, there are many situations that are not covered by rules or detailed codes. In these situations, directors or accountants with integrity can be trusted to 'do the right thing' and act in an ethical way.

43   Public interest

The public interest is the collective well-being of society or the community of people an institutions in which an individual lives and works.

Showing a concern for the public interest means recognizing responsibilities to the public. For a professional accountant, the public includes employers, clients, government, investors, employees, creditors, customers, the business and financial community and all people who rely on the objectivity and integrity of professional accountants to maintain the orderly functioning of business and commerce.

Professional accountants are required to show a concern for the public interest in the work that they do. They should put the public interest before their responsibilities to their employer or clients, for example when the employer or a client is acting illegally.

Accountants also have an obligation to the public in their everyday life, because they help to create public trust in business.

The public has a right to expect that:

- auditors will try to ensure the reliability of financial statements that are issued by companies
- financial managers will help to ensure the efficient and effective use of resources by the companies or other entities they work for
- tax experts will ensure a fair application of the tax rules
- accountants will give competent business advice to management.

44   Business and professional ethics

(a)   A business code of ethics is developed for a company and is a statement of the ethical stance of the company. It is also a statement by the company about how it expects its employees to behave, in order to uphold the ethical values of the company.

A professional code of ethics for accountants is for all individual professional accountants, and is a statement of how they are expected to behave as individuals. It includes a requirement that accountants should consider the public interest.

    © International Financial Publishing Limited

(b)   An accountant might face an ethical dilemma in the following situations.

(1)   The accountant is under pressure from a senior manager to agree with the manager's point of view and provide formal support, even though the accountant does not agree.

(2)   The accountant is expected to support a decision taken by management, which might also be in the accountant's personal interests, even though the accountant knows the decision to be wrong. (For example, the accountant might be expected to keep quiet about an illegal activity by the company.)

(3)   The accountant is asked to do something that is contrary to an accounting standard, or other professional or technical standard, in order to present information in a more favourable way.

(4)   The accountant is asked to keep quiet about a mistake made by a boss. The accountant might feel obliged to agree, out o f loyalty to the boss.

(5)   The accountant misleads his boss of his client about this technical expertise and knowledge, in order to be given some work.

45   Two clients

(a)

(1)   The first step in assessing the situation is to decide whether an ethical issue does exist. The partners have agreed a valuation for the business, and an amount that the remaining partner will pay the retiring partner to take over the entire business. There is a concern that the valuation of the balance sheet might have been based on a balance sheet valuation of assets, and that the value of the workshop might not have been brought to the attention of the retiring partner. If these are the actual facts, the retiring partner will be paid less than his or her fair share of the business on retirement.

If possible, as much information about the valuation of the business should be obtained, without (yet) alerting the partners to your concerns. There may be a written agreement between the partners about what should happen on the retirement of one of the partners. For example, there may be a written partnership agreement in which a process is specified for valuing the business on the retirement of a partner. If the partners have reached their agreed valuation of the business in a fair and open way, there is no ethical problem for the accountant.

If there are doubts about whether the valuation of the business has been fair, there is an ethical issue to resolve, because one of the clients could be treated unfairly by the other.

(2)   The next step is to assess the threats to the accountant's compliance with the fundamental ethical principles. The two clients could have a conflict of interests. This raises threats to the accountant's integrity (objectivity) and ability to treat the affairs of each client with confidentiality.

Integrity is threatened because at some stage, the accountant might have to take sides, and support the interests of one client against the interests of the other. Confidentiality is threatened because by raising concerns with one client, the accountant would be breaching confidentiality for the other client.

The threats would seem to be sufficiently significant to make the accountant consider whether additional safeguards could be introduced to eliminate the risk.

(3)   The next step is therefore to consider safeguards. In a large accounting practice, it might be possible to appoint another senior member of staff to take over dealing with the affairs of one of the client partners. Since the accountant here is a sole practitioner, this is not possible in this situation.

There are no other obvious safeguards that can be introduced, and the accountant is therefore faced with a significant threat to compliance with the fundamental ethical principles. He should not allow this to happen.

(4)   A solution to the problem has to be found. The most suitable solution in this case would be to arrange a meeting with both partners, where the accountant should inform them that he is unable to continue providing professional services to both of them.

At the meeting, the partners might agree that the accountant should continue to provide a service to one of them, but the accountant should not 'take sides' and indicate any preference for one client.

46   Errors in the numbers

(a)   Judy did not learn about the error in the figures for the board until after they had been submitted. The consequence of the error could have been very serious, and the board might have taken a big investment decision based on misleading and incorrect information.

There is a threat to the integrity of Tom and the members of his team, including Judy, when information is provided that is known to be materially incorrect.

Judy was probably correct to wait until the board made its investment decision. Since the board decided not to invest, the failure of Tom to report the corrected figures to the board did not have any immediate consequence.

However, Judy was also correct to recognise that a similar problem might happen again in the future, and she looked for a suitable safeguard. She thought that she had found a safeguard by obtaining agreement from Tom to involve his team more closely in the future in preparing and checking figures.

In conclusion, the action by Judy in this first instance was probably appropriate, and she complied with the fundamental ethical principles (even though Tom did not).

© International Financial Publishing Limited

However, she should maintain documentary evidence or a documentary record of the incident, in case she needs to raise the matter again at some time in the future.

(b)   The second incident showed to Judy that the safeguard she agreed with Tom earlier had not worked. Tom submitted figures to Will that were presumably not checked by anyone else in Tom's team. However, Judy would need to check this point: errors in checking Tom's figures could have been made by someone else in the team.

Another ethical issue arises, however, because Tom has asked Judy not to correct all the errors she found, only those that Will knows about. If Judy agrees to do what Tom has asked, she will be in breach of the fundamental principle of objectivity. Accountants should not be involved in the provision of information that is materially incorrect or misleading.

There is pressure from Tom to make her do what he wants, possibly by asking her to act out of a sense of loyalty to him (a familiarity threat) or because Judy feels intimidated by the possible consequences of arguing with her boss and refusing to comply with his instructions.

Judy is in a very difficult position. She must comply with the fundamental ethical principles, but in doing so she will inevitably cause problems in her working relationship with Tom.

I recommend that Judy should take the following action.
(1)   She should speak to Tom about her concerns, and explain that she cannot agree to do what he has asked.
(2)   She should discuss the failure of their previous agreement and her concern that there could be more similar situations in the future where Tom prepares incorrect information and asks his staff to cover up the errors.
(3)   She should explain that she will provide corrected figures to Will with corrections to all the errors that she has found. She will draw the additional errors to the attention of Will.
(4)   She should tell Tom that she is concerned with his unprofessional conduct, and that she cannot continue to work for him in the future. She will therefore need to consider her position.

This leaves a problem unresolved. If Judy asks for a transfer to another department, she will be leaving tom to continue to do what he has done in the past, preparing figures without due care and covering up any errors. This is likely to be a serious situation for the company. Judy might therefore decide that she needs to inform Will about the problems she has experienced. She should inform him about Tom's reluctance to admit to his mistakes (and she could explain the consequences by giving Will another set of figures containing corrections only to the errors that he had found, so that he can compare them with Judy's own corrected figures). She should also mention the earlier incident about the errors in the board papers and Tom's similar refusal on that occasion to admit to the errors.

Will can then make a decision about what action is appropriate.

47   Discount

The problem here is that by offering to sell a necklace to Peter at a discount, the finance director might be trying to influence Peter by obtaining his goodwill. The risk is to Peter's objectivity, which is a fundamental ethical concept.

Peter does not have to reject the offer from the finance director without consideration. He can begin by establishing some basic facts.

(1)   He should decide whether he would he want to buy any of the necklaces. If he didn't, he could politely refuse the offer from the finance director.

(2)   If he is interested in buying a necklace, he should ask what the price would be both without the discount and with the discount.

(3)   He should ask whether the company normally offers discounts, and if so what a normal commercial discount to a customer would be.

He could then tell the finance director that he is grateful for the offer and is interested in buying a necklace, but he must first clear the matter with his audit manager. He can explain that this is a professional requirement.

He can tell the audit manager about the offer from the finance director. If the size of the discount is one that is normally offered to other customers of the company, or if it is insignificant in amount, they might agree that Peter can accept the offer without any threat to his objectivity. Otherwise he should politely thank the finance director for the offer, but say no.

48   Principles and rules

A rules-based code of ethics is one in which detailed rules are specified about the way in which professional accountants must behave or act in particular circumstances.

In practice, there are many different situations, with differing circumstances, where accountants might have an ethical dilemma. It would be difficult to foresee every type of situation and specify the exact rule for each. The appropriate resolution of an ethical problem might also vary between countries, according to the differing cultures and ethical outlook of each country.

For this reason, except where particular behaviour is required from accountants by the law (for example, with regard to reporting suspicions of money laundering activities by a client), accountants are required to act in accordance with a principles-based code of ethics.

The code of ethics for accountants requires compliance with five fundamental ethical principles: integrity, objectivity, professional competence and due care, confidentiality and professional behaviour and care.

© International Financial Publishing Limited

49   Imported meat

(a)   A professional accountant has the following responsibilities to his or her employer:

■   To act with integrity and diligence and with the highest standard of care, in all situations.

■   As far as possible, to observe the confidentiality of information obtained during the course of work. This requirement to maintain confidentiality applies even when the accountant has left the job and no longer works for the employer.

■   To act in the interests of the shareholders as far as possible.

■   To show loyalty to the employer, although only within the limits of what is legal and ethically proper.

(b)   As a 'professional', an accountant has a responsibility to comply with additional ethical requirements.

■   The accountant must comply with the law.

■   The accountant must comply with any relevant professional codes that apply.

■   In the absence of any specific codes, the accountant must comply with the fundamental ethical principles (of integrity, objectivity, professional competence and due care, and so on).

■   Crucially, the professional accountant must also act in the public interest, even if this means in an extreme case reporting an employer to the authorities for a breach of the law or other regulations.

(c)   Even though the problem in this case does not relate to accountancy and finance, Ben cannot ignore the problem. The company's management appear to be breaking the law on food health and safety, and could be putting the public health at risk.

He must decide what the most suitable course of action is. He should try to obtain evidence of the law-breaking. If he cannot obtain documentary evidence, he should make a record of all relevant conversations and actions.

He should report his concern. Senior management are involved in the crime, and he should therefore begin by reporting his concern outside the normal hierarchical channels. He might report the problem to the company chairman, for example, or another director.

It should then be the responsibility of the chairman or board of directors to take action.

If no action is taken internally, Ben Meakin will probably be obliged to report to an external agency, such as a food standards agency or a public health agency. However, this would be an extreme measure, and internal procedures for dealing with the problem should be tried first.

50   Footprint

An environmental footprint is a term used to mean the mark that has been left behind on the environment, usually by social and economic activities. All economic activity has an effect on the environment, and so leaves a 'footprint' after it has occurred.

A company might report on its environmental footprint by providing information about three things:

(1)   The quantities of natural resources it has used, and (in some cases) the quantity of land that it uses for its business purposes. An environmental report may indicate the quantities of natural resources consumed where these are important renewable resources (such as timber and fish stocks) or where they are valuable non-renewable resources (such as mineral deposits, oil and natural gas).

(2)   The amount of pollution or emissions created by its activities. These could be emissions into the air or into the sea, lakes and rivers which pollute the air or water. They might also be emissions that contaminate land.

(3)   Another aspect of the environmental footprint is the effect that the use of natural resources and the creation of pollution have on the environment. In addition to quantifying resources consumed and pollution created, there should be an assessment (in qualitative or quantitative terms) of how the environment has been affected. For example a company that uses large amounts of timber might report on the amount of timber it has used, and also specify the amount of deforestation (allowing for re-planting of new trees) that this has created in different parts of the world.

51   Sustainability

(a)   Sustainability refers to the ability of a company to achieve a sustainable business. Sustainable development has been defined as business development that meets the needs of the present without compromising the ability of future generations to meet their own needs. An important aspect of sustainable development is the effect of business on the environment. Companies meet the needs of present-day customers by using resources. When these resources are non-renewable, or when the rate of use of the resources exceeds the rate of renewal, current business activity obviously reduces the ability of future generations to meet their needs.

Another definition of sustainability, which is possibly easier for companies to accommodate, is expressed in terms of value creation. Value creation is measured in three dimensions: economic, social and environmental. Sustainability could be described as creating more value in these three dimensions than the cost of the resources consumed (economic and environmental).

A sustainability report typically provides performance measurement in three dimensions: economic, social and environmental. This is called 'triple bottom

© International Financial Publishing Limited

line reporting', which is advocated by organisations such as the Global Research Initiative (GRI).

(b) Users of sustainability reports should have a right to believe that they can trust and accept the information in sustainability reports.

When a sustainability report presents measures of performance as a triple bottom line, the economic performance can be verified from information in the published financial statements. However, there is no way in which the audit of financial statements can provide verification of performance measures relating to social and environmental performance.

Unless the published social and environmental information can be formally verified, there is no way of assessing whether the company is telling the truth or not. The claims that a company makes could be misleading, or even totally wrong.

Verification of sustainability report information can be provided by an environmental audit, provided that the audit is conducted by independent experts. Specialist firms have been established to provide environmental audits. The major audit firms have also established environmental audit groups within their firm.

(c) Social and environmental reports might provide quantifiable or qualitative information about the effects that a company has had on society and the environment. They do not necessarily discuss social and environmental strategy concerns or even social and environmental strategy – although they might.

Social and environmental risk reports are reports about the social and environmental risks facing a company and how these have been managed. In the UK for example quoted companies are required to include a section on social and environmental risks in their annual business report to shareholders.

© International Financial Publishing Limited

Appendix

THE UK COMBINED CODE ON CORPORATE GOVERNANCE

© Financial Reporting Council (FRC). Adapted and reproduced with the kind permission of the Financial Reporting Council. All rights reserved.

CODE ON CORPORATE GOVERNANCE

PREAMBLE

1. This Code supersedes and replaces the Combined Code issued in 2003. It follows a review by the Financial Reporting Council of the implementation of the Code in 2005 and subsequent consultation on possible amendments to the Code.

2. The Financial Services Authority, as the UK Listing Authority, is obliged by statute to carry out a separate consultation before listed companies can be formally required under the Listing Rules to disclose how they have applied this new version of the Combined Code. This consultation is expected to begin in September 2006 and, subject to views received, the Listing Rules would be expected to apply to the new version of the Combined Code with effect from some time in the second quarter of 2007.

3. In the meantime, in view of the limited nature of the changes and the strong support that they have received, the FRC would encourage companies and investors to apply the revised Code voluntarily for reporting years beginning on or after 1 November 2006.

4. The Code contains main and supporting principles and provisions. The Listing Rules require listed companies to make a disclosure statement in two parts in relation to the Code. In the first part of the statement, the company

has to report on how it applies the principles in the Code. This should cover both main and supporting principles. The form and content of this part of the statement are not prescribed, the intention being that companies should have a free hand to explain their governance policies in the light of the principles, including any special circumstances applying to them which have led to a particular approach. In the second part of the statement the company has either to confirm that it complies with the Code's provisions or – where it does not – to provide an explanation. This 'comply or explain' approach has been in operation for over ten years and the flexibility it offers has been widely welcomed both by company boards and by investors. It is for shareholders and others to evaluate the company's statement.

5. While it is expected that listed companies will comply with the Code's provisions most of the time, it is recognised that departure from the provisions of the Code may be justified in particular circumstances. Every company must review each provision carefully and give a considered explanation if it departs from the Code provisions.

6. Smaller listed companies, in particular those new to listing, may judge that some of the provisions are disproportionate or less relevant in their case. Some of the provisions do not apply to companies below the FTSE 350. Such companies may nonetheless consider that it would be appropriate to adopt the approach in the Code and they are encouraged to consider this. Investment companies typically have a different board structure, which may affect the relevance of particular provisions.

7. Whilst recognising that directors are appointed by shareholders who are the owners of companies, it is important that those concerned with the evaluation of governance should do so with common sense in order to promote partnership and trust, based on mutual understanding. They should pay due regard to companies' individual circumstances and bear in mind in particular the size and complexity of the company and the nature of the risks and challenges it faces. Whilst shareholders have every right to challenge companies' explanations if they are unconvincing, they should not be evaluated in a mechanistic way and departures from the Code should not be automatically treated as breaches. Institutional shareholders and their agents should be careful to respond to the statements from companies in a manner that supports the 'comply or explain' principle. As the principles in Section 2 make clear, institutional shareholders should carefully consider explanations given for departure from the Code and make reasoned judgements in each case. They should put their views to the company and be prepared to enter a dialogue if they do not accept the company's position. Institutional shareholders should be prepared to put such views in writing where appropriate.

8. Nothing in this Code should be taken to override the general requirements of law to treat shareholders equally in access to information.

© International Financial Publishing Limited

CODE OF BEST PRACTICE

SECTION 1 COMPANIES

A. DIRECTORS

A.1 The Board

Main Principle

Every company should be headed by an effective board, which is collectively responsible for the success of the company.

Supporting Principles

The board's role is to provide entrepreneurial leadership of the company within a framework of prudent and effective controls which enables risk to be assessed and managed. The board should set the company's strategic aims, ensure that the necessary financial and human resources are in place for the company to meet its objectives and review management performance. The board should set the company's values and standards and ensure that its obligations to its shareholders and others are understood and met.

All directors must take decisions objectively in the interests of the company.

As part of their role as members of a unitary board, non-executive directors should constructively challenge and help develop proposals on strategy. Non-executive directors should scrutinise the performance of management in meeting agreed goals and objectives and monitor the reporting of performance. They should satisfy themselves on the integrity of financial information and that financial controls and systems of risk management are robust and defensible. They are responsible for determining appropriate levels of remuneration of executive directors and have a prime role in appointing, and where necessary removing, executive directors, and in succession planning.

Code Provisions

A.1.1 The board should meet sufficiently regularly to discharge its duties effectively. There should be a formal schedule of matters specifically reserved for its decision. The annual report should include a statement of how the board operates, including a high level statement of which types of decisions are to be taken by the board and which are to be delegated to management.

A.1.2 The annual report should identify the chairman, the deputy chairman (where there is one), the chief executive, the senior independent director and the chairmen and members of the nomination, audit and remuneration committees. It should also set out the number of meetings of the board and those committees and individual attendance by directors.

A.1.3 The chairman should hold meetings with the non-executive directors without the executives present. Led by the senior independent director, the non-executive directors should meet without the chairman present at least annually to appraise the chairman's performance (as described in A.6.1) and on such other occasions as are deemed appropriate.

A.1.4 Where directors have concerns which cannot be resolved about the running of the company or a proposed action, they should ensure that their concerns are recorded in the board minutes. On resignation, a non-executive director should provide a written statement to the chairman, for circulation to the board, if they have any such concerns.

A.1.5 The company should arrange appropriate insurance cover in respect of legal action against its directors.

A.2 Chairman and Chief Executive

Main Principle

There should be a clear division of responsibilities at the head of the company between the running of the board and the executive responsibility for the running of the company's business. No one individual should have unfettered powers of decision.

Supporting Principle

The chairman is responsible for leadership of the board, ensuring its effectiveness on all aspects of its role and setting its agenda. The chairman is also responsible for ensuring that the directors receive accurate, timely and clear information. The chairman should ensure effective communication with shareholders. The chairman should also facilitate the effective contribution of non-executive directors in particular and ensure constructive relations between executive and non-executive directors.

Code Provisions

A.2.1 The roles of chairman and chief executive should not be exercised by the same individual. The division of responsibilities between the chairman and chief executive should be clearly established, set out in writing and agreed by the board.

A.2.2 The chairman should on appointment meet the independence criteria set out in A.3.1 below. A chief executive should not go on to be chairman of the same company. If exceptionally a board decides that a chief executive should become chairman, the board should consult major shareholders in advance

© International Financial Publishing Limited

and should set out its reasons to shareholders at the time of the appointment and in the next annual report.

A.3 Board Balance and Independence

Main Principle

The board should include a balance of executive and non-executive directors (and in particular independent non-executive directors) such that no individual or small group of individuals can dominate the board's decision taking.

Supporting Principles

The board should not be so large as to be unwieldy. The board should be of sufficient size that the balance of skills and experience is appropriate for the requirements of the business and that changes to the board's composition can be managed without undue disruption.

To ensure that power and information are not concentrated in one or two individuals, there should be a strong presence on the board of both executive and non-executive directors.

The value of ensuring that committee membership is refreshed and that undue reliance is not placed on particular individuals should be taken into account in deciding chairmanship and membership of committees.

No one other than the committee chairman and members is entitled to be present at a meeting of the nomination, audit or remuneration committee, but others may attend at the invitation of the committee.

Code Provisions

A.3.1   The board should identify in the annual report each non-executive director it considers to be independent. The board should determine whether the director is independent in character and judgement and whether there are relationships or circumstances which are likely to affect, or could appear to affect, the director's judgement. The board should state its reasons if it determines that a director is independent notwithstanding the existence of relationships or circumstances which may appear relevant to its determination, including if the director:

- has been an employee of the company or group within the last five years

- has, or has had within the last three years, a material business relationship with the company either directly, or as a partner, shareholder, director or senior employee of a body that has such a relationship with the company

- has received or receives additional remuneration from the company apart from a director's fee, participates in the company's share option or a performance-related pay scheme, or is a member of the company's pension scheme

- has close family ties with any of the company's advisers, directors or senior employees

- holds cross-directorships or has significant links with other directors through involvement in other companies or bodies

- represents a significant shareholder, or

- has served on the board for more than nine years from the date of their first election.

A.3.2 Except for smaller companies3, at least half the board, excluding the chairman, should comprise non-executive directors determined by the board to be independent. A smaller company should have at least two independent non-executive directors.

A.3.3 The board should appoint one of the independent non-executive directors to be the senior independent director. The senior independent director should be available to shareholders if they have concerns which contact through the normal channels of chairman, chief executive or finance director has failed to resolve or for which such contact is inappropriate.

A.4 Appointments to the Board

Main Principle

There should be a formal, rigorous and transparent procedure for the appointment of new directors to the board.

Supporting Principles

Appointments to the board should be made on merit and against objective criteria. Care should be taken to ensure that appointees have enough time available to devote to the job. This is particularly important in the case of chairmanships.

The board should satisfy itself that plans are in place for orderly succession for appointments to the board and to senior management, so as to maintain an appropriate balance of skills and experience within the company and on the board.

Code Provisions

A.4.1 There should be a nomination committee which should lead the process for board appointments and make recommendations to the board. A majority of members of the nomination committee should be independent non-executive directors. The chairman or an independent non-executive director should chair the committee, but the chairman should not chair the nomination committee when it is dealing with the appointment of a successor to the chairmanship. The nomination committee should make available4 its terms of reference, explaining its role and the authority delegated to it by the board.

© International Financial Publishing Limited

A.4.2   The nomination committee should evaluate the balance of skills, knowledge and experience on the board and, in the light of this evaluation, prepare a description of the role and capabilities required for a particular appointment.

A.4.3   For the appointment of a chairman, the nomination committee should prepare a job specification, including an assessment of the time commitment expected, recognising the need for availability in the event of crises. A chairman's other significant commitments should be disclosed to the board before appointment and included in the annual report. Changes to such commitments should be reported to the board as they arise, and included in the next annual report. No individual should be appointed to a second chairmanship of a FTSE 100 company.

A.4.4   The terms and conditions of appointment of non-executive directors should be made available for inspection6. The letter of appointment should set out the expected time commitment. Non-executive directors should undertake that they will have sufficient time to meet what is expected of them. Their other significant commitments should be disclosed to the board before appointment, with a broad indication of the time involved and the board should be informed of subsequent changes.

A.4.5   The board should not agree to a full time executive director taking on more than one non-executive directorship in a FTSE 100 company nor the chairmanship of such a company.

A.4.6   A separate section of the annual report should describe the work of the nomination committee, including the process it has used in relation to board appointments. An explanation should be given if neither an external search consultancy nor open advertising has been used in the appointment of a chairman or a non-executive director.

A.5 Information and Professional Development

Main Principle

The board should be supplied in a timely manner with information in a form and of a quality appropriate to enable it to discharge its duties. All directors should receive induction on joining the board and should regularly update and refresh their skills and knowledge.

Supporting Principles

The chairman is responsible for ensuring that the directors receive accurate, timely and clear information. Management has an obligation to provide such information but directors should seek clarification or amplification where necessary.

The chairman should ensure that the directors continually update their skills and the knowledge and familiarity with the company required to fulfil their role both on the board and on board committees. The company should provide the necessary resources for developing and updating its directors' knowledge and capabilities.

Under the direction of the chairman, the company secretary's responsibilities include ensuring good information flows within the board and its committees and between senior management and non-executive directors, as well as facilitating induction and assisting with professional development as required.

The company secretary should be responsible for advising the board through the chairman on all governance matters.

Code Provisions

A.5.1 The chairman should ensure that new directors receive a full, formal and tailored induction on joining the board. As part of this, the company should offer to major shareholders the opportunity to meet a new non-executive director.

A.5.2 The board should ensure that directors, especially non-executive directors, have access to independent professional advice at the company's expense where they judge it necessary to discharge their responsibilities as directors. Committees should be provided with sufficient resources to undertake their duties.

A.5.3 All directors should have access to the advice and services of the company secretary, who is responsible to the board for ensuring that board procedures are complied with. Both the appointment and removal of the company secretary should be a matter for the board as a whole.

A.6 Performance Evaluation

Main Principle

The board should undertake a formal and rigorous annual evaluation of its own performance and that of its committees and individual directors.

Supporting Principle

Individual evaluation should aim to show whether each director continues to contribute effectively and to demonstrate commitment to the role (including commitment of time for board and committee meetings and any other duties). The chairman should act on the results of the performance evaluation by recognising the strengths and addressing the weaknesses of the board and, where appropriate, proposing new members be appointed to the board or seeking the resignation of directors.

Code Provision

A.6.1 The board should state in the annual report how performance evaluation of the board, its committees and its individual directors has been conducted. The non-executive directors, led by the senior independent director, should

© International Financial Publishing Limited

be responsible for performance evaluation of the chairman, taking into account the views of executive directors.

A.7 Re-election

Main Principle

All directors should be submitted for re-election at regular intervals, subject to continued satisfactory performance. The board should ensure planned and progressive refreshing of the board.

Code Provisions

A.7.1   All directors should be subject to election by shareholders at the first annual general meeting after their appointment, and to re-election thereafter at intervals of no more than three years. The names of directors submitted for election or re-election should be accompanied by sufficient biographical details and any other relevant information to enable shareholders to take an informed decision on their election.

A.7.2   Non-executive directors should be appointed for specified terms subject to re-election and to Companies Acts provisions relating to the removal of a director. The board should set out to shareholders in the papers accompanying a resolution to elect a non-executive director why they believe an individual should be elected. The chairman should confirm to shareholders when proposing re-election that, following formal performance evaluation, the individual's performance continues to be effective and to demonstrate commitment to the role. Any term beyond six years (e.g. two three-year terms) for a non-executive director should be subject to particularly rigorous review, and should take into account the need for progressive refreshing of the board. Non-executive directors may serve longer than nine years (e.g. three three-year terms), subject to annual re-election. Serving more than nine years could be relevant to the determination of a non-executive director's independence (as set out in provision A.3.1).

B. REMUNERATION

B.1 The Level and Make-up of Remuneration

Main Principle

Levels of remuneration should be sufficient to attract, retain and motivate directors of the quality required to run the company successfully, but a company should avoid paying more than is necessary for this purpose. A significant proportion of executive directors' remuneration should be structured so as to link rewards to corporate and individual performance.

Supporting Principle

The remuneration committee should judge where to position their company relative to other companies. But they should use such comparisons with caution, in view of the risk of an upward ratchet of remuneration levels with no corresponding improvement in performance.

They should also be sensitive to pay and employment conditions elsewhere in the group, especially when determining annual salary increases.

Code Provisions

Remuneration policy

B.1.1 The performance-related elements of remuneration should form a significant proportion of the total remuneration package of executive directors and should be designed to align their interests with those of shareholders and to give these directors keen incentives to perform at the highest levels. In designing schemes of performance-related remuneration, the remuneration committee should follow the provisions in Schedule A to this Code.

B.1.2 Executive share options should not be offered at a discount save as permitted by the relevant provisions of the Listing Rules.

B.1.3 Levels of remuneration for non-executive directors should reflect the time commitment and responsibilities of the role. Remuneration for non-executive directors should not include share options. If, exceptionally, options are granted, shareholder approval should be sought in advance and any shares acquired by exercise of the options should be held until at least one year after the non-executive director leaves the board. Holding of share options could be relevant to the determination of a non-executive director's independence (as set out in provision A.3.1).

B.1.4 Where a company releases an executive director to serve as a non-executive director elsewhere, the remuneration report7 should include a statement as to whether or not the director will retain such earnings and, if so, what the remuneration is.

Service Contracts and Compensation

B.1.5 The remuneration committee should carefully consider what compensation commitments (including pension contributions and all other elements) their directors' terms of appointment would entail in the event of early termination. The aim should be to avoid rewarding poor performance. They should take a robust line on reducing compensation to reflect departing directors' obligations to mitigate loss.

B.1.6 Notice or contract periods should be set at one year or less. If it is necessary to offer longer notice or contract periods to new directors recruited from outside, such periods should reduce to one year or less after the initial period.

© International Financial Publishing Limited

B.2 Procedure

Main Principle

There should be a formal and transparent procedure for developing policy on executive remuneration and for fixing the remuneration packages of individual directors. No director should be involved in deciding his or her own remuneration.

Supporting Principles

The remuneration committee should consult the chairman and/or chief executive about their proposals relating to the remuneration of other executive directors.

The remuneration committee should also be responsible for appointing any consultants in respect of executive director remuneration. Where executive directors or senior management are involved in advising or supporting the remuneration committee, care should be taken to recognise and avoid conflicts of interest.

The chairman of the board should ensure that the company maintains contact as required with its principal shareholders about remuneration in the same way as for other matters.

Code Provisions

B.2.1 The board should establish a remuneration committee of at least three, or in the case of smaller companies8 two, independent non-executive directors. In addition the company chairman may also be a member of, but not chair, the committee if he or she was considered independent on appointment as chairman. The remuneration committee should make available9 its terms of reference, explaining its role and the authority delegated to it by the board. Where remuneration consultants are appointed, a statement should be made available of whether they have any other connection with the company.

B.2.2 The remuneration committee should have delegated responsibility for setting remuneration for all executive directors and the chairman, including pension rights and any compensation payments. The committee should also recommend and monitor the level and structure of remuneration for senior management. The definition of 'senior management' for this purpose should be determined by the board but should normally include the first layer of management below board level.

B.2.3 The board itself or, where required by the Articles of Association, the shareholders should determine the remuneration of the non-executive directors within the limits set in the Articles of Association. Where permitted by the Articles, the board may however delegate this responsibility to a committee, which might include the chief executive.

B.2.4 Shareholders should be invited specifically to approve all new long-term incentive schemes (as defined in the Listing Rules) and significant changes to existing schemes, save in the circumstances permitted by the Listing Rules.

C. ACCOUNTABILITY AND AUDIT

C.1 Financial Reporting

Main Principle

The board should present a balanced and understandable assessment of the company's position and prospects.

Supporting Principle

The board's responsibility to present a balanced and understandable assessment extends to interim and other price-sensitive public reports and reports to regulators as well as to information required to be presented by statutory requirements.

Code Provisions

C.1.1   The directors should explain in the annual report their responsibility for preparing the accounts and there should be a statement by the auditors about their reporting responsibilities.

C.1.2   The directors should report that the business is a going concern, with supporting assumptions or qualifications as necessary.

C.2 Internal Control

Main Principle

The board should maintain a sound system of internal control to safeguard shareholders' investment and the company's assets.

Code Provision

C.2.1   The board should, at least annually, conduct a review of the effectiveness of the group's system of internal controls and should report to shareholders that they have done so. The review should cover all material controls, including financial, operational and compliance controls and risk management systems.

C.3 Audit Committee and Auditors

Main Principle

The board should establish formal and transparent arrangements for considering how they should apply the financial reporting and internal control principles and for maintaining an appropriate relationship with the company's auditors.

© International Financial Publishing Limited

Code Provisions

C.3.1 The board should establish an audit committee of at least three, or in the case of smaller companies13 two, members, who should all be independent non-executive directors. The board should satisfy itself that at least one member of the audit committee has recent and relevant financial experience.

C.3.2 The main role and responsibilities of the audit committee should be set out in written terms of reference and should include:

- to monitor the integrity of the financial statements of the company, and any formal announcements relating to the company's financial performance, reviewing significant financial reporting judgements contained in them

- to review the company's internal financial controls and, unless expressly addressed by a separate board risk committee composed of independent directors, or by the board itself, to review the company's internal control and risk management systems

- to monitor and review the effectiveness of the company's internal audit function

- to make recommendations to the board, for it to put to the shareholders for their approval in general meeting, in relation to the appointment, re-appointment and removal of the external auditor and to approve the remuneration and terms of engagement of the external auditor

- to review and monitor the external auditor's independence and objectivity and the effectiveness of the audit process, taking into consideration relevant UK professional and regulatory requirements

- to develop and implement policy on the engagement of the external auditor to supply non-audit services, taking into account relevant ethical guidance regarding the provision of non-audit services by the external audit firm; and to report to the board, identifying any matters in respect of which it considers that action or improvement is needed and making recommendations as to the steps to be taken.

C.3.3 The terms of reference of the audit committee, including its role and the authority delegated to it by the board, should be made available14. A separate section of the annual report should describe the work of the committee in discharging those responsibilities.

C.3.4 The audit committee should review arrangements by which staff of the company may, in confidence, raise concerns about possible improprieties in matters of financial reporting or other matters. The audit committee's objective should be to ensure that arrangements are in place for the proportionate and independent investigation of such matters and for appropriate follow-up action.

C.3.5 The audit committee should monitor and review the effectiveness of the internal audit activities. Where there is no internal audit function, the audit committee should consider annually whether there is a need for an internal audit function and make a recommendation to the board, and the reasons for the absence of such a function should be explained in the relevant section of the annual report.

C.3.6 The audit committee should have primary responsibility for making a recommendation on the appointment, reappointment and removal of the external auditors. If the board does not accept the audit committee's recommendation, it should include in the annual report, and in any papers recommending appointment or re-appointment, a statement from the audit committee explaining the recommendation and should set out reasons why the board has taken a different position.

C.3.7 The annual report should explain to shareholders how, if the auditor provides non-audit services, auditor objectivity and independence is safeguarded.

D. RELATIONS WITH SHAREHOLDERS

D.1 Dialogue with Institutional Shareholders

Main Principle

There should be a dialogue with shareholders based on the mutual understanding of objectives. The board as a whole has responsibility for ensuring that a satisfactory dialogue with shareholders takes place.

Supporting Principles

Whilst recognising that most shareholder contact is with the chief executive and finance director, the chairman (and the senior independent director and other directors as appropriate) should maintain sufficient contact with major shareholders to understand their issues and concerns.

The board should keep in touch with shareholder opinion in whatever ways are most practical and efficient.

Code Provisions

D.1.1 The chairman should ensure that the views of shareholders are communicated to the board as a whole. The chairman should discuss governance and strategy with major shareholders. Non-executive directors should be offered the opportunity to attend meetings with major shareholders and should expect to attend them if requested by major shareholders. The senior independent director should attend sufficient meetings with a range of major shareholders to listen to their views in order to help develop a balanced understanding of the issues and concerns of major shareholders.

© International Financial Publishing Limited

D.1.2   The board should state in the annual report the steps they have taken to ensure that the members of the board, and in particular the non-executive directors, develop an understanding of the views of major shareholders about their company, for example through direct face-to-face contact, analysts' or brokers' briefings and surveys of shareholder opinion.

D.2 Constructive Use of the AGM

Main Principle

The board should use the AGM to communicate with investors and to encourage their participation.

Code Provisions

D.2.1   At any general meeting, the company should propose a separate resolution on each substantially separate issue, and should in particular propose a resolution at the AGM relating to the report and accounts. For each resolution, proxy appointment forms should provide shareholders with the option to direct their proxy to vote either for or against the resolution or to withhold their vote. The proxy form and any announcement of the results of a vote should make it clear that a 'vote withheld' is not a vote in law and will not be counted in the calculation of the proportion of the votes for and against the resolution.

D.2.2   The company should ensure that all valid proxy appointments received for general meetings are properly recorded and counted. For each resolution, after a vote has been taken, except where taken on a poll, the company should ensure that the following information is given at the meeting and made available as soon as reasonably practicable on a website which is maintained by or on behalf of the company:

- the number of shares in respect of which proxy appointments have been validly made

- the number of votes for the resolution

- the number of votes against the resolution, and

- the number of shares in respect of which the vote was directed to be withheld.

D.2.3   The chairman should arrange for the chairmen of the audit, remuneration and nomination committees to be available to answer questions at the AGM and for all directors to attend.

D.2.4   The company should arrange for the Notice of the AGM and related papers to be sent to shareholders at least 20 working days before the meeting.

SECTION 2 INSTITUTIONAL SHAREHOLDERS

E. INSTITUTIONAL SHAREHOLDERS

E.1 Dialogue with Companies

Main Principle

Institutional shareholders should enter into a dialogue with companies based on the mutual understanding of objectives.

Supporting Principles

Institutional shareholders should apply the principles set out in the Institutional Shareholders' Committee's "The Responsibilities of Institutional Shareholders and Agents – Statement of Principles", which should be reflected in fund manager contracts.

E.2 Evaluation of Governance Disclosures

Main Principle

When evaluating companies' governance arrangements, particularly those relating to board structure and composition, institutional shareholders should give due weight to all relevant factors drawn to their attention.

Supporting Principle

Institutional shareholders should consider carefully explanations given for departure from this Code and make reasoned judgements in each case. They should give an explanation to the company, in writing where appropriate, and be prepared to enter a dialogue if they do not accept the company's position. They should avoid a box-ticking approach to assessing a company's corporate governance. They should bear in mind in particular the size and complexity of the company and the nature of the risks and challenges it faces.

E.3 Shareholder Voting

Main Principle

Institutional shareholders have a responsibility to make considered use of their votes.

© International Financial Publishing Limited

Supporting Principles

Institutional shareholders should take steps to ensure their voting intentions are being translated into practice. Institutional shareholders should, on request, make available to their clients information on the proportion of resolutions on which votes were cast and non-discretionary proxies lodged.

Major shareholders should attend AGMs where appropriate and practicable. Companies and registrars should facilitate this.

Schedule A: Provisions on the design of performance related remuneration

1. The remuneration committee should consider whether the directors should be eligible for annual bonuses. If so, performance conditions should be relevant, stretching and designed to enhance shareholder value. Upper limits should be set and disclosed. There may be a case for part payment in shares to be held for a significant period.

2. The remuneration committee should consider whether the directors should be eligible for benefits under long-term incentive schemes. Traditional share option schemes should be weighed against other kinds of long-term incentive scheme. In normal circumstances, shares granted or other forms of deferred remuneration should not vest, and options should not be exercisable, in less than three years. Directors should be encouraged to hold their shares for a further period after vesting or exercise, subject to the need to finance any costs of acquisition and associated tax liabilities.

3. Any new long-term incentive schemes which are proposed should be approved by shareholders and should preferably replace any existing schemes or at least form part of a well considered overall plan, incorporating existing schemes. The total rewards potentially available should not be excessive.

4. Payouts or grants under all incentive schemes, including new grants under existing share option schemes, should be subject to challenging performance criteria reflecting the company's objectives. Consideration should be given to criteria which reflect the company's performance relative to a group of comparator companies in some key variables such as total shareholder return.

5. Grants under executive share option and other long-term incentive schemes should normally be phased rather than awarded in one large block.

6. In general, only basic salary should be pensionable.

7. The remuneration committee should consider the pension consequences and associated costs to the company of basic salary increases and any other changes in pensionable remuneration, especially for directors close to retirement.

Schedule B: Guidance on liability of non-executive directors: care, skill and diligence

1. Although non-executive directors and executive directors have as board members the same legal duties and objectives, the time devoted to the company's affairs is likely to be significantly less for a non-executive director than for an executive director and the detailed knowledge and experience of a company's affairs that could reasonably be expected of a non-executive director will generally be less than for an executive director. These matters may be relevant in assessing the knowledge, skill and experience which may reasonably be expected of a non-executive director and therefore the care, skill and diligence that a non-executive director may be expected to exercise.

2. In this context, the following elements of the Code may also be particularly relevant.

   (i) In order to enable directors to fulfil their duties, the Code states that:
   - The letter of appointment of the director should set out the expected time commitment (Code provision A.4.4), and
   - The board should be supplied in a timely manner with information in a form and of a quality appropriate to enable it to discharge its duties. The chairman is responsible for ensuring that the directors are provided by management with accurate, timely and clear information. (Code principle A.5).

   (ii) Non-executive directors should themselves:
   - Undertake appropriate induction and regularly update and refresh their skills, knowledge and familiarity with the company (Code principle A.5 and provision A.5.1)
   - Seek appropriate clarification or amplification of information and, where necessary, take and follow appropriate professional advice. (Code principle A.5 and provision A.5.2)
   - Where they have concerns about the running of the company or a proposed action, ensure that these are addressed by the board and, to the extent that they are not resolved, ensure that they are recorded in the board minutes (Code provision A.1.4).
   - Give a statement to the board if they have such unresolved concerns on resignation (Code provision A.1.4)

3. It is up to each non-executive director to reach a view as to what is necessary in particular circumstances to comply with the duty of care, skill and diligence they owe as a director to the company. In considering whether or not a person is in breach of that duty, a court would take into account all relevant circumstances. These may include having regard to the above where relevant to the issue of liability of a non-executive director.

© International Financial Publishing Limited

Schedule C: Disclosure of corporate governance arrangements

Paragraph 9.8.6 of the Listing Rules states that in the case of a listed company incorporated in the United Kingdom, the following items must be included in its annual report and accounts:

- a statement of how the listed company has applied the principles set out in Section 1 of the Combined Code, in a manner that would enable shareholders to evaluate how the principles have been applied

- a statement as to whether the listed company has

    - complied throughout the accounting period with all relevant provisions set out in Section 1 of the Combined Code, or
    - not complied throughout the accounting period with all relevant provisions set out in Section 1 of the Combined Code and if so, setting out:
        - (i) those provisions, if any, it has not complied with
        - (ii) in the case of provisions whose requirements are of a continuing nature, the period within which, if any, it did not comply with some or all of those provisions; and
        - (iii) the company's reasons for non-compliance.

In addition the Code includes specific requirements for disclosure which are set out below:

The annual report should record:

- a statement of how the board operates, including a high level statement of which types of decisions are to be taken by the board and which are to be delegated to management (A.1.1)

- the names of the chairman, the deputy chairman (where there is one), the chief executive, the senior independent director and the chairmen and members of the nomination, audit and remuneration committees (A.1.2)

- the number of meetings of the board and those committees and individual attendance by directors (A.1.2)

- the names of the non-executive directors whom the board determines to be independent, with reasons where necessary (A.3.1)

- the other significant commitments of the chairman and any changes to them during the year (A.4.3)

- how performance evaluation of the board, its committees and its directors has been conducted (A.6.1)

- the steps the board has taken to ensure that members of the board, and in particular the non-executive directors, develop an understanding of the views of major shareholders about their company (D.1.2).

The report should also include:

- a separate section describing the work of the nomination committee, including the process it has used in relation to board appointments and an explanation if neither external search consultancy nor open advertising has been used in the appointment of a chairman or a non-executive director (A.4.6)

- a description of the work of the remuneration committee as required under the Directors' Remuneration Report Regulations 2002, and including, where an executive director serves as a non-executive director elsewhere, whether or not the director will retain such earnings and, if so, what the remuneration is (B.1.4)

- an explanation from the directors of their responsibility for preparing the accounts and a statement by the auditors about their reporting responsibilities (C.1.1)

- a statement from the directors that the business is a going concern, with supporting assumptions or qualifications as necessary (C.1.2)

- a report that the board has conducted a review of the effectiveness of the group's system of internal controls (C.2.1)

- a separate section describing the work of the audit committee in discharging its responsibilities (C.3.3)

- where there is no internal audit function, the reasons for the absence of such a function (C.3.5)

- where the board does not accept the audit committee's recommendation on the appointment, reappointment or removal of an external auditor, a statement from the audit committee explaining the recommendation and the reasons why the board has taken a different position (C.3.6), and

- an explanation of how, if the auditor provides non-audit services, auditor objectivity and independence is safeguarded (C.3.7).

The following information should be made available (which may be met by placing the information on a website that is maintained by or on behalf of the company):
- the terms of reference of the nomination, remuneration and audit committees, explaining their role and the authority delegated to them by the board (A.4.1, B.2.1 and C.3.3)

- the terms and conditions of appointment of non-executive directors (A.4.4) (see footnote 6 on page 8), and

- where remuneration consultants are appointed, a statement of whether they have any other connection with the company (B.2.1).

The board should set out to shareholders in the papers accompanying a resolution to elect or re-elect directors:
- sufficient biographical details to enable shareholders to take an informed decision on their election or re-election (A.7.1)

- why they believe an individual should be elected to a non-executive role (A.7.2), and

- on re-election of a non-executive director, confirmation from the chairman that, following formal performance evaluation, the individual's performance continues to be effective and to demonstrate commitment to the role, including commitment of time for board and committee meetings and any other duties (A.7.2).

The board should set out to shareholders in the papers recommending appointment or reappointment of an external auditor:

© International Financial Publishing Limited

- if the board does not accept the audit committee's recommendation, a statement from the audit committee explaining the recommendation and from the board setting out reasons why they have taken a different position (C.3.6).

© The Financial Reporting Council 2006

© International Financial Publishing Limited

Index

D

E

© International Financial Publishing Limited

© International Financial Publishing Limited

T

U

V

W

© International Financial Publishing Limited